COMPLETE HANDBOOK OF PROFITABLE
MARKETING RESEARCH TECHNIQUES

Complete Handbook of Profitable Marketing Research Techniques

Robert P. Vichas

Prentice-Hall, Inc.
Englewood Cliffs, New Jersey

Prentice-Hall International, Inc., *London*
Prentice-Hall of Australia, Pty. Ltd., *Sydney*
Prentice-Hall of Canada, Ltd., *Toronto*
Prentice-Hall of India Private Ltd., *New Delhi*
Prentice-Hall of Japan, Inc., *Tokyo*
Prentice-Hall of Southeast Asia Pte. Ltd., *Singapore*
Whitehall Books, Ltd., *Wellington, New Zealand*

This publication is designed to provide accurate and authoritative information with regard to the subject matter covered. It is sold with the understanding that the publisher is not engaged in rendering legal, accounting, or other professional advice. If legal advice or other expert assistance is required, the services of a competent professional person should be sought.

—From a Declaration of Principles jointly adopted by a Committee of the American Bar Association and a Committee of Publishers and Associations.

Library of Congress Cataloging in Publication Data

Vichas, Robert P.

  Complete handbook of profitable marketing research techniques.

  Includes index.
  1. Marketing research. I. Title.
HF5415.2.V49   658.8′3   81–15796
ISBN 0-13-161158-5   AACR2

Printed in the United States of America

THE AUTHOR

Robert P. Vichas has gained practical and academic experience in scientific market research, corporate policy and strategy formulation, financial management, and business-government relations. Early in his career he became a sales manager with Capitol Service, Inc., and later, in sales and marketing, became associated with Dun & Bradstreet, Inc. Also, he was Vice President-International of Executive Management Consultants, Inc., and manager of commodity funds. Additionally, he has taught marketing management to MBA students at Catholic University and Interamerican University, and policy and strategy at Old Dominion University and The University of Connecticut. He is also a member of the Product Development and Management Association.

Articles authored or co-authored by Dr. Vichas have appeared in *Tradelook*; *Managerial and Decision Economics*; *Human Events*; *Long-Range Planning*; *The Envoy*; *Journal of Management Studies, Management World*; various *Proceedings*; and he has presented papers at the Institute of Marketing and Management in New Delhi, India, and a conference sponsored jointly with the European International Business Association in Barcelona, Spain, among others.

His published books include these:

Handbook of Annotated Financial Forms, Prentice-Hall, Inc.
Handbook of Financial Mathematics, Formulas, and Tables, Prentice-Hall, Inc.
Getting Rich in Commodities, Currencies, or Coins, Arlington House Publishers.
Coeval Economics, McCutchan Publishing Co.

To
   my
      wife,
         Dolores

ACKNOWLEDGMENTS

The author acknowledges the assistance of many individuals and organizations, although unnamed, whose numerous small contributions added up to a large result.

Particularly, the author thanks (in alphabetical order) several part-time researchers who came and went during the two-year project.

Don Breen
Mary Cookson
Dennis D'Angelo
Timothy Hoffman
Jeffrey Lebert
Mary Nemecek
Scott Parsons
Jack Shea
Robert Sopher
David Stearns

Also, the author is grateful for the contributions of these persons and organizations:

The *Boston Globe*, Boston, Massachusetts.

Kimon J. Constas, Managerial Economist and Statistician, The University of Connecticut, Storrs, Connecticut.

Maurice Kogon, Industry and Trade Administration, U.S. Department of Commerce, Washington, D.C.

Alan B. Miller, Jr., Vice President, Selling Areas-Marketing, Inc. (SAMI), New York, New York.

Duane B. Reutter, Data Control Manager, Electro-Methods, Inc., South Windsor, Connecticut.

The University of Connecticut Research Foundation, Storrs, Connecticut.

Paul L. Zorfass, Vice President, Waters Business Systems, Inc., Framingham, Massachusetts.

Regional staff personnel of the Bureau of the Census, U.S. Department of Commerce, Boston, Massachusetts.

In addition, the author personally thanks each purchaser of this book and hopes that every reader finds profitable application of some of these marketing research techniques.

"When I applied mine heart to know wisdom, and to see the business that is done upon the earth:

"Then I beheld the work of God, that a man cannot find out the work that is done under the sun: because though a man labour to seek it out, yet he shall not find it; yea, farther; though a wise man think to know it, yet shall he not be able to find it."

Ecclesiastes 8:16-17

USING THIS BOOK FOR CORPORATE AND PERSONAL PAYOFF

How Would You Handle These Challenges?

(A) You have a new product in the design stage. Sales will not be large, but they can be profitable if costs are kept down. Which combination of product features, colors, design and packaging will appeal to the most customers at the lowest cost to yield you the highest profits?

(B) You are a retailer who wants to begin advertising. Where should you advertise? What should the ads say? How do you gauge ad effectiveness? How much do you now know about your present customers: Where do they come from? How much do they earn? Do they think of your store as their primary source of supply? Who spends how much on what?

(C) You are planning a program of market penetration to increase market shares. Do you know what customers really think about your company? Your product(s)? Your service? Your pricing? Do you know what your customers think about the competition: their companies, products, service, pricing? Do you know what *potential* customers think about your firm and your competitors? How do you discover major weaknesses of competitors?

(D) You own or manage a business in a deteriorating neighborhood. Relocation is desirable, but to where? Where can you find inexpensive already available information?

These are a few typical marketing research problems. Answers to these and even tougher problems are available to any owner, manager, or market researcher *armed with the 35 powerful tools and techniques of data collection and analysis explained and illustrated in this book of profit ideas—techniques aimed at the reduction of judgment errors and business losses.*

No business in the 1980's can afford to make costly errors. No business can proceed very far with inadequate information. No business can sustain wasted expenditures of funds due to incorrect decisions made at any level of marketing.

Any business that is not future-looking will not grow. Any concern that is not future-looking will probably drop out of existence. Marketing research is future-looking. It holds the key to market position, saturation, and new streams of profit.

Any size of organization, a one-person consulting firm, or service station, or manufacturer, can afford to allocate a few dollars, and a few hours weekly, to marketing research. The techniques in this book are organized so that most can be implemented within a limited budget of time and money and *without* special skills or knowledge. In other words, these marketing research techniques are for the busy manager who wants to grow, with profits.

Marketing research is a planned and organized effort to obtain new facts and new knowledge, and to understand the old ones, with the goal of making better, more profitable decisions. For businesses without a fully staffed market research department, the manager confronts the issue of, first, discovering available research tools, and then learning how each one can contribute to more effective decisions.

To make that task simpler and cheaper, some of America's most successful marketers were surveyed to learn which marketing research techniques the big corporations spend their money on. About 40 basic techniques surfaced. These were the most economical and most productive ones.

Then this question was posed: How can even the smallest firm profit from the application of these techniques? Of these 40 techniques, 35 of them seem most practical for the smallest to the largest organizations.

This led to the devising of a format that provides for basic inexpensive instruction and demonstration—with many practical examples and applications—for *all types of organizations*, and for management who has had *no previous marketing research experience*.

Application examples support the text explanation of each tested and tried profit-building research technique. You will learn how other concerns solved specific marketing problems—problems you face now, or will face in the future. The multiple examples are a fruitful source of ideas, offering new twists and thought motivators for many types of business situations.

But this is not all! Besides examples, there are applications, problems and solutions, forms, checklists, and sample questionnaires that show you how to apply these marketing research ideas to your marketing problems in a practical manner that leads to more sales dollars.

And if you are still hampered with a tough issue, you will find reference to a number of money-saving sources of information or research assistance.

Of course, research data have some limitations. One of the most difficult tasks you face is to forecast market size. To identify problems after they have occurred is always easier with 20/20 hindsight. But an important issue this book addresses is the reduction of the failure rate of new (or recycled) products or services (some seven out of ten don't make it).

The answer lies in marketing research. Dik Twedt, a well-known corporate marketer, writes: "The first law of marketing is, 'Make what people want to buy; don't try to sell what you happen to make.' So the marketer tries through research to find out what people want to buy. The ultimate criterion of research effectiveness must be whether the research provides a better basis for making decisions than was previously available."

Here are just a few of the tips, ideas, methods and solutions to better decision-making you will discover in this book. (Section references—in parentheses—follow each item.)

- One hundred and fifty specific sources of information, statistics, and marketing data, and where to find hundreds more sources on your competitors, markets, and customers. (I.1)
- The three laws of successful marketing. (III.2)
- One hundred examples of survey questionnaires, checklists, analytical formulas, and numerical tables. (All sections)
- Ten steps that lead to an effective mail survey campaign. (I.5)
- How to discover what customers really think of your products. (III.5)
- Ten crucial steps to profitable test marketing. (II.1)
- Formats for market share analysis and market potential analysis. (I.2, I.7)
- Fifty life style factors for questionnaire design. (II.3)
- A high-powered method to test effectiveness of different sales presentations. (V.4)
- Checklist of 11 key points to remember with personal interviewing. (I.3)
- Eight steps to predict tomorrow's sales today with regression analysis. (VI.3)
- Three key formulas for projecting test market outcomes. (II.1)
- How to test a new product without test marketing. (I.6)
- When cobras are safer to handle than data revelations. (VI.3)
- A sure-fire, shortcut approach to sales predictions. (VI.3)
- A method to learn what customers think of competitors' products. (I.6)
- Crucial elements of an analysis of competitors. (I.1)
- A time-saving checklist for new industrial products. (I.2)
- Asset growth opportunities with a computer. (VI.1)
- How to obtain maximum amount of data at minimum costs. (IV.1)
- Cross-cultural factors in foreign market penetration. (II.3)
- How to identify new customer potential in a newly opened establishment. (III.1)
- A low-cost data collection technique for new products ideas. (I.6)
- How to develop a systems approach to marketing research. (VI.1)

- How to reduce promotion risks with a correlation index. (VI.2)
- Fourteen benefits from test marketing. (II.1)
- Fourteen programs for micro-computers. (VI.1)
- Five low-cost steps to semantic differential measurement for small firms with sales under $5 million. (III.1)
- How to evaluate individual sales performance. (V.1)
- Nine benefits and nine limitations of telephone surveys. (I.4)
- How to use time series analysis for key trend projections. (VI.4)
- How to use Latin Square and randomized designs in low-cost experimentation. (II.4)
- How to reduce large quantities of data to a single meaningful profit figure. (V.1)
- How to pry out how much (or how little) your customers like you and your products, and what to do about it. (III.1)
- Six key formulas to improve market estimates and market results and make better decisions. (V.2)
- Nine profit-generating steps to the successful application of Delphi techniques. (II.5)
- How to figure out the chance of making a small sale, no sale, or a super sale. (V.4)
- The hidden profits in stories and other tall tales. (III.2)
- How to fill an interview quota without cheating. (IV.3)
- How to test statistical computations to control risks and reduce losses. (V.3)
- How to measure sales effectiveness of advertising expenditures. (I.8)
- Five steps to better decision-making with Likert scales. (III.3)
- Six steps to profits with store audits. (I.8)
- How to analyze sales activity by region, by sales representative, and by characteristics of buyers. (IV.6)
- Basic data in profit analysis and basic steps in profit-supporting experimental designs. (I.2, II.2)
- How to structure personal interviews and informal designs for straightforward answers. (I.3, II.2)
- How to employ sample data to increase sales with greater confidence. (V.3)
- When *not* to test market. (II.1)
- How to construct a sales index for use during periods of inflation. (VI.4)
- When to use the fishbowl method. (IV.1)

- How to apply the principle of optimum allocation. (IV.2)
- Twelve profit-making steps in marketing research. (VI.1)
- Q-sort technique for big-money answers. (III.4)
- Three crucial steps in quota sampling. (IV.3)
- Where to find resource material for semantic design or other survey questionnaires. (I.1, III.1)
- How to avoid the shortcut trap to shortcuts. (V.1)
- When to use cross-tabulations to improve profits. (IV.6)
- How to determine the best sample size and implement a survey on a low-cost budget. (IV)
- Two cost-saving techniques to convert market averages into profit-producing decisions. (V.1, V.2)
- How to stratify the universe into subgroups to lower sampling costs. (IV.2)
- How to conduct top-drawer interviews any weekend or after business hours. (I, II)
- How to construct a correlation index for more effective marketing that picks winners. (VI.2)
- Twelve variance analysis formulas to keep sales on target and reduce risks. (V.4)

Even the smallest part-time venture is underpinned by three legs of the profit stool: marketing, finance, and production. This idea book will help improve the first of these three important business functions—marketing.

The author has researched marketing research techniques employed by the most successful marketers in American business. He has presented 35 techniques in a most practical manner. They can be quickly understood, and used profitably, by even the least experienced businessperson, without preparation in mathematics or statistics or research methodology. In presenting and explaining these techniques one overriding purpose arises: to improve your profits.

Some of these techniques have a long track record, are economical to use, and have transformed basement enterprises into money giants. A few of the newer techniques are sophisticated and require considerable expenditure of time, energy, and resources, and employ complex computer programs. The five most costly and most complicated ones were excluded.

Nevertheless, this important and unique reference book, whether you use it today or several years from now, is aimed toward that one end—profits. Profits, tangible or intangible, result from careful application of these money-saving practical techniques.

Presumably, the reader and user of this manual, when s/he opens it, is asking this question: "Which method will provide me with the best answers at the lowest costs?"

Certainly you should not expect to study three or four courses in statistics in order to obtain an answer needed yesterday. Two-thirds of the ideas presented here require nothing more than basic arithmetic—grammar or high school level.

About 20 percent of the techniques do require a very elementary notion of statistics; however, studying the examples and cameos only briefly *will provide you with all the information immediately necessary to solve your marketing research problems*.

Roughly 15 percent of the methods do require a nodding acquaintance with statistical theory, but anyone who can spend a few hours (not weeks, or months, but hours) with an elementary statistics book will become adept enough to qualify as an expert. The illustrations in the book will lead you the rest of the way to more sales.

The 35 most widely used marketing research techniques are arranged in a manner that will minimize your cost (time) in finding the best technique(s) appropriate to your problem.

How This Handbook Is Organized

Notice that this handbook does not fall into the usual chapter subdivisions. It is divided into six sections plus appendices of tables to help you solve problems faster and to communicate additional information sources:

I. Data Collection
II. Research Design
III. Attitude Measurements
IV. Sampling Procedures
V. Data Analysis
VI. The Computer and Other Techniques

Then, each section is further subdivided into four to eight subsections which highlight each of these powerhouse techniques. Each technique is carefully explained, fully illustrated. Examples drawn from actual applications show how to wring the most out of each technique.

Moreover, you can get some idea of whether the method is too costly, beyond personnel capability, or just about right for your organization. No punches are pulled, either; you will learn not only potential benefits from using a technique but also its limitations.

Sometimes a combination of research methods is the best option. Frequent cross-references will lead you to other parts of the book. And several *actual sample questionnaires* demonstrate how to tie several research techniques together into one survey.

If you wonder what kinds of questions to ask, how many to ask, where to get ideas for panels or interviews, many examples and sources throughout this book will lead you right to the money.

In fact, if you were to follow through on every one of the ideas in this book, your staff could generate enough information and statistical data to keep your organization occupied in analysis for the next 1,000 years.

How can you find exactly the right information you require without reading the entire volume? First, the table of contents carries the title of each section and subsection. Here are just a few of the crucial items each section contains.

I. *Data gathering*, of course, is pivotal in any marketing research project. The value of any research depends upon the quality of data input. Poor data in—solid profits out (way out).

Even the most superior research design cannot offset poor information collected. For this reason you must select carefully from among the data-gathering options discussed—analysis of trade journals and trade association data, analysis of internal company records, personal interviews, telephone surveys, mail surveys, consumer panels, or store audits—constrained by time, money, and level of sophistication desired, and then carefully apply the technique(s) to obtain the best data. Better data—better profits.

II. *Research design* and experimentation, the second section of the profit-book, offers the following techniques: test marketing, life style analysis, formal and informal experimental designs, and the Delphi technique.

Research projects may be descriptive or experimental. Experiments more effectively pinpoint cause and effect relationships. This section also points out how to avoid increased costs, possible losses, produced by obscure or confusing information.

III. *Measurement* principally means attitude measurement, observational studies, and questionnaire construction procedures that provide an answer to "Why do people buy?" questions. You will learn why, when, where, and how often through the application of these techniques: semantic differential, projective psychological techniques, ranking, Likert and other scales, multidimensional scaling, and the Q-sort technique.

IV. *Sampling* is a commonplace idea because everyone is accustomed to drawing conclusions (generalizing) about large groups of people from observations of small numbers. These conclusions are often wrong. One can conclude, from very small samples, that all Africans are black, all Asiatics are short, or all Americans are blond and blue-eyed. Herein lies the danger.

The best information is to observe all (100%) of Africans, Asians, or Americans. But the magnitude of information is so overwhelming that no conclusions would be forthcoming.

Ideally, a small sample of persons who are representative of the entire population will provide inexpensive information about many persons. The trick is to obtain the right sample—at the lowest cost.

Money-saving techniques discussed here include simple random sampling, stratified sampling, quota sampling, judgmental sampling, cluster sampling, convenience sampling, area sampling, sample size, plus cross-tabulation.

V. *Analysis* of data means getting your money's worth out of data collected from samples, and then transforming that hard-won information into customers and profit-dollars. Proper analysis also will tell you something about the quality of data and how much confidence you can have in the projected outcomes from budget expenditures.

VI. *More techniques* represent a few more cat-skinning instructions that can even be linked to your micro, mini, or large computer main frame. These future-looking devices focus on asset growth, relationships, and trend analysis.

The Table of Contents is not the only means for finding the technique that fits your current needs. The introduction to each section can lead you to bell-ringing ideas.

Generally, each section progresses from the most popular to the least popular technique. But you should recognize, too, that a technique popular among retailers will be employed not at all by manufacturers because it does not fit specific needs. Nevertheless, the author spent more time and space on those sections, and on those specific techniques, that you are most likely to apply to your business questions.

Notice too, in the front of the book there is a list of figures. The lead to the idea you seek may pop out during a scanning of this list, for it includes sample surveys, checklists, solutions to problems, questionnaires, examples, and forms.

Frequent cross-references in the text material provide another key source of further information. Of course, do not overlook the comprehensive Index as an additional way to corner market ideas.

Market research is only one step, although a crucial one, in the profit-maximizing process. Nevertheless, it can open the way to a high volume of sales and huge profits. What follows is a very small sample of the kinds of questions market researchers try to answer. How many of them fit your situation?

> Why do people spend money on (especially the other fellow's) products?
> Where are the potential customers? Who are they?
> Are seasonal and cyclical factors present?
> What are the competitive and alternative products or services?
> What is our marketing problem? Are there any cheap solutions?
> What are normal sales expectancies?
> What are present and future trends for the industry?
> Should we expand regionally, nationally, internationally?
> Do we have sufficient marketing data for long-range planning?
> How much should we buy, sell, stock, order?
> What is the expected cash flow for next month? In six months? In the next 12, 18, or 24 months?
> Where should we advertise? How should we advertise?
> What will happen to profits if we raise (lower) prices?
> What are the chances that our new product (service) will be a market success? How can we make it a winner?
> What customers will switch brands (or when)?
> How can we increase our market share?

Will our new product (service) be accepted? What are potential sales?

Why are sales declining?

How can we project sales potential? Who are our best sales representatives? (Volume alone may mislead you.)

Why do our competitors have a better (store/product/safety) image than we?

How can we double sales and triple profits?

Where will the big markets be ten years from now?

Where can we get new product ideas? How do we know they are good ideas?

Did several of those questions lead you right to the mine shaft? Questions for which you would like better answers or more information than you are now obtaining? Sinking a mine shaft may be a good idea, but it is not the objective, not the end purpose. To convert a good idea into solid gold requires tools and techniques and energy. The tools and techniques are laid out for you in the following pages. They're yours—for the taking.

Robert P. Vichas

TABLE OF CONTENTS

LIST OF FIGURES

SECTION *I*

DATA COLLECTION

"Behold, this have I found, counting one by one, to find the account: Which yet my soul seeketh, but I find not."

Ecclesiastes 7:27-28

INTRODUCTION

Data collection follows along a logical path, like any other decision-making process. Understanding this process is the key to data collection design and to transformation of the ideas and techniques developed in the following eight subsections into profit dollars.* The nine-step approach provides a logical framework to guide you in the application of Section I material.

STEP I: Objectives of the research project need to be agreed to, stated, known among the people involved in designing the project, and understood, for without objectives data gathered become gathered data, without point or purpose—or profitable application.

STEP II: Because not everyone who is the object of surveys eagerly cooperates, a plan must be designed to secure cooperation and reliable answers from a representative sample of respondents, whether the data are collected from personal or telephone interviews, mail surveys, focus groups and panels, or via store audits. People are involved, not numbers; therefore, empathize.

STEP III: Building upon Steps I and II, review and expand the questions to be answered. The basic who, what, why, which, when, and where formula applies, plus another very important "w": *W*ill the customer buy our product again?

STEP IV: Next, think about which questionnaire format will be best to administer, given your personnel resources and budget, and best to code and analyze after data are accumulated. In this first sec-

---

*Although the term "dollars" is employed throughout this book, it expresses the popular sense of the term rather than any reference to its real connotation. A better term is "Federal Reserve Notes," those decorative rectangles of paper printed by the federal government (and other counterfeiters, too) designed to substitute for real money. However, given the awkwardness and unfamiliarity of the term "FRN," the "dollar" designation is retained, however reluctantly.

tion of the book, as well as in following sections, several types of questionnaires are illustrated: multiple-choice, open-ended questions, scaling and ranking alternatives, informal.

STEP V: Develop some ideas about sequencing of questions and quality of instructions. Sequencing means to place questions in a logical order, grouped by topic or subject. Start with easy or innocuous questions; save the toughest ones for last. Instructions must be crystal clear. Regardless of your efforts here, an instruction with even the remotest chance of being misunderstood will probably be misunderstood.

STEP VI: Now review those questions and instructions. Pretest them among employees, or on an informally selected outside group of persons. Some questions and instructions may be ambiguous, incomprehensible, unanswerable, or even unintentionally offensive.

STEP VII: Revise and improve the survey questionnaire, or even redesign it, if necessary. That is, get it right before spending a great deal of money on research that may turn out to be unprofitable due to unsuitable questionnaire design.

STEP VIII: Before the entire research budget is committed, still another step can save money. Test your creation with a subsample of respondents, a trial run. This test is more formalized than the Step VI pretest. Testing should be done live (even though the actual survey is done by mail) to learn whether instructions were understood clearly and to register respondents' reactions to the questionnaire. During the test more time is spent with each respondent than during actual data collection, because the test objective is to clean up the questionnaire.

STEP IX: Revisions may be light or heavy, according to what developed during Step VIII procedures. This is the last opportunity to make it right before full and final commitment.

Therefore, keep these steps in mind as you read and apply material in Section I pertinent to your needs, and design a research project that will produce sales growth and profits.

I.1: WHERE TO FIND A TREASURE CHEST OF INFORMATION ON COMPETITORS, MARKETS, AND CUSTOMERS

Imagine yourself in this situation: your Board has just agreed to a new company policy that will require marketing research proposals for certain new product ideas. No one in sales or marketing is experienced with marketing research. So, you decide to coordinate the first project yourself, until the marketing department can be reorganized.

Since you need basic information before finalizing a plan, you ask the marketing manager to provide data developed from internal company records, and you ask John, his assistant, to visit the library and dig out some basic facts on general characteristics of the projected market area.

Beyond those minimal instructions you have provided no additional guidance. John's knowledge of libraries extends no further than his college days back in the 1960's when he used a hidden library alcove as a private motel. John discovers still another use of libraries and is overwhelmed by floors of books and pamphlets. He looks for an alcove out of habit.

Beyond that he is uncertain where or how to begin. Besides, much data, sometimes available in abundant quantities, often are not presented in a format convenient to specific marketing needs.

You can

(a) pull John out of the stacks and send him back to his old job.
(b) do the work yourself evenings (learn-as-you-go) and risk unhappiness on the homefront.
(c) hire a marketing research consultant or firm to do the job.
(d) bend company policy and perform only a cursory study by asking the sales people what they think.
(e) do none of the above.

Or you can apply ideas from Section I.1 of this book to your particular marketing needs. The next several pages suggest what to look for in secondary sources, where to look for it, and what to ask for when you still need more information.

The references listed at the end of this subsection should substantially lessen research costs, and save time, because the information is all together in one place in the book. And you'll be able to give John specific and knowledgeable direction.

On the other hand, someone in your organization may challenge the expense of secondary research. This challenge can be successfully answered by pointing out that successful firms with sizable marketing research budgets value highly the information derived from secondary sources. Here are only a few ways your firm may benefit from these valuable resources:

- ◎ If research can be segmented into information derived from primary and secondary resources, obtain as much as possible from secondary ones in order to lower costs. Secondary research costs are substantially less than primary collection costs.
- ◎ Besides, a solution to the question may develop during data accumulation from secondary sources, obviating the need for expensive primary research. Or you may discover that someone else has already done the research you require and has published the results.
- ◎ Starting with secondary sources contributes to the planning process by isolating areas for most productive work, and helps plan primary research. Secondary research may be considered preliminary work in order to better define the problem and hypothesize about its solution.
- ◎ Published statistical series provide bench marks for comparing company performance against general economic conditions.
- ◎ And, such data provide background to round out the entire market picture and to help define the market sample for primary research.

Three Critical Questions

Because of its diversity and volume of potentially available information, a huge research library can overwhelm and discourage a researcher. Some answers to a specific marketing problem probably lie within, but access to them can prove difficult or unnecessarily costly. For an inexperienced market researcher, pinpointing data from secondary sources at first seems impossible, especially if other duties encroach on the market researcher's time. The objectives of this first subsection are

- ◎ to make that task easier and cheaper,
- ◎ to reduce the cost of gathering information, and
- ◎ to direct you to high payoff sources.

Nevertheless, three critical questions must be seriously considered before committing funds.

• *The first critical question*: Do you know precisely what you need, and where to look for it?

Many secondary sources and indices and references to these sources exist. One of the most valuable bonuses in this section is its list of sources.

Assume that you begin research by previewing published articles. Even knowing precisely what you are seeking may not correspond to how an experienced periodical indexer perceives the contents of magazine articles, for example. Since it may not be indexed in a manner that directly relates to your specific needs, a little imagination is in order.

Suppose your key term is "downstream mergers," but no available reference source lists this term. (Remember that indexers may not be trained in your area of specific needs.) What other terms might you try? "Mergers," "acquisitions," "consolidations," "statutory mergers," "divestitures," "spinoffs," "split-offs," etc. Even if none of these are helpful, do not despair.

Keep trying. It's like the children's game of trying to enumerate all the uses of a brick. In our example, "combinations" or "business combinations" may yield the required wealth of referential sources. In other words, don't expect everything to be laid out neatly and orderly. Research is hard work, requiring patience and imagination.

• *The second critical question*: Are the data gathered from these secondary sources in a format applicable to your research problem or sufficiently complete to provide worthwhile answers to your questions?

The data should meet your needs, be consistent with your research objectives, and compatible with the requirements of your marketing program. If the data fail to furnish necessary detail or are in an unusable form, it may be best not to try to stretch research dollars as a substitute for unassimilable data. Inadequate investment is a poor investment.

• *The third critical question*: Are the data generated technically sound?

In using data from secondary sources, you must deal with liars, lunatics, the loquacious, the libertine, and the ludicrous, as well as the learned, the legitimate, the lucent, the logical, and the luminous.

Bias is ever present. The sponsoring organization is biased. The researchers are biased. The interviewees are biased. The editors are biased. And the results are biased . . . despite the best intentions of all.

Aside from this, the research design may or may not be technically sound. The methodology may be faulty. The sample size or population may be unreliable for the level of accuracy desired. The statistical analysis may not be consistent with the quality of data. Still, decisions must be made—but not blindly!

Six Important Advantages

Despite the cautious tone on the use of secondary statistical sources, they frequently represent a low-cost, readily accessible avenue of information sufficiently reliable for planning and decision-making. After all, what is the alternative?

(a) Either gather the information yourself, at your expense (or hire someone to do it), from primary sources, if available;

(b) Or forge on by trial and error, and hope that financial resources hold out for a lot of trials and errors.

Nevertheless, distinct advantages arise in using information, from whatever sources:

1. Data developed support short- and long-range planning and strategic resource deployment to achieve company goals.
2. Good information reduces costs and losses through trial and error tactics; lower costs should generate higher profits.
3. Searching secondary sources may produce a real gold mine of information; someone may have already done precisely (or nearly so) the exact kind of study you need.
4. Even though you know the market well—either intuitively or from a synthesis of experiences—you may not know everything you should, and secondary material may well fill in an important, profit-bleeding gap.
5. Fresh information may trigger an entirely new concept for market penetration or introduction of a new product or service.
6. Statistical series can provide a standard against which to measure your own firm's performance. (Remember that the Swiss watch companies in the 1950s, while discounting the advances of Timex, began to realize that something was amiss when disposable incomes of Americans were climbing but Swiss watch sales were not matching this growth.)

As you sort through data, preparation of an analysis of competitors, or potential competitors, will influence type, amount, and quality of promotion. One suggested format for organizing a competitor analysis appears in Figure I.1.A. Data on 16 separate items are called for. Chances are that all of this information will be available from secondary sources listed on the following pages.

To make your research efforts more pleasant and profitable, here is an enumeration of some of the major sources of information, statistical data, and services, and suggestions as to where to obtain more data. We'll begin with indices as an important channel to get a lead on further information and follow this with a short list of firms offering search services and then an exposition of nongovernmental sources of statistics and data. Then we can examine some principal governmental sources, followed by a short list of major business directories, marketing and advertising journals, and trade associations.

Indices of Business Data

Business and technical articles provide a wealth of information on trends, competition, new product developments, economic and regulatory changes, shifts in demand, and data on specific research. Most libraries subscribe to several of these indices. Twenty-eight major ones appear below in alphabetical order.

Accountants' Index. Don't let the title mislead you. It has been around since 1921 and currently covers a lot more than accounting subjects and includes some Canadian and British journals as well. Well indexed and easy to use.

American Statistics Index. A real winner if you are looking for government-generated statistical information. It classifies information by geographic, economic, and demographic factors.

Applied Science and Technology Index. Indexes more than 225 engineering and technical periodicals including chemistry, construction, metallurgy, and transportation.

COMPETITOR ANALYSIS

(Use separate form for each competitor.)

Name and Address of Current or Potential Competitor:

Organization (Principal Officers):

Geographical Coverage:

Sales and Earnings over Past Five Years:

Net Worth:

Inventory:

Number of Employees:

Number and Location of Branches, Plants:

Field Service Capability:

Market Share:

Characteristics of Leading Competitive Product or Service:

Advertising and Promotion Methods:

Product Cost:

Distribution Channel:

Sales Force Effectiveness:

Advertising Effectiveness:

Figure I.1.A: COMPETITOR ANALYSIS

Bibliographic Index: a Cumulative Bibliography of Bibliographies. If you want quantity, this index catalogs more than 2,000 periodicals, books, and pamphlets.

Biological and Agricultural Index. Covers biology, agriculture, and related sciences.

Business Literature. This Newark Public Library publication covers books, magazines, government publications and pamphlets.

Business Methods Index. This index embraces a variety of Canadian and British sources including 300 business magazines and journals.

Business Periodicals Index. A popular source, by subject index, of well over 150 business periodicals. Published monthly for current information.

Business and Technology Sources. The Cleveland Public Library brings together a wide range of sources, usually focusing on a narrow range of topics.

Congressional Record Index. This biweekly index to the *Congressional Record* is available in all governmental depository libraries.

Consumer Index to Product Evaluations and Information Sources. Since 1973 this publication has indexed articles from approximately 125 magazines which report product test results and consumer goods evaluations.

Current Contents. This bi-weekly from The Institute for Scientific Information publishes tables of contents of periodicals dealing in marketing and other business areas.

Encyclopedia of Business Information Sources. Refers to bibliographies, articles, handbooks, encyclopedias, directories, etc.

F & S Index of Corporations & Industries. Indexes financial and business news from more than 1,000 publications.

F & S Index International. Summarizes, on a monthly basis, articles from business literature with bibliographic information. Contains information on production, market trends, end uses, government regulations, shipments, resource and materials supply, unit costs and prices, management procedures, etc., in Latin America, Canada, Japan, Oceania, the Mid-East, Asia, and Africa.

Guide to Reference Books. Although this one, too, includes areas outside of marketing, it does refer to government documents, dissertations, directories as well as bibliographies.

Index to U.S. Government Periodicals. Since 1974 it has been indexing more than 150 government periodicals.

Marketing Information Guide. Lists marketing information from various sources: government agencies, state and local organizations, trade associations, universities.

Marketing Review. Published in Toronto, Ontario, this weekly publication lists articles from general and advertising periodicals.

Newspaper Index. Around since 1972, it now includes the following newspapers: *Chicago Tribune, Detroit News, Houston Post, Los Angeles Times, Milwaukee Journal, New Orleans Times-Picayune, San Francisco Chronicle, The Washington Post*.

The New York Times Index. Here's an idea! Since most newspapers tend to copy the *Times*, finding the date of an event in this index may help to pinpoint the date of an important article in your own newspaper.

Official Index of the London Times. This index is indispensable for organizations operating in an international environment.

Periodicals and Sources: a List of Federal Statistical Periodicals and Their Issuing Sources. If this index is not available at a library or information center, it may be obtained from Congressional Information Service, Inc., Washington, D.C.

Public Affairs Information Service. Covers government pamphlets and other factual publications with emphasis primarily on political science.

The Readers' Guide to Periodical Literature. Published since 1900, it indexes currently more than 160 general and nontechnical magazines; list is updated monthly.

Statistical Sources. Indexes approximately 8,000 subjects monthly.

Tables of Contents of Selected Advertising and Marketing Publications. Compiles tables of contents of over 25 marketing and advertising publications from England, Canada, and the United States.

Wall Street Journal Index. Since 1957, a monthly index on information on corporations.

Computer Data Bases

The newest and probably most efficient, albeit more costly, way to research secondary sources is to use the new computer data bases, most of which are keyed to recently published materials. These commercial services are available around the country and in major research libraries. The purpose is to locate more information faster than traditional research techniques permit. Reference is made to *The Electronic Library* for specific uses of data bases and for information on more than the examples listed below. The fifth and sixth sources indicated below are a handbook on services and a catalog of computer programs for analyzing data.

1. CAPITAL SYSTEMS GROUP, INC. (Rockville, Maryland 20852). Searches information on business, agriculture, food, health, medicine, and technical data.

2. CENTRAL ABSTRACTING & INDEXING SERVICE (New York, New York 10016). Monitors business news publications and technical journals.

3. DATA COURIER, INC. (Louisville, Kentucky 40202). Abstracts business, health, medicine, and technical publications.

4. FIND/SVP (New York, New York 10036). Searches information on agriculture, food, health, medicine, business, economics, new products, sports, travel, etc.

5. *Handbook of Commercial & Financial Information Services.* A valuable reference volume.

6. *IPC QUARTERLY.* This is a catalog of available computer programs which includes sales analysis, forecasting, simulations, market research, computer letter writing, mailing lists, management, etc.

7. INTERNATIONAL FOOD SERVICE INFORMATION SERVICE (Reading, England RG2 9BB). Abstracts about 18,000 items worldwide on food science and technology.

8. NATIONAL AUTOMATED ACCOUNTING RESEARCH SYSTEM (NAARS) (New York, New York 10036). Data base on more than 4,000 published annual reports.

9. SYSTEM DEVELOPMENT CORP. SEARCH SERVICE (Santa Monica, California 90406). Information on laws, new products, food, agriculture, sports, scientific and technical data, etc.

10. WITS is a data base organized by the U.S. Department of Commerce to encourage exports by small and medium-sized firms by matching foreign needs and inquiries to subscriber interests. The system is explained in more detail in Section VI.1.

Data and Statistics from Private Sources

Statistical data are available from many private sources which either compile data or provide information on data which can lead the researcher to the source for greater detail. Following are 25 sources on data and statistics.

American Metal Market. Publishes statistics on prices, production, stocks, and consumption.

The Book of the States. A guide to sources of state statistical data and other information on state governments.

Chicago Mercantile Exchange Yearbook. Publishes future and spot prices along with other data on futures contracts traded on the exchange.

Commercial and Financial Chronicle. A twice-weekly publication that includes weekly highs and lows and volumes on major Canadian and American exchanges and information on state and local bonds.

Commodity Year Book. Historical data on many commodities including trends, marketing methods, and long-term outlook.

The Conference Board Business Record. Monthly publication provides indices on production, commodity prices, distribution, etc., and changes in inventories, costs of living, wages, etc.

Current Statistics. Monthly indices of business activity in basic industries.

Data Sources for Business and Market Analysis. Addresses a variety of marketing information with references to business forms, trade associations, and journals and magazines.

The Economic Almanac. Statistical information of practical interest to businesses; a good source to check on statistical data from other sources.

Editor and Publisher Market Guide. Publishes estimates on household incomes and retail sales and market data related to more than 1500 daily newspaper markets in the United States and Canada.

Europa Yearbook. Provides statistics, administration, education and other data on many countries in Europe, Africa, and Asia.

A Graphic Guide to Consumer Markets. Statistical data on population, income, expenditures, production, prices, markets, and advertising on consumer goods and services.

Information Please Almanac. Compilation of facts and selected statistical data; complements the *World Almanac.*

Metal Statistics. Annual data on metal prices, stocks, production, consumption.

The Mining Yearbook. An annual British publication which furnishes data on mining companies.

Moody's Manual of Investments. Various volumes on transportation, public utility, industrial securities, bank and finance.

Population Index. Quarterly bibliography of articles, books, and studies on population throughout the world.

Rand McNally Commercial Atlas and Marketing Guide. Maps and statistics coverage worldwide; marketing tables containing over 40 statistical items for each U.S. county; population figures for over 6,000 American localities.

Statesman's Yearbook. Published since 1864; contains information on economic conditions, agriculture, commerce, education, defenses, and other data on governments of the world.

Statistics Sources. American and international statistics on industry, business, finance, advertising, agriculture, foreign trade, marketing, etc.

Trade and Securities Statistics. Statistical material on general business conditions, prices, cost of living, financial data, and major Canadian statistics.

Weekly Desk Sheet of Business Indicators. A single page of the more important indices measuring business activity.

World Advertising Expenditures. Includes trend data for advertising expenditures for 86 countries; market information on number of newspapers, magazines, television, radio sets and cinemas in 55 countries.

World Almanac. Statistics on business, population, governments, industries, sports, associations, societies. Complements *Information Please Almanac*.

Worldcasts. Organizes over 50,000 published forecasts on 50 major products in 52 countries. Forecasts abstracts include base period data, projected growth rates, bibliographic references. Product series data include revenues, expenditures, consumption, sales, shipments, capacities, new equipment purchases, production, major economic indicators, etc.

Forty-One Government Sources

Among the many governmental sources of information, possibly the most attractive to market researchers are those many statistics collected by the Bureau of Census, of which only a few sources are indicated below. However, like all macro-level data these must not be considered necessarily the ultimate or even the best source of information; statistics from government sources have at least as many limitations as statistics gathered by any other research team. Exclusive of these limitations they may prove to be the cheapest sources. A number of them appear below.

AGRICULTURAL MARKETING SERVICE. This service of the Department of Agriculture includes information on specific agricultural products, market news, and marketing agreements, and provides marketing services for nearly all agricultural commodities.

Agricultural Statistics. This annual publication of the Department of Agriculture includes data on production, prices, costs, consumption, etc.

Business Statistics. Published annually by the Department of Commerce, it summarizes national data on population, vital statistics, income and expenditures, prices, housing, manufacturing and other business activities, distribution, communications, transportation, etc.

BUREAU OF ECONOMIC ANALYSIS. This Department of Commerce bureau publishes basic economic data on the national economy, current analysis of the economic situation, and macro-economic research figures on the economy.

Directory of Federal Statistics for States. A guide to many sources of statistics for regions, states, counties, and cities.

Federal Reserve Bulletin. This monthly publication includes monetary statistics, and indices of industrial production, cost of living, construction, employment, retail sales, etc.

Marketing Information Guide. A monthly Department of Commerce publication, this is an annotated bibliography of current governmental and nongovernmental materials on domestic and international marketing information.

Monthly Catalog of U.S. Government Publications. This monthly catalog contains information on materials potentially of value to market researchers.

Statistical Services of the U.S. Government. This describes the main statistical publications of federal agencies.

Survey of Current Business. Published monthly by the Department of Commerce, it contains a weekly statistical supplement of such areas as commodity prices, business indicators, population, communications, transportation, review of the current business situation, etc.

UNESCO, *International Bibliography of Economics*. An annual publication of the United Nations.

UNITED NATIONS: Two other U.N. publications:

    Statistical Yearbook.   Issued annually since 1948.

    Demographic Yearbook.   Emphasizes special types of population statistics.

U.S. BUREAU OF CENSUS

Catalog of United States Census Publications. This quarterly publication describes upcoming reports and other material, and data files and special tabulations.

CENSUS OF AGRICULTURE. Tabulates farm size, acreage value, farm expenditures, value of products, crops and livestock, use of fertilizers, facilities and equipment and other information on a county basis.

CENSUS OF BUSINESS:

    Distribution of Manufacturers.

    Retail Trade.

    Service Businesses.

    Wholesale Trade.

CENSUS OF GOVERNMENTS. Value of taxable property, public employees and payrolls, governmental revenues and expenditures, debt, financial assets, etc.

CENSUS OF HOUSING. Data on types of structures, year built, equipment, fuel used, rent paid, value, number of persons per room, ethnic category of occupants, mortgage status, condition of dwelling, water source, etc., broken down by city blocks.

CENSUS OF MANUFACTURERS. Statistics on number and size of entities, payrolls, man-hours, sales by customer class, inventories, selected costs, book value of fixed assets, capital expenditures, industrial water use, value added, energy consumed, etc.

CENSUS OF MINERAL INDUSTRIES. Number of companies, mines, plants, employees, and value of shipments, capital expenditures, principal expenses, power equipment, and energy consumption, etc.

CENSUS OF RETAIL TRADE, WHOLESALE TRADE, AND SELECTED SERVICE INDUSTRIES. Data on total sales, number of employees, payrolls, number of firms, etc.

CENSUS TRACTS. Very convenient for marketing surveys; includes such population characteristics as race, sex, age, citizenship, education, families, employment status, occupation, income, etc.

CENSUS OF TRANSPORTATION. Covers commodity transportation, truck inventory, national travel and related data.

County and City Data Book. Provides about 200 statistical items for each county or city equivalent.

Current Housing Reports. Quarterly data on number of television sets, housing vacancies, and other housing data.

Current Population Survey. A scientific sampling (see Section IV on sampling procedures) of population mobility, income characteristics and buying behavior, school enrollment, and other personal characteristics.

Monthly Retail Trade Report. Reports on value and volume of sales broken down by kind of business and region or city.

Monthly Wholesale Trade Report. Provides information on sales and inventories, trends, ratios, etc., by type and location of business.

Statistical Abstract of the United States. Covers vital statistics, immigration, population, commerce, finance, railroads, etc.

United States Census. Includes population characteristics, housing data, and block statistics.

U.S. BUREAU OF LABOR STATISTICS

BLS Catalog of Publications.
BLS Handbook of Methods.
Employment and Earnings Statistics.
Employment and Wages of Workers.
Handbook of Labor Statistics.

Monthly Labor Review.
Occupational Outlook Handbook.
Occupational Outlook Quarterly.

Major Business Directories

Of course, there are many hundreds more than the 21 business directories catalogued below. Listed are the major, better known ones, but any one of a number of specialized directories will yield specific categories of information. Usually they inventory names of officers, sales, size, addresses, and related information about companies. The listing may be international, U.S. only, by region or state, metropolitan area or local.

American Guide to Business Directories. A directory to the directories.

American Guide to Directories. A Prentice-Hall publication listing 2200 titles.

Dun & Bradstreet Middle Market Directory. This directory includes businesses with reported or estimated net worths between 500,000 and one million dollars. It includes names of officers and directors, type of business activities, annual sales, total number of employees, firm's name and state of incorporation.

Dun & Bradstreet Million Dollar Directory. Covers same data as the above directory except that it reports on firms worth one million dollars or more.

Directory of Business and Financial Services.

Directory of Discount Stores.

Directory of Industrial Distributors.

MOODY'S MANUALS. Includes only the largest corporations in industry, public utilities, banking and finance, and transportation.

Shopping Center Directory.

STANDARD & POOR'S CORPORATION publishes several guides:

    Bond Guide.
    Bond Outlook.
    Industry Surveys.
    Listed Stocks Report.
    The *Outlook.*
    Register of Corporations, Directors & Executives.
    Stock Guide.

Sources of State Information and State Industrial Directories. Information on state and regional directories.

Sweet's Catalog. Annual. A catalog of manufacturers, catalogs for architecture, light construction, industrial construction, product design, metal-working equipment, plant engineering, which includes trade names, products, and marketing data.

25,000 Leading U.S. Corporations. Companies by about two dozen indices including earnings, number of employees, sales, etc.

Thomas' Register of American Manufacturers. Arranged by product, geography, and manufacturer.

Trade Directories of the World. Covers U.S. and foreign countries.

Marketing and Advertising Journals

There are, of course, many more marketing and advertising journals than the eight recorded below. References to these journals and trade magazines will appear in the indices indicated earlier in this section, of which there are hundreds. The trade magazines, especially, focus on specific industries or product lines and often compile and publish current statistics and market data that are available to the researcher for the cost of retrieving them.

Advertising Age. A weekly newspaper concerned mainly with developments in the field of advertising, it is also a source for other marketing data. Also, it publishes advertiser expenditures on media, along with other information on top advertisers.

Industrial Marketing. A monthly publication that covers industrial marketing and business publication advertising.

Journal of Advertising Research. Good source for listings, reviews, and résumés of the current literature.

The Journal of Marketing. A quarterly from the American Marketing Association, it publishes general readership and academic articles on marketing.

Journal of Marketing Research. Also a quarterly publication of the American Marketing Association, it focuses on methodology and technical problems of statistical analysis.

Journal of Retailing. Quarterly. Articles focus on retailing and developments in the field.

Sales and Marketing Management. A semi-monthly issue that covers current trends and marketing management. "The Survey of Buying Power" appears mid-year.

Survey of Buying Power. (See above.) Provides details on consumer income and expenditures, retail sales, population, and potential marketing applications of the survey data. The buying power index is a weighted index that uses a combination of population, effective buying income and retail sales as a measure of the market's ability to purchase and expresses it as a percentage of the potential of the American market.

Trade Associations for Specific Data

Trade associations are the source of much specific information that may not be readily accessible from other sources. Trade associations often compile statistics and information on their industry, or may interpret research results of other agencies and organizations, which may be made available only to the membership. The *Encyclopedia of Associations* is the major source book for names and addresses of all types of associations, many of which are of only peripheral interest to the market researcher. Below are listed only a few associations of general interest to the market researcher and a few guides to trade associations.

Association of National Advertisers. Offers assistance in developing accurate information on promotional activities and advertising but does not provide industry statistics.

Association for Systems Management. Publishes 35 publications and offers statistical and informational matters in the business systems field.

Council for Agricultural Sciences and Technology. Provides information on food and agricultural issues and issues a bimonthly newsletter.

Directory of British Associations. Lists approximately 8,000 British and Irish associations.

Directory of European Associations. Lists about 7,500 associations of western and eastern Europe.

The Encyclopedia of Associations. Since 1956 this directory has kept count on currently more than 13,000 trade, fraternal, and special interest associations.

Governmental Research Association. An organization of individuals professionally involved in governmental research.

Information Industry Association. Covers creation, retrieval, marketing, publishing, and utilization of information and data, documents, and literature.

Institute for Monetary Research, Inc. Offers information searches on industry, business, economics, monetary matters, and politics.

Municipal Yearbook. An annual publication of the International City Managers' Association.

National Association of Manufacturers. A trade association that represents the majority of American manufacturers before Congress and regulatory agencies.

National Trade and Professional Associations of the U.S. Lists approximately 4,500 national associations and available materials.

Besides these very important secondary sources of information, a wealth of data exists within your own organization.

I.2: AN ACRE OF DIAMONDS IN YOUR COMPANY RECORDS

A lode of valuable information at this moment awaits excavation in the mine of company records. Data may be used alone, or combined with information from secondary sources. Although company financial records have been organized for financial analysis, a persistent market researcher will rework the data to extract gems of marketability.

Which of the following company record jewels will embellish your sales and profits?

◎ Screening new product ideas for viability and profitability.
◎ Determining the return on advertising expenditures.
◎ Assessing return from different types of customers.
◎ Ascertaining geographic and economic areas of present customers.
◎ Making a profit analysis by product line and customer size or type.

Screening for Profits

In the process of new product or service development, after idea generation, the next discrete stage is screening. Screening relies on secondary data generated externally, and internally, and on qualitative judgments.

A conceptualization of the new product development process is shown in Figure I.2.A. It indicates that the entire process engages at least six distinct stages leading from idea generation to screening. Screening relies on secondary data and qualitative judgments which suggest a broad analysis during these early stages. Business analysis, which follows, requires collection of primary data on potential demand coupled with a more exhaustive analysis of technical flexibility. Background for this research begins with internal records. From this stage onward, more attention is paid to risk—the chance of failure—and areas of uncertainty, as funds are allocated for product development, testing, and finally commercialization. The objective at each stage is cost reduction, and the elimination of potentially low-payoff ideas.

Sometimes a firm may prefer to list evaluation criteria in a checklist such as the example that appears in Figure I.2.B, developed by Richard Christian. Or management may prefer a broader examination of key areas of uncertainty. Such analysis may encompass not only new products and services but also evaluation of marketing effectiveness of existing lines in terms of profitability and penetration.

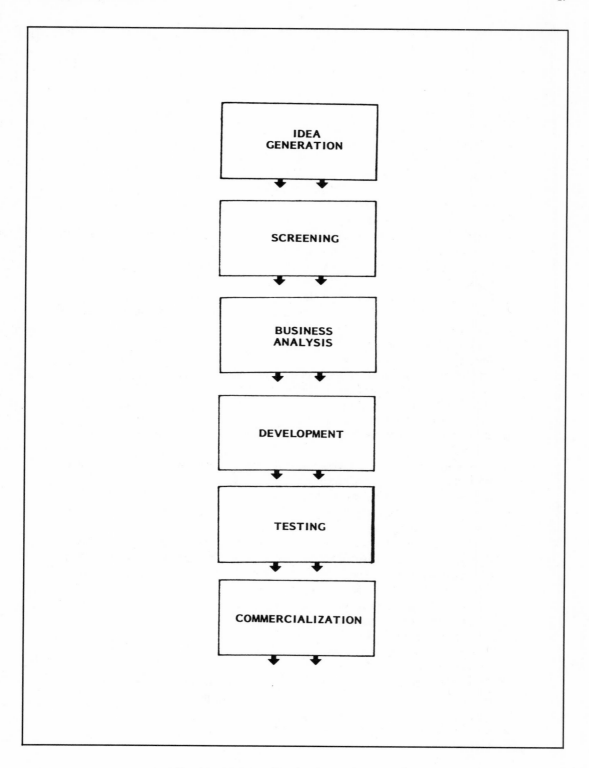

Figure I.2.A: THE PRODUCT DEVELOPMENT PROCESS

A CHECKLIST FOR NEW INDUSTRIAL PRODUCTS

---

1. Purposes of New Product:
   a. Round out company's present line?
   b. Fill idle time of plant and equipment?
   c. Help long-range growth and security of business?
   d. Seasonal effects can be leveled?
   e. Impact of business cycles is lessened?
   f. Excess capital is put to work?
2. Qualifications of the Proposed New Product:
   a. An entirely new product that will be accepted in adequate volume because it satisfies some need and sells at a price prospective buyers will pay?
   b. In an already developed field, a new product that offers some important competitive advantages?
   c. A new product, even without competitive superiority, in a relatively undeveloped field where there appears to be ample opportunity for another product to obtain satisfactory volume by sales to new users?
3. Legal and Related Problems:
   a. Who controls all rights to the new product?
   b. Are all outstanding claims to royalties or other indemnities settled?
   c. Has maximum patent and trade-mark protection been secured?
   d. What patent, trade, legal, or similar restrictions, if any, are there on the production, distribution, sale or use of the new product?
   e. Will marketing agreements or other industry agreements in any way limit production, sales, or use of the product?
   f. Is there anything in pricing policies, trade practices, or selling setup which might be in violation of a statute, law, or ordinance?
   g. Have all local licensing and tax problems been considered?
   h. Are there any other legal problems, peculiar to the new product, to be considered?
4. Financial Considerations:
   a. What capital investment will be required in plant, equipment, engineering etc.? Show description, unit value, life expectancy and total value of equipment, facilities, tools, patterns, etc., necessary for production.
   b. How much—if any—new capital is required?
   c. Have budgets been made up estimating, at various volume levels, the following:
   — Manufacturing and distribution costs?
   — Prices and gross margins?
   — Selling and administrative expenses?
   — Net profit or loss?
   d. Does prospective profit warrant risk under the most adverse circumstances anticipated?
   e. How large in amount are excess funds over current operating requirements?
5. Production Facilities:
   a. Can new product be made at existing plant? How adaptable are present production facilities?

Figure I.2.B: A CHECKLIST FOR NEW INDUSTRIAL PRODUCTS

  b. Will new facilities interfere with present operations?

  c. Is wholly new plant required?

  d. If so, have all factors determining location been considered?

  e. Will plant operation be flexible enough for adjustment to periods of unexpected heavy or low demands?

6. Raw Materials:

  a. What new materials are required?

  b. Are adequate supplies assured?

  c. Are sources of supply dependable?

  d. What inventories will be required?

  e. What substitutes are available?

  f. How will substitution affect quality? Cost?

7. Product Research and Development:

  a. What preliminary laboratory research is needed?

  b. What is estimate of time it will take? Cost?

  c. Will successful small-scale operations insure successful large-scale operations?

  d. Will plans allow for ample time before test marketing?

  e. Is the engineering group supplied with sufficient talent?

8. Number of Prospective Users:

  a. What industries will use the new product?

  b. Can the product be sold to the federal government, including armed forces? To state and local governments?

  c. How many potential customers are there in this country? Estimate number of prospects, either firms or individuals, for each type of user.

  d. What factors cut down the size of the total market?

  — Does computation of potential customers include deduction for sections of country where there is little use for product?

  — What percentage will be poor prospects because they use smaller-scale or larger-scale equipment than this product?

  e. Is the market for this type of product likely to increase or decrease in size during the next two, five, or ten years?

  f. Are there foreign sales possibilities for the product?

9. Users' Buying Habits:

  a. What is frequency of purchase and use? Order size that can be expected?

  b. How do users generally pay for such products? For cash, open-account credit, time-payment, other?

  c. Will product sell evenly throughout year, or will bulk of sales be concentrated in one or more seasons?

  d. If seasonal:

  — When will immediate customers buy?

  — If present customers are not the final users, when will users buy?

  — Is there any way to level out seasonal fluctuations in sales by balancing sales to different groups of purchasers?

  e. Are purchasers of this type of product accustomed to buying it ahead of need, or do they tend to place spot orders for instant shipments?

Figure I.2.B (continued)

   f. Will some purchasers of new product buy only on basis of unusual technical specifications or other special buying procedures? If so, can their requirements be met?
   g. Are potential users accustomed to relying on trade names or firm names, or do they buy mainly on the basis of technical specifications?
   h. How do major users or distributors of product negotiate for it?
   i. How receptive are prospects to new products?
10. Distribution:
   a. In what parts of country are prospects?
   b. How, if at all, does location of prospects affect plans for distribution channels?
   c. Might it pay, for a preliminary trial period, to confine distribution to one or a few selected regions of the country?
   d. Through what channel or channels are users accustomed to buying products of this kind? What channel or channels are planned?
   e. On what sort of franchise, if any, do competitors usually sell products like new product?
   f. What about the franchise matter?
   g. Will contemplated selling methods fit the company's present sales organization?
   h. If not, what about this type of distribution?
   i. How do proposed selling methods compare with competitors' methods?
   j. What changes in or additions to present sales force will be needed?
   k. If products like new ones usually have a service guarantee (factory or distributor guarantee), will distributors conform?
   l. If products like this are usually installed by the manufacturer or distributor, will distributors conform?
   m. What is the best way of getting product to customers? Consideration of carriers from the viewpoint of rates, territory served, accessibility to plant, losses in transit, packaging requirements, speed in handling and transit, and so on?
   n. How should product be prepared for shipment?
   o. Where will stocks of product be maintained?
   p. Where will servicemen and spare parts be available?
   q. Is test marketing needed?
11. Competition:
   a. How firmly entrenched is present competition?
   b. What firms make products that will compete with product?
   c. What advantages has each competitor over company, for example, in terms of nearness to market?
   d. What is reputation of:
   — Leading competitive firms?
   — Leading competitive products?
   e. Are competitors or potential competitors likely to enter the field with products similar to this?
   f. To what extent do unrelated products indirectly compete with new product?
   g. Are changes in materials or methods likely to reduce the need for product? Are changes in material or methods likely to increase present competitors' sales?
   h. What past, current, and prospective technological trends might affect the competitive situation?

Figure I.2.B (continued)

    i.   Is name and reputation of company already established, in the minds of the people who will distribute new product and the people who will use it, with respect to:

— Similar products already made?

— A general reputation for quality and engineering progressiveness?

    j.   Is it best to trade on company name in introducing the product, or would it be easier and more satisfactory to build up a separate name for the product itself?

    k.   Can new product compete favorably with similar products on the market as to:

— Price?

— Quality?

— Performance?

— Finish and appearance?

— Durability and length of service?

— Length-of-service guarantee?

— Other guarantees?

— Package or method of packing?

— Other respects?

    l.   Has product received controlled-engineering performance tests side by side with the products of competitors?

    m.   What unique advantages, if any, can be claimed for product over those of competitors?

    n.   Do customers buy competitors' products mainly on the strength of:

— Technical specifications?

— Reputation of the company?

— Reputation of the brand or trade name?

— Other factors, such as reciprocal sales arrangements, company affiliations, personal friendships?

    o.   Which of the following methods will be used to obtain share of market?

— Reducing total competitors' sales for this type of product?

— Expanding the demand for the product, so as to sell full output without cutting sales of competitors?

— Partly by cutting competitors' sales and partly by increasing total effective demand?

12. Price Policy:

    a.   What will price policy be?

    b.   Has profit margin been computed as accurately as possible?

    c.   Which: a big-volume/small-margin price policy, or a small-volume/big-margin price policy?

    d.   What about insurance costs as well as manufacturing-and-selling costs in determining price?

    e.   What about transportation costs, including basic rates, yard-and-switching charges, if any, and other handling costs?

    f.   How much will packaging and packing costs be?

    g.   How will installation costs, if any, affect price policies?

    h.   Will company service or help service the product? If so, will the user pay directly for the service?

    i.   Will distributors help to service the product?

    j.   Have complete factory-price schedules been worked out for spare parts?

    k.   What classes of customers will be entitled to trade discounts?

    l.   Will cash discounts be offered to customers?

Figure I.2.B (continued)

13. Sales Force and Selling:
    a. In terms of direct-selling costs, what will it cost per unit to promote and sell product?
    b. Is sales force already handling other products?
    c. If yes:
       — Can it take on new product and do justice to it without harming the sale of regular line?
       — Or will present organization need to be changed or expanded?
       — Or would it be best to establish an entirely separate sales staff to handle the new product?
    d. If decision is to expand or change present organization to handle the new product, what about the following?
       — Increase the size of the staff?
       — Decrease the size of territories?
       — Give salesmen special training to sell the new product?
14. Advertising and Sales Promotion:
    a. Have general policies been formulated for promoting product among:
       — Users?
       — Distributors?
    b. What sales-promotion and advertising methods are used by competitors?
    c. What sales-promotion practices are followed by distributors in reselling type of product?
    d. Are advertising and sales-promotion activities planned now, or for later?
    e. What engineering and design or other features of product can be stressed in advertising and promotional work?
    f. What message, in general, will be the basis of advertising appeal?
    g. How much and what type of sales-promotion assistance will salesmen need to help them sell to distributors or users, or both? For example, engineering advice, marketing data, printed catalogs, drawings, samples, briefcase portfolios, educational slides or films.
    h. What general advertising and promotional support for distributors?
    i. Are there to be sales-and-service manuals, parts lists, tables of shipping weights, and the like for the use of distributors and users of the product?
15. Personnel:
    a. Background of executive experience—what talent going beyond the existing product line is available?
    b. What additional personnel will be necessary? Production? Clerical? Marketing? Other?
    c. Can present departments handle the new work load, or will separate departments with new personnel be needed?

Figure I.2.B (continued)

Consider this example: A company conducted a detailed cost analysis of three of its distributors. When they discovered that not all products handled by their distributors were profitable, they forged a marketing program that increased profitability. The firm began by selecting three distributors. For each one, the supplier did a one-year cost analysis by product classification. Overall operations of the three distributors were profitable.

However, analysis of details revealed that one distributor was losing money on 28% of the 28 product classifications handled. Another was losing on 21% of the product classifications. A third one was losing on 25% of the product classifications carried. That is, overall profitability, the big picture, hid the little profit leaks.

Each company moved to plug them. One distributor dropped some of the biggest money losers. Another increased the price on high volume losers and turned these items into profit makers. A third one reshuffled inventories and increased profits.

Pinpointing Money Makers

One enterprise analyzed costs and profits not only by products but also by type of customer. Initially this may involve some effort to pry appropriate figures out of accounting; but this financial information, coupled with data from the sales or marketing department, will pinpoint the money losers, and the money makers. Profit-building builds on data relevant to profit analysis. The form in Figure I.2.C illustrates one method of organizing such data.

BASIC DATA FOR PROFIT ANALYSIS

By Products:

	PRODUCTS		
	A	B	C
Cost per Unit			
Unit Selling Price			
Number of Units			
Sales per Period			

- -

By Customer Type:

	CUSTOMER CATEGORY		
	I	II	III
No. of Sales Calls			
Total Sales Expenses			
Sales Cost per Call			
No. of Orders			
Total Billing Cost			
Billing Cost per Order			
Sales of Product:			
A			
B			
C			
Inventory Control Cost:			
No. of Units			
Total Cost			
Cost per Unit			

Figure I.2.C: BASIC DATA FOR PROFIT ANALYSIS

There are two parts to this form:

1. The upper section focuses on the various products, market A, B, C, in the example.
2. The lower section highlights category of customer, indicated I, II, III.

For example, an apparel manufacturer may produce dresses, pants, and jackets (Products A, B, C) and sell them to department stores, discount stores, and boutiques (I, II, III). Cost data will come from accounting, sales call data and costs from the sales department. These figures underpin profit and loss statements by type of customer, exhibited in Figure I.2.D.

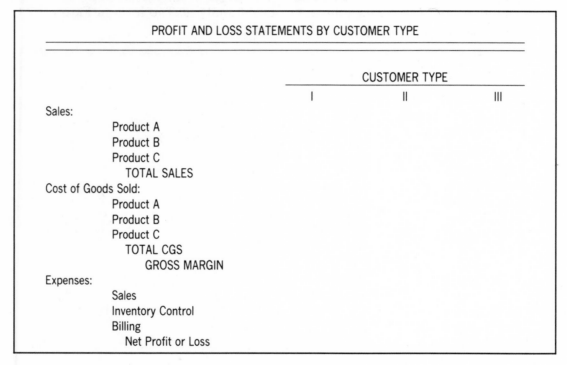

	CUSTOMER TYPE		
	I	II	III
Sales:			
Product A			
Product B			
Product C			
TOTAL SALES			
Cost of Goods Sold:			
Product A			
Product B			
Product C			
TOTAL CGS			
GROSS MARGIN			
Expenses:			
Sales			
Inventory Control			
Billing			
Net Profit or Loss			

PROFIT AND LOSS STATEMENTS BY CUSTOMER TYPE

Figure I.2.D: PROFIT AND LOSS STATEMENTS BY CUSTOMER TYPE

There is an important advantage to this method: It provides crucial evidence for strategic planning by pinpointing profit-makers and high-cost sales.

Broadly, such facts will encourage the decision-maker to modify present and future policies so that total profitability rises. This is valuable information for screening new product ideas. It is valuable information for formulating promotional strategies that yield higher return per dollar spent in advertising or in direct sales. Carried out in sufficient detail, this analysis highlights not only type of customer but also customer size and product line in relation to type of customer.

Eliminating Money-Losing Bids

Another type of problem experienced by a small manufacturer of aircraft parts appeared when the cost of bidding rose dramatically. Although this was a small manufacturer, or small business as rated by the SBA, its sales were world-wide. So the executive vice president ordered a simple analysis on all quotations by geographical location, by customer size, by product type (broad definition), and by whether the customer was new or old. The firm followed the format in Figure I.2.E.

	(1) Number Quoted	(2) Number Sold	(3) Sales Ratio
QUOTATION ANALYSIS			
I. Territory:			
Northeast			
East			
Southeast			
Midwest			
Southwest			
West			
International			
II. Customer Size: (No. of employees)			
1 – 99			
100 – 499			
500 – 999			
1000 – 2499			
over 2500			
III. Product Type:			
A			
B			
C			
IV. New or Old Customers:			
New—never sold			
No sales in past year			
Presently selling			

Figure I.2.E: QUOTATION ANALYSIS

Some of the information was already available on the computer; the remain-der required some research hours by the clerical staff, i.e., low cost labor. Customer size absorbed the most research time. Because old customers were well known, someone in the office could provide a good estimate of size. Fortunately, their only international salesman was in the office when the analysis was initiated; he furnished data on international customers. Dun & Bradstreet directories (see references in I.1.) filled in missing facts on new accounts, together with state directories. In two instances the firm telephoned small manufacturers on whom they had no information.

The executive vice president learned from this simple analysis that most high-cost quotations sprang from new accounts in four product categories. After pointing a finger at the cost drain, management did two things immediately:

1. They stopped bidding in those categories where the success ratio was low.
2. They personally visited or telephoned a number of these firms to explore what further changes were necessary. Profits rose dramatically on the same volume of business.

Analyzing Market Shares

Another question that internal data can deliver leads on, coupled with some statistics from external secondary sources, is this: How well are we really doing? This questions leads to two types of analysis:

(a) market share analysis, and
(b) market potential analysis.

The analysis may be done by

1. sales or marketing territory,
2. a political subdivision such as city, county or parish, state, region, or country, or,
3. marketing area that may embrace several small countries.

Examples shown are for state-wide analysis. The market share analysis somewhat parallels quotation analysis in that it attempts to nail down where the business is headed, by plant size and by product line.

The firm that conducted the analysis along the lines of data in Figure I.2.F sold industrial cleaning supplies, equipment, and services. However, a manufacturer and renter of uniforms employed similar type analysis over the five counties that make up the greater Atlanta area. Similarly, a commercial collection agency analyzed a region covering greater New York and suburbs extending to Fairfield County in Connecticut, all of New Jersey, and the Philadelphia area. In this latter case, the collection firm contacted only firm headquarters or regional credit offices rather than plants.

• *First*, the manufacturer categorized its sales by broad product line; in this example there were 32. Then, number of plants sold was subdivided into those employing fewer than 100 employees, the small manufacturers, and those employing over 500, the larger customers; a third column was allocated for all plants sold.

Product Line	No. of Plants Sold			No. of Plants in State			Percent Plants Sold		
	Plants > 100 Employees	Plants < 500 Employees	All Plants	Plants > 100 Employees	Plants < 500 Employees	All Plants	Plants > 100 Employees	Plants < 500 Employees	All Plants

MARKET SHARE ANALYSIS FOR STATE OF _____

Figure I.2.F: **MARKET SHARE ANALYSIS FOR STATE OF**_____

• *Second*, from state directories they totaled the number of plants within the state by the same breakdown. Because it proved difficult to relate potential customers to actual products the company sold, they resorted to SIC numbers to classify plants and adjusted their product lines correspondingly.

• *Third*, the percent of plants sold was a simple arithmetic task of dividing the number sold by the number existing for each product category to obtain this result: the number of plants sold. By this technique the firm readily saw wherein lay their strengths and weaknesses. The marketing strategy they developed was simple: "We'll build on our strengths and avoid putting money in efforts that spring from our weaknesses." Although this may not be tackling weaknesses and competition head on, it was a practical solution for this firm. Sales, and profits as a percentage of sales, rose.

Assessing Market Potential

A producer of business forms wanted to assess the market potential for their line which included business forms, printing services, selected office items, and a new line of sales presentation items they were adding. Also, they wanted to compare sales force effectiveness, but they had difficulty comparing results from

Rhode Island, Washington, D.C., Virginia, and New York, for example. They decided that a simple, low-cost way around this problem was to base their analysis on number of employees. The format used appears in Figure I.2.G. (For alternative methods see Section V.4, VI.2 and VI.3.)

• *First*, they divided their product into five categories for an analysis of current customers: columns 1, 2, and 3. This information gave them a better idea of the source of business plus a comparison among states, which revealed the average annual sales per employee of their existing customers. (Subsequently, they repeated this analysis by sales territory.)

• *Second*, they wanted to project state-wide potential by simple extrapolation. Since everyone was a potential customer for their products and services, they could not classify potential customers by product category, so they used totals only.

Market Potential: By multiplying average annual sales per employee of existing accounts (column 3) times state-wide employment in all businesses, they developed a "State Market Potential."

Market Penetration: Then, dividing present total annual sales (column 1) by the state market potential (column 5) resulted in a figure, a percentage, which they interpreted as "market penetration." (This was the subject of sales meetings over the next several months, since they had barely penetrated 2-to-3% of the market in most instances.)

For a company with a distinct product line that can be subdivided by SIC numbers, this same analysis carried across all columns produces detailed information. Such details are preferable when allocating budget and time within the organization. They are valuable in determining whether or not to enter new markets. For example, a regional pickle packer can substitute adult population figures for number of employees.

A cross-sectional analysis not only by product line but also by ethnic group, for example, may suggest a particular market strategy for introducing products into a virgin region; or data may imply that more fertile possibilities lie in another hitherto unexploited region; or the figure may simply say: "You haven't been doing very well in your own region, so why move on at this time and increase expenses to generate questionable profits?" Of course, marketing research will not give the final answer. Decision-makers still make decisions. But supplementary information helps raise decisions to more profitable levels.

MARKET POTENTIAL FOR STATE OF _____

Product Line	(1) Total Annual Sales to Present Customers	(2) Number Employees in Customers' Businesses	(3) Average Annual Sales per Employee $(1) \div (2)$	(4) State-Wide Employment	(5) State Market Potential $(3) \times (4)$	(6) Penetration of State Market (%) $(1) \div (5)$

Figure I.2.G: MARKET POTENTIAL FOR STATE OF _____

59

I.3: SECRETS OF GETTING RIGHT RESPONSES IN PERSONAL INTERVIEWS

Most marketing research—even that done with external secondary materials or in conjunction with internal company records—probably should involve some interviewing, either personal or telephone, for profit protection. The market researcher ought to perform at least some of this interviewing, even though hired interviewers complete the bulk of the basic research. (Even politicians occasionally escape from their ivory towers and meet the voters.)

By talking with consumers the researcher observes other, more subtle, feedback (body movements, voice intonation, etc.) and learns from unsolicited comments (sometimes rough on the ego) information that may not turn up at all during secondary research or mail surveys. However, competent interviewing pivots on preparation, practice, and proficiency.

Essentially there are four types of personal interviews:

1. Structured and direct.
2. Unstructured and direct.
3. Structured and indirect.
4. Unstructured and indirect.

Which Interview Technique Is Best?

A *structured* interview requires the interviewer to follow questions in the exact words and in the exact order given. No deviation is permitted.

Structured formats are preferred for interviewers of low-level training:

(a) to overcome interviewer bias,
(b) to compare results consistently among several interviewers, and
(c) to provide continuity among respondents from diverse backgrounds.

In other words, comparison among questionnaires is easier and answers tend to be more consistent. We come across structured interviews in shopping centers, or in supermarkets, or in many door-to-door surveys.

An *unstructured* interview, being flexible, seemingly follows no fixed pattern or order of questioning. Nevertheless, the goal, or end result, is clearly fixed in the interviewer's mind. Only highly trained, experienced interviewers should be entrusted with this approach, and only if they understand and agree with the objectives of the survey. The unstructured approach is more appropriate on the professional or industrial level where a company representative visits an executive in another firm. This approach permits the interviewer to explore important peripheral subjects that can well yield more information than that developed through a formal questionnaire. Its disadvantage is that it may yield nothing at all.

The *direct* interview starts with the purpose clearly evident to interviewer and respondent. "Our new infrared circuits are not selling as well as we thought they would. I'd like to get your reaction to them."

On the other hand, in the *indirect* technique, the interviewee does not know the primary reason for the questionnaire. For example, a respondent may be asked about a number of similar products without knowing that the real purpose is to ascertain data on brand preference. Indirect questions can generate information on opinions, attitudes, brand preferences. An unstructured, direct interview frequently crops up in exploratory studies to analyze attitudes, suggestion, personal experiences, etc.

How Do You Know What the Customer Wants?

An example, or pre-measure to research design, was a test run on various women's groups in two towns. The hypothesis was that the more a woman uses a specific brand the more she would know about that brand. Each woman was asked to classify the brands from three product categories—spray cologne, regular coffee, and fabric softener—according to her purchase/use experience: "Purchase" meant a current user; "familiar" meant had not bought within the past two years; and "unknown" meant never bought. By controlling the previous brand experience factor in the experiment, a sampling of a specific group of respondents led to controlled experiment on each of these products.

From this information, a hypothesis may be proposed and a more formal sampling may then follow. (See Section IV on sampling and sample size.) Of course, more difficult to tabulate are results from an unstructured approach. The structured direct interview, probably the most common, is naturally preferred by statisticians because they can more easily tabulate and manipulate outcomes mathematically (Section IV.6). Too, cost per interview is lower because data are more cheaply tabulated, and lower-priced interviewers are hired.

The purpose of interviewing is to find out what the buyer wants. For example, the chairman of International Flavors and Fragrance states that his company goes to the source, the buyer, for information. They search out new markets, and new product ideas, worldwide, by asking people what they want.

Of course, when we read of survey results, it all sounds simple and cheap. For instance, the National Family Opinion, Inc., conducts a survey with 5,000 households for The Conference Board and compiles a consumer buying-plans index which foreshadows changes in overall economic activity. Or Citibank, in its six-times-yearly survey, measures consumers' pessimism or optimism about the economy.

These questionnaires are not a simple: "Well, what do you think is going to happen?" A great deal of careful planning precedes the interviews.

A. *Preparation*.
  1. Why do you want to interview?
  2. What do you hope to learn from interviews?
  3. Specifically, what are your objectives? (Write them out.)
B. *Questionnaire*.
  1. Can any question be misinterpreted? (They will be.)
  2. Does any question offend or slur any group?
  3. Does each question ask for only one item, or one answer?
  4. Are the questions short? (Twenty words or less is about right.)
  5. Were the big words left at the office? (Use the KISS approach: Keep It Simple and Straightforward.)
  6. Is the questionnaire short? (For on-the-street or mall interviews, three minutes is about tops.)
  7. Will the questions provide the quality and quantity of answers necessary to justify the expense of this survey?
C. *Target*.
  1. Where should I interview?
  2. Whom should I interview?
  3. When should I interview?
D. *Revision*.
  1. After a trial run, be prepared to revise the questions; it pays to do several yourself in the beginning. Ask: How can I revise the questionnaire to make it more effective?
E. *Common Sense*.
  1. Whatever it is, use it. For example, if you want a good cross-section, interview at times of the day that will provide it.

     Remember: More than one-half the wives work today; more young wives than mature ones work; interview hours influence the sample.

For example, Carl J. Nelson, Inc., did a study for *The Boston Globe*. Interviewing began and ended on a Saturday. From Tuesday through Friday, interviewing hours were from 3 P.M.; on Saturdays, from 10 A.M. to 4 P.M. They selected these hours because that is when more adult family members were available. They avoided Mondays in order to avoid confusion over questions concerning daily newspapers read yesterday. In some cases they had to adjust interviewing hours to accommodate availability of family members.

What Goes Into a Good Questionnaire?

A questionnaire need not be complicated to produce useful information. In fact, a simple, but workable, technique may be the desirable, low-cost answer, especially if your firm does not have even a part-time marketing research department.

To illustrate, when consumers were presumably more brand conscious than price sensitive, the American Oil Company conducted personal interview surveys in selected markets, randomly selected from the state vehicle registration lists in specified counties. Part of the survey asked the gasoline purchasers what they thought about eight major brands and three leading independent brands of gasoline and asked them to rate each as follows: very favorable; moderately favorable; slightly favorable; neither favorable nor unfavorable; slightly unfavorable; moderately unfavorable; very unfavorable. (Also, refer to "Attitude Measurements" in Section III.) The approach lends itself well to firearms, computers, electronic calculators; stereo equipment, and other consumer products.

Techniques for ranking and analyzing are discussed in Sections III, V, and VI of this book. However, to provide the flavor of a personal interview, the questions in Figure I.3.A are taken from a survey conducted among a sample of 7500 persons. As you read through these questions, try to determine survey objectives.

AN EXAMPLE OF A PERSONAL INTERVIEW

Automobile Questionnaire

Respondent is   Census Region _____

_____   Area _____

Head of household _____   City _____

Other _____   State _____

                          Cluster # _____

Market Facts Representative _____   Date _____

City and State _____   Cluster # _____

◆◆◆◆◆◆◆◆◆◆◆◆◆◆◆◆◆◆◆◆◆◆◆◆◆◆◆◆◆◆◆◆◆◆◆

How do you do? I'm with Market Facts, Inc., and we're doing a national survey about automobiles. May I ask you some questions please?

〜〜〜〜〜〜〜〜〜〜〜〜〜〜〜〜〜〜〜〜〜〜

1a. Does anyone in this household happen to have an automobile?
    Yes ____ No ____
1b. (If "yes" to 1a) How many cars do you have? [Circle one.]
    1 2 3 4 or more

〜〜〜〜〜〜〜〜〜〜〜〜〜〜〜〜〜〜〜〜〜〜

(Ask questions 2-5 for each car owned; if more than one car owned, use this introduction: "Would you please give me some information about each of these cars? Let's take any one of them first.")

〜〜〜〜〜〜〜〜〜〜〜〜〜〜〜〜〜〜〜〜〜〜

Figure I.3.A: AN EXAMPLE OF A PERSONAL INTERVIEW

2a. What make and year is this car?

2b. Do you use this car mainly for business, for pleasure or both?

2c. About how many miles would you say the car is driven each year?

2d. How many people drive this car?

2e. Are any of these people under 25 years old?

3a. Is this car insured? [*If "yes" ask questions 3–4; if "no" go on to question 17.*]

3b. In round figures, about how much does insurance for this car cost you each year?

4a. Does this car have the kind of insurance that pays for damage to other people if you have an accident—that is *liability* insurance?

4b. With what company is this insurance carried?

4c. Does it have the kind of insurance that pays for damage to your car if you have an accident—that is *collision*?

4d. With what company is this insurance carried?

4e. Does it have the kind of insurance that pays for loss from fire, theft of your car—that is *comprehensive*?

4f. [*For each company mentioned*] How long have you been carrying insurance with this company? [*Specify years or months.*]

5a. Which member of the family drives this car the most?

5b. How old is he/she?

5c. Which member of the family would you say knows the most about choosing auto insurance?

~~~~~~

(Ask questions 6-16 only if car is insured.)

~~~~~~

6a. How did you first get in touch with your present company—that is, how did you first hear about it?

6b. The last time you bought auto insurance did you "shop around"—that is did you get prices from different companies?

6c. [*If yes*] How did you go about finding the names of companies to contact?

6d. What reasons are most important to you in choosing the company you did? Any others? [*Probe.*]

7a. With what company did you carry auto insurance before this one?

7b. [*If company named*] Why do you no longer carry your car insurance with this company?

8a. Do you think that there is a big difference in what different companies would charge you for the same kind and amount of auto insurance, or a small difference, or do you think that they all charge about the same?

8b. [*If difference between companies indicated*] Do you think that the cost of your present car insurance is higher than most companies would charge, lower than most, or about the same?

8c. [*If higher or lower*] Why do you say that?

9a. When you bought your present policy, did you contact the agent, or did he contact you?

9b. [*If respondent contacted agent*] How did you first get his name?

10a. What were the main sales points the agent made about your present insurance?

10b. Did the agent show you any printed material?

10c. [*If yes*] Do you remember what it was about?

Figure I.3.A (continued)

11a. Did you get any kind of insurance company identification to put on your car?

11b. [*If yes*] What was it?

11c. Did you put it on your car?

11d. Why?

12. How would you prefer to pay for your car insurance? Would you rather pay the whole amount once a year, pay half the amount twice a year, or make smaller payments more frequently?

13a. Are you satisfied with the evidence of auto insurance coverage that you now get from the company—such as the policy, a file card for your wallet, etc.?

13b. [*If no*] Why not?

14a. Have you ever had any occasion to use the insurance you carry with your present company— that is, have you ever had any claims with this company?

14b. [*If yes*] About how many times have you dealt with this company on a claim? [*Circle one.*] 0 1 2 3 4 5 6 7 8 or more

14c. In general, how well satisfied are you with the way (present company) handled your claims? Would you say you were very well satisfied, fairly well satisfied, or not at all satisfied?

14d. [*If not at all*] Why?

15a. Is there anything you would like to see changed in your present auto insurance company?

15b. [*If yes*] What would you like to see changed?

16a. What other types of insurance besides auto insurance does your present company sell?

16b. When you take out auto insurance do you usually discuss it with your wife/husband?

17a. What do you think is the principal difference between a mutual insurance company and other kinds of insurance companies?

17b. In general would you prefer to insure your car with a mutual insurance company or a stock insurance company?

17c. [*If any preference is expressed*] Why do you say this?

18. People give different reasons for taking out auto insurance. Which of the following do you think is most important to most people? Which do you think is least important?

_____To cover yourself against damage to your car.

_____To cover your responsibility for damage to the other fellow.

_____Because it's required by law.

_____Other.

19a. Do you think there should be a law requiring anyone who drives to have some kind of auto insurance that protects the other fellow?

19b. Does (your state) have any special law that requires drivers to carry auto insurance?

19c. [*If yes*] Briefly, what are its provisions?

19d. Would you say that the law that (your state) has is a good law or a poor law?

20. Here are some of the things about auto insurance companies that some people feel are important. [*Show set of cards.*] Now can you tell me which of these is most important to you personally? [*Record 1 below and ask:*] And of these left, which is the most important? [*Record 2 and proceed until all cards have been ranked.*]

_____ Quick settling of claims	_____ Claims adjusters in all
_____ Low cost of insurance	parts of the U.S.
_____ Good service from local agent	_____ Fair treatment by company
_____ Well-known company	
	_____ Installment plan for payment

_____ Other [Explain.] _____

Figure I.3.A (continued)

21. Besides your present company, what auto insurance companies can you think of offhand? . . . Any others?

22a. Of all the auto insurance companies you have ever heard of, and regardless of cost, which one do you think gives the best service in settling claims quickly and fairly?

22b. Why do you happen to think so?

23a. Of all the auto insurance companies you have ever heard of, which one do you think gives the poorest service in settling claims quickly and fairly?

23b. Why do you happen to think so?

24a. Here is a list of eight insurance companies. [*Show card.*] Which ones have you ever heard of before?

    ____Allstate, ____Farm Bureau Mutual, ____Farmers' Insurance Group,
    ____U.S. Fidelity & Guaranty, ____Hartford Accident, ____Liberty Mutual,
    ____State Farm Mutual, ____Travelers.

24b. Have you ever bought insurance from any of these companies?

24c. [*For each mention*] Why do you no longer carry (each company's) insurance on your car?

24d. What do you think of this company? [*Interviewer, rate respondent's attitude.*] Why?

24e. Does (each company heard of) sell other kinds of insurance besides auto insurance? What other kinds?

24f. One of these companies sells more auto insurance than any other company in the world. Which company would you guess that is?

25a. Of the eight auto insurance companies, which company would you say probably offers insurance at the lowest cost?

25b. [*If respondent has insurance, but not with company mentioned in 25a*] How does it happen that you don't carry (least expensive company's) insurance on your car?

26a. Have you ever heard of or seen advertising for any of these four companies? [*Show card.*]

    ____Allstate, ____State Farm Mutual, ____Travelers, ____Liberty Mutual

26b. Where did you hear or see the advertising?

26c. What did the advertising say?

26d. How does that strike you?

26e. [*For all four companies.*] You probably don't know exactly, but just as a guess, what percent of (each company's) policyholders would you say are farmers?

27a. In the last four years have you ever driven your car without any insurance for any length of time—that is, as long as six months?

27b. [*If yes*] What was the main reason you did not carry any insurance at that time? . . . . any other reasons?

28a. [*Ask if car insurance not carried now*] Have you had any auto insurance in the past 12 months?

28b. [*If yes*] What company was it with?

28c. Why did you drop this insurance?

29. About how many years do you usually keep a car before trading it in?

30a. When you first got the car you are now driving, did you sell or trade in another car at the same time?

30b. [*If yes*] At that time, when you changed cars, did you also change insurance companies?

30c. [*If yes*] Can you tell me why?

31a. How many people are there in your family?

Figure I.3.A (continued)

31. How old are they?
32. Age of respondent
    16–20 ____21–24 ____25–30 ____31–40 ____41–50 ____51–60 ____61 and over ____
33a. In what business trade or profession does the head of the household work?
33b. What is his or her exact job? In other words, exactly what kind of work does he or she do?
34a. Can you receive cable television in this area?
34b. Do you have a television set?
34c. What is your name please?
34d. What is the address?
35a. Income class: [*Show income card and enter letter here.*]
35b. How was this obtained? From respondent ____By observation ____
36. This respondent is: White ____Non-White ____[by observation]

◆◆◆◆◆◆◆◆◆◆◆◆◆◆◆◆◆◆◆◆◆◆◆◆◆◆◆◆◆◆◆◆

Date ____Time interview began ____Time interview ended ____

Figure I.3.A (continued)

Did you discern the purpose(s) of the survey? These personal interviews were done for an automobile insurance company to learn about their customers' attitudes toward that particular company and to compare it with attitudes consumers have about other insurance companies specifically and about insurance companies generally.

Through an analysis of answers the company learned: (a) why persons chose a particular insurance company; (b) how much comparison shopping they do; (c) whether the customers felt they were paying more or less than they would with another company; (e) why people bought more or less coverage; and, (f) an economic profile of interviewees.

Do You Know the Key Points?

To summarize, here are some important points to remember about personal interviewing:

- Both the questionnaire and the interviewing must be carefully planned and rehearsed to obtain valid results.

- Questions must be unambiguous, not subject to too many interpretations.

- Questions should be neutral to the extent possible, not likely to evoke an emotional response or cause the respondent to want to live up to an image. (An example of this occurred when a publishing firm asked people which books they would buy if out-of-print editions were reprinted. Most people answered "Shakespeare," or one of the classics. To double-check responses, the interviewer offered interviewees a book as a "token of thanks for your time." The books ranged from classics to porn. Invariably the respondents, who had just stated that they preferred the classics, would choose a free book with a title something like "Sex Murders in Love Motel.")

o→ Because of abuses and phony surveys, persons to be interviewed must not be suspicious of your motives. They must be convinced of your genuine intentions if you expect valid answers. They should be aware of the real purpose of interview. Identification, interviewers' paraphernalia such as clipboards or product samples may lower today's resistance to invasion of privacy.

o→ Which means that interviewers should be well trained. Instruction to them should be precise. One or several practice sessions are a must. Observation in the field by a supervisor will weed out abrasive personalities.

o→ There is always the temptation for the interviewer to fill in the blanks of uncooperative respondents or even to invent data, like some irresponsible news and credit reporters who fill quotas and write "reports" sitting in a bar. Follow-up postcards to respondents can help verify data. Inconsistencies or confused data turned in by an interviewer signal potential problems.

o→ This seventh key point relates to the attitude of interviewers, which is partly controlled by source and screening of applicants plus close supervision in the field.

o→ The questionnaire should be interesting to respondents (likewise, enthusiasm should be generated in the interviewer since it is contagious). The respondent should feel that he or she is benefiting, too, by answering the questions.

o→ Of course, paying respondents may kindle their interest, but paid respondents may hedge answers, too.

o→ Interviewers need to be persuasive (not dominating), must be able to create a friendly and cooperative environment, and especially must know when *not* to talk (very important in unstructured interviews).

o→ The interviewer should be well organized and prepared through practice, and the questionnaire pretested, tested, and revised where, when, as, and if necessary.

Even for mail surveys, the questionnaire must be tested and retested and revised, and ambiguous questions rooted out, because no interviewer is present to answer inquiries; but telephone interviews, while briefer than either personal or mail interviews, combine some advantages of each.

I.4: NINE BENEFITS AND NINE LIMITATIONS OF TELEPHONE SURVEYS

Whether your phone call meets with an alluvial voice or one of the finest cut, consider each potential respondent a diamond in the rough. The same persistence and courtesy that paid off in personal interviews will crystallize into flawless responses in telephone surveys if you incorporate these profit-ringing ideas in your next survey.

Almost everything written about personal interviewing applies to telephone interviewing, although telephone surveys do have certain cost advantages. But there are information disadvantages, too. Typically, telephone surveys are briefer, with fewer questions than personal interviews. Many businesses use telephone surveys. They are quite appropriate for small and medium-sized concerns stretching results from a restrictive marketing research budget.

The Short-Term Trends

Changes in consumer buying habits and business capital expenditure projections are often monitored through telephone surveys. For example, *The Wall Street Journal* staff conducts interviews in such major cities as Los Angeles, Chicago, New York, and Atlanta to determine the level of pessimism (or optimism) about the economy because such attitudes foreshadow changes in spending patterns.

National Family Opinion Survey, Inc., maintains contact with about 5,000 households for input in a consumer buying-plans index which reflects consumer confidence in the economy. Such information helps to decipher changes in shortterm trends and inventory planning. Minor business trends can change rapidly, and frequent updating of indices and time series devours quantities of information. But information on broad trends is readily available.

A Test for Brand Loyalty

Perhaps you want to know whether buyers of television sets in your marketing area display any strong degree of brand loyalty. One solution, an informal research design, is to poll (preferably through a research organization) selected households with a simple questionnaire such as the one in Figure I.4.A.

A SIMPLE SAMPLE SET OF QUESTIONS

1. Have you replaced a television set within the past 18 months?
2. Did you replace it with the same brand? [If yes, go to Question No. 3; if no, go to Question No. 4.]
3. YES
   (a) How many brands were considered while you were deciding? (More than 5; less than 5; none other.)
   (b) Was the old brand the first set you looked at?
   (c) Why did you finally decide to repurchase the old brand?
4. NO
   (a) How many brands did you consider? (More than 5; fewer than 5; only one.)
   (b) Did you consider the old brand at all? Why?
   (c) Which brand did you finally purchase? Why?
5. What is the single most important reason you considered in buying a television set?
6. How much did you pay for your television set?
7. How old was your last television set? Why did you replace it?
8. Personal data: age; marital status; type employment; etc.

Figure I.4.A: A SIMPLE SAMPLE SET OF QUESTIONS

A Test Market Telephone Panel

Several open-ended questions can generate additional information without burdening the respondent with too many questions. Too, the telephone survey approach can be combined with any of several other research techniques discussed in this handbook.

Here's a bell-ringer: Create a telephone panel for test market evaluation. Suppose you are introducing a new brand of a household item and want to know how consumers react to it. (Sales to stores alone will not reveal the extent of repeat buying; only total sales count.)

Such information will help plan advertising expenditures, market penetration, and portend potential market shares. Calling the same group of consumers periodically, say twice a month, will register the march of progress, at least among the consumers sampled. The questionnaire can be quite simple; e.g.,

1. Have you bought any (whatever the product is) within the past two weeks (since I last telephoned you)?
2. If yes, which brand did you purchase?
3. Which size did you buy (if that is applicable)?
4. How many (boxes, bottles, whatever) did you buy?
5. How long will that supply last you?

Survey results denote the import of advertising or special deals, whether small or large packages are preferred, and some indication as to how to space the promotional campaign. And this information flows from essentially the same group of consumers over a fairly long period. It can work effectively if

- ◎ rapport is established and maintained with each panel member;
- ◎ interviewers are well trained and courteous, and have pleasant voices (and preferably the same interviewers are telephoning the same panel members);
- ◎ the questionnaire is kept short and easy to answer;
- ◎ an inexpensive gift is sent initially or promised later; and
- ◎ it is done by an independent concern.

(For more specifics on use of panels, refer to Section I.7, and for test marketing to Section II.2.)

Another Bell-Ringer

Another practical application of the telephone method is to combine it with a mail survey. (Mail survey techniques are discussed in Section I.5.)

Unanswered mail-outs may be followed up a second, third, and even fourth time, but some persons who will not respond even to the 100th request for information will freely answer the same questions over the telephone. Consequently, the response rate from a specific sample will rise. This may be the least costly alternative to surveying a larger sample by repetitive mail follow-ups.

Which raises the other issue of when is the best time to call. It depends on the targeted respondents. Common sense usually will lead you in the right direction. The first and last hours of the workday, Monday mornings, and Friday afternoons are obviously not the best time for business surveys; but if you are telephoning housewives and female household heads, Monday morning is indeed the best time.

One survey found that the highest percentage of one-time calls could be completed between 9:00 A.M. and noon. Evenings, 7-10:00 P.M., were second best. Results from afternoon calls were quite poor. By day of week, the best to worst days ranked as follows: Monday, Wednesday, Thursday, Tuesday, Saturday and Sunday, about equal, and, on the bottom, Friday. So, ring on Monday morning!

The Rewards of Telephone Interviews

There are both benefits and limitations from telephone surveys; you should be aware of at least the main ones.

(a) A small amount of information can be collected from many persons (or businesses) quickly: certainly ideal for studies necessary to determine brand preference product knowledge.

(b) Per interview cost is lower than with personal interviews, but per unit of data (i.e., answer) is not necessarily cheaper. (More questions per respondent can be asked usually in personal interviews.)

(c) The cooperation rate tends to be higher on the assumption that more people will cooperate if it does not cost them much inconvenience or time.

(d) The interviewer can reschedule telephone callbacks easier and cheaper than personal interview callbacks.

(e) Telephoning is probably less flexible than personal interviewing but more flexible (especially with unstructured interviews) than mail surveys.

(f) Similarly, greater rapport can be established over the telephone than by mail, but probably less than with personal interviews; and an unrehearsed response can be expected.

(g) Telephoning can reach a wider geographical area (especially with cheaper evening or Saturday rates or WATS lines) cheaper than personal interviewing. (Although mail surveys may *reach* a wider geographical area, the *response rate* will be lower.)

(h) It is fast. An immediate answer is requested. A mail questionnaire is easily postponed, which requires expensive follow-up with second and third mailings and possibly phone calls. A regional, national, even international sampling can be completed in a few days, even in one day, by an effective team.

(i) Most households have telephones; a representative cross-section of potential respondents can be readily assembled from a crisscross directory, or the telephone directory alone in smaller cities.

Know the Limitations

(a) Not every household has a telephone; some groups are impossible to reach by phone. There is an increasing number of unlisted numbers (although this presents no problem with random dialing). In some areas a directory name may be starred to indicate that that person does not wish to be disturbed by unsolicited phone calls. Or if the phone sends out repeated busy signals because it is tied up by household teenagers, for all practical purposes the adults in that household do not have a telephone.

(b) Respondents' reactions cannot be observed as in personal interviews.

(c) A potential respondent may more readily refuse to cooperate than if he or she were accosted in a shopping mall by a personal interviewer.

(d) The scope of the interview is limited by the necessity of shorter questions; long distance toll charges are a constraint as well to longer interviews.

(e) Dispensable personal information that may be generated in personal interviews may be either not forthcoming or inaccurate. (Observation can at least confirm data on age, income, etc.)

(f) For certain consumer categories effective telephone interviews may be conducted only between dinner hour and television prime time—a short interval—to secure cooperation and reliable answers. For business people, getting past secretaries and assistants may be a serious obstacle.

(g) Products cannot be sampled or a free gift quickly given as in the case of personal interviews, and, to a lesser extent, in mail surveys.

(h) Because of repeated misuse of the telephone to develop sales leads under the guise of marketing research, respondents are more likely to be uncooperative, if not downright nasty. (Let professional researchers absorb the verbal abuse and rebuffs.)

(i) With the quest for privacy on one hand and the drive of governments for more information on its subjects, especially its dissidents, answers may be deliberately shaded for protective cover.

The Final Ring

Nevertheless, the telephone remains a practical instrument in marketing research in free societies. For a manufacturer, or supplier, an unstructured survey among present customers can turn up potential problems, generate ideas for product or service improvement, and establish closer links between supplier and customer.

That is, a marketing survey done by the marketing department is not a wasted telephone call even if it produces no quantifiable marketing research data. Such contacts can often produce valuable information that should be made available to other managements. But such contacts should be for legitimate market research purposes.

A distinct cost advantage may already exist in your organization if a WATS line is in place and available. Using it for telephone surveys beyond the local range makes sense, especially if it is currently underutilized. With time zone differentials, equipment need not be tied up during peak business hours. Evening calls to consumers may be stretched out another couple of hours calling from the East to the West, or they may be begun to businesses a couple of hours early, before the normal business day begins, when telephoning from the West to the East.

Data gathered by trained interviewers on a part-time or occasional basis will typically depend on a structured interview, a limited questionnaire that focuses on a set of specific questions and frequently for a single purpose.

For example: Who reads our magazine? How often? And where do they rank ours relative to other magazines? Or, do you plan to buy a new car this year? Or do you prefer presidential candidate X, Y, or Z? Or how many overseas telephone calls did you make last month? Where? And how much do you typically spend each month on overseas calls? Or to use in before-and-after studies such as assessing the impact of a promotional campaign, or in attitude surveys (more on this later)—consumer attitude toward a product, store, service—or measurement of consumer awareness of a product, store, service. If you require more information, however, then consider a mail survey.

I.5: TEN GILT-EDGED STEPS TO A SUCCESSFUL MAIL SURVEY

Because of the increased use, and misuse, of mail survey methods of market research, a successful, legitimate survey is in a race with the trash collector. Many questionnaires, especially poorly constructed ones, end up in the household or corporate wastebasket.

Managers of organizations especially have been inundated with forms and mandatory requests for inconsequential information from local and federal government agencies, from university professors writing about vague theories to support tenure and promotion, or from others who disguise their real purpose for information under the market research umbrella. Legitimate market survey questionnaires must compete for precious time.

Initial costs of a well-organized mail survey are considerable. A mail survey is costly if it generates a low return. A good mail survey is cheaper than either telephone or personal interviews, if a high response rate is explicitly planned for. A high response rate is also desirable for important reasons other than cost:

- ◎ quality of answers,
- ◎ representative sample response, and
- ◎ sufficient quantity of data for analysis.

Careless planning can render a 5 or 10 percent response rate. Careful planning can turn out a 50, 60, 70, or even 80 percent response rate. The magic answers expected from marketing research result from

- ◎ intelligent planning,
- ◎ high quality organization,
- ◎ expenditure of a reasonable sum to support the effort, and
- ◎ some common sense in the interpretation of data received.

Let's explore ten steps that can lead to an effective and successful mail survey campaign.

First: Sample Size

—Who should be targeted?
—How large should the sample be?
—Where are some sources of names?

A mail survey is best targeted to a specific group of respondents with several common dimensions. The broadest criterion is to include all human beings;

only the U.S. Bureau of Census spends that kind of money. Therefore, we must narrow the target to the group of persons who best fit our interests and purposes of the survey and budget.

In the sample questionnaires appearing in this section, notice that "our customers" is a common denominator. In Figure I.5.C the survey is directed to American book authors, a specific audience.

The state of Vermont hands out a brief questionnaire (illustrated in Figure II.2.B) to most persons who stop at a visitor center and request information—a rather hit-or-miss survey since it is not known whether certain categories of people stop, and, of those, which types of persons will actually return the completed card after the visit. And not everyone is handed a card. Such a leaky survey design is chancy for crossing a statistical lake of unknown depth.

Suppose you want to poll chiropractors with offices in Jacksonville, Florida. You may as well send questionnaires to all of them since the total population is rather small, and the cost not prohibitive. On the other hand, if you want the opinions of chiropractors throughout the United States concerning medical equipment you manufacture, then cost and common sense dictate that you select a representative sample.

Sampling procedures are explained and illustrated for you in Section IV of the handbook; but, obviously, the sample selected must sufficiently characterize other chiropractors in order to draw universally valid generalizations. Generally, the smaller the sample the more carefully you must select potential respondents. Even then, the issue arises whether chiropractors who answer questionnaires represent the general population of chiropractors.

Therefore, we can conclude the following about who, and how many, will receive questionnaires:

◎ Look for homogeneity in the group selected (e.g., chiropractors).
◎ If not homogeneous, look for common interest or problem (e.g., American book authors, or people against yellowjackets [wasps or drinks], or our customers).

From where do names originate? Company records harbor the most valuable source: credit customers, warranty cards, coupon respondents, inquiries from advertising, sales prospects, association lists from someone in your organization, suppliers' registration lists from trade shows.

From the directories listed in Section I.1, substantial lists by individuals, companies, or job titles can be easily assembled. Yellow pages of telephone directories bear fertile data. Still another source is public records: registered voters, property owners, vehicle registration lists, filings of motor transport companies, licensed professionals, 10-K forms, fish and game hatcheries, . . . and the list goes on.

Of course, purchased specialized mailing lists will subsume nearly any subgrouping of individuals or businesses imaginable: commodity futures speculators, parents with teenagers, congressional staffers, DP managers, etc.

Second: Composing Questions

—How to go about it?

—What kinds of questions?

This is crucial to an efficient campaign, a most difficult hurdle for the inexperienced. Unless questions are properly constructed, all other expenditures are wasted.

For example, with telephone or personal interviews, someone is available or present to discuss the purpose of the survey, to induce cooperation, and to clear up any obscure or thorny questions or issues. The mail questionnaire must be so constructed as to overcome resistance, inertia, and obscurity. A cover letter can explain the purpose.

A major problem centers on the unclear or misunderstood question—and respondents will misinterpret questions if at all possible. For instance, take a look at the example in Figure I.5.C. Researchers sent this questionnaire to book authors. One set of questions relates to authors' income; but authors receive advances which may or may not be chargeable against royalties, flat fees, income from book sales earned in one year but not paid until the next, and other combinations and possibilities not clearly explainable within the constraints of the questionnaire. Although the central purpose of this survey relates to author incomes, this set of questions will likely churn out some inconsistent answers.

The first step, then, in writing questions, is to decide clearly the aims of the mail survey. Write all questions with these objectives clearly up front. However, to eliminate invalid answers, the questionnaire should begin with one or more screening questions.

> *An example*: "Have you bought a new typewriter within the past 18 months? If not, please fold the questionnaire and return to us in the enclosed self-addressed, stamped envelope. Thank you for your cooperation."

The screening question cuts the cost of worthless tabulation of results. Return of the questionnaire helps to keep tabs on responses.

After writing the questionnaire, *the second step* is rewriting it, followed by a *third step*—revision. The objective of this revision is clarity. Are all questions clear as sin? Can they possibly be misunderstood?

Now continue to the *fourth step*: Rewrite it again. After all, it costs a lot of research money to gather this information, so why invalidate results with sloppy questions? Also, questions may be structured—as they usually are in most questionnaires—or semi-structured, or unstructured. Unstructured questionnaires produce feedback difficult to key and tabulate. They are more expensive to interpret but probably yield more interesting answers.

Figure I.5.A presents an example of a mail questionnaire sent to small manufacturers. Since it requires considerable effort from the respondent, returns tend to be lower than on one that is easily answered.

A SAMPLE MAIL QUESTIONNAIRE

Section I. General Production Marketing ● ● ● ● ●

1. What percentage of your sales volume is:
   A. production of standard products for inventory?
   B. custom (or "made-to-order") items?
   C. jobbing for other manufacturers?
   D. other?
2. What percentage of your total sales volume is:
   A. local (within 150-mile radius of your firm)?
   B. Northwest (remainder of Washington, Oregon, and Idaho)?
   C. entire West (remainder west of the Rocky Mountains)?
   D. U.S., east of Rockies?
   E. international?
3. Which company do you regard as the leading firm for your major product line, in your principal marketing area? _____
4. With respect to your distribution policy:
   A. Do you sell through your own sales organization?
   B. If "yes," how many full-time salesmen do you employ?
   C. Do you sell through manufacturers' agents?
   D. What percentage of your sales volume is sold through the following channels?
      (1) Direct to consumer
      (2) Direct to industrial user
      (3) Direct to retailer to user
      (4) Through wholesalers (or jobbers)
      (5) Through brokers
      (6) Other
   E. If you sell through wholesalers (or jobbers) is it your usual policy to grant:
      (1) exclusive territories?
      (2) semi-exclusive territories?
      (3) non-exclusive ("open") territories?
5. Is the size of your firm a handicap in your industry?
   If "yes," indicate in what ways you are handicapped.
6. Is your ability to compete adversely affected by the competitive practices of larger national competitors?
   If "yes," please indicate the types of practices and how they affect your company.
7. Do you have any special advantages in competing with large national competitors?
   If "yes," please indicate.

Section II. Cost Analysis ● ● ● ● ●

8. Do you make a "break-even point" analysis based upon a separation of actual fixed costs (expenses) and actual variable or semi-variable costs?

Figure I.5.A: A SAMPLE MAIL QUESTIONNAIRE

If "yes," how often is your break-even point analysis made available to the company's management?

9. In making a break-even point analysis, what percentages of the following cost categories do you consider fixed and what percentage variable?
   A. Raw materials
   B. Purchased parts and sub-assemblies
   C. Direct labor
   D. Indirect labor
   E. Other manufacturing expense
   F. Selling expenses
   G. General and administrative expenses

10. Do you compute actual costs per unit at various production levels?

11. Do you compute actual total costs for your individual products?

12. Does this break-even point analysis influence your management in making:
    A. pricing decisions?
    B. other decisions?
       (Please explain) _____

Section III. Pricing ● ● ● ● ●

13. In selecting your selling prices, is it your policy to:
    A. realize a specific percentage share of the market?
    B. realize a predetermined rate of profit on capital investment?
    C. realize a predetermined rate of profit on sales?
    D. mark up a predetermined percentage on total costs?
    E. mark up a predetermined percentage on direct costs?
    F. other (please indicate)?
    If "yes" to any of the above, please indicate percentage target.

14. In making calculations for pricing decisions, do you normally use:
    A. actual costs?
    B. predetermined standard costs?
    C. no costs in setting prices?
    D. other (please explain)?

15. Do you normally set your prices:
    A. at the same level as your principal competitor?
    B. above the level of your principal competitor?
    C. below the level of your principal competitor?
    D. other (please explain)?
       (1) Set prices independently.
       (2) Usually bid on job.
       (3) On basis of costs.
       (4) Trades association average or franchise grantor.
       (5) According to work load, location of buyer, buyer's needs, and ability to pay.

16. Please indicate how you determine your selling prices. For example, show the formula or the method used for pricing a representative product: _____

Figure I.5.A (continued)

17. What considerations would cause you to alter the previous prices of your products?
    A. "Competition and market conditions"
    B. "Change in costs"
    C. "Changes in volume"
    D. "If profit margin is not realized"
    E. "Improved methods"
18. What do you regard as a "fair" net profit before taxes for a firm in your industry?
    A. As a percentage of sales?
    B. As a percentage of total investment or net worth?
19. Do you have plans to expand your plant?
    If "yes", within the next:
    A. 12 months
    B. 3 years
    C. 5 years
20. What were your net profits before taxes as a percentage of sales for:

1981 _____	1977 _____
1980 _____	1976 _____
1979 _____	1975 _____
1978 _____	

    A. If all figures are not available, please indicate for the 1975-1981 period your:
    High _____
    Low _____
    Average _____
21. With respect to your ability to expand plant and facilities:
    A. Does your firm have sufficient retained earnings to:
       (1) replace machinery?
       (2) purchase additional machinery?
       (3) make a major expansion?
    B. Is your firm able to get long-term capital funds from conventional financial institutions to undertake:
       (1) minor expansions?
       (2) major expansions?
    C. Has your firm ever acquired funds from public sale of its capital stock for expansion purposes?
    D. Does your firm plan to sell its stock at public sale in the near future?

Figure I.5.A (continued)

Third: Questionnaire Length

—How many questions?
—How many pages?

Somehow we associate length with worth. A college student asks how long his term paper should be. A market researcher asks how many questions.

Let's turn the whole issue around, and ask: What is the objective of the study? How many questions (or pages) will it take to accomplish the objective? Sprinkle some common sense on your answers, and you will know how many questions to ask.

Is short better than long? Warranty cards have fewer consumer questions. Yet returns are typically low, even under the implied threat that the product guarantee is invalid without its return. Even among serious users of a product, such as firearm purchasers, the return is low. Marlin Firearms of New Haven, Connecticut, receives about 10 to 15 percent return of its warranty cards.

Some researchers say six to eight pages of questions are about right. But that is not a magic number, because we do not know the number or complexity of questions or interests of respondents.

Interest prevails over length, unless, of course, coercion is implied—such as by those mail surveys sent out by various governmental agencies. The number of pages is a function of the number and length of questions and format. Since format (the fifth point, discussed below) overrides length, we will pay more attention to that important step.

Fourth: Keying

—Should questions be keyed or precoded?
—If so, how?

The purpose of keying or precoding questions is for inputting in the computer for subsequent analysis. The operator need only refer to the coding and enter the data. Even for a purely mechanical operation, keying allows a clerk to transfer data onto coding sheets in a uniform manner, not subject to vagaries of interpretation. Two keying variations are illustrated in Figures I.5.B and I.5.C. (Also, refer to Section IV.6 on tabulation.)

For small quantities of data, hand tabulation on accounting paper is a low-cost alternative. It may well be the fastest alternative.

> *An example*: You have just surveyed 100 of your distributors on a single issue; breakdown of data by geographical area, size of distributor, number of years in business, etc. are not essential to the study.

On the other hand, if you have a large quantity of data from many respondents and require rather complex analysis, then machine-read answers, which transfer data directly from the form to the computer, eliminate staff time used for inputting data.

Magazine Letterhead
Address

Dear Reader:

This is the survey we wrote to you about a few days ago.

We are conducting this survey among our subscribers so that we may more closely match the editorial content of our magazine to your specific interests and needs.

We have selected random names from our subscriber list, and since yours was one of the ones selected, your answers are essential to the accuracy of our research.

We would be most grateful if you could take the time now to fill out the enclosed questionnaire and return it to us in the enclosed postage-paid envelope.

Our subscribers are the most important people we know, since without you, we would have no reason to exist.

Many thanks for your help.

Sincerely yours,

Editor

Figure I.5.B: READER SURVEY

EDITORIAL SURVEY

PAGE 1

Please answer by drawing only one "**X**" in the appropriate box for each question.

1023400

A. FROM THE JUNE TABLE OF CONTENTS LISTED BELOW
1. PLEASE GIVE US YOUR OPINION OF EACH ARTICLE
   BY MARKING

-1- EXCELLENT -2- GOOD -3- FAIR -4- POOR

PAGE	EDITORIAL	
16	THE NUCLEAR TRUTH	01
PAGE	ARTICLES	
26	GROW CARROTS IN ANY SOIL	02
34	THE ALTERNATIVE POTATO	03
38	MOTHER NATURES BUG-KILLER	04
46	GET THE DROP ON WATERING	05
52	BEAT THE BEET LEAF MINER	06
55	SUCCESS WITH CUTTINGS	07

PLEASE FOLD ON DOTTED LINE.

Figure I.5.B (continued)

EDITORIAL SURVEY

Please answer by drawing only one "**X**" in the appropriate box for each question.

1023400

A. (CONT.) FROM THE JUNE TABLE OF CONTENTS LISTED BELOW
1. PLEASE GIVE US YOUR OPINION OF EACH ARTICLE
   BY MARKING

-1- EXCELLENT -2- GOOD -3- FAIR -4- POOR

PAGE	ARTICLES	
60	LAYERING PLANTS FOR SURE PROPAGATION	08
64	THE MANY MOODS OF MULCH	09
75	KEEPING YOUR GARDEN HOSES UNDER CONTROL	10
82	GOURMET DISCOVERY IN FLAVOR -- VEGETABLE JUICE ASPICS	11
96	WHAT MAKES ORGANICS SO GOOD	12
104	ORGANICALLY GROWN BERRIES WIN TASTE TEST	13
108	TYING THE KNOT ON A SMALL HOMESTEAD	14

PLEASE FOLD ON DOTTED LINE.

Figure I.5.B (continued)

EDITORIAL SURVEY

Please answer by drawing only one "**X**" in the appropriate box for each question.

1023400

A. <CONT. FROM THE JUNE TABLE OF CONTENTS LISTED BELOW

1. PLEASE GIVE US YOUR OPINION OF EACH ARTICLE
   BY MARKING

   -1- EXCELLENT -2- GOOD -3- FAIR -4- POOR

PAGE	SHORT ITEMS	
57	BUILDING A ROOTING BOX	15
58	SEASONAL CUTTING CHART	16
63	MULTIPLY BY DIVIDING	17
70	CAUTION ON PAPER AND PLASTIC	18
90	DOLOMITE FOR HEALTH	19
103	PINE MOTH FACES NATURAL DEATH	20
105	EARLY-BIRD COMPOSTING	21

PLEASE FOLD ON DOTTED LINE.

Figure I.5.B (continued)

EDITORIAL SURVEY

Please answer by drawing only one "**X**" in the appropriate box for each question. 1.

1023400

A. <CONT. FROM THE JUNE TABLE OF CONTENTS LISTED BELOW
1. PLEASE GIVE US YOUR OPINION OF EACH ARTICLE
   BY MARKING

   -1- EXCELLENT -2- GOOD -3- FAIR -4- POOR

PAGE	DEPARTMENTS	
4	READERS LETTERS	22
16	QUESTIONS AND ANSWERS - GARDENING	23
66	READERS FORUM	24
81	ORGANIC LIVING EDITORIAL - UNTIL JULY	25
88	QUESTIONS AND ANSWERS - FOOD AND NUTRITION	26
92	HEALTH HARVEST -- STRAWBERRIES - THE LUSCIOUS HEALTH FOOD	27
117	GARDEN CALENDAR	28

PLEASE FOLD ON DOTTED LINE.

Figure I.5.B (continued)

EDITORIAL SURVEY

Please answer by drawing only one "X" in the appropriate box for each question.

10 2 3 4 0 0

A. (CONT. FROM THE JUNE TABLE OF CONTENTS LISTED BELOW
1. PLEASE GIVE US YOUR OPINION OF EACH ARTICLE
   BY MARKING

   -1- EXCELLENT -2- GOOD -3- FAIR -4- POOR

PAGE   DEPARTMENTS

126   GOINGS-ON   29

142   ORGANIC GARDENING ALMANAC   30

B. READING OUR MAGAZINE
1. WOULD YOU LIKE US TO CARRY MORE OR LESS
   OF THE FOLLOWING ARTICLES

   MARK -1- MORE -2- LESS -3- THE SAME

   INDOOR GARDENING - HOUSEPLANTS   31

   ENERGY CONSERVATION   32

   TIPS FOR BEGINNING GARDENERS   33

PLEASE FOLD ON DOTTED LINE.

Figure I.5.B (continued)

86

EDITORIAL SURVEY

1023400

Please answer by drawing only one "X" in the appropriate box for each question.

B. <CONT. READING OUR MAGAZINE
1. WOULD YOU LIKE US TO CARRY MORE OR LESS
   OF THE FOLLOWING ARTICLES

MARK -1- MORE -2- LESS -3- THE SAME

COMPOSTING	34
COMPANION PLANTING	35
GARDENING TOOLS	36
PEST CONTROL	37
VEGETABLE GARDENING	38
FLOWER GARDENING	39
BEE RAISING	40
SMALL LIVESTOCK RAISING	41
ADVANCED GARDENING TECHNIQUES	42

PLEASE FOLD ON DOTTED LINE.

Figure I.5.B (continued)

EDITORIAL SURVEY

Please answer by drawing only one "**X**" in the appropriate box for each question.

1023400

B. <CONT. READING OUR MAGAZINE
1. WOULD YOU LIKE US TO CARRY MORE OR LESS
   OF THE FOLLOWING ARTICLES

MARK -1- MORE -2- LESS -3- THE SAME

GREENHOUSES		43
ORCHARDS		44
KEEPING HEALTHY NATURALLY		45
NUTRITION		46
CANNING, FREEZING, DRYING		47
LAWN CARE		48
BUILD-IT-YOURSELF PROJECTS		49
COOKING AND RECIPES		50
HERBS		51

PLEASE FOLD ON DOTTED LINE.

Figure I.5.B (continued)

EDITORIAL SURVEY

1023400

Please answer by drawing only one "X" in the appropriate box for each question.

B. <CONT. READING OUR MAGAZINE
1. WOULD YOU LIKE US TO CARRY MORE OR LESS
OF THE FOLLOWING ARTICLES

MARK -1- MORE -2- LESS -3- THE SAME

SOIL BUILDING   52

C. ABOUT YOURSELF

1. DO YOU PRACTICE ORGANIC GARDENING   -1- YES -2- NO   53

2. DO YOU EAT ORGANIC FOODS   -1- YES -2- NO   54

3. HAVE YOU EVER PURCHASED A PRODUCT BY
MAIL FROM AN AD IN OUR MAGAZINE
-1- YES -2- NO   55

4. SEX   -1- MALE -2- FEMALE   56

5. AGE   -1- UNDER 25 -2- 25-39 -3- 40-65 -4- OVER 65   57

PLEASE FOLD ON DOTTED LINE.

Figure I.5.B (continued)

EDITORIAL SURVEY

Please answer by drawing only one "X" in the appropriate box for each question.

1023400

C. ABOUT YOURSELF

6. HOW LONG HAVE YOU BEEN SUBSCRIBING
   -1- UNDER 1 YR -3- 3-5 YRS
   -2- 1-2 YRS -4- OVER 5 YRS   58

7. WHAT IS THE APPROXIMATE SIZE OF YOUR PROPERTY
   -1- NONE -3- 1-5 ACRES
   -2- UNDER 1 ACRE -4- OVER 5 ACRES   59

8. WHAT IS THE APPROXIMATE SIZE OF YOUR GARDEN
   -1- UNDER 10,000 SQ FT -3- 22,000-44,000 SQ FT
   -2- 10,000-22,000 SQ FT -4- OVER 44,000 SQ FT   60

9. ABOUT WHAT PERCENTAGE OF YOUR VEGETABLE AND FLOWER
   PLANTS DO YOU START FROM SEED
   -1- NONE -2- 33% -3- 66% -4- 100%   61

10. DO YOU OWN A SOIL TEST KIT
    -1- YES -2- NO   62

PLEASE FOLD ON DOTTED LINE.

Figure I.5.B (continued)

EDITORIAL SURVEY

Please answer by drawing only one "**X**" in the appropriate box for each question.

1023400

C. (CONT.) ABOUT YOURSELF

11. IF YOU OWN A SOIL TEST KIT - DID YOU BUY IT OR WAS
IT GIVEN TO YOU AS A GIFT
-1- BOUGHT IT -2- GIFT   63

12. IF YOU OWN A SOIL TEST KIT - ABOUT HOW MANY TIMES A
YEAR DO YOU USE IT

-1- ONCE A YEAR   -3- THREE TIMES A YEAR
-2- TWICE A YEAR -4- FOUR OR MORE TIMES A YEAR   64

13. WE ARE VERY INTERESTED IN FINDING OUT WHAT OTHER
PUBLICATIONS YOU READ. PLEASE MARK -1- FOR EACH OF
THE FOLLOWING PUBLICATIONS WHICH YOU READ
VERY REGULARLY
<THAT IS - 3 OUT OF EVERY 4 ISSUES

BESTWAYS   65

BETTER NUTRITION   66

LETS LIVE   67

----- PLEASE FOLD ON DOTTED LINE.

Figure I.5.B (continued)

EDITORIAL SURVEY

Please an only one "**X**" in the appropriate box for each question.

1023400

C. <CONT. ABOUT YOURSELF

13. WE ARE VERY INTERESTED IN FINDING OUT WHAT OTHER
PUBLICATIONS YOU READ. PLEASE MARK -1- FOR EACH OF
THE FOLLOWING PUBLICATIONS WHICH YOU READ
VERY REGULARLY
<THAT IS - 3 OUT OF EVERY 4 ISSUES

	MOTHER EARTH NEWS	68
	PREVENTION	69
	TODAYS LIVING	70

14. WHICH OF THE FOLLOWING POWER EQUIPMENT DO YOU OR
OTHER MEMBERS OF YOUR HOUSEHOLD PRESENTLY OWN
<PLEASE CHECK BOX -1- FOR EACH ONE OWNED

	TILLER	71
	GARDEN TRACTOR	72
	SHREDDER-GRINDER	73

PLEASE FOLD ON DOTTED LINE.

Figure I.5.B (continued)

92

EDITORIAL SURVEY

Please answer by drawing only one "**X**" in the appropriate box for each question.

10234900

C. (CONT. ABOUT YOURSELF

14. WHICH OF THE FOLLOWING POWER EQUIPMENT DO YOU OR
OTHER MEMBERS OF YOUR HOUSEHOLD PRESENTLY OWN
(PLEASE CHECK BOX -1- FOR EACH ONE OWNED

RIDING LAWN MOWER   74

15. FOR THE POWER EQUIPMENT PRESENTLY OWNED - WAS IT
BOUGHT BEFORE OR AFTER YOU SUBSCRIBED TO OUR
MAGAZINE   -1- BEFORE -2- AFTER

TILLER   75

GARDEN TRACTOR   76

SHREDDER-GRINDER   77

RIDING LAWN MOWER   78

PLEASE FOLD ON DOTTED LINE.

Figure I.5.B (continued)

EDITORIAL SURVEY

Please answer by drawing only one "X" in the appropriate box for each question.

1023400

D. PLEASE WRITE ANY ADDITIONAL COMMENTS OR SUGGESTIONS
   ABOUT OUR MAGAZINE ON THE BACK OF THIS SHEET

THANK YOU VERY MUCH. PLEASE RETURN SURVEY IN
ENCLOSED POSTPAID ENVELOPE

THE EDITORS

PLEASE FOLD ON DOTTED LINE.

Figure I.5.B (continued)

THE AUTHORS GUILD FOUNDATION, INC.
234 WEST 44TH STREET, NEW YORK, N.Y. 10036 • (212) 398-0838

Dear Colleague:

We have commissioned the Center for the Social Sciences at Columbia University to do a professional study of the economic condition of authors in the United States. We hope to correct whatever distorted ideas people may have about writers' incomes. Authors themselves, many of them, have only a limited perspective on the careers of others in their own profession. We expect that the study will provide an accurate up-to-date body of fact.

We need your help. Your name was selected either from The Authors Guild membership list or from a separate list of authors who are not members of the Guild. We urge you to complete the enclosed questionnaire. It should not take more than a few minutes of your time. We are depending on your cooperation and that of several thousand other writers to preserve the integrity of the sample.

The survey asks for information that most people consider private, but we can assure you that, as the enclosed letter indicates, the Columbia research center will treat all replies with strict concern for your privacy.

We want this study to present a realistic picture of the economic condition of authors. You can help to make the survey effective by completing the enclosed questionnaire and sending it on to Columbia, as soon as you can. Many thanks.

Sincerely,

Peter S. Prescott
President

Figure I.5.C: MAIL SURVEY BY INDEPENDENT RESEARCHERS

Columbia University in the City of New York | *New York, N.Y. 10027*

CENTER FOR THE SOCIAL SCIENCES   420 West 118th Street

Dear Author:

On the request of the Authors Guild Foundation, we have designed a questionnaire to elicit information about the economic circumstances of authors. If we receive a sufficient number of completed questionnaires, it will truly provide the necessary data for the first accurate portrait of authors' economic circumstances. We would be able to report on authors in general as well as on specific types. Since this survey is so promising, we would like to reiterate Peter Prescott's request for your cooperation.

In considering the survey questions, you will find most of them to be straightforward. We recognize that none of the responses to a few questions may fully reflect your own experience--this is an inevitable problem with surveys--but we ask you to check the response that best approximates your situation or attitude. In addition, we welcome any written comments explaining your answers or raising other issues. Your comments will certainly be taken into account in our reports.

Without qualification, we assure the confidentiality of your responses. No names will ever appear on any questionnaire, computer tape, working paper, or finished report. The names of those in the sample, known only to the project staff at the Center for the Social Sciences, will be destroyed immediately after the final mailing. Each person in the sample has been assigned a number which appears on the survey form (so that we may prompt those not responding to our first request), but this name-number list is locked away and available only to the project staff. It will also be destroyed after the last mailing. We are providing this detail to assure you of our professional commitment to protecting your confidentiality.

Of course you have the option of not answering particular questions. Should you not wish to respond to some questions, we hope that you will still complete the rest of the questionnaire.

Sincerely,

Jonathan R. Cole
Director

Paul W. Kingston
Research Associate

Figure I.5.C (continued)

CENTER FOR THE SOCIAL SCIENCES
SURVEY OF AMERICAN AUTHORS

I. OCCUPATION

1. Would you characterize your occupation as full-time, freelance author or writer?

    Yes_____₁   No_____₂   11

2. On average, in the last year how many hours per week did you spend writing or directly working in some other way on your own book or article?

    Hours/week_____   12-13

3. On average, in the last year how many hours per week did you work in a paying activity besides book or article writing? (Count regular and irregular work.)

    Hours/week_____   14-15

4. In 1979 did you give any paid lectures or readings or do any irregular, fee-for-service editing, translating, etc.?

    Yes_____₁   No_____₂   16

5. Do you now hold a paid position besides freelance writing? (Do not count occasional lectures or readings or irregular, fee-for-service editing, translating, etc.)

    Yes_____₁   No_____₂   17

Questions 6 and 7 should be answered only by authors who hold a paid position besides freelance writing. All others should skip to Question 8.

---

6. What kind of paid position do you hold besides freelance writing? (If you hold more than one type of position, indicate the one from which you earn the most income.)   18-19

    _____ University teaching   _____ Primary/secondary teaching   _____ Public Relations
    _____¹Editor/publisher   _____⁵Clerical/secretarial   _____⁹Other Professional
    _____²Journalist   _____⁶Blue collar/service   _____¹⁰Other: Specify:
    _____³Manager/proprietor   _____⁷Sales/technical   _____¹¹
                 ⁴   ⁸   _____

    6a. Do you consider this a relatively permanent type of position for you?   20

         Yes_____₁   Possibly_____₂   No_____₃

7. Have you ever been a full-time writer for at least a year?   _____₁Yes _____₂No   21
    7a. If yes: Indicate which years: _____   22-36

Questions 8-10 should be answered only by authors who do not hold a paid position besides freelance writing.

---

8. For how many years have you been a full-time, freelance writer? _____Years   37-38
    8a. Indicate which years: _____   39-53

9. Since the end of your formal schooling, how many years have you primarily supported yourself by income from a position besides freelance writing? _____Years   54-55

10. What type of position did you have immediately before becoming a full-time freelance writer? (If you held more than one job, indicate the one from which you earned the most income.)

     _____ None   _____ Manager/proprietor   _____ Public Relations
     _____¹Primary or secondary teaching _____⁵Sales/clerical   _____⁹Other Professional   56-57
     _____²University teaching   _____⁶Clerical/secretarial   _____¹⁰Other: Specify:
     _____³Editor/publisher   _____⁷Blue collar/service   _____¹¹
                  ⁴   ⁸   _____

Figure I.5.C (continued)

II. INCOME

1) Please provide your <u>best estimate</u> of the amount (pretax) that you received in each of the following categories for the calendar years 1978 and 1979. <u>We do not expect you to check your financial records.</u>

   <u>N.B.</u> All income earned for salaried employment, <u>even if it involves writing</u>, (e.g., newspaper reporter, editor, writing teacher), should be included in Line 3, "Income from Salaried Employment." If you received no money in a particular category, mark an "0." Please do not simply leave it blank.

ROUND ALL FIGURES TO THOUSANDS	1978 Calendar Year	1979 Calendar Year
1. Income·Directly Related to Writing		
A. Books		
1. Royalties Hardcover Editions	____58-63	____141-146
2. Royalties Paperback Originals	____64-69	____147-152
3. Royalties Paperback Reprints	____70-75	____153-158
4. All Subsidiary Rights	____76-81	____159-164
5. Total Income From Books (Sum of 1A1-1A4)	____82-87	____165-170
B. Magazine and Newspaper Articles (Not reprints of books)	____88-92	____171-176
C. Motion Pictures/Television/Radio (Not including subsidiary rights in published books)	____93-98	____177-182
D. Total Income Directly Related to Writing (Sum of 1A5, 1B, and 1C)	____99-104	____183-188
2. Income from Other Freelance Writing Work (Lecturing, reading, consulting, editing, translating, etc.)	____105-110	____189-194
3. Income from Salaried Employment	____111-116	____195-200
4. Income from Investments/Pensions/Social Security (Include income from investments jointly held with spouse)	____117-122	____201-206
5. Total Personal Income (Sum of 1D, 2, 3, and 4)	____123-128	____207-212
6. Spouse's Income (All personal income, including income from investments separately held)	____129-134	____213-218
7. TOTAL FAMILY INCOME (Sum of 5 and 6)	____135-140	____219-224

2) Please provide your best estimate of the most, and the least, income that you have derived from <u>one book</u> (including all subsidiary rights) throughout your career.

   Most $_____225-230   Least: $_____231-236

Figure I.5.C (continued)

3) In what year did you earn the most writing-related income: 19___   237-238
   3a. Indicate the amount: $_____   239-245

4) Indicate the source(s) of any grants for writing that you have received in the past
five years.
        ____Public agency   ____Both public and private sources   246
           1
        ____Private foundation   ____Haven't received any
           3   4

5) Do you have an agent?   ____Yes$_1$ ____No$_2$
                                                              247

6) What was the largest advance you ever received for a book? $____   248-253
   6a. How much of an advance did you receive from your last book? $____   254-259

III. ATTITUDES TOWARD WORK

1. Do you expect to continue writing? ____Yes ____No ____Unsure   260
                                       1   2   3

2. In choosing among ideas for books, how frequently have you given up or postponed
the personally most interesting project in favor of one that promised greater sales:
       ____Often ____Occasionally ____Once ____Never   261
          1   2   3   4
Comments:_____
             _____
             _____

3. How significant are economic considerations for you now in choosing among writing
projects?
   ____Decisive ____Important ____Some influence ____A small concern ____Irrelevant   262
      1   2   3   4   5
Comments:_____
             _____
             _____

```
┌──────────────────────────────────────────────────────────────┐
│ Questions 4 - 6 should be answered only by authors who have paying work │
│ (regular or irregular) besides book or article writing.  All others should │
│ skip to the next section. │
└──────────────────────────────────────────────────────────────┘
```

4. What is your primary motivation for having a paying work besides book or article
writing? (Check one.)   263
      ____Necessary income for living
          1
      ____A desirable, complementary source of income
          2
      ____Both complementary income and nonmonetary satisfaction
          3
      ____Derive most work-related satisfaction from this other work
          4
      ____Do not like writing full-time
          5
      ____Other: Specify_____
          6
          _____

5. How do you evaluate the personal satisfaction of writing as compared to your other
work?   264
      ____Other job much more satisfying
          1
      ____Writing much more satisfying
          2
      ____About equally satisfying
          3
      ____Other job somewhat more satisfying
          4
      ____Writing somewhat more satisfying
          5
      ____Not sure
          6

6. If you could at least match your present total income by writing full time, would
you drop your other work?   265
      ____Yes ____Possibly ____No ____Don't know
        1   2   3   4

Figure I.5.C (continued)

IV. WRITING ACTIVITY

1) How many books have you published?_____   266-267

    1a. Of this total, how many were fiction? _____ poetry? _____
                                         268-269   270-271
                            non-fiction? _____
                                         272-273

2) List below the publication date, publisher, and <u>approximate</u> number of copies sold for your (a) last book, (b) first book, and (c) biggest selling book. Also, check whether each book is fiction/poetry or non-fiction.

	Year of Publication	Publisher	Copies Sold Hardcover	Paperback	Type Fiction/ Poetry	Non-fiction	
Last book:	19___ 274-275	___ 276	___ 277-282	___ 283-288	___1	___2	289
First book:	19___ 290-291	___ 292	___ 293-298	___ 299-304	___1	___2	305
Biggest seller:	19___ 306-307	___ 308	___ 309-314	___ 315-320	___1	___2	321

3) Do you currently belong to the Authors Guild? _____ Yes₁ _____ No₂   322

4) Have any of your books been reviewed in the <u>New York Times Book Review</u> in 1978 or 1979?

                             _____ Yes₁   _____ No₂   323

    4a. At any other time in the past? _____ Yes₁ _____ No₂   324

5) Did you have a book on one of the <u>New York Times</u> best seller lists (i.e., one of the top fifteen positions on the fiction or non-fiction hardcover lists or the mass or trade paperback lists) at any time in 1978 or 1979?

                           _____ Yes₁   _____ No₂   325

    5a. At any other time in the past? _____ Yes₁ _____ No₂   326

6) List all awards (including nominations for awards) that you have received for your writing. _____ None   327

    _____

    _____   328

7) What <u>single</u> category best describes the type of books to which you have given the most and second most time in your writing career?

Type of book	Most time spent on: (check one)	Second most time spent on: (check one)
"Genre fiction" (e.g., westerns, thrillers, mysteries, science fiction, historical romances, and gothic/occult novels)	___1	___1
General adult fiction	___2	___2
Academically-oriented non-fiction	___3	___3
Adult non-fiction (e.g., current events; popularizations of history, science, psychology, etc.; and biographies)		
"How-to" books (sex, gardening, cooking, etc.) or travel guides	___4	___4
Technical reports--manuals--textbooks	___5	___5
Poetry	___6	___6
Children's books	___7	___7
Religious -- inspirational	___8	___8
Translations	___9	___9
Other	___10	___10
	___11	___11

                                   No secondary type
                                   of publication _____12
                                   329-330   331-332

Figure I.5.C (continued)

V. BASIC BACKGROUND MATTERS

1) Your sex: ____ Male ____ Female   2) Your age: ____   333
   1   2   334-335

3) Your highest educational attainment:
   ____ Less than a high school degree ____ High school degree ____ Some college
   1   2   3
   ____ B.A./B.S. ____ M.A. (arts & science) ____ Professional Degree ____ Ph.D.   336
   5   6   6   7

4) If you at least attended college, write out the name of your undergraduate school.
   (Do not abbreviate)_____   337

5) Your marital status: ____ Single ____ Married ____ Divorced or separated   338
                        1   2   3

6) Number of children:_____   339

7) Your predominant religious background:
   ____ Roman Catholic ____ Jewish ____ Protestant ____ Other ____ None   340
   1   2   3   4   5

8) Your race:
   ____ White ____ Black ____ Asian ____ Hispanic ____ Other   341
   1   2   3   4   5

9) Did either of your parents or any close relatives ever publish a book: 342
   ____ Yes ____ No
   1   2

10) Your father's main type of work while you were in high school: 343
    ____ Educator   ____ Author   ____ Other professional
    1   2   3
    ____ Clerical/sales/technical ____ Blue collar/service ____ Manager/proprietor
    4   5   6
    ____ Other: Specify:_____
    7

11) Highest educational attainment of your better educated parent: 344
    ____ Less than high school   ____ High school
    1   2
    ____ Some college   ____ B.A./B.S.   ____ Post-college degree
    3   4   5

12) Your spouse's main type of work now: 345-346
    ____ Freelance author ____ Publisher/Editor ____ Homemaker
    1   2   3
    ____ Journalist   ____ Manager/proprietor ____ Clerical/sales/technical
    4   5   6
    ____ Blue collar/service ____ Educator   ____ Other Professional
    7   8   9
    ____ Retired   ____ Other: Specify_____
    10   11

13) Primary area of residence: 347
    ____ New York metropolitan area ____ South   ____ California
    1   2   3
    ____ Other Northeast   ____ Midwest   ____ Other West
    4   5   6

Figure I.5.C (continued)

VI. CONNECTIONS WITH OTHER AUTHORS

1) Do you seriously discuss ideas for books or work in progress with other authors?

   ___Always   ___Usually   ___Sometimes   ___Never   348
      1   2   3   4

   1a) With how many authors did you seriously discuss your most recent work? _____   349

   1b) How have these discussions affected your work?_____
   _____

2) Besides your relatives, do you seriously discuss ideas for books or work with people who are not authors?

   ___Always   ___Usually   ___Sometimes   ___Never   350
      1   2   3   4

3) How often do you meet with other authors in some social setting? (Exclude your spouse).

   ___At least once a week ___At least once a month ___Every few months ___Rarely 351
      1   2   3   4

4) How many other authors (excluding your spouse) do you count as a good friend? _____ 352-353

5) Of the three contemporary authors who have most significantly influenced your own writing, what is the closest relationship you have?

   ___None have significantly influenced my work
      1
   ___"Know" him or her only through published writing
      2
   ___Have had some conversations
      3
   ___Friendly acquaintanceship
      4
   ___Friend
      5
   ___Other - Specify:_____   354
      6

Comments:

   If you desire, please write any comments below. We welcome comments explaining your responses to our questions or raising additional issues related to your career, including proposals to improve the economic circumstances of writers.

**NO POSTAGE
NECESSARY
IF MAILED
IN THE
UNITED STATES**

BUSINESS REPLY MAIL
FIRST CLASS   PERMIT NO. 9259   NEW YORK, N.Y.

POSTAGE WILL BE PAID BY ADDRESSEE

Authors Guild Study
Center for the Social Sciences
420 West 118th Street, Room 814
New York, New York 10027

Figure I.5.C (continued)

Fifth: Layout

—What comprises an interesting format?
—How many pages?

The entire length of the questionnaire is determined by

(a) the number of questions, and
(b) alternative answers for each question.

The number of pages should conform to an interesting format, for an uninteresting form competes for space with other discarded papers in the trash barrel.

Of course, an attractive and uncrowded format will not substitute for dull questions, an apparently purposeless survey, or one to which the respondent cannot relate his or her own interests. But a poorly planned layout, on the other hand, can negate other planning efforts. Here are some ideas to keep in mind when planning your mail survey.

- ◎ Adequate white space; i.e., let wide margins frame the questionnaire.
- ◎ Sufficient space to answer all questions, and please, enough space between lines to allow for reasonably sized handwriting (or typewriting).
- ◎ Space enough between questions to avoid a crowded look.
- ◎ Subheadings to break up copy and give it a more pleasing appearance.
- ◎ Boldface type for emphasizing words in a question and for subheadings.
- ◎ A logical sequence of questions so that one naturally follows another, and a logical order so that one set of questions flows into another; subheadings provide transitions from one group of questions to another.
- ◎ Interesting, sharp, crisp, intelligent, logical questions, but not "cutesy" ones.
- ◎ Questions that can be quickly answered or easily estimated, and that do not require record research. (Avoid "How many gallons of gasoline did you use from June 14th to August 27th?")
- ◎ KISS: Keep It Simple and Straightforward—simple, clean organization.

Since you will again face the questionnaires when surveys are returned, a sloppily organized questionnaire will come back to haunt when you try to work with it. If funds are in short supply, then consider a shorter questionnaire rather than reducing 11-point type (about the height of the letters of this book) by 75 percent and then printing the entire questionnaire on the front and back of a single sheet. You could spend more for less information due to a low percentage of returns.

Sixth: Cover Letter

—Is a cover letter a necessary expense?
—If so, how should it be written?

The answers are: *yes*, and *well*. If you receive an unsolicited résumé in the mail without a cover letter, what is your first impression? Mine, too!

One important function of the cover letter is to cover the purpose of the survey. In the 1980 Census mail survey, although there was no cover letter, the accompanying instructions emphasized why certain questions were necessary, the purpose of the data, and generally how resulting information affects the respondent. But the purpose must be so stated that it shows a benefit to the respondent:

(a) The survey is important (serious business).
(b) It has a valid purpose.
(c) The respondent will benefit (in some stated way).

Notice, for instance, the cover letters in Figures I.5.B and I.5.E. They state why the survey is being conducted, and why answers are important. The benefits are better articles, better books, better service, etc., for the reader or the user of the service.

After all, is that not why we use surveys—to provide better services to our customers? Should not respondents know that? Even so, put in the benefits right at the top of the letter on the assumption that many respondents may not even read beyond the first paragraph or two. Does the survey get answered or tossed away? What the opening statements of your cover letter say may make the difference.

Obviously a cover letter should not be a dull piece of work. If you are not a good letter writer, don't let vanity stand in the way of a high response rate; hire someone to write it for a reasonable fee. The letter need not to be long—a couple of hundred words is plenty—but make every word sparkle; arouse interest; don't go so far as to destroy its serious purpose; and then show the finished documents to your enemies for comments.

As with the questionnaire, appearance is important. Some of the same suggestions listed above apply here as well:

◎ white space,
◎ crispness,
◎ straightforwardness in a creative way.

Paper quality may or may not be important, depending on the respondents. The choice is always between good and deluxe paper, never poor quality material.

The printing, however, is important, because it affects the general appearance of the package. It conveys a message to the respondent: *well dressed, well received*.

Too, use a letterhead—your own if it is a company mailing, the research organization's if it is done independently, or even both for impact—which will be demonstrated in the ninth step.

Should letters be individually signed? In the examples here all are machine-signed. The simulated signature seems adequate at least in these instances—and better than no signature or name at all—but, of course, recipients readily detect the difference. The related question is whether cover letters should be individually addressed. Once again, in all the samples in this section, none are addressed to an individual; therefore, a simulated signature seems consistent with the rest of the letter.

Preferably, each letter is addressed personally, and directed to a specific individual with title, if applicable, and personally signed. This adds to the cost. The marginal increase in responses may not justify such additional costs.

This is probably a safe set of rules to follow:

1. If respondents are to remain anonymous, a printed letter with simulated signature may actually help to convey the idea of confidentiality.
2. If the respondent is identified, as in Figure I.5.A, then an inside address and actual signature convey an idea of importance and seriousness.

Seventh: Testing and Rewriting

—Is testing really necessary at this point?
—Why rewrite for the tenth time?

Since you have already spent considerable time and money in the preparation of the mail survey, it seems prudent to strain the questionnaire for any defects that may have missed your keen eye. Each person who scans your document will interpret according to his or her own set of interests; each does not perceive the issues as you do.

A quick internal test: Ask co-workers to complete the questionnaire, or ask them to critique it.

An external test: (1) Select a small number of respondents from your sample and send them the questionnaire. (2) Follow up with telephone calls to get their various reactions.

If you have done a careful job, any rewriting will be minimal. Sometimes changing only a word or two in a key question may greatly improve the value of returns. Test the cover letter, too. You may show friends the letter typed on plain paper without indicating to them it is your work of art. But if you are a sensitive type, or do not have friends to spare, avoid this method.

Eighth: Production

—What's so important about production?

We have really covered this point above. Respondents judge the organization by what they see and feel. Sloppy or cheap printing, poor organization, and low quality paper may work in some charity appeals; that is not the message you want to transmit. On the other hand, a personally written note on colored, high rag content paper is an unnecessary expense.

Keep these critical points in mind:

1. The entire package should be attractive; questions easy to answer.
2. If pictures and drawings are necessary to a question, then use them, even though reproduction costs a little more. They should be used for a purpose other than entertainment value.
3. The questionnaire should follow good organizational principles.
4. If typeset, make your instructions clear to the typesetter.

5. In general, you want to convey two basic messages:
   (a)"We're proud of our firm. That's why we used quality planning, preparation, printing, and paper in this survey."
   (b)"We value your opinion highly. That's why we have enclosed a first-class package. We respect your ideas."

If you have conveyed that message, then you are on the right track.

Ninth: Increasing Participation Rate

—How can I generate more responses per mail-out?

Although some surveys generate only a 10 percent (or less) response rate, others can claim an 80 percent return. The 1980 Census mail survey generated a high return rate, but the government employs a weapon businesses cannot use: coercion. Aside from coercion, or implied threat, there are techniques for persuading respondents to answer.

The most important ingredient to a high number of returns is interest. A close relationship between the sample selected and the purpose of the survey must prevail.

For example, respondents receiving the questionnaire in Figure I.5.C will have a strong interest in the results because it is linked to their incomes. What will diminish the number of responses are the very personal questions included in that survey.

To counter this resistance, two cover letters were included: (a) one from the sponsoring agency (a nonprofit organization in this instance), and (b) a second from the researchers. Since the researchers personally are unknowns, they have used the letterhead of the well-known university with which they are associated.

As in the census survey, confidentiality is stressed here too, since confidentiality is the weak link in both surveys. The author's survey has an identifying number stamped on each form, but it is promised that the master list will be destroyed. (Nevertheless, it would not take much research to identify the respondent by correlating books published to public information available.) Therefore, the respondent is assured of complete privacy by (a) the participating association, (b) the researchers, and (c) the implied prestige of the university whose name appears on the letterhead.

Another technique is spaced follow-up. After a couple of weeks, a second cover letter with the questionnaire is sent to respondents who have not replied (or to everyone if it is truly an anonymous survey), urging them to reply now. A reminder postcard may later follow. Even fourth and fifth reminders are possibilities as long as incremental returns exceed incremental costs.

A variation of this technique: Follow up with a telephone call at some point and even be prepared to take the information over the phone. Talkers may not like writing.

A departure from this method was practiced by the company conducting the mail survey illustrated in Figure I.5.B.

First, they sent a brief letter to all respondents in the sample telling them in advance about the survey, advising them they would receive a questionnaire, and solicited their cooperation.

Second, a questionnaire, with the cover letter illustrated, was mailed.

Third, a follow-up card was sent about two weeks later.

This is a very effective technique for communicating the seriousness of the survey and reducing cost per response.

A common practice is to include an S.A.S.E.—a self-addressed, stamped envelope. This seems as fundamental to the survey package as the cover letter. Its purpose is to make it easy for the respondent to return the completed questionnaire. Use of a postage permit reduces some postage costs on one hand but probably not very much in cases of high returns.

Some researchers prefer placing postage stamps on the envelope, and using several four or five-cent stamps rather than a single stamp. Similarly on the outside envelope, first-class postage, hand stamped, is more personal than a postage meter mark.

Of course, there's always the shiny new dime trick, which may have been a great stunt before the clad-coin era. Today, a dull, old, pre-1965, silver dime worth several times its face value, is a clever twist to this idea. Since every one likes a gift, especially money, attaching a federal reserve note to the survey tends to obligate the respondent, and a higher response rate materializes.

An inexpensive but attractive mailable gift still represents a winning approach, especially if your company produces the product or service. Do not offer the item, or money, as a bribe, or suggest it as payment for filling in the questionnaire (unless that is the case). Make the gift say thanks to the respondent in advance.

Gimmicks sometimes cause a piece of mail to stand out: colored envelopes, priority mail, special delivery (which may not really get special attention), or certified mail. These expensive attention-getters, which may have worked well in the past, and may work well again in the future, probably add an unnecessary expense. A couple of exceptions surface.

Certainly certified mail gets attention. It conveys seriousness of purpose. But it is too expensive for most surveys. The other possibility is foreign air mail for noncommercial respondents. A large exotic stamp from a foreign country will get attention. It has been used successfully by some mail order firms. It should be tied in to the survey or the product to make it believable.

Tenth: Some Examples

—How should I go about writing up a questionnaire?

1. Apply the suggestions and ideas presented above.
2. Remember to break down the information you desire into small subunits, much as you would an assembly operation.
3. Provide for a reasonable spectrum of answers, but avoid bias.
4. Don't assume anything.

You have already seen a mail survey example earlier in this section (Figure I.5.A); you have seen other types of questionnaires illustrated in the section on personal interviews. Here are four more types to study.

Figure I.5.B is longer (as was I.5.A); Figure I.5.C digs deeper. The next one, Figure I.5.D, is a quickie for the purpose of identifying types of customers.

The last one, Figure I.5.E, although a 28-question survey, is very easily answered. It requires no more than five minutes—about two minutes if no written comments are made—but does furnish the basis for considerable information. The first 28 questions illustrate a structured survey; the space at the end is an open-ended approach that can draw out extremely valuable information from those persons who react strongly enough to answer. The problem here is that we do not know whether those persons who write additional comments necessarily represent all customers.

MAIL SURVEY AND SOLICITATION

Dear Customer:

    Since you have been a valued customer in the past, I would like to make certain that we are mailing our circular to you properly.

    I would be very grateful if you would take a moment to answer the questions below and return to me in the enclosed pre-paid envelope:

_____ Is your mailing label above correct as is? If not, please provide corrections in the blanks below (please print or type):

    YOUR NAME _____

    ORGANIZATION _____

    STREET _____

    CITY, STATE _____

    ZIP CODE _____

1) _____Are you a library of any kind (public, religious, school, corporate, special, etc.)?
    If yes, to whose attention should we mail the circular?
    _____

2) _____Are you a bookseller of any kind?
    If yes, are you:
    _____a bookstore?
    _____a wholesaler?
    _____a non-bookstore retailer who sells books also?
    _____a mail order company?
    Do you specialize in selling any particular category of books?

3) _____Are you an individual who happens to receive the circular where you work? If yes, please print the name here to make sure we have it correctly, if it is not already correct on the label shown:
    _____
    _____

Figure I.5.D: MAIL SURVEY AND SOLICITATION

4) ____If questions 1, 2 and 3 don't apply, would you be kind enough to tell us what kind of business or institution you are affiliated with?

_____

5) ____Do you have friends or colleagues who might enjoy receiving the circular? If so, please provide their names and addresses below, and we will gladly add them to our mailing list.

NAME _____   NAME _____

STREET _____   STREET _____

CITY _____   CITY _____

STATE _____   STATE _____

ZIP CODE _____   ZIP CODE _____

Sincerely,

_____

Samuel Clemens, Vice President

SC/rv

Figure I.5.D (continued)

Book Club

9933 Alliance Road · Cincinnati, Ohio 45242

August, 1979

Dear Member,

The enclosed survey is important to you and to me.

I want to know more about you *so I can make the Writer's Digest Book Club work for you even better* than it's working now. I want to know about your needs, your interests, and what you like (and what you don't like) about Writer's Digest Book Club.

I want to know about you so *we can provide more books you can use* — to become a better writer, to sell more of what you write, or just to relax and get a little inspiration from.

I also want to know about you so we can find more people like you to join Writer's Book Club. If the Book Club grows, that's to your benefit. *Together, we'll have more clout* with the publishers from whom we purchase books. "Clout" means that other publishers won't give exclusive rights to books about writing to another book club—they'll think of us, too. And it means that *I'll be able to purchase larger quantities of books at better prices*—better prices I will pass along to you.

So grab a pen, sit down and fill out the survey form. Then send it back to us in the enclosed postpaid envelope. And watch *Looks at Books* for a report on the results of this survey.

Thanks,

Mert Neal

Mert Neal
Director

Figure I.5.E: CUSTOMER INTEREST SURVEY

WRITER'S DIGEST BOOK CLUB MEMBER SURVEY

Demographics

1. Sex: a. Male   ( )   b. Female   ( )

2. Age: a. Under 18 ( )   d. 35 - 44 ( )   g. 65 & Over   ( )
     b. 18 - 24   ( )   e. 45 - 54 ( )
     c. 25 - 34   ( )   f. 55 - 64 ( )

3. Marital Status: a. Single   ( )   b. Married   ( )

4. Number of Children: a. None   ( )   c. 3 - 4   ( )
     b. 1 - 2   ( )   d. 5 or more   ( )

5. Education: a. Some High School   ( )   e. Post Graduate   ( )
     b. High School Graduate ( )   f. Master's Degree   ( )
     c. Some College   ( )   g. Doctorate   ( )
     d. College Graduate   ( )   h. Professional School ( )

6. Total Annual **Family** Income: a. Under $10,000   ( )   d. 30,001 - 40,000   ( )
     b. 10,001 - 20,000   ( )   e. 40,001 - 50,000   ( )
     c. 20,001 - 30,000   ( )   f. Over 50,000   ( )

6. Occupation:_____

About Writing

7. Check the type of writing you do for the love of it. Underline the area in which you hope to earn the most income:
     a. Poetry   ( )   j. Scientific   ( )
     b. Short Stories   ( )   k. Business   ( )
     c. Novels   ( )   l. History   ( )
     d. Writing for Children   ( )   m. Technical   ( )
     e. Writing for Young People ( )   n. Newspaper   ( )
     f. Confessions   ( )   o. Script (TV, Film)   ( )
     g. Humor   ( )   q. Fillers   ( )
     h. Religious   ( )   r. Other:_____
     i. Article   ( )

8. Have you taken writing courses?   a. Yes ( )   b. No ( )

9. If answer to 8 is yes, where?
     a. College   ( )   d. Correspondence   ( )
     b. Adult Education Classes   ( )   e. Workshops   ( )
     c. Seminars   ( )   f. Other:_____

10. How many manuscripts have you submitted for publication in the past 12 months?
     a. One   ( )   d. Four   ( )
     b. Two   ( )   e. Five or more   ( )
     c. Three   ( )   f. _____ ( )

11. How many articles, short stories, poems or other manuscripts have you sold or had published in the past 12 months?
     a. One   ( )   c. Three   ( )   e. Five or more   ( )
     b. Two   ( )   d. Four   ( )   f. _____ ( )

About Writer's Digest Book Club

12. How did you learn about Writer's Digest Book Club?
     a. Direct Mail   ( )   d. A friend   ( )
     b. Ad in Writer's Digest   ( )   e. News Article   ( )
     c. Ad in The Writer   ( )   f. Other   ( )

Figure I.5.E (continued)

13. Which of the following was the main reason you joined the Club?
   a. Offer — 3 Books for $4.95   (   )   d. Books at discounted prices   (   )
   b. Specially selected books for writers   (   )   e. Can't get at book stores   (   )
   c. Writer's Digest affiliation   (   )   f. Convenience of ordering by mail   (   )
                                    (   )   g. No risk guarantee   (   )

14. How satisfied are you with the selection of books offered?

   a. Excellent (   )   b. Good (   )   c. Adequate (   )   d. Poor (   )

15. Which one subject area would you most like covered in upcoming books?
   a. Books on how to write (Subject area)_____   (   )
   b. Specific problem-area help books (plotting, style, etc.)   (   )
   c. Guides to mechanics of writing (grammar, syntax, etc.)   (   )
   d. How writers work (Insight)   (   )
   e. The business of writing (finance, legal, tax)   (   )
   f. Writers' general reference books   (   )
   g. Annotated anthologies of superior stories, plays, etc.   (   )
   h. Literary classics   (   )
   i. Best-selling novels with critiques   (   )
   j. Biographies and autobiographies of writers   (   )
   k. Publishing scene insights   (   )
   l. How-to or other books on photography   (   )
   m. Other-specify_____

16. How is the program living up to your expectations?

   a. Better than expected (   )   b. As expected (   )   c. Less than expected (   )

17. Does **Looks at Books** adequately describe the selections?
           a. Yes (   )   b. No (   )

18. Do you save your **Looks at Books** bulletins for future reference?
           a. Yes (   )   b. No. (   )

19. **Looks at Books** was recently expanded to 12 pages to include feature articles and interviews with authors. What do you think of the new format?

           a. New format much better   (   )
           b. New format OK   (   )
           c. Don't like new format   (   )

20. Which feature of the Club most influences you to continue as a member?

   a. Good selection of books   (   )   e. Free postage on prepaid orders   (   )
   b. Books at discounted prices   (   )   f. Features, editorial content
   c. Bonus Plan   (   )   of **Looks at Books**   (   )
   d. Special sales   (   )   g. Other: _____   (   )

21. What non-book items would you like offered in the Club?

   a. Records   (   )   g. Calendars (designed to writer's needs)   (   )
   b. Tapes   (   )   h. Desk Equipment (desk sets, etc.)   (   )
   c. Typewriters   (   )   i. Wall flow chart for writers   (   )
   d. Tape Recorders   (   )   j. Manuscript Criticism   (   )
   e. Book Bags   (   )   k. Other:_____
   f. Book Cases   (   )   _____

22. What has most impressed you about the Book Club?

   a. Prices   (   )   d. Selection of books   (   )
   b. Service   (   )   e. Special sales   (   )
   c. Bulletins   (   )

Figure I.5.E (continued)

General Information

23. Do you currently subscribe to Writer's Digest?

          a.   Yes ( )   b.   No ( )

24. How long have you been a subscriber?

    a. Not a WD subscriber   ( )   d. Two years   ( )
    b. Less than one year   ( )   e. Four years   ( )
    c. One year   ( )   f. Over five years   ( )

25. Approximately how many hardcover books do you normally purchase in a year?

    a. 1 - 5 ( )   b. 6 - 9 ( )   c. 10 - 14 ( )   d. 15 - 19 ( )   e. More than 20 ( )

26. Do you prefer the books you buy to have jackets?

          a. Yes ( )   b. No. ( )   c. No opinion ( )

27. From which of the following sources did you purchase books during the past 12 months?

    a. Book Club   ( )   d. Department store   ( )
    b. Mail order (other than Book Club)   ( )   e. Newsstand   ( )
    c. Bookstore   ( )   f. Other:_____   ( )

28. To which other book clubs do you belong?

    a. Book-of-the-Month   ( )   f. Mystery Guild   ( )
    b. Literary Guild   ( )   g. Quality Paperback   ( )
    c. Doubleday Book Club   ( )   h. Reader's Digest Condensed Books   ( )
    d. Preferred Choice Bookplan   ( )   i. Other: _____   ( )
    e. Reader's Subscription Book Club ( )

Feel free to use the following space for your personal comments about Writer's Digest Book Club:

Figure I.5.E (continued)

I.6: HOW TO USE FOCUS GROUPS FOR PROFIT-MAKING IDEAS

Group interviewing differs from personal interviews. Group interviewing typically will be unstructured; personal interviewing generally is structured around a questionnaire.

Group interviewing, a popular and widely used technique since the 1950's, can be done fairly inexpensively either (a) by someone within the firm, or (b) at a higher cost by hiring a marketing research firm, or (c) by a psychologist trained in group dynamics. A psychologist unfamiliar with the product, service, or purpose of the focus group will not generate the same quality of information as will someone from within the marketing organization of the firm.

The purpose of group interviews is to draw out opinions and feelings about a product or service, but not judgments; therefore, a free flow of information from and among participants is essential to success. It is the moderator's job to probe below the surface of opinions and ideas of the group members.

Some Profitable Applications

Which types of situations lend themselves to group interviewing? For instance, suppose you are seeking a new product idea. Getting together an amateur think-tank of persons who have a stake in solving the problem is one method.

Pillsbury was seeking an easy-to-prepare dessert and had come up with a number of ideas. Most of the ideas originated with marketing and research executives within the company. However, in a focus group session a fruit dessert emerged as a favorite among consumers of the group.

Of course, between ideas and profits lies considerable hard work. The profit process can fail at any point due to no fault of the focus group technique. Still, this method breeds product or service ideas that solve specific problems or tastes. It is management's task to shape these ideas into a winning mold.

A focus group can also test a new product. The new product need not be yours; it can be a competitor's. Blue Plate Foods tested Orville Redenbacher Popcorn (ORP), only ORP did not know about it. A total of 300 Dallas women participated in the test—one-half of them receiving ORP and the other half receiving Jolly Time Popcorn the first week. Then for the second week Blue Plate switched popcorn between the groups. For the clincher, the third week, they asked: "Would you be willing to pay twice as much for Orville Redenbacher's Gourmet Popping Corn?" And the women said, "Yes."

Along similar lines you can test for product acceptance, or lack of it, or identify potential markets, or discover what pluses consumers see in your product. Here is a case that illustrates the latter.

A company developed a new automobile air conditioning filter. From focus group interviews, management learned that family members with allergies or respiratory problems were top prospects, along with persons concerned with air pollution. On the negative side were those persons who could see no need for the product, or were concerned whether the filter would affect operating efficiency of the cooling system, or were not prepared to pay the price for changing filters periodically.

In this instance, the company conducted further studies. This saved thousands of dollars from being dumped into a low-payoff marketing strategy. Consequently, they bridged the gap between marketing management at the manufacturing level and interests of the final user.

In addition to sparking the evolution of new products or ideas, this approach can zero in on trends among specific groups, as in the next example.

Seagram's wanted to know how drug usage was influencing alcohol consumption for the under-age-30 group. Such information helps to predict the trend of future alcohol sales—other things being equal, which they seldom are. Besides in-depth personal interviews, focus groups help draw out further reasons for trend development so that the company can incorporate such data into strategic planning.

Attitudes toward products and services are not the only reason for organizing focus group interviews. Politics account for much marketing research. Organizations profit from all types of research designs—from well-tested to experimental. An illustration of the focus group interview technique is an eight-member panel in New Hampshire put together by a polling firm commissioned by *The Wall Street Journal*. The purpose of the two-hour session was "to probe for the perceptions, attitudes and feelings" which shape decisions of Republican voters in a presidential election year. Each person was paid $15.00 to participate.

Here is another thought: It may be interesting to experiment with video-taping potential store managers or potential salespersons in experimental situations and then gauge the reactions of focus groups to these potential key personnel.

An electric utility company used the focus group approach when management wanted to push through a rate hike. Theirs was a three-part analysis.

First, they analyzed internal company resources: interviews with executives and employees, audit of past record of consumer complaints, audit of past company advertisements. Next, they conducted 12 focus group interviews to learn (a) customer opinions of a rate increase, and, (b) reasons for customer resistance to proposed rate increase. Finally, they conducted telephone interviews of 700 randomly sampled adults.

Often you will discover that a combination of marketing research techniques will provide the most information of value to immediate operating decisions at a reasonable cost. Information generated in a focus group interview can be quite valuable to copywriters, to an advertising campaign, or, as in this last example, to counter potentially adverse reactions to a proposed price increase.

Or suppose you want to discover what motivates customers to buy your products. Although you may have very complete records on sales, even on customer types, you may not know with any precision why some people are motivated to buy your product(s). Is it appearance? Brand name? Company reputation? Guarantees? Price? Or do certain attitudes grow out of circumstances beyond the influence and knowledge of the company?

Buying attitudes may originate in childhood experiences; or a color, for example, may connote a whole class of images different for each category of consumers. Information on price, appearance, guarantees, etc., can be obtained through other techniques. Mail surveys or telephone interviews are two common ones.

But a well-conducted focus group session can expose extremely useful relationships not precipitated by other information-gathering methods. Too, the focus group can pretest an ad or promotional campaign. Does the ad motivate them to buy? Why or why not? Information generated in a focus group interview can provide guidelines for constructing questionnaires preparatory to telephone or mail surveys.

Seventeen Consecutive Winners

Along the lines of pretesting promotional material is new product testing. For example, major movie studios such as Warner Brothers or Columbia may use focus groups to test audience reactions to different possible endings of a film. Schick Sunn Classics Productions, Inc., backs up the marketing research process to *before* (also, refer to Section II.2) a decision to film. The firm consolidates a variety of methods to prescreen movie ideas.

The film company generally begins by conducting on-the-street interviews with all types and ages of persons to find out what people prefer in movies. After learning *what* people prefer the company's management want to know *how much* people prefer it. In this case they use focus groups with a slight twist. They show them a variety of short films or have them listen to story lines on an audio cassette, and then ask them to fill out questionnaires to indicate preference for actors, settings, costumes, plot sequences, etc., which is really a combination of research methods. Theirs is a sophisticated, and expensive, marketing research program that cost $5 million to develop and another $1 \frac{1}{4}$ million annually to operate.

The payoff? Seventeen consecutive winners, no losers, and a quintupling of gross revenue in five years. Since this research technique has broad applications, the company applies it to other entertainment areas as well.

All types of products and ideas can be pretested in similar ways, such as which fragrance best matches a product's claim to cleanliness, effectiveness, or whatever. Color, odor, print size or design—all, for example, convey a message perceived differently by different consumer segments.

Or a product may be tested first and then discussed in focus group interviews, such as a taste test of a new cereal. If it doesn't taste right, appearance alone will not make the product a winner. Therefore, focus groups help to generate hypotheses in the qualitative stage of marketing research.

Up from Mediocrity

Do you really want to know what customers think about your products?

Many insignificant variables, which altogether can spell the difference between mediocrity and a winner, may crop up in focus group interviews: the product may be hard to use; directions difficult to follow or decipher with either too little, or highly irrelevant, information; the safety child-protection lid can only be opened by a child, while arthritic women (a main buyer category) can get the container open only by smashing the lid with a hammer; the color is wrong, or right, or too dull, or too bright; or once the package is opened there is no way to store the unused tacks, candy, staples, fuses, etc.

Although you wish to learn of product virtues—why people buy it—it is also critical to design, pricing, and packaging policies to know why people do not buy it—the negative attitudes.

This is why a meat packer used focus groups—to discover why sales were off in one region. They soon learned of a serious packaging problem with their line of luncheon meats. The package conveyed the wrong message: poor image on quality and quantity; difficult to open; inconvenient sizes.

What did management do with this information? They designed a package that communicated the brand's qualities and reinforced this with a new marketing strategy to regain lost market shares.

Word-processing equipment manufacturers learned that they had to make keyboards less awesome for the concept to be acceptable to final users, i.e., user oriented.

Food products, too, must be user oriented, as in the case of frozen pizza. A manufacturer held focus group interviews around the country and discovered from 2,000 participants what consumers did not like about frozen pizza. Mostly they disliked the cardboard taste of the crust. To a company that can solve the problem, this information can raise profits. One company did manage to solve the problem and successfully promote the new product.

The profit payoff? Market share rose from 18 percent to 30 percent; and the product now adds another $60 million a year in sales. This is a variation of that well-known truism: "Find a need, and fill it."

Products may not sell well because too many people think the product is dangerous, or unhealthy, or at least appears to be so. The truth of the assertion does not matter; but how others perceive the product, or its use, does count.

Lack of information can mean increasing costs: throwing money into a promotional campaign that promises only a low payoff at best. The gathering of information, even though incomplete, can turn a slow-mover into a profitable item; such information can emanate from low-cost focus group interviews.

Three Key Points

What are some key factors in productive interviewing?

For effective results, an interview will last about two hours. Don't expect two hours of top-drawer ideas to pour forth. It takes time to warm up the group. It takes time to develop rapport. It takes time to wear off the strangeness and uneasiness that usually pervades for the first 15 minutes or so. Conversation should come naturally, with ease, as in a friendly luncheon. Beyond two hours the subject matter begins to bore; the quality of responses rapidly diminishes around this time.

Groups should be homogeneous. Which does not mean a group of 27-year-old females, all born on January first, five feet tall, and weighing 123 pounds. Those, of course, may be your parameters (for whatever reasons), but homogeneity, in this instance, refers to interests common or related to the product service. If the subject is treatment of athlete's foot, persons who have never had it will not get very excited discussing the new product. Still, if a product is widely used, like deodorant, you should probably group participants by sex, age, race, and occupation. On the other hand, some researchers prefer that the entire group consist of strangers for better balance of discussion. Friends may talk to each other or dominate the group. Other researchers have had good success where all members were drawn from the same group—church, club, school, office—where each was known to the others, as long as all had an interest in, or could relate to, the product. Social and intellectual homogeneity helps, too.

Should groups be large or small? A large quiet group churns out less than a small active one. About 10 to 15 seems about right. That number is easy for the moderator to handle. They can get comfortable with one another within a reasonable time. Preferably, to eliminate the show-offs and to generate spontaneity, they should not have participated in focus group interviews previously.

Guidelines to Productive Interviewing

The moderator's role is decisive, although with spontaneous and productive groups his task is easier, his influence on the group minimal. The crucial question may be one of these:

(a) Should you or someone from your company play the role of moderator? Or,
(b) Is it better to hire a psychologist experienced in focus group interviews? Or,
(c) Should you engage a marketing research firm for the task?

You can do it, if you prepare for it. Of course, if you seek rather sensitive information, a neutral third party should extract it from the group. In this last instance, a company representative probably ought to observe or listen in, and even prompt the third-party group leader, during a break, on matters to explore. Naturally, the group will not be aware of this.

Following these guidelines should turn out all-star interviews:

★ *Be relaxed.* Get the group to relax and respond productively as soon as possible. Although you can be both relaxed and firm, measured firmness lends direction to the group.

★ *Be prepared.* The right kind of group will need little prompting, while other groups require considerably more structuring. Therefore, have ready a list of materials, questions, and topics, in an organized sequence. Of course, questions or materials cannot be so explicit that they evoke only short, multiple-choice type answers. The focus group is to raise the questions, the issues, or the ideas, so as long as the discussion proceeds along profitable lines, abandon the structured format. On the other hand, a barren bull session yields one thing: a barren bull.

★ *Be aware* that group members often tacitly elect a leader. Followers will defer to a leader (or leaders) by not speaking up first and often by not offering any new ideas contrary to those suggested by more active group participants. However, this does not mean that the quieter ones have no worthwhile ideas, or are, in reality, very quiet. Get them alone and they'll wear your ears off. They may have some excellent ideas quite contrary to those of the natural group leader. Therefore, the moderator must encourage everyone to speak and offer challenging notions. This may require considerable skill and practice.

★ *Be a little dense at times.* As moderator you should not pretend either to know or to understand everything being said (even if you do). Try to probe more deeply into ideas to prevent early-on development of habits of shallow responses. If necessary ask questions, or make statements that are phrased in questioning tones, but do not supply the missing phrases or ideas for those incompletely expressed thoughts. Of course, do not interrogate group members either. A third-degree routine may scare off all except the very boldest.

★ *Be ready* to handle all types of participants in such a way that a productive interview results. There are all types: the wallflowers; the show-offs; the talkers who spin long yarns to make short points; the yes-people or no-people; the slow speaker or one who pauses so long that a more active participant may jump in; the ones with bored looks (who are really interested); and the ones with eager looks (who hear or contribute nothing). Mainly you want many persons to contribute something, which suggests that the moderator must encourage and stimulate personal interest and involvement to avoid the generation of banalities and panaceas. (An interesting way of circumventing some problems typical of face-to-face groups is the Delphi technique, explained in Section II.5.)

★ *Record the sessions* so that they can be transcribed, or at least listened to, by as many persons in your organization as practical, for each listener may perceive something you missed. Too, there are other physical requirements such as the practical matter of choosing the right type of room and physical appointments—comfortable but not to the point of distraction, adequate recording equipment and microphones properly spaced around the room, and a seating arrangement that contributes to informality. As moderator you will want to make everyone feel comfortable quickly. That may be done by asking for self-introductions from each person. Also, the moderator can introduce the subject matter (product, idea, etc.) and discuss the purpose of the session, and convey to the group that each person's ideas and thoughts do matter.

Beyond these basic guidelines you may wonder how many sessions are necessary for a respectable sampling. After a time, ideas will begin to cluster around certain basic themes. When you perceive a definite pattern forming (also, read Section IV.5 on selecting a sample size), that may be the time to halt the focus group project.

I.7: CONSUMER PANELS—THE SECRET OF USING THEM FOR PROFITABLE EFFECT

Panels, while similar to focus group interviews, usually consist of the same persons from one survey to the next. For the purposes of testing a product or idea, a permanent or fixed sample of individuals functions for both exploratory and conclusive studies: a jury, if you wish to think of them that way. Essentially these panels attempt to gauge consumer, or final user, preferences.

Job shops, subcontractors, and those businesses producing according to specifications do not have the same measurement problems that many other businesses do. Marketing uncertainties mostly arise with the production and sale of standardized goods, style merchandise, and new product acceptance. Promotion of these products typically depends upon differentiation either at the product or packaging level or at the service level.

Detection of perceived differentiation, more decisive than any real differences, springs from properly designed consumer panels. Consumer panels can test new product acceptance and promotional campaign effectiveness as well.

The Modern Way to Profits

The most modern application of consumer panels is to keep on tap a group of participants for a variety of research projects. Often they participate in one-time experiments.

To continue the example from the previous section, Pillsbury developed the idea of an easy-to-prepare fruit dessert in a focus group session. The company carried forward the idea, deciding on apples, for what can be more American than apple pie? Consumer panels helped pick a name; "Appleasy" stood out as the name that best exemplified the product and its purpose. Consumer panels also took part in subsequent taste tests.

Many product ideas get zapped at this stage. Another Pillsbury example was a high-quality frozen croissant. It scored high in taste tests but was discarded after some panel members made remarks like: "It sure tastes good, but I don't know what it is. Do I eat it for dinner or breakfast?"

Later we will note that one of the disadvantages of consumer panels is that not all population segments are necessarily represented on panels. Pillsbury did not want to risk the expense of "trying to educate the public."

121

Then, again, were they wrong about the public? Thriving French bakeries in places as diverse in size and population composition as Santa Fe, Atlanta, and New York, suggest that consumer panels represent only a part of the chain from product development to promotion to sales and profits.

Several firms set up their juries in this way:

◎ *First*, they contact a cross-section of persons within their immediate marketing area to determine interest in panel participation.
◎ *Second*, they pre-screen these "volunteers" and develop personal and demographic profiles.
◎ *Third*, when they are ready to put together a panel for a specific purpose, management calls upon those persons who best match the purpose(s), which means that some persons will appear more often on panels than others.

Participants are paid. There are two basic methods of compensation: money and products. One approach for acquiring names of potential panel participants is to prepare a colorful poster with a pocket of mailers inviting persons to mail in a pre-addressed envelope in order to receive "free gifts" in exchange for opinions on products. However, clubs, organizations, social groups, newspaper classified ads will turn up a stream of local volunteers.

Additional Profitable Applications

A variety of techniques are used and products tested by various companies. Marketing majors from a nearby university tested various products such as mouthwash and ice cream flavors. The football team from the same university offered their skin for bandage strips and skin moisturizers. In Boston, members of a teenage hockey team made themselves available for the testing of an acne product.

Nuns are sometimes used to test products for people who already have fine skin, for nuns typically have beautiful skin since they apply no cosmetics. Gillette maintains a test population of about 1,000 women who, for a small fee, subject themselves to antiperspirant testing. In some cases, these are not truly consumer panels but simply persons who allow products to be tested on them without comment. In other cases, the combination method both tests products on individuals and then seeks their evaluations subsequently.

There are some problem areas in consumer panel designs, whether consumer panels are maintained for a variety of research projects as discussed above or whether they participate in long-term projects as discussed below.

(a) One issue centers on the type of people who comprise a panel. They may not portray the actual buying population. Then, despite all the research and advertising expenditures, the product flops. A month-long test, in full public view, on sleep and dreams took place at the Museum of Science and Technology. Obviously, the volunteers do not represent the entire population. Would you do it, for example?

(b) Opinions for pay may not elicit the most spontaneous, or even the most honest, responses. One respondent said, "If I always bad-mouth their products, they'll kick me off their panels. I like the extra money, so I'm careful what I say."

(c) Consciously or unconsciously some panel members may try to influence results so that data do not represent real consumer reactions. "What kind of books do you read for pleasure?" may evoke the response, *The Rage of Edmund Burke*, when, in fact, the member had just reread *The Happy Hooker* for the tenth time. The self-proclaimed expert is another form of vanity or petty dictatorship that must be guarded against.

The other object of consumer panels is for ongoing experimentation and measurement. This is the older use of consumer panels. Of course, its importance as an information-gathering device continues. In each instance, the group remains structurally the same throughout the experiment from which the same type of data is collected at intervals.

There are at least three key considerations in developing this approach.

- The sample population, that is, the persons on various panels, must describe the entire market. (Sampling techniques are discussed in Section IV.) One difficulty is that participation tends to be low among certain socio-economic groups—usually the low and high ends of the scale—which complicates the sampling procedure. Those who drop out of the experiment should be replaced with persons of fairly identical characteristics to maintain integrity of results.

- The participants should represent a stable group, with staying power. A high-turnover geographical area—frequent transfers, seasonality, transient nature of the immediate population—spells difficulty for long-term projects. If these are your target customers, then a different experimental design may prove more appropriate.

- Assuming reliability of data, it must be properly analyzed—mined, squeezed, and wrung for all it will yield. (Data analysis is discussed in Section V.) Frankly, this particular application of consumer panels is less practical for many smaller businesses. A marketing research company probably can develop the information more economically.

Profit-Generating Panel Designs

In order to better understand applications of consumer panels, let's examine some design examples.

First, consider a test market panel, designed for test marketing (more on test marketing in Section II.1) a new consumable product in a given geographical area. Suppose a new mustard preparation qualifies as the test product. The panel records all purchases; and the percentage of first-time buyers is noted during the campaign, which, let's say, lasts six months (26 weeks). These results are tabulated. By computing the rate of change from the, say, bi-weekly tabulations, we can project the probable final purchase level.

This figure represents market penetration. Let's presume that projections indicate 17 percent of the consumers will try the product. Profits, however, arise from repeat business. By examining panel data, we can readily calculate how many persons bought the mustard again. Assume that the repeat purchase rate registers 10 percent. Now we can arrive at a formula for predicting the long-term market share for the product.

FORMULA: Market Share = Market Penetration times Repeat Purchase Rate

= 17.5% × 10% = 1.75% of the market

This technique applies to product modifications and innovations, as well as to new products. In before-and-after results it tests the effectiveness of an advertising or promotional campaign. Before and after results matched against additional promotion expenditures determine whether revenue increments exceed cost increments. Naturally, if a campaign adds more to costs than to income, the operation will be unprofitable.

Another use, the retail store panel, also requires collection of data either continuously or at regular intervals on sales of individual products at various prices, by store types, with different retail mark-ups, by size or package types, or any other factor pivotal in promotion.

The largest cost is the fixed one, the initial investment in putting together appropriate panels and urging participants to respond. Unless these heavy initial costs are spread over many projects, the approach is not practical for many businesses. Engaging a research firm that specializes in this type of data-gathering seems like a preferred option in these cases.

Typically, families chosen through proper sampling techniques must record all purchases over a specified period, say, 12 weeks.

An application example: A firm, in a nationwide sampling of 15,000 households, combined personal interviewing (discussed in Section I.3) and consumer panel techniques. In this particular instance the research firm sought information on purchases of big ticket items (automobiles) as well as on consumable daily and weekly purchases. Data on the large, infrequent purchases were obtained in personal interviews and recall by the purchaser. Household items were recorded in a diary when the item was bought. Information solicited included description of the item, place or type of store where bought, day of week purchased, price, reason for purchase. This was a very broad study to gather data of the type summarized in Figure I.7.A. The data were also classified by personal characteristics including age, marital status, number of children, education, and household income.

PERCENTAGE OF TOTAL EXPENDITURES AMONG PRINCIPAL PURCHASES

	Household Income Before Income Taxes						
	Under $5,000	$5,000 to $10,000	$10,000 to $15,000	$15,000 to $20,000	$20,000 to $25,000	$25,000 to $30,000	$30,000 or More	ALL HOUSE-HOLDS
Total Annual Expenditures per Household								
Percent of Total Expenditures								
Food, Beverages, Tobacco								
Clothing, Accessories								
Home Operation, Improvement								
Home Furnishings, Equipment, Appliances								
Medical, Personal Care								
Automotive[1]								
Recreation								
Other[2]								
Total U.S. Households (000's)								
Sample Base								
Average Number of Persons per Household								

[1] Expenditures on automobiles in this category refer to net outlays after trade-in allowances.
[2] Includes life insurance premiums and nonmedical professional services.

Figure I.7.A: PERCENTAGE OF TOTAL EXPENDITURES AMONG PRINCIPAL PURCHASES

Such a study need be neither as broad nor as extensive. Whether for one product, a group of related products, in one geographic area only, by type of consumer, or any other classification, you slice the sample in any way that increases profits.

Be aware of shortcomings, too.

(a) For one, respondents may lose interest; therefore, periodic follow-up in person or by telephone will encourage them to keep on with it.

(b) For another, overenthusiasm at the beginning and underenthusiasm at the end suggest dropping first and last data.

(c) Most importantly, the information should be recorded when items are acquired rather than filling in the diary hurriedly the day before it is due.

Similar to the store panel, television, reading, or activity panels serve the same ends. A family records the times the television set is turned on and which programs are watched (not always the same). Although some respondents will fudge data and enter information corresponding to the image they wish to portray, overall the technique seems sufficiently reliable.

The reading survey applies mostly to newspapers and periodicals. It asks what was looked at, or read, which articles, whether articles were read with interest or skimmed, etc. An example of a reader's survey (Figure II.1.B) pins down the reader. Designed to diminish fudging and second guessing, the information is valuable in editorial planning. Of course, about half the questionnaire is devoted to reader demographics and life style. (See Section II.3 on Life Style Analysis.)

Activity analysis, widely used by others besides market researchers, has many applications other than for leisure products and services. It can apply to store hours, shopping mall activities, telephone sales, for example.

Another use of panels is trend projection. A panel of business executives is queried on sales forecast, general business trends, or projected capital expenditures. Consumer panels furnish details on purchase intentions, or saving intentions, or on the most irksome national problem of the moment. Some surveys are conducted on an ongoing basis; the periodic reports are available to managers, for a fee, from various marketing research organizations.

Panels, too, may be designed for a specific project or to test a hypothesis. For instance, researchers hypothesized that some market segments of young women respond more readily to new clothing fashions than others, and that this market segment would externalize some traits that typify opinion leaders and other innovators.

A quota sample (quota sampling is explained in Section IV.3) of 200 post-high school teen women, i.e., first-year college students, rated local clothing stores according to "innovativeness," that is, those keeping up with styles from ski pants to beachwear. The respondents were interviewed to determine

(a) new clothing items owned;

(b) magazines read;

(c) memberships in organizations;

(d) income, education, and occupation of father (on the assumption that lifestyles of late teenagers still closely resemble their families'); and

(e) inner-and-other-directedness as measured by the I-O Social Preference Scale.

Such studies are valuable because teenagers represent a consumer segment with substantial available, and willing, purchasing power.

Some Profit-Leaking Caveats

Despite the popularity of panels there are still a number of drawbacks, six of which follow.

1. One problem is sampling. (See Section IV for solutions to sampling obstacles.) If the sample does not represent customers, or intended customers, the data have limited value. Some types of persons will not serve on any panel, for pay or for free. Some persons willingly participate, but due to lack of discipline, education, or whatever, they contribute only limited, partial, or questionable data. And these may be the very persons from whom you need accurate opinions.

2. Another problem is the "I-want-to-look-good" attitude. Does the panel member, when "being watched," knowing that recorded data will be analyzed, perform differently than in more normal situations? Does he or she record "top sirloin" when he or she actually put chicken wings and backs in the shopping cart? Or during the survey period, are shopping habits altered in fact? We may never know for certain—not even the hairdresser knows!

3. Requiring too much information from panelists may destroy the incentive to cooperate. However, premiums or periodic incentives, and even follow-up contacts, can help to offset this dis-incentive. An even more serious problem is when initial positive reaction meets with rapidly developing disinterest, regardless of the number of details requested. Some lopsided, invalid results can turn up if too many persons of this type participate.

4. A related problem is the difficulty in maintaining a stable, and representative, panel. Turnover affects results. Although replacing departees with persons of similar personal and economic characteristics does help, enough small differences can invalidate the entire research project.

5. The method is expensive enough to make a one-time project for smaller businesses impractical except through another organization that has already made the substantial outlay of funds required to establish panels.

6. Too, competitors may learn of the project and act to invalidate the results through price changes, coupon offers, or a blitz campaign.

Some Profit-Making Advantages

All is not bleak, however. There are advantages. Consider these:

1. Consumer panels are especially valuable in ascertaining trends, or a ve-ridical pattern of buying, because they do involve time studies.
2. Interviewers, because of personality, inadequate training, or physical presence alone, can influence responses. The panel member is on his own. No specific questions are being asked. No one else is present to be impressed.

3. We can measure consumer reactions to changes: for example, changes in advertising or responses to promotional gimmicks. Or, how loyal are customers to a brand name and over what range of price increases? And we may gain further insight into consumer preferences.

4. Data, presumably, do not depend upon the imperfect memory of consumers. Recording data in the diary near time of purchase means that the consumer is less likely to forget important items or details, which should produce better data and more dependable results.

5. If respondents regularly serve on panels for the same organization, the rapport developed is a decided plus quality for cooperation and dependable data.

6. This form of research yields informational details not accessible through other research techniques. It can save the firm from spending large sums in misdirected undertakings or can create profit opportunities that would otherwise have been missed. As panels continue in a widening array of uses, considerable refinement and data manipulation suggest that further improvements in design and data-gathering can be an even more valuable aid to decision-making.

I.8: WHEN WISDOM IS BETTER THAN RUBIES: STORE AUDITS

The purpose of a store audit is to determine how well a product is currently selling. But isn't that information available from internal company records? Yes and no.

Sales records tell us how many manufactured, processed, or packaged products have entered the distribution pipeline. Because the pipeline extends from factory to household shelves, variable flow, delays in purchase decisions, and stocking up, sales records provide lagged results. Which does not tell us how well a current advertising campaign, for example, is doing, or how well the product is being accepted at the end of distribution line.

The chart in Figure I.8.A implies that although internal company records indicate how much volume has been sold to wholesale distributors (and a check of wholesalers can indicate how much has been moved to the retailers), we still do not know what is happening at the point of sale. From factory to consumer may well take a year or more.

How can we measure the effectiveness of expenditures for major marketing efforts? The answer: Physically count the movement of merchandise at the retail store level; ergo, the store audit.

You may wonder how a store audit is superior to a consumer panel. For one thing, an audit of a single store represents the buying preferences of a large number of people—the families who shop in the store. For another, a store audit represents real, not hypothetical, purchases.

Six Steps to a Successful Store Audit

So what is involved in a store audit? The mathematics of it can be expressed in a simple formula:

$$\text{Beginning inventory} + \text{purchases} - \text{shrinkage (theft and losses)} - \text{ending inventory} = \text{sales}$$

These are the steps to a successful store audit.

FIRST: Why conduct an audit? What do you expect to accomplish? What action will the audit lead to? In other words, if management, marketing, and other personnel do not understand the purpose, do not expect viable outcomes from fuzzily stated objectives. In fact, if goals are that hazy, postpone a store audit until they take shape. Results should lead you to do something, such as more or less advertising, a chance in packaging, better service, or whatever.

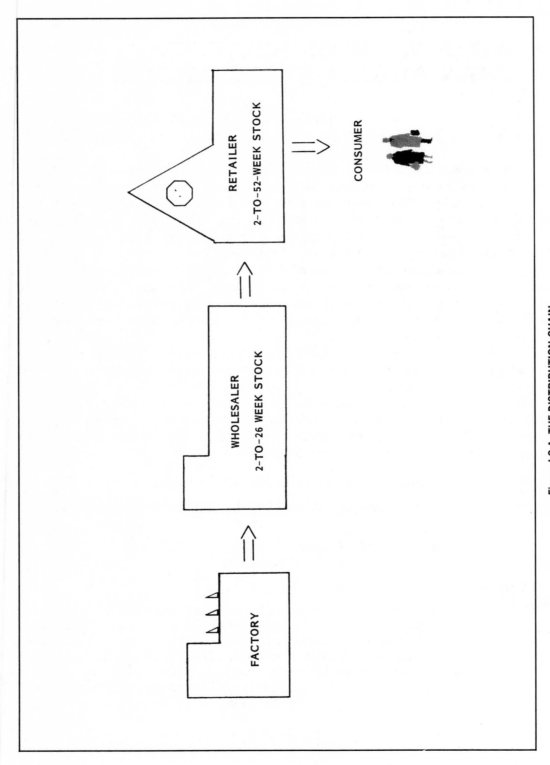

Figure I.8.A: THE DISTRIBUTION CHAIN

SECOND: Where are you going to conduct your audits? A little knowledge of sampling helps here. (Be sure to read Section IV on sampling techniques in this handbook.) If the product is sold in a variety of outlets, then your sample should reflect elements of the entire population of stores. Including all stores from all geographic areas will be prohibitively costly. Suppose that the product is sold in chain supermarkets, large independent supermarkets, medium-sized stores, and convenience stores. A sample should reflect both diversity of stores and sales volume. For instance, if 40 percent of the stores that carry your product are convenience stores, but they represent only 10 percent of total volume; then 40 percent of your sample should *not* reflect convenience stores; that is, a disproportionate sample tends to reflect more high-volume stores rather than a large number of stores.

THIRD: Are you ready to begin now? No, for you still must obtain cooperation of retail stores. Some chains will not let any outsider in their stores (other than customers, of course). Others do not want to be bothered; they fail to see benefits to them. Still others may maintain poor records, or are inconsistent, which raises the cost of a store audit and the question of dependability of data. Secure store management's cooperation not just one time but throughout the audit, which may take several weeks, and preferably maintain good relations that allow for future audits. Personal contacts are advisable. You may even have to pay for the store's cooperation.

FOURTH: How often does the store send in a report? The store's management does not. You generate your own reports by going to the store and physically counting what is on the shelves. And if you do not do it personally, train your people as well as you can *before* sending them out on the road. Even if the merchandise is not sitting on the proper shelf, it must be located and counted; the audit should be completed on one trip. How often? That really goes back to the first step, which may dictate a bimonthly or monthly schedule, or some other period. Remember to apply the formula to determine how much of your merchandise has sold during the period. That means reviewing purchase invoices as well as counting what is lying around in the store.

FIFTH: Should you monitor products of competitors as well? If store management will cooperate, such information is extremely valuable to you. It certainly is not unethical, for the consumer benefits in the long run from improvements arising from audits. And while you are at it, audit some stores in another area, too, a control group. Assume that the purpose of audits is to gauge response to a promotional campaign in a specific geographical area. Wouldn't you like to know, also, what might have happened had you not made the additional expenditures? The technique is to audit stores that have not been exposed to the promotional material. At least you will enjoy the comfortable feeling that increased sales are more likely attributable to your campaign than to exogenous or unobserved factors.

SIXTH: How long should you continue the audits? You may prefer to end them shortly after the completion of a promotional campaign, or you may discover that such information is so valuable that audits should continue indefinitely. Your budget and needs dictate that decision, in part. If you plan on using your own sales force to perform store audits, lower expectations. Salespersons sell; auditors audit. Each job requires different personality traits and preferences. The rest you can decide when the issue arises.

An Alternative to Do-It-Yourself Store Audits

Suppose, however, that although information from store audits is valuable in developing a marketing strategy, audits are not practical or economical, given present organizational capabilities and staff.

The alternative is to purchase this service from any of several firms engaged in store audits. The principal disadvantage arises when no auditing firm presently monitors your particular line of products.

One well-known service is the Nielsen Retail Index, established in 1934. This particular index provides these categories of information:

(a) Reported nationally, by region, sales area, and store type, are sales and sales share for your product and your competitors', and total product class sales.

(b) Total merchandise purchased by retailers by brand, product class, major market divisions.

(c) Retail inventories to assess retailer intentions and to evaluate inventory sufficiency relative to current and future sales rates.

(d) Average price charged consumers for each brand by type, size, and area.

(e) Out-of-stock figures.

(f) Separate reporting for special deals and offers.

(g) Cooperative advertising, in-store advertising and displays, and special prices.

(h) Compilation of network television, magazine and newspaper advertising by media type and brand name.

(i) Special reports and analyses such as variance analysis, regression analysis, co-variance, etc. (These analytical techniques are explained in Sections V and VI of this handbook.)

A national firm offers the advantage of width and depth of information. For example, Nielsen covers continental U.S., maintains a 1600 store sample, which, according to them, represents about 4,000,000 people spending close to $2 billion annually. A major disadvantage, this index reflects the distribution of drug and grocery products; it is a disadvantage if you sell neither of these.

A Lesson from Store Audits

What can you learn from store audits? You can use them for more than gathering raw data; you can use them during times of experimentation.

For instance, is horizontal or vertical shelf arrangement better for your product(s)? Horizontal arrangement means spreading one brand along one or two shelves, and separating brands by shelves. Vertical placement of your product means placing it in one store section ranging from top shelf to bottom shelf. Of course, Campbell soup marketers performed such a test years ago and discovered that vertical spacing for them produced the maximum sales volume for a given amount of shelf space.

From the retailers' viewpoint, shelf space is a valuable resource. They prefer the highest returns of sales and profits from the use of any given shelf area. High return per unit of shelf space also improves the relationship between producer and retailer.

You can calculate the impact of shelf space on unit sales for your product and even for your competitor's. This is referred to as space elasticity. By definition it is the ratio of a relative percentage change in unit sales to a relative percentage change in shelf space. Here is the formula for computing space elasticity.

$$E_S = \frac{(U_t - U_{t-1})/U_{t-1}}{(S_t - S_{t-1})/S_{t-1}} \quad \text{or} \quad \frac{U_1 - U_2}{U_1 + U_2} \div \frac{S_1 - S_2}{S_1 + S_2}$$

E_S = space elasticity
U = unit sales
S = shelf space
t = present time period
$t-1$ = previous period (such as last month or last quarter)

What does the coefficient of space elasticity convey? Suppose the answer were 5. *An interpretation*: A 1 percent increase in shelf space will give rise to a 5 percent increase in unit sales. Of course, the relationship between shelf space and unit sales represents a loose link.

Other variables, not immediately evident, can overshadow research outcomes and predictions. For example, package size, brand type, retail price, availability of substitutes, prices of substitute and complementary products, shelf capacity, frequency of restocking in the household (or seasonality such as hot cereals in the winter and cold cereals in the summer), whether the item is fast selling or slow selling—all can subvert space elasticity measurements. (The reader is also referred to the Drop Factor Formula discussed under "Test Marketing" in Section II.1.)

Due to unforeseen variables, store audits impart partial answers. There is the story of the successful introduction of a new product. An early audit verified that the product was a fast sellout. That should call for a celebration. Some time later, when "reorders" proved dismal, the truth came out. Salesmen from competing companies bought the product by the case and sent it to their labs for analysis.

Moreover, store audits keep tabs on advertising campaigns: who's about to grab the rabbit? A.C. Nielsen helps Pepsi-Cola and Coca-Cola keep score on market shares; and executive careers rise and fall with each turn of advertising successes and failures.

Price Estimation with Store Audits

Store audits also figure in pricing policies. Pricing itself derives from the estimated demand equation for the group of products; but price-setting is also strongly influenced by prices of competing products (as substitutes), and of complementary products (those things that go together like bacon and eggs).

Through product differentiation, or brand loyalty, the manufacturer or processor strives to delay brand switching if price differences become too great. Some products reflect more sensitivity to price spreads than others.

To illustrate, an experiment was conducted with peas and chili. It was discovered that chili enthusiasts are reluctant to surrender their favorite brand even when a competing brand sells at a substantial discount. Pea consumers are not nearly so loyal. They switch as often as a cow's tail in summer.

Warehouse withdrawal records offer another method of determining the flow of goods through the distribution channel. Nielsen points out that as a substitute for measuring sales at the point of sale, this method has certain weaknesses:

(a) The records actually report movement of products from one point in the distribution chain to another, rather than the actual final sales.
(b) The records exclude those goods shipped directly from factory to retailers.
(c) Uncooperative warehouses provide no records and still represent a substantial part of the market.
(d) Records do not provide the breadth and depth of information from on-the-spot measurement.

Nevertheless, important answers can appear in warehouse withdrawal data. In 1966, SAMI (Selling Areas-Marketing, Inc.) began testing various methods and now offer data (see Figure I.8.B and I.8.C) supplied by chains, wholesalers, rack operators, and frozen food warehousemen on the movement of all dry grocery and household supplies, frozen food, health and beauty aids, and certain warehouse refrigerated items. In all, the marketing research firm reports on 68 product groups, in 39 marketing areas, and over 400 categories. Data are generated every four weeks.

In Figure I.8.B appears a sample SAMI item detail report that shows caseload product movement of every single warehoused item measured versus the food operator's own movement on that item for the current 12 weeks and the past 52 weeks. Buyers and merchandisers use this report to ascertain how many cases of a given item they moved compared to the total market.

Mainly these data help determine which items buyers should, or should not, handle. Decisions on which new products to add usually are based on information supplied by manufacturers. But deciding which brands to drop often is done on a rule-of-thumb figure based on sales volume such as "drop it if at least one case per week per store is not purchased." If a product does well within a limited geographical area, probably it should not be dropped.

SAMI — FOOD OPERATOR ITEM DETAIL REPORT

MARKETING AREA ISSUE 162-164 REPORT NUMBER 162 162 PERIOD COVERED JAN 13 - APR 06, 1979 INITIAL PERIOD APR 08 - MAY 05, 1978 PAGE 0701-01

REPORT	SIZE	PACK PER CASE	TMM CASE VOL 12 WK	TMM CASE VOL 52 WK	DOLLAR SHARE CAT 12 WK	DOLLAR SHARE CAT 52 WK	SARDI DISTR ACV % 12 WK	CASE VOL 1 WK	CASE VOL 3 WK	FO SHARE CASE VOL 12 WK	FO SHARE CASE VOL 52 WK	SARDI DISTR ACV % 12 WK	SARDI ADD.CASES IF 100% 12 WK	SAMI FO SHIPPING 12 WK	NEW ITEM PERIOD ENDING
COFFEE — TOTAL - COFFEE: REGULAR			247,051	1,017M	100.0%	100.0%	100	44M	148M	17.6%	14.6%	100		14	
TOTAL - PRIVATE LABEL			40,674	151,108	16.0%	14.4%		19M	53,112	47.7%	35.1%			12	
PVT LABEL CASE SHR OF CATEGORY					16.5%	14.9%									
PVT LABEL CASE SHR OF FO VOL										44.6%	35.9%				
TOTAL - BRIM			2,552	9,643	1.4%	1.3%	94	373	1,390	14.6%	14.4%	100		12	
BRIM COFFEE A P DECAF	1 LB	24	2,492	9,405	1.4%	1.2%	94	373	1,390	15.0%	14.8%		0	12	
BRIM COFFEE ELC PRK DECAF	1 LB	24	60	238	.0%	.0%	5			.0%	.0%			*	
TOTAL - MAX PAX			1,161	6,210	.5%	.6%	60	256	946	22.0%	15.2%	88		12	
MAX PAX COFFEE REG 10S	12 OZ	24	348	1,944	.1%	.2%	14			.0%	.0%			6	
MAX PAX COFFEE ADC 10S	12 OZ	24	185	719	.1%	.1%	17			.0%	.0%			4	
MAX PAX COFFEE ELC PRK 10S	12 OZ	24	628	3,547	.3%	.4%	32	256	946	40.8%	26.7%	88	35	6	0922N
TOTAL - MAXWELL HOUSE			96,583	410,325	40.0%	41.4%	100	13M	41,059	13.2%	10.0%	100		13	
MAXWELL HOUSE COF REG	1 LB	24	23,687	123,418	9.7%	12.4%	98	4,334	13,405	18.3%	10.9%	100	0	13	
MAXWELL HOUSE COF REG	2 LB	12	12,799	34,900	5.3%	3.5%	85	701	2,889	5.5%	8.3%	100	0	13	
MAXWELL HOUSE COF REG	3 LB	8	168	696	.1%	.1%	10		10	.0%	.0%			*	
MAXWELL HOUSE COF DRP	1 LB	24	6,052	32,945	2.5%	3.3%	96	989	3,629	16.3%	11.0%	100	0	13	
MAXWELL HOUSE COF DRP	2 LB	12	1,786	5,983	.7%	.6%	50	264	1,090	14.8%	18.2%	100	0	7	
MAXWELL HOUSE COF ADC	1 LB	24	19,789	94,724	8.2%	9.5%	100	3,355	8,861	17.0%	9.4%	100	0	13	
MAXWELL HOUSE COF ADC	2 LB	12	16,345	43,466	6.9%	4.4%	86	987	3,734	6.0%	8.6%	100	0	12	
MAXWELL HOUSE COF ADC	3 LB	8	245	897	.1%	.1%	12			.0%	.0%			*	
MAXWELL HOUSE COF FNE	1 LB	24	258	1,119	.1%	.1%	9			.0%	.0%			*	
MAXWELL HOUSE COF ELC PRK	1 LB	24	8,926	50,195	3.6%	5.1%	97	1,763	5,828	19.8%	11.6%	100	0	13	
MAXWELL HOUSE COF ELC PRK	2 LB	12	6,494	21,769	2.8%	2.2%	76	390	1,623	6.0%	7.5%	100	0	11	
MAXWELL HOUSE COF ELC PRK	3 LB	8	34	213	.0%	.0%				.0%	.0%			0	
TOTAL - SANKA			5,872	23,842	3.2%	3.1%	99	688	3,152	11.7%	13.2%	100		13	
SANKA COFFEE REGULAR	1 LB	24	2,743	11,848	1.5%	1.5%	93	211	1,151	7.7%	9.7%	72	82	13	
SANKA COFFEE DRIP	1 LB	24	749	2,855	.4%	.4%	22			.0%	.7%			4	
SANKA COFFEE DRIP-MATIC	1 LB	24	1,951	7,393	1.1%	1.0%	69	306	1,367	15.7%	18.5%	88	42	9	
SANKA COFFEE ELEC PERK	1 LB	24	429	1,746	.2%	.2%	26	171	634	39.9%	36.3%	88	23	*	
TOTAL - YUBAN			906	3,349	.4%	.4%	57	180	744	19.9%	22.2%	96		7	
YUBAN COFFEE ALL PURPOSE	1 LB	24	288	1,121	.1%	.1%	22			.0%	.0%			*	
YUBAN COFFEE REGULAR	1 LB	24	618	2,228	.3%	.2%	34	180	744	29.1%	33.4%	96	8	5	
TOTAL - MELLOW ROAST			1,812	12,577	.6%	1.1%	81	215	1,850	11.9%	14.7%	100		11	0728N

M-000 W-000,000
ACV = ALL COMMODITY VOLUME
* = 3 OR LESS FOOD OPERATORS SHIPPING
NA = SARDI DATA NOT AVAILABLE

Figure I.8.B: SAMI FOOD OPERATOR ITEM DETAIL REPORT
(Courtesy of Selling Areas—Marketing, Inc. (SAMI))

Paralleling the report in Figure I.8.B is the SAMI standard dollar report illustrated in Figure I.8.C, which is issued every 12 weeks. The average shelf price on each item is a weighted average for the market. Market shares shown are a percent of each item's contribution to the brand total as well as share of the market. The report also records the number of food operators in the market shipping the item and identifies new and discontinued items.

In tandem with research methods explicated in this book, the SAMI reports are used to work toward solutions of a variety of marketing problems, such as these:

◎ Do you enjoy favorable turnovers of sales but still meet buyer resistance?
◎ How can you get a new product in the store?
◎ Is the buyer not stocking your fast-moving items?
◎ Does the purchaser carry your complete line?
◎ Do you need to prove you're entitled to additional shelf facing?
◎ Does your brand movement justify better shelf position (off the floor)?
◎ Do you want buyers to discontinue marginally profitable items?
◎ Do you need evidence of promotional strength?
◎ Can you point out a weak competitive promotion?

In other words, with adequate information food operators can allocate shelf space more efficiently, and manufacturers and processors, with top product exposure, can bring in the big bucks per unit of space.

Another service offered by the same firm is SARDI (SAMI Retail Distribution Index), which prepares reports from store-by-store shipping pattern figures every four weeks. The data indicate the volume of your product and your competitors' sales and the relationship of these sales to product availability in stores. Several SARDI reports are published. The brand trend report on peanut butter in Figure I.8.D illustrates the reporting format.

Line A of the sample SARDI report shows dollar volume (SAMI). Line B is the percent distribution or availability in large supermarkets. Line C is Line A divided by Line B. Line D reflects how much more of the product might have been sold had more of it been available.

Line C represents sales per percentage point of distribution, which reduces all brands to a common measurement level. Other things being equal, Line C tells which brand outsells others.

The key to high sales is not only distribution to all stores, or even distribution to all large stores, but distribution to those large stores that sell a lot of your product category. The purposes of these various reports, and of marketing research, is to pinpoint outcomes (effects) and causes, so that you can alter, or work with, causes to bring about bigger effects.

SAMI

STANDARD DOLLAR REPORT

MANUFACTURER: NON-CONTRACT
CONTRACT NO.:
MARKET AREA:

CATEGORY: COFFEE. REGULAR

ISSUE NUMBER: 116

CURRENT 4 WK. PERIOD: 07/05/75 - 08/01/75

UNITS: DOLLAR VOLUME, CASE VOLUME

PAGE: 0701-002

PERIOD COVERED: 07/30/74 - 08/01/75

STANDARD DOLLAR REPORT	ITEM SIZE	PACK PER CASE	AVG. SHELF PRICE	MEASURED CASE VOLUME 4 WEEKS	MEASURED CASE VOLUME 52 WEEKS	MEASURED DOLLAR SALES 4 WEEKS	MEASURED DOLLAR SALES 52 WEEKS	DOLLAR SHARE OF BRAND 4 WEEKS	DOLLAR SHARE OF BRAND 52 WEEKS	DOLLAR SHARE OF CATEGORY 4 WEEKS	DOLLAR SHARE OF CATEGORY 52 WEEKS	* SUB TOT PGS weeks	NEW IN/DROP (D)/ITEM IN MARKET PERIOD ENDING
YUBAN COFFEE ALL PURPOSE	2 LB	12	2.068	675	6.204	16.752	190.655	30.611%	21.999%	1.197%	.971%	*	
YUBAN COFFEE REGULAR	2 LB	12	2.710	46	.377	1.496	12.447	2.734%	1.436%	.107%	.063%	*	
YUBAN COFFEE DRIP	2 LB	12	2.700	35	2.572	1.134	84.937	2.072%	9.801%	.081%	.432%	7	
YUBAN COFFEE ELECTRAMATIC	1 LB	24	1.374	232	3.918	7.648	130.937	13.975%	15.108%	.546%	.667%	7	
YUBAN COFFEE ELECTRAMATIC	2 LB	12	2.130	767	10.544	19.600	325.775	35.815%	37.590%	1.401%	1.658%	6	
FOLGERS				14.405	193.431	446.064	5.916.015	100.000%	100.000%	31.874%	30.116%	8	
FOLGERS COFFEE REG	8 OZ	24	.721	26	.410	450	7.052	.101%	.119%	.032%	.036%	*	
FOLGERS COFFEE REG	1 LB	24	1.297	2.385	22.585	74.248	710.901	16.645%	12.017%	5.305%	3.619%	8	
FOLGERS COFFEE REG	2 LB	12	2.604	1.039	24.027	32.469	747.589	7.297%	12.637%	2.230%	3.806%	8	
FOLGERS COFFEE REG	3 LB	8	3.821	1.448	20.109	44.262	589.614	9.923%	9.966%	3.163%	3.001%	8	
FOLGERS COFFEE DRIP	1 LB	24	1.300	1.529	14.073	47.717	443.029	10.697%	7.489%	3.410%	2.255%	8	
FOLGERS COFFEE DRIP	2 LB	12	2.624	826	15.670	26.013	485.829	5.832%	8.212%	1.859%	2.473%	8	
FOLGERS COFFEE FINE	3 LB	8	3.801	1.176	13.365	33.932	394.721	7.607%	6.672%	2.425%	2.009%	8	
FOLGERS COFFEE FINE	1 LB	24	1.287	259	2.606	7.999	82.444	1.793%	1.394%	.572%	.420%	5	
FOLGERS COFFEE FINE	2 LB	12	2.599	89	1.691	2.776	53.292	.622%	.901%	.198%	.271%	8	
FOLGERS COFFEE ELECTRIC PRK	1 LB	24	1.306	2.574	24.814	80.672	778.244	18.085%	13.155%	5.765%	3.962%	8	
FOLGERS COFFEE ELECTRIC PRK	2 LB	12	2.599	1.181	28.425	36.832	682.427	8.257%	14.916%	2.632%	4.492%	8	
FOLGERS COFFEE ELECTRIC PRK	3 LB	8	3.796	1.933	25.656	58.694	740.873	13.158%	12.523%	4.194%	3.771%	8	
HIGH POINT				874	6.487	32.051	239.690	100.000%	100.000%	2.290%	1.220%	8	
HIGH POINT COF DRIP DECAF	1 LB	24	1.535	261	2.300	9.616	85.685	30.002%	35.748%	.687%	.436%	8	0214N
HIGH POINT COF DRIP DECAF	2 LB	12	3.048	124	.757	4.536	27.666	14.152%	11.542%	.324%	.141%	5	0214N
HIGH POINT COF EL PERK DECAF	1 LB	24	1.535	275	2.081	10.133	77.278	31.615%	32.241%	.724%	.393%	8	0214N
HIGH POINT COF EL PERK DECAF	2 LB	12	3.024	214	1.349	7.766	49.061	24.230%	20.469%	.555%	.250%	7	0214N
CHASE SANBORN				583	21.733	17.951	653.726	100.000%	100.000%	1.283%	3.328%	4	
CHASE SANBORN COF REG	2 LB	12	2.576	224	8.193	6.923	249.779	38.209%	38.566%	.495%	1.272%	4	
CHASE SANBORN COF DRIP	2 LB	12	2.596	98	3.288	3.053	96.177	17.007%	14.712%	.218%	.490%	4	
CHASE SANBORN COF ELC PRK	2 LB	12	2.546	261	10.252	7.975	307.770	44.426%	47.079%	.570%	1.567%	4	
FRENCH MARKET				4	18	62	280	100.000%	100.000%	.004%	.001%	*	
FRENCH MARKET COF CHIC REG	1 LB	12	1.292	4	18	62	280	100.000%	100.000%	.004%	.001%	*	0314N
OLD JUDGE				1.847	33.829	54.275	1.060.584	100.000%	100.000%	3.878%	5.399%	6	
OLD JUDGE COFFEE REG	1 LB	24	1.304	299	6.418	9.360	203.224	17.246%	19.162%	.669%	1.035%	5	
OLD JUDGE COFFEE REG	2 LB	12	2.322	474	6.389	13.205	199.850	24.330%	18.843%	.944%	1.017%	6	
OLD JUDGE COFFEE REG	3 LB	8	3.822	59	2.510	1.804	77.465	3.324%	7.304%	.129%	.394%		
OLD JUDGE COFFEE DRIP	1 LB	24	1.303	127	1.892	3.972	59.711	7.318%	5.630%	.284%	.304%		

*ASTERISK INDICATES 3 OR LESS FOOD OPERATOR SHIPPING.

Figure I.8.C: SAMI STANDARD DOLLAR REPORT
(Courtesy of Selling Areas — Marketing, Inc. (SAMI))

SAMI SARDI BRAND TRENDS

MANUFACTURER: ABC COMPANY INC.
CONTRACT NO:
MARKET AREA: PHILADELPHIA
ISSUES COVERED: 115 – 120
PERIOD COVERED: 6/7/75 – 11/21/75

CATEGORY: PEANUT BUTTER & PEANUT BUTTER COMBINATIONS

UNITS: DOLLARS

PAGE 0001

DESCRIPTION DETAIL:
A — 4 WEEKS DOLLAR VOLUME
B — 4 WEEKS ACV DISTRIBUTION
C — SALES PER POINT OF DISTRIBUTION
D — ADDITIONAL SALES IF DISTRIBUTION IS 100%
E — AVERAGE PRICE PER POUND

DESCRIPTION SIZE PACK		ISSUE NUMBER / PERIOD ENDING	115 7/4/75	116 8/1/75	117 8/29/75	118 9/26/75	119 10/24/75	120 11/21/75	115-117 8/29/75	118-120 11/21/75
PEANUT BUTTER & COMBINATIONS	A		$ 1,207M	$ 1,025M	$ 1,134M	$ 1,141M	$ 1,313M	$ 1,366M	$ 3,366M	$ 3,820M
	B		100	100	100	100	100	100	100	100
	C		12,070	10,252	11,341	11,414	13,128	13,657	33,663	38,199
	D		0	0	0	0	0	0	0	0
	E		.739	.769	.764	.763	.771	.780	.757	.772
BRAND A	A		179,140	172,371	206,839	215,766	241,159	270,761	558,350	727,686
	B		100	100	100	100	100	100	100	100
	C		1,791	1,724	2,068	2,158	2,412	2,708	5,584	7,277
	D		0	0	0	0	0	0	0	0
	E		.779	.790	.789	.806	.810	.814	.786	.810
CREAMY SMOOTH 18 OZ.	A		48,273	45,597	48,893	52,411	50,186	54,405	142,763	157,002
	B		86	84	87	93	90	95	89	97
	C		561	543	562	564	558	573	1,604	1,619
	D		7,858	8,685	7,306	3,945	5,576	2,863	17,645	4,856
	E		.743	.784	.754	.770	.780	.794	.759	.782
CREAMY SMOOTH 28 OZ.	A		47,563	37,899	58,913	55,039	81,104	57,239	144,375	193,382
	B		90	86	94	92	100	96	95	100
	C		528	441	627	598	811	597	1,520	1,934
	D		5,285	6,170	3,760	4,786	0	2,416	7,599	0
	E		.756	.759	.771	.798	.766	.795	.763	.784
CHUNKY 18 OZ.	A		27,317	22,968	26,656	33,071	25,735	38,383	76,941	97,189
	B		64	62	63	68	66	72	66	72
	C		427	370	423	486	390	533	1,166	1,350
	D		15,366	14,077	15,655	15,562	13,257	14,927	39,636	37,796
	E		.793	.784	.808	.810	.825	.829	.796	.821

Figure I.8.D: SAMI/SARDI BRAND TREND REPORT
(Courtesy of Selling Areas— Marketing, Inc. (SAMI))

TABLE
Maximum Coverage of SAMI Market Areas
When Distribution Checks Are Restricted To:

	Metropolitan Areas Only	Stores With Annual Volume		Metropolitan Area Stores With Annual Dollar Volume	
		Over $2 Million Only	Over $1 Million Only	Over $2 Million Only	Over $1 Million Only
TOTAL 39 MARKETS	80%	70%	79%	60%	66%
Albany	64	66	77	47	52
Atlanta	→68	→66	→77	→51	→57
Baltimore/Washington	84	78	83	68	72
Birmingham/Montgomery	70	51	65	37	47
Boston/Providence	92	77	83	73	78
Buffalo	66	68	75	51	54
Charlotte	→36	→62	→73	→24	→28
Chicago	90	76	82	70	75
Cincinnati/Dayton/Columbus	72	67	78	53	60
Cleveland	87	69	79	63	71
Dallas/Fort Worth	→81	→73	→83	→63	→71
Denver	79	77	83	65	68
Des Moines/Omaha	60	68	82	47	53
Detroit	96	65	74	64	73
Houston	→91	→79	→86	→74	→81
Indianapolis	69	74	85	56	62
Jacksonville/Tampa	81	78	83	66	70
Kansas City	75	68	84	56	66
Los Angeles/San Diego	98	81	86	80	85
Memphis/Little Rock	40	54	67	28	32
Miami	86	76	82	67	71
Milwaukee	83	74	83	64	70
Minneapolis/St. Paul	72	70	81	57	64
Nashville/Knoxville	53	46	65	30	38
New Orleans	67	62	74	49	56
New York	94	67	73	63	69
Norfolk/Richmond	69	62	76	49	57
Oklahoma City/Tulsa	60	70	81	44	49
Philadelphia	→95	→68	→74	→66	→71
Phoenix/Tucson	74	83	91	66	70
Pittsburgh	→64	→56	→69	→38	→46
Portland, Oregon	64	73	86	51	58
Raleigh	52	52	62	33	37
St. Louis	83	74	88	67	75
Salt Lake City	57	77	88	48	53
San Antonio/Corpus Christi	75	74	81	62	67
San Francisco	88	74	82	67	74
Seattle/Tacoma	71	77	86	57	63
Syracuse	68	56	75	51	52

→Note the great differences in market-by-market coverage when in-store
checks are conducted only in large Metropolitan Area stores.

Figure I.8.E: THE 39 SAMI MARKET AREAS
(Courtesy of Selling Areas—Marketing, Inc. (SAMI))

The SAMI market area coverage is restricted to 39 major markets. Since it may be of interest to you to know which markets are included, even for your own research purposes, they are listed in Figure I.8.E. From the figures in the table, we can also learn in which areas food sales are concentrated more or less in urban (versus suburban) settings.

All together you now know the major sources and methods of data collection. Next we want to take a close look at research design.

SECTION *II*

RESEARCH DESIGN

"I applied mine heart to know and search, and to seek out wisdom, and the reason of things, and to know the wickedness of folly, even of foolishness and madness."

Ecclesiastes 7:25

INTRODUCTION

===

As we have already seen in Section I, and will see in Sections II and III, asking questions is the chief way to get answers in marketing research. Therefore, the art of asking questions, and the design of the questionnaire, are crucial in turning silver-star responses into gold-star sales dollars.

The various techniques presented in Sections I, II, and III are designed basically to elicit three types of responses, or sets of data:

ONE: *Demographic characteristics* of consumers or potential buyers: location, occupation of consumer or type of firm, age, income or sales level, education, family status, etc. Much of Section I material is focused on demographic factors.

TWO: *Attitudes and opinions* of customers and others: buying habits; intent to purchase (expand); reaction to product, service or idea; attitudes toward specific advertising; opinions on selected product attributes; *inter alia*. Several of the research designs both in Sections II and III aim to disinter this kind of information buried in the brains of individuals.

THREE: *Behavioral characteristics*, whether related to past or projected, or current, patterns: reaction to a promotional or advertising campaign; spending habits and age, income level; race or national origin; and the accumulation of information that respondents are unable or unwilling to articulate through direct questioning.

Of the five techniques that follow in this section, test marketing is most highly favored among industrial companies and firms in the communications industry. It is a close second among the techniques preferred by consumer concerns.

Taking all types of concerns together, consumer and industrial, test marketing ties for first place with informal experimental designs among the favorite techniques explained in this section and favored by successfully managed business organizations.

Test marketing focuses on how buyers will really react under actual market conditions, not on how they say they will react under hypothetical conditions. A controlled test market lowers risks associated with a full-scale new product launch. Test marketing procedures serve to gather data on all three sets of characteristics listed above.

An alternative to the fairly well-controlled test market approach is experimentation with informal designs, to discover which variables influence behavior in the market place. That is, this technique responds more to the type 3 design, discovering behavioral characteristics of buyers. Too, both test marketing and informal experimental designs have found considerable popularity among small and medium-sized companies.

After these two research techniques, life style analysis is favored about equally with formal experimental designs by firms selling into the consumer market. Neither of these two techniques finds much interest among industrial suppliers. Life style analysis is popular among utility, consulting, insurance, personal finance, and market research companies. The focus is mainly type 2 research: attitudes, interests, and opinions.

Formal experimental designs popularly substitute for sampling because, often cheaper to initiate, they give rise to easily obtainable results. Thrusts are behavioral, primarily, type 3, and attitudinal, secondarily, type 2. Two basic experimental designs in this subsection provide easy access to market information for firms of any size, although their popularity predominates among the largest firms, those with sales of $200 million or more.

The Delphi technique has been employed almost exclusively by large industrial organizations, practically not at all by smaller firms, and relatively little by consumer companies. Its focus is on attitudes and opinions, type 2, that affect long-term policy formulations. It is linked more to trend predictions than to routine decision-making.

II.1: TEN CRITICAL STEPS TO PROFITABLE TEST MARKETING

Testing is better than asking. Test marketing measures, on a miniature scale, how consumers really react to a new product (or service)—not how they say they *may* react.

This technique is especially decisive for new products because historical data on them typically do not exist, or are unreliable as a proxy measure. Of course, the term "new product" may connote only slight variations of the old product, or no differences at all, but a new marketing approach, or possibly new packaging, or appeal to a new market segment.

A Practical Answer

What do you really want to know? Whether enough consumers will spend their money on your product (or service), again and again, in sufficient periodic volume, at a price several times basic costs, which will add something to the firm's total profits. How can you learn that without making a full-fledged market invasion investment?

Test marketing is a practical, asset-protecting tool recommended for many businesses and for many products. Most often test markets are conducted with consumer goods, usually supermarket items, because such concentrated area testing does not lend itself well to big ticket, capital equipment items. But there are other profitable applications.

For example, Shick Sunn Classic Pictures employs a sophisticated computerized test marketing system to select stories, actors, advertising strategy, and even premier dates for its movies. Sunn's system cost about $5 million to develop, and another $1 ¼ million annually to maintain. Then again, this system has enabled them to gross an average $14 million per movie.

But test marketing need be neither as expensive nor as complex as that. The ten profit-building steps in this section will guide you in test market designs.

Risk Reduction with Market Intelligence

Test marketing is a particular type of marketing intelligence: a mini-marketing program for a new product with maxi-potential. Or at least that's what you want to discover. If you ever participated in market gap analysis, you probably churned up scores of excellent, potentially high-profit, new product and service ideas. Analysis beyond the idea stage will separate truly potential winners from mirages. Sometimes an idea is good, but ahead of its time, such as the cartridge television systems offered by Cartridge Television Inc. in 1971–72. Buyers must be receptive in order for successful marketing to turn a good idea into tangible bucks.

Test marketing may be likened to experimental marketing—a form of risk control, or asset protection. Risk dimensions are a vital factor in deciding whether to test market a product.

Although not all products should be test marketed, others are excellent candidates. Test-market truly unique products, even if only on a very limited scale. Unfamiliarity with the marketplace increases the urgency for test marketing. If the new product threatens to take a big bite out of the market for successful, existing products of the company (through product differentiation, for example), then test profitability impact on the total product line. If producing and selling the new product will require substantial investment, test marketing figures prominently in the evaluation process.

If the competition gets wind of the test, and can outflank you both in timing and financial backup, then you must decide whether to swallow the risks and push onward and outward without benefit of test marketing.

When Lever Brothers tested an ammoniated household cleaner a number of years ago, competition read the message, accepted some risks, and led Lever to the national market by several months.

> *The lesson*: Protection of marketing ideas or concepts is nearly impossible, and these things do not lend themselves to test marketing. Better candidates are found among those products not easily duplicated.

The test market should be a microcosm of the total market—an ideal not always realized—that omits no major buying segment. Too, you will probably prefer to test in more than one market (more on that later).

Suppose you plan to market nationally a new "hot" mustard: Aunt Harriet's Favorite Mustard. A single test area will not generate information on regional differences in tastes, if they exist. Testing may reveal that New Englanders like a spicier mustard packed in ten-ounce jars, while Californians prefer a less spicy, nine-ounce package.

Typically three markets are tested because relying on data from a single market does not adequately reduce risk of failure. Statistical odds indicate a greater chance of error in using one market instead of more than one.

Vlasic Pickles presents an interesting variation to this thesis. Vlasic Foods, Inc., expanded regionally until it was acquired by Campbell. It discovered that the New England market was essentially one of price competition. The company penetrated the market by developing new and aggressive marketing concepts, an innovative approach to pickle departments in supermarkets. Before entering untried markets they test vigorously for taste and packaging differences. Some regions like more or less spice in the kosher pickles; some varieties sell better in one region, or state, than in another; and packaging matches the preferences of local consumers. For Vlasic, testing is an important ingredient in the marketing formula.

Profitable Application of the Technique

To help discover whether test marketing is for you, let's list in random order some purposes or benefits of test marketing.

• 1. One bell-ringing appeal: it's *money-saving*. Naturally, test marketing is justified only if it is likely to save money.

> *A general rule*: We can state that it will save money whenever the financial and operating risks of launching the product exceed the cost of conducting the test.

Testing a product on a limited basis and risking a specified amount of funds is more prudent than exposing total capital. Of course, a series of test failures can add up to one big mistake. But if you have done your homework well, a big winner will turn up. Learning does occur. Test marketing indicates whether to kill the dog—or teach it new tricks.

• 2. A test failure does not necessarily imply a bad product. Consumers may not like the packaging; they may not respond to your promotion; or they may need more assurance. Through test marketing and consumer surveys you can learn of consumer objections. Then correct them, and shake the money tree.

• 3. Careful study and analysis of consumer reception to your product will incubate valuable information for the regional or national campaign.

• 4. Test marketing in several market areas allows experimentation with advertising appeals, and affords an opportunity to perfect them before the big push.

• 5. Another area of experimentation is with price. What price do you charge when no appropriate guidelines exist? For example, a newly formed non-profit organization in Connecticut, the American Backgammon Association, struggled for months over the issue of pricing. Experimentation holds the key.

• 6. Naturally, the information developed in Nos. 3, 4, and 5 above will provide valuable clues to sales expectations. These are projected sales, not guaranteed sales.

• 7. Probably the overriding benefit—and perhaps this one should have been placed above or right below money-saving—is that testing imparts real information on how consumers react and not speculation on what they may do under *if* conditions. Either they buy the product or they do not. Either they return for more of it or they do not.

There is no acid test like parting the consumer from his money, and often. Test data can signal why he or she did buy, did not buy, bought again, or did not buy again, by using any of the several techniques suggested in Section I of this handbook.

Consumer panels, telephone surveys, personal interviews, and store audits, for example, offer follow-up techniques after test marketing and for developing a market profile: who likes it, why (or why not), and who buys, among other factors.

Only actual market experience can feed your organization data from which to make reasonably reliable predictions on the effects of changes in marketing expenditures on contribution to profits, or on the physical volume of sales, of each customer segment, or sales area, or effect of product differentiation, or other factors that influence the successful operation of your organization. (Also refer to Figure II.1.B.)

• 8. Test marketing is critical in strategy formulation—between new product development and a national campaign effort. At this stage, new product decisions typically fall into one of these categories:

(a) drop it altogether;
(b) delay introduction;
(c) continue testing and experimentation;
(d) authorize full commitment of company resources.

• 9. It also allows time to position yourself for greater profitability, assuming positive test results. For instance:

(a) The testing period makes available time to sharpen estimates of unit costs.
(b) You can reasonably project profit potential—a real *must* prior to seeking venture capital.
(c) It should offer better perspective on market price strategy formulation: skimming, penetration, etc.

• 10. With careful test design, incoming data permit comparisons with similar products already being sold, and even data on complementary goods, if prices of the latter figure in the marketing strategy.

• 11. Proper test design helps to identify specific factors—i.e., the marketing mix, those most likely to transfer the product into a financial success.

• 12. If you already sell nationally, adverse effects of one really bad product, marketed in a test area, do not spill over onto the main product line. On the other hand, if a successful product steals sales from the rest of your line, analyze total profitability; i.e., do profits from the new product outweigh losses of sales of established products?

• 13. A cost problem that may surface during testing is the expense of dealer training or store personnel education. With promotion of a new type of camera film, this issue does not arise. Selling something that when attached to the carburetor promises to save gasoline, involves training and education expenses—which can be estimated during the test marketing period.

• 14. This is a weak benefit: a chance to keep ahead of the competition. To the extent that testing efforts and results are shielded from outsiders, a marketing edge may accrue. However, testing can backfire because such activity defies total secrecy.

Three Stages of Consumer Attitude Research

The choice of specific research methods, from other parts of this handbook, is a function of reasons for test marketing, learning objectives from test marketing, and the variables tested in the program. Suppose that you want to measure consumer attitudes and reactions to the new product; you will probably conduct research in three stages. For instance:

Stage One: This is the *base line survey* stage. Its purpose is to establish the base, or reference points, against which to compare future data: a before-and-after approach. The purposes of the base stage survey are

1. to measure the extent of knowledge consumers currently have about products related to the new one, or to measure the potency of national (or local) advertising that precedes the actual test;
2. to determine current attitudes toward the product, or idea, and reasons for those attitudes; and
3. to establish base data against which to measure operability of selected variables (such as advertising, packaging, sales promotion, etc.) from data derived in follow-up interviews.

Figure II.1.A illustrates a simple mini-survey used by a company introducing a new product, like a new type of glue. The same survey was conducted six months apart—in April and again in October. Area advertising preceded the first interview. The variables analyzed in this instance were the effect of advertising on consumer awareness and acceptance of the product.

Stage Two: Interviewing during the initial trial stage begins soon after the actual test gets under way. Evidence from these interviews delivers some feedback on preliminary usage levels and consumer attitudes. These audits and interviews continue periodically during the test period to project peak level and stable level consumption, useful data for predicting likely outcomes in other markets. (This formulation is explained more clearly below.)

Stage Three: This is the final stage. Interviews may take place at the end of six months, as illustrated in Figure II.1.A, or even as much as a year later to determine current usage levels, repurchases, and attitudes toward the product (or advertising, pricing, or some other variable) after continued exposure. Any type of interview, or combination, presented in Section I of this handbook is acceptable.

Ten Time-Saving Steps

Now that we know the general sequence of testing, let's examine these stages in more detail in ten practical time-saving steps. Although these steps are

BASE LINE AND FOLLOW-UP SURVEY

1. (a) Several new types of glue have been introduced in recent months: Have you heard of any of these?

_____YES
_____NO
_____DON'T KNOW

(b) What were they?

_____OURS
_____OTHERS
_____DON'T KNOW

2. One manufacturer has developed a glue strong enough to glue two elephants together; they can't pull apart without tearing off hide. Have you heard of such a glue?

_____YES
_____NO
_____DON'T KNOW

3. As you understand it, would you find the glue extremely dangerous to use?

_____YES
_____NO
_____DON'T KNOW

4. (a) Have you heard the name of the company that makes this glue?

_____YES
_____NO

(b) (If Yes) Which?

5. We would like to know whether a super glue appeals to you?

_____DOES APPEAL
_____DOES NOT APPEAL
_____UNDECIDED
_____NEED TO KNOW MORE ABOUT IT

Figure II.1.A: BASE LINE AND FOLLOW-UP SURVEY

alterable according to circumstances and budget, keep in mind that the key variable is to determine the volume of annual unit sales of the new product at various prices.

This input ranks high in cash budgeting and forecasting. Actually all budgets begin with sales forecasts. They are no better than management's ability to predict reasonably how many units the business can sell, at a price that yields something above the minimum required rate of return.

The other variable, the market's annual sales, supports calculations on market shares and marketing strategy consistent with company goals. These are the fundamental steps in test marketing.

STEP 1: Clearly Establish Objectives.

First of all, who defines the objectives? Although goals may represent input from several individuals of the organization, top management must agree to them. After the market researcher—even if s/he is part of the top management team—clearly understands what management wants to test, s/he can forge a proper test market design (Steps 2 and 3 below) and establish the controls essential to a valid test (Step 4 below).

Projecting regional or national sales is not a simple matter of determining how many consumers buy the product and then multiplying the figure by number of markets. When a new product is introduced, consumer preferences range from eyes-closed acceptance to eyes-closed rejection.

Persons between these extremes, ranging from those who display qualified acceptance to those who exhibit disinterest, may be influenced to move toward the buyer end of this spectrum. The question is, what will move them?

Test marketing, then, is a means of testing the relative efficiencies of alternative marketing mixes, testing such variables as: periodicity and type of advertising; promotional experiments (couponing, discounts, displays, samples, etc.); packaging (size, shape, color); and certainly pricing, or any other variable. "What are we trying to accomplish?" remains a pivotal question in strategy formulation.

Consequently, it is necessary to compose a formal, carefully planned program of research not only to determine the effectiveness of introductory marketing policies but also to improve the marketing plan. Even suggesting plan reformation can bend some egos. But management should not approve any "concrete" plan: i.e., one that is all mixed up and set forever.

The research team must agree, in advance, that any plan can be improved, and demonstrate willingness to make changes. Funds ought to be budgeted in advance, to compensate for modification and experimentation aimed to enhance the plan.

In other words, test-market planning rests with profit-oriented people, not ego-bound ones. The time to amend the plan is now, in the initial testing stages, not at a later, more expensive time. Therefore, objectives should include *doing it better*.

Too, test marketing does not mean verifying two dozen variables simultaneously. If there are several variables to confirm, then test them in different markets to allow for some degree of experimental control.

The case of Montgomery Ward catalog sales represents an example of goal-setting. Management wanted to determine whether selling advertising space to outsiders in their catalog was a practical idea. For more than a year they experimented with a few mail order ads for RCA and Columbia records and for book clubs. Because the test was successful, Wards rapidly expanded outside ad sales at the rate of several million a year to auto producers and to noncompetitive companies selling food, pharmaceuticals, and household products. Of course, Wards did not have to develop a consumer profile, and this was a strong advertising sales benefit. They had already ascertained these catalog readership statistics: 55 percent female, 45 percent male; heavily rural; families with average annual incomes of $20,000.

Unless you know where you are going, the remaining steps make little sense.

STEP 2: Establish Success Criteria.

Against which standards will test market performance be evaluated? And what can be learned from the test marketing experience?

There is still time to back away from a test marketing plan, and evidence uncovered here may point away from it. In fact, such tests make sense only when the potential financial loss (assuming product or market plan failure) exceeds the cost of the proposed test marketing plan. If calculations warrant moving forward, then establish realistic criteria, proportionate to expected sales volume at the national (or total market) level.

To solve the problem of projecting test market results (more on that in Steps 9 and 10) to the national level, three formulas appear below. Although none of these is perfect, each points in the direction of profitability. Try the last one first.

(a) Buying Income Method:

$$\text{National Sales Estimate} = \frac{\text{Total U.S. income}}{\text{Test area income}} \times \text{Test market sales}$$

(b) Sales Ratio Method:

$$\text{National Sales Estimate} = \frac{\text{National Sales of related product}}{\text{Test area sales of same product}} \times \text{Test market sales}$$

(c) Share of Market Method:

$$\text{National Sales Estimate} = \text{Share of market ratio in test area} \times \text{National sales of the product class}$$

Although the formulas are geared to national sales, either regional sales or state-wide sales may be substituted in the computations. If you wonder where to obtain some of the data for these formulations, the answer may lie in Section I.1 of this book. However, this means that evaluation must be rational and objective, and influenced neither by fiery enthusiasm nor cold-noodle pessimism.

Here is what one concern wanted to learn from its test marketing experience. First, they wanted to create a market profile: income and age characteristics of consumers, purchase history, frequency of use, how purchase is decided.

Then, they wanted to know minimum and maximum profitability after a full-scale launch. Effective test marketing should establish the best combination of volume and price, marketing expenses, and expected profits based on minimum share of market calculations. (Notice the initial focus on minimum market share.)

Next, the firm's management set up criteria to evaluate viability of a marketing program. In this instance they rated the interaction of television advertising expenditures and samples on householders. Also, the company wanted to gather other trade and consumer attitude data, both on the new product offered and on competing products, which leads to the next step.

STEP 3: Mesh the Test Plan into the Total Marketing Program.

The problem centers on consistency. Test market efforts should be consistent with the general marketing policy of the organization and with the larger marketing program that will eventually be settled upon for the new product.

A high advertising budget, or the use of top salesmen only in the test area, or an exaggerated promotional push may well give very favorable returns, but are these policies consistent with what the company normally does, and will special or unusual efforts turn a profit? Here are some ideas to keep up front, to avoid unrealistically optimistic projections.

Most of this discussion has been tailored for the retail trade. Test marketing works at the wholesale or distributor level as well, or even for OEM accounts.

Customers may buy only small amounts of the product at first, to test it before placing big orders. (Obviously, test results will not be evaluated in the usual ways discussed above.)

Or a buyer may purchase a small quantity to test the acquired product on his own customers. This is an evaluative problem dealing with several factors: the form of repeat sales, order size, time lags. Such test marketing should occur over a longer period, with greater emphasis placed on the second round of purchases.

Actually, data on repeat sales are crucial bits of information, exposed during testing, because they tell more about the longevity of market demand and determine the type of marketing strategy.

The chief issue is whether enough people who buy the product the first time will come back again and again, because we know that as a general rule, about 20 percent of the buyers account for 80 percent of the sales.

Normally, with the introduction of a new product, sales rise rapidly, peak, and then settle at some stable level. How rapidly they peak and settle is important for market strategy. How to calculate and use the "drop factor" will be demonstrated in Step 10.

Another issue concerns type of buyer. Some are always among the first to try a new product; some are risk takers. Others are trend followers; others are adverse to risk. Some delay entering the market, possibly because they do not expose themselves to the same advertising media, are slow to hear about new products or ideas, are extremely cautious and slow to change, are waiting for price reductions, or whatever.

Nevertheless, late-comers still represent solid market potential, while innovators have moved on to new things. Forecasting ability depends on knowledge of who is buying, and why, timing of purchases, and some idea of the likely market cycle of the product.

Another point to consider when integrating the test market plan into the full-scale plan deals with types of end users. Some are high-volume buyers, others low-volume buyers.

The different consumption rates can affect the profits of some new products; e.g., bathroom fixtures. Builders represent high-volume purchasers; replacement means a low-volume buyer. The question arises: To what extent does our new product appeal to different market segments?

STEP 4: Set Up Controls.

Just why do some people buy much, others less, some none? Do some people buy, or not buy, because of the color of the package, too much or too little advertising, or price?

Many people believe that all marketing problems are solved with advertising. By how much can sales be pushed up with an increase in the advertising budget? Did sales drop off because advertising declined or because competitors lowered their prices? The problem centers on the separation of cause and effect. Two events occurring at the same time does not mean that one causes the other to happen. Pinpointing significant variables in the test market takes on high priority.

The fourth step is to establish controls so that we can make valid judgments about the key variables. As a general rule, test only one variable in each market.

Further, it is better to have a control group. Therefore, it is better to use two markets to test one variable—a pairing of markets; so that, for example, in a pair of test markets, if we want to measure the consequence of advertising, we will spend nothing on advertising in one of the two markets.

The difference in sales between the two markets represents the theoretical effect of advertising *provided that all other variables are unchanged*. If competition spoils the experiment by playing around with prices of their products during the test period, test outcomes are marred, perhaps rendered totally unreliable.

New buyers and brand-switchers account for product sales. Knowing something about the composition of buyers provides some indication of market size and market share projections. Some buyers are loyal, some fickle. The fickle ones, probably more price sensitive, respond to small price differences. They may not comprise a stable market during short-run price movements. Therefore, marketing strategy should fit the market targeted.

Preferably the testing period will be segmented into several stages—for example, three, as discussed earlier in this section.

• *First*, ascertain the market situation at the beginning of the test period. This may mean utilizing sound research approaches discussed in Section I of this handbook, especially beginning the research with ideas developed in Sections I.1 and I.2.

• *Second*, keep an eye on what happens during the test period. This stage may last for several months and require continued monitoring.

• The *final* stage consists of data-gathering at the end of the test period. It may even be desirable to do a post-mortem some months after the testing has ended.

STEP 5: Select Representative Test Cities.

The purpose of testing in a limited market area is to extrapolate results in order to typify a wider market area, such as a regional market or a national market.

Extending such extrapolations to international markets is unwise, because distinct cultural differences necessitate distinct marketing strategies for each nation or country.

The following critical factors will impart initial guidelines for test city selections.

• **Size**. Ideally, the city selected should be small enough to keep costs down but large enough to fairly characterize the larger market area, similar to those issues encountered in any sampling procedures. (See Section IV on various sampling procedures.)

One question that crops up: How many units of the new product must be produced to supply the test market(s)?

If a fixed amount of productive facilities is set aside for the new product, or if a pilot plant has been constructed to supply the item, then the test market's absorption of the product should just about match production—neither more nor less; otherwise, select some new test areas.

Smaller size keeps certain budgets down, e.g., advertising. Please keep in mind, however, that marketing budgets in the test market should also be proportional to expenditures projected in the larger market area. Proportion is better measured with volume of advertising, for example, than actual dollar expenditures. In the case of television, a local, smaller company probably will offer rates lower than those charged for comparable network advertising. Because the same dollar spent in a test city can produce greater ad frequency than that projected for the major launch, some sense of proportion will maintain the desired parallel between the test and national markets.

Typically, a city of 100,000 seems about right. This allows for high coverage of fewer stores and close monitoring of results during the second stage of data-gathering.

• **Location**: Not only should the city be representative of the region, but also it should be suitable for the product being tested. Obviously Miami is an unsuitable test market for a new chemical de-icer; but it may be less obvious whether a window cleaner can be suitably tested in Phoenix. Although one firm did test a window cleaner in Phoenix some years ago, afterward researchers observed that windows did not get dirty as rapidly as in downtown Cleveland.

Aggressive researchers like to test 2 to 5 percent of the total market, which signals heading straight for Chicago or New York City. That resembles a full-scale market entry, hardly a test.

Some researchers say stay away from San Francisco and Los Angeles because consumers there tend to overreact to new products. Many cities and towns do not make the best candidates: one-industry towns; towns with seasonality and migratory factors, which rule out the Catskills and Palm Beach; cities having had a recent strike or a potential strike of a major employer; towns in hard or soft water areas; cities with a high welfare or food stamp component; bedroom towns; etc. The exception to the rules: if your product is designed for special situations or markets, such as beach wear or a water softener, some of these towns or cities are appropriate.

Finally, do not let external, unrelated factors sway your decision. Fort Lauderdale in the winter and Lake Geneva (Wisconsin) in the summer may provide the right tax deductions but the wrong test facts. Nevertheless, there are probably 25 or more cities that will fit your criteria.

• **Demographics**. The term "representative market" has been used repeatedly. But what does it mean?

Family size, racial or language composition, average income and income ranges, categories of employment, etc., should be in proportions that typify the intended larger market area. Both Stamford, Connecticut and Hamtramck, Michigan are ruled out as potential test areas: neither typically represents markets in Hartford or Ann Arbor, for instance.

In other words, consumer profiles in the test market should parallel those in the full-scale launch market. Recall the example earlier in this section on Montgomery Wards sales of catalog advertising space. They had pegged their consumers; consequently, advertising of the type solicited will have its biggest impact on the selected market segment.

For some products (or services) a user profile can evolve from a mail survey. (Section I.5 spells out the profitable application of this data-gathering technique.) Most of the entries in the questionnaire in Figure II.1.B aim to develop these timely details, beginning with Question No. 6. Knowing your customer helps you to avoid disappointments.

1. How long have you been a REASON subscriber?

___ 0-12 months
___ One-two years
___ Two-three years
___ Over three years
___ No longer subscribe

2. How many people (other than yourself) read your copy of REASON?

___ One
___ Two
___ Three
___ Four
___ Five or more
___ None

3. What do you think of the following features?

	Usually Good	So-so	Bad	Don't Read
Editorial	___	___	___	___
Editor's Notes	___	___	___	___
Brickbats	___	___	___	___
Trends	___	___	___	___
Viewpoint				
Davidson	___	___	___	___
Reynolds	___	___	___	___
Rothbard	___	___	___	___
Money	___	___	___	___
Taxes	___	___	___	___
Spotlight	___	___	___	___
Book Reviews	___	___	___	___
Movie Reviews	___	___	___	___
Rudebarbs	___	___	___	___

4. What is your opinion of our articles in the past year?

	Consistently	Mostly	Sometimes	Never
Well-written	___	___	___	___
Interesting	___	___	___	___
Timely	___	___	___	___
Could be shorter	___	___	___	___
Too brief	___	___	___	___
Too intellectual	___	___	___	___
Too political	___	___	___	___
Too general	___	___	___	___

Figure II.1.B: QUESTIONNAIRE TO DETERMINE READER'S INTERESTS AND PROFILE

5. How much time do you usually spend on an issue of REASON?

___ A half hour

___ One hour

___ Two hours

___ Over two hours

6. Following are eight articles that have appeared in REASON over the last year. We'd like to know your reaction to each.

	Liked	Didn't Like	Didn't Read At All	Don't Remember it
a) Radiation Fantasies (Mar. '80)	___	___	___	___
b) Who's Bankrolling the UFW? (Nov. '79)	___	___	___	___
c) SALT-Free Defense (Mar '80)	___	___	___	___
d) Alienation: Was Marx Right? (Sept. '79)	___	___	___	___
e) Slash Your Phone Bill (Mar '80)	___	___	___	___
f) Another Side of Oscar Wilde (Jan. '80)	___	___	___	___
g) American Gestapo (April '80)	___	___	___	___
h) Anticommunist? Yes. Cold Warrior? No. (Taft, July 1979)	___	___	___	___

7. Which of these areas would you like to see REASON feature:

	More Of	Less Of	About the Same
Book reviews	___	___	___
Examples of free enterprise	___	___	___
Feminist issues	___	___	___
Foreign news	___	___	___
History	___	___	___
Humor	___	___	___
Interviews	___	___	___
Investigative reporting	___	___	___
Investments/financial	___	___	___

Figure II.1.B (continued)

	More Of	Less Of	About the Same
Libertarian movement	__	__	__
Personality profiles	__	__	__
Psychology/self-help	__	__	__
Reviews of art, music, theatre	__	__	__
Short stories	__	__	__
Theoretical discussions of human rights, economics, etc.	__	__	__

8. What other magazines do you read regularly?

__ Atlantic Monthly   __ New Republic
__ American Spectator   __ Playboy/Penthouse
__ Fortune   __ Politics Today
__ Harper's   __ Progressive
__ Inquiry   __ Psychology Today
__ Libertarian Review   __ Rolling Stone
__ Mother Jones   __ Saturday Review
__ Ms.   __ Scientific American
__ The Nation   __ Wall St. Journal
__ National Review   __ Washington Monthly
                                       __ Others (please list)

9. In the last two years, have you had any subscription problems with REASON? If so, please specify.

__ Unexplained interrupted service
__ Interrupted service for a long period after moving
__ Faulty or confusing subscription and/or renewal notices
__ Lack of response from REASON on complaints
__ Other

10. How would you describe your political views?

__ Conservative
__ Liberal
__ Libertarian
__ Anarchist
__ Moderate
__ Other (_____)

11. In the past 12 months, which of these have you done:

__ Contributed to a political campaign
__ Circulated a petition
__ Run for office
__ Attended meetings of a political group
__ Written letters to the editor and/or elected politicians
__ Worked as a political campaign volunteer
__ Other

Figure II.1.B (continued)

12. Are you: ___ Male ___ Female

13. Your age is: ___ years

14. Approximately what is your total household income (before taxes) for the year? $___

15. Do you: ___ Rent ___ Own your home ___ Live with relatives

16. What is your occupation? (Choose single best response)

Business Executive
___ Owner
___ Partner
___ President
___ Vice president
___ Manager/supervisor
Student
___ Undergraduate
___ Graduate

Professional
___ Educator
___ Doctor
___ Lawyer
___ Tax analyst
___ Accountant
___ Stock broker
___ Government
___ Journalist
___ Engineer
___ Data processing
___ Other professional

___ Skilled/technical
___ Secretarial/clerical
___ Blue collar
___ Self-employed
___ Homemaker
___ Other

17. What kind of decisions do you make for your employer/company?

___ Hiring/firing decisions
___ Office equipment, supplies purchasing decisions
___ Legal decisions
___ Investment decisions
___ Long-range planning decisions
___ Other

18. What is the highest level of education you have completed?

___ High school graduate
___ A.A. or equivalent of two-year college degree
___ B.S., B.A., or equivalent
___ M.S., M.A., or equivalent
___ Ph.D., M.D., or equivalent

19. Which of the following credit cards do you hold?

___ American Express
___ Carte Blanche
___ Diners Club
___ Mastercharge
___ Visa/Bankamericard
___ None of these

20. Do you use a computer?

At work: ___ No ___ Yes
At home: ___ No ___ Yes

21. During the past 12 months, have you bought or sold any form of gold or silver investments?

___ No ___ Yes

Figure II.1.B (continued)

22. During the past 12 months, have you bought or sold stocks, bonds, or other similar investments?
    __ No __ Yes

23. Do you currently subscribe to any investment advisory services or letters?
    __ No __ Yes. If yes, how many? __

24. Are you currently investing in real estate (other than your own home, if applicable)?
    __ No __ Yes

25. During the past 12 months, how many hardcover books have you purchased? __ How many paper-backs? __

26. What kind of books do you generally buy?

    __ Political   __ Fiction
    __ Bestsellers   __ Psychology
    __ Humor   __ How-to books
    __ Science Fiction   __ Biographies
                          __ Other _____

27. Do you purchase books through book clubs? __ No __ Yes
    Records through record clubs? __ No __ Yes

28. In the past 12 months, which of the following have you ordered by mail?

    __ A language course   __ A gift
    __ A speed-reading course   __ A weight-loss/diet item
                                __ An electronic gadget

29. Do you drink:

    __ Liquor   __ Soft drinks
    __ Wine   __ Diet soft drinks
    __ Beer   __ Mineral water

30. Do you smoke? __ No __ Yes
    If so:
    __ Cigar __ Cigarette __ Pipe

31. How many passports do you and your family hold?
    __ One __ Two __ Three or more __ None

32. Have you or your family traveled out of state in the past 12 months?
    __ No __ Yes
    Out of the United States?
    __ No __ Yes

33. Were any of these trips on business? __ No __ Yes

34. How many times have you or members of your family traveled by plane in the last 12 months? (Count each ticket bought per trip, per person, as a separate number.)
    __ One __ Two __ Three __ Four __ Five __ Six or more

Figure II.1.B (continued)

35. Which of the following items have you purchased?

___ Recreation vehicle   ___ Boat (power or sail)
___ High fidelity stereo   ___ Vacation home or property
___ Camera/darkroom equipment   ___ Manual typewriter
___ Flying lessons   ___ Electric typewriter
___ B/W television   ___ Calculator/computer
___ Color television   ___ Backpacking/camping equipment

36. Would you like us to continue to publish a special book review issue each year? ___ Yes ___ No
—a special financial issue each year? ___ Yes ___No

37. If we included a stamped postcard in your issue of REASON each month, asking your opinion of the articles in that issue, would you be likely to fill out and return it?

___ Every month   ___ Sometimes
___ Only if I felt strongly about an article   ___ Never

Figure II.1.B (continued)

The attempt of Kronenbourg Beer (a French beer) to lay claim to a share of the American market failed. They test-marketed, but in areas unrepresentative of likely buyers of imported beer. They worked from a profile of all American beer drinkers instead of fashioning a profile of foreign beer drinkers. Again using Stamford and Hamtramck as examples, Stamford is a better place than Hamtramck to test acceptance of Kronenbourg beer; but acceptance in Stamford does not mean it will sell well in Hamtramck either.

• **Insularity**. The test market selected must be insulated from other trading areas to eliminate the transshipment problem. Unfortunately, this proviso may eliminate several good test market areas; but without experimental control, judging results and extending them as predictors is difficult. The same is true of the media used in advertising.

Is there spillout beyond the immediate geographic test area? Lack of insularity in both product movement and advertising spillout eliminates both Stamford and Hamtramck as test areas.

• **Advertising Efficiency**. Except for spillout problems, buying advertising space and time should be performed efficiently.

For testing a new consumer item, television is a major vehicle. As in "demographics," the objective is to duplicate the larger regional or national market as closely as possible. Local TV spots substitute for national television—not perfect, but a fair substitute to allow for reasonable measurement of advertising efficiency in this medium.

Although radio does not substitute for any other medium, it is particularly valuable when appealing to specific market segments. Audiences of various radio stations, even at different times, tend to fall within very distinct boundaries. Most radio stations cater to a narrow market segment, rather carefully defined.

Newspapers figure prominently in consumer product sales through space ads, coupons, or special deals for getting distribution in stores. Supermarkets, being heavy users of newspaper space to promote weekly specials, are more likely to highlight your new product if offered trade allowances or discounts.

In addition to the above essential factors, some others carry greater or lesser importance, depending upon purposes of the test, especially for new products:

1. The market should not be overtested. Syracuse; Columbus, Ohio; Des Moines; Denver; and Albany have been popular test areas, for example. On the plus side, these markets already have a track record, and some good reasons explain the popularity of these markets. The nonprofessional may prefer to follow the professional researchers.
2. The markets should have "normal" historical development for the product class tested, and be typical regarding competitive advertising.
3. The markets selected should represent different geographical regions to test sales variables, and increase the projectability of results; but the area should not comprise groups not normal to the product's market—which purges both El Paso, Texas and Hamtramck, Michigan.
4. The market should be neither so small as to cast doubt on results (which excludes Cavendish, Vermont) nor so large that the test looks like an expensive, full-scale campaign (eliminating Chicago).

STEP 6: Pick Number of Markets.

How many test markets should you use? One survey revealed that test marketers seldom entered more than three or four test markets. Two is a bare-bones minimum. Sears uses three; in the event something happens to one (volcanic eruption, tornado, strike or other unforseen events), there are still two left.

For experimental control, pair the cities to estimate the influence of a variable, so that two becomes four, and three, six. If the product will be distributed nationally, then there should be at least four test markets to reflect regional differences.

Also, testing more variables necessitates more markets. To test six variables (test only one in each market), a total of six markets becomes 12, when matched against the control group.

One large national retailer tests three markets based on incomes, as compared with the national average: above, similar, and below. The limit to the number of markets tested is really a function of your budget. A small budget may suggest going regional rather than national.

Not everyone agrees on the validity of test marketing. Those who question it can cite many examples of wide divergence between projected and actual results. Still, ranking test marketing first in this section of the handbook establishes its popularity. This tool must be producing good results for many firms.

The problem seems to focus on the number of test and control markets. More is better than one or two. By using a larger number of markets, data will reflect greater reliability and more sensitivity to small but important differences in sales as a result of changes in copy and advertising media exposure. If you can afford it, try eight to ten markets. If not, then a compromise must be reached between accuracy desired and money available.

STEP 7: Establish Variables and Variations.

How effective are new package designs? Various shelf arrangements? Competitors? Different display methods? Given sales copy? Pricing variations? Alternative advertising approaches? Coupons? Cooperative ads? Different marketing plans?

Test marketing lends itself to new product testing and also to testing new selling approaches of existing products. For example, suppose that your organization has assembled two competing marketing plans. The whole package may be tested as a plan rather than being tested for performance of individual variables. Two pairs of cities (or trading areas) are selected. Plans II and I are activated in the first pair; Plans I and II in the second pair. The standard for comparison is present sales levels. A control city can also be monitored, if desired. Hence, even small data variations in sales furnish fruitful figures.

Generally, in new product testing, the variables or variations tested must be significant enough to register measurable differences, given constraints of time and budget. If appropriate, test fewer variables, but more thoroughly. For example, try two levels (in two markets) of advertising and promotion expenditures: a minimum figure and a maximum figure.

It is possible to run tests within tests, i.e., subtests, to achieve maximum return from efforts. New products should be carefully evaluated before committing funds to a test. The 12-point questionnaire in Figure II.1.C provides for basic information in the initial evaluation. However, the form can be completed again, during the test and possibly by other persons as well, to evaluate the product of later development stages and spot and plug any potential profit leakers.

It is essential to learn not only whether consumers will buy your product (or service), but also how much they will buy, how often, and what profit this volume of sales will generate.

For many products, recommendations by friends, relatives, or acquaintances sway up to 25 percent of first-time buyers. To illustrate the importance of this type of advertising, this category of first-time buyer will probably become repeat purchasers.

Shelf facings are important, too. Recall the experiment mentioned in Section I on vertical versus horizontal display? There is an optimum number of shelf spacings for each type of product. Vlasic Pickles has made good use of this factor.

NEW PRODUCT EVALUATION

(Rank answers from 5 (best) to 1 (worst) or 0 if not known.)

1. How does the new product fit into existing marketing and corporate strategies? _____

2. Does the product conform to the image the firm wants to maintain? _____

3. How easily can competitors develop a similar or substitute product? (5 = not easily) _____

4. Will the company's good name and image influence customer purchases? _____

5. How well can the product be marketed with the firm's current level of knowledge and management resources? _____

6. For the new product, how well qualified are personnel in:

    Production? _____
    Sales? _____
    Engineering? _____
    Physical Distribution? _____

7. Do we have distinct advantages over competitors in: (5 = high advantages)

    Technology? _____
    Production? _____
    Product uniqueness? _____
    Patents / processes? _____
    Marketing? _____
    Experience? _____
    Customer relations? _____
    Raw materials? _____

8. Due to our various advantages [will not (5)/will (1)] competitors compete? _____

9. Are there conflicts with other company: (5 = no conflict)

    Products? _____
    Divisions? _____
    Customer relations? _____

10. Will our present market position yield a strong advantage (5) or disadvantage (1)? _____

11. Does our product present any safety hazards (5 = none) for our:

    Customers? _____
    Employees? _____

12. Are there potential (5 = none)

    Regulatory problems? _____
    Patent suits? _____

Figure II.1.C: NEW PRODUCT EVALUATION

Most often the best advertising is free advertising, like personal testimonials, or an article appearing in a popular magazine or newspaper. Reputable third-party endorsements are priceless, although sales may peak quickly and drop sharply. And of course, ill-timed publicity can wreck a test.

All important variations should be tested about the same time. Time alone can make a significant difference. Changes in expectations of the future can sharply alter consumption patterns. Therefore, any differences in test results, due to time, ought to be eliminated. Too, actual versus projected sales may diverge because of events occurring over a period of time, after the experiment. This is not the fault of test marketing but rather the inability of researchers and management to forecast accurately the future business environment.

STEP 8: Decide On Duration of Test.

What is the optimum testing period? Unfortunately, budget constraints will limit the number of markets, but it is decidedly unproductive to cut short a testing period for lack of funds.

Typically, it costs $100,000 to $150,000 per market per year, assuming three or four markets are tested simultaneously. Smaller firms can realize some economies by taking on the extra workload. But keep in mind the underlying objective of test marketing, viz., risk reduction. A short testing period that produces questionable results may increase rather than reduce risk. It may be worse than no test at all.

Look at some of the problems. How do you know customers are satisfied with your product based on high initial sales alone? You don't. They may not return in the same large numbers. If it takes time to use up the product—such as automobile tires—the test period must be longer than that needed to test a dog shampoo, and at least long enough to complete one consumption cycle.

The number of repeat customers is the critical variable. Grocery products usually require six months of testing. If the test began with an intensive introductory campaign (coupons, specials, etc.), allow enough time for sales to return to normal; then start counting. If you want to evaluate the accumulative effects of advertising, the test period may well stretch into a year, or even two years.

But costs crop up on the other end, too. The more information desired, the more it costs. The more you want to reduce potential risks, the more it will cost. And as risks approach a low level, most likely everyone else, including competitors, knows what has taken place. Any market advantages evaporate.

Procter and Gamble has scooped Lever Brothers on more than one occasion. The reverse happens as well. Then too, competitors have a habit of frustrating test results when they become aware of the test: lowering their prices, increasing their advertising, buying the competition's products, and using other tactics that may qualify for the dirty tricks department.

STEP 9: Evaluate Results.

If you have survived to this juncture, you are now prepared for the final steps: first, evaluation of the results, and second, projection of these findings.

Evaluation occurs at two points: (a) the market potential, and (b) rate of return, which is related to the company's resources and profit targets.

Once final results are locked up, there is no time to dawdle, for speed may be vital in order to take advantage of market opportunities speedily before they slip by—or into your competitor's hands.

Therefore, preparation for these final steps must take place before the test even begins. That is the essence of good planning. Data should have been gathered, ready for analysis, from every significant aspect of marketing: pricing, packaging, advertising, promotion, publicity, distribution, customer profile, other considerations. Data must represent best efforts, and analysis must be accurate, for management to make alpha-plus decisions. Although success is not guaranteed, failures are minimized if careful planning goes on throughout the test period.

Successful product acceptance depends not solely on marketing but on the harmonious operation of the entire organization. To that end it is necessary to solicit expert opinion from manufacturing, finance, shipping, accounting, etc. Completion of the information in Figure II.1.D will produce rate-of-return projections over the next five years. Without fairly reasonable estimates on items 1 and 2, the bottom line figure is untrustworthy, despite the accuracy of information plugged into items 3 through 22.

Since many types of problems can crop up, close consultation with other functional operations opens up an opportunity to work out potential difficulties. Marketers should discuss with production management their test-marketing proposals, the finance people will have to arrange for availability of funds, sufficient computer time must be commited to the experiment, etc. In other words, cool planning rather than fiery reaction to early, positive test market results underpins long-term profitability.

STEP 10: Make Forecasts and Projections.

Test-market data yield many different kinds of testimony. Two decision disclosures called for on the form in Figure II.1.D are unit sales and unit price. How else can test intelligence be utilized?

Typically sales will follow a distinct pattern during precursory stages. During introduction, sales will build up from zero until they peak out, and then decline—not to zero but to a stable level of purchases. The rise and decline may occur rapidly or fairly slowly, or get off to a fast start followed by a slow decline, or vice versa. None of these data alone are very beneficial.

However, to track the sales pattern, store audits, not factory shipments, for reasons already discussed in Section I.8, supply the pertinent details. With these facts we can compute the *drop factor* (DF), a predictor of how sales will behave in other test areas. The formula follows:

RATE-OF-RETURN COMPUTATIONS

	198A	198B	198C	198D	198E
1. Unit Sales					
2. $ Sales					
3. Unit Manufacturing Cost					
4. Cost of Goods Sold					
5. Gross Profit					
6. Selling Expenses					
7. Administrative Expenses					
8. Earnings before Tax					
9. Marketing Start-Up Expenses					
10. Product Development Expenses					
11. Production Start-Up Expenses					
12. Other Development Costs					
13. Total Nonrecurring Expenses					
14. Opportunity Costs					
15. Earnings (Losses) before Taxes					
16. Estimated Income Taxes					
17. Earnings after Taxes					
18. Depreciation Expenses					
19. Operating Cash Flows					
20. Depreciation on New Capital					
21. Nondepreciable Capital Requirements					
22. Investment Cash Flows					
23. New Cash Flows					
24. Rate of Return					

Figure II.1.D: RATE-OF-RETURN COMPUTATIONS

$$DF = \frac{\text{Peak Sales} - \text{Stable Sales}}{\text{Peak Sales}}$$

The drop factor will range in value between 0 and 1. The nearer peak sales and stable sales levels are to one another, the closer will the DF be to zero. The greater the distance between peak and stable sales, the closer will the DF approach 1.

At the extremes, if the DF equals one, then stable sales have dropped to zero—at which time you will have worries other than the computation of a drop factor.

For example, let's say that the DF in the first market is 60 percent. In the second market if a peak level of 30 percent were established, then the projected stable sales level would be 18 percent (60% × 30%). Several guidelines should be kept in mind:

o—x Generally, the peak level is lower the longer the period of audit, and different audit periods do not produce comparable results; therefore, comparisons should occur over identical audit periods.

o—x According to E.J. Davis, if at any point during the build-up stage sales exceed a rate twice as high as the stable sales target level, the probability is about 3:1 that the target will be met or exceeded.

o—x Also, unless the peak sales exceed the target level by at least 50 percent, the probability is about 3:1 that the product will not maintain target sales over the long run.

With these points in mind, you may want to forecast sales on a format similar to the one summarized in Figure II.1.E. Forecasts of the new product's unit sales depend on

(a) the specific marketing strategy;
(b) pricing strategy;
(c) market and business environments (including government regulations);
(d) prices of competing products;
(e) forecast of total market demand;
(f) share of market achieved, given assumptions above.

REGISTER SALES FORECAST FORM

Product _____ Market Plan No. _____ Date _____
Estimated by _____ Reviewed by _____
Marketing Strategy _____

Description of Market _____

Year	Expected Level Unit Sales Total Market	Expected Unit Price Our Product	Expected Annual Sales Level Our Product	Cumulative Expected Level	Profitability of Success (%)	Expected Market Share (%)
198A						
198B						
198C						
198D						
198E						
199A						

Figure II.1.E: REGISTER SALES FORECAST FORM

Forecasting and Planning

To repeat, many different types of data can be generated during the test; e.g., characteristics of one-time buyers of various marketing variables, minimum and maximum profitability. Within the company, forecasts should be made of

1. amount of investment;
2. timing of investment requirements;
3. source and cost of funds at various stages;
4. residual value, or use, of investment at end of product's market life;
5. one-time costs;
6. estimate of opportunity costs;
7. economies to be achieved: (a) over the learning curve, (b) volume;
8. assessment of risk at each stage—probability of success (or failure);
9. risk-adjusted rate of return at each stage;
10. the expected values of additional marketing information and contribution to profits.

Obviously, test marketing does not furnish the definitive answer, for all types of tests have serious drawbacks to the extent that they fail to duplicate the projected market conditions. Less a test of whether the product is acceptable to the consumer, test marketing is more a method of testing a marketing plan for the intromission of a new product or variations on an existing one. That is, being gauged is the measured response of how you offer and promote the product.

A Test Market Profile

Let's examine a complete test market profile, considerably scaled down from the recommendations in this section. The following example is intended to show not how to do it but rather what was done in a particular case.

As you read through the story you will readily spot deviations from many of the precepts set forth in the preceding pages. But this project was funded by a government grant and mainly involved nonbusinessmen: government officials, university professors and personnel, biologists, marine food technologists, food scientists, public university employees, et al. Business's role in test marketing was largely passive. If your firm had participated, we are confident you would have brought the project, and its outcomes, into sharper focus.

From the consumer's viewpoint, the product is new, a finfish, called *Macrozoarces Americanus* (and no jests about Holy Macro!). (If you are puzzling over whether the *macro* is the grown-up version of a *microzoarces*, I don't know.) Apparently prior to World War II days a limited consumer market existed for this product. Since that era the fish has been harvested only for industrial use (fertilizers, animal food, etc.).

Obviously, the scientific name is not the best choice for consumer testing. Neither are the more common names—"yellow eel," "eel pout," and "ocean pout." Practically everyone able to talk can create a product name more appealing than any of these; and a creative marketing person will state "product name" as one of the chief test variables.

But federal legislation mandates that the most common name be used. That alone is sufficient to cause an entrepreneur to turn profit sights elsewhere, except that, in this case, the fish has been known by at least 39 names, which may inspire some poetic digressions.

With a two-year, $67,000 government grant in hand, the University of Rhode Island decided to use a portion of the funds for a two-phase test marketing project. The government agency (not the fish industry) prescribed the parameters, one of which was that marketing thrusts must concentrate on fresh fish fillets.

The preliminary steps included chemical analysis and consumer panels (refer to Section I.7 for more on consumer panels) to test for taste. The initial results were positive:

(a) The consumer panel rated the fish's taste (cooked, presumably) more highly than the high-priced brand, viz., flounder.
(b) They found no significant difference between this fish and flounder in regard to texture, color, odor, and after-taste.
(c) The panelists could not distinguish taste differences between fresh fillets and 12-day-old iced fish of the same kind.
(d) They rated the fish as good, white, lean fish. (Food scientists confirmed that the fish is low in cholesterol and exhibits minimal seasonal variation in protein content.)

The plan established followed this sequence:

1. Product analysis.
2. Consumer panels.
3. Product testing in households.
4. Product testing in stores.

After favorable reception in Step Numbers 1 and 2, the team proceeded with Step Number 3, product testing in homes. First they conducted a telephone survey to determine who would accept an unidentified fresh fish fillet, prepare and cook it in a customary way, and then submit to a subsequent telephone interview.

From among persons who responded favorably, they randomly selected 29 households in the Rhode Island towns of South Kingstown and Narragansett, and 27 households in North Kingstown.

In follow-up telephone interviews (more on telephone surveys in Section I.4), 80 percent of the households reported favorably on the fish. When asked how much they would pay for fish fillets, two-thirds of the answers fell into three distinct categories: (a) 25 percent would pay $1.19 per pound (the price of pollack at the time of the survey); (b) 27 percent would pay $1.69 per pound (the price of cod); and (c) 15 percent would pay $1.99 per pound (the price of flounder). Cumulating the figures, computations show that one-half of the households would pay at least $1.39 per pound.

The feedback encouraged the researchers to proceed to Step 4, product testing in stores. As you will see, this continues to be a low-budget test, certainly subject to substantial errors if data were projected regionally, but certainly better than no information at all in this instance.

For implementation of Step 4, they selected only five fresh-fish retail markets in Rhode Island. The test lasted only five weeks. The two variables observed were price and repeat purchases. Additionally, store personnel were interviewed for information on customer reactions. The three per-pound prices tested were $1.89, $1.69, and $1.19.

Initial data suggested inelastic demand with respect to the range of prices tested; or at least all inventory sold out. These data are not entirely free of distortion because the fish fillets were delivered free. Without question the stores involved in the test put forth an extraordinary sales push. Nevertheless, consumers did return, and they reported favorably on the fish.

The researchers had insufficient funds to segment their test market. Early results in Step 3 suggest two or three distinct markets.

All of this interesting activity led to a fifth step, inducing corporate chains and independent fish markets to sell the critter. (By now it was being marketed under the name "ocean pout.") They then did the following:

(a) Presentations were made to several supermarket chains in Rhode Island, Massachusetts, and Long Island, New York.
(b) Corporate kitchens conducted their own taste tests with favorable results.
(c) The entire distribution channel was identified, which linked the processor (cutting house), wholesaler, retailer, and consumer.
(d) From information gathered in (c), it appeared that a retail price of $1.69 would cover costs and contribute to profits and still be acceptable to final consumers.
(e) A marketing plan was developed.

It may be of interest to know something about the promotional element of the marketing mix settled upon. Promotion consisted of the following factors:

1. Publicity:
   (a) newspaper articles;
   (b) newspaper food page coverage—recipes and project story;
   (c) radio news broadcasts, interviews, talk shows;
   (d) television news coverage, talk shows.
2. Advertising:
   (a) product featured in food chain newspaper ads.
3. Personal selling:
   (a) to trade (by project personnel);
   (b) to management of chains and independents (all levels);
   (c) to primary handler;
   (d) to cutting house;

      (e) to fishing vessels;

      (f) to wholesaler;

      (g) to consumer-store demonstrations.

4. Sales promotion:

      (a) to trade: project description; taste test results; in-store posters; recipe booklet samples;

      (b) to consumer: recipe booklets; in-store posters; demos.

What was the payoff? Checking fish landings at Galilee, Rhode Island, the researchers said these rose from zero to one million pounds, which generated revenue at various stages of production and sales of roughly one-half million dollars. Will test marketing work as well for you, or do you prefer an informal market research design?

II.2: 24-KARAT PROFITS FROM A 14-KARAT BUDGET FOR INFORMAL DESIGNS

Although the researchers on ocean pout, in the preceding subsection, labeled their program "test marketing," the entire procedure more nearly resembles experimental design. Research projects are descriptive or experimental in design.

Experiments pin down cause and effect relationships. In experimentation one or more variables are manipulated under specified conditions in order to collect data that communicate straightforward answers. In one sense, experiments are contrived for testing purposes; but evidence is organized to produce fairly clear-cut, action-oriented interpretations.

Of course, it is not possible to maintain the ideal, a tightly controlled experiment—holding all variables unchanged except the experimental one—because we are dealing with the complexity and individuality of humans. But rigidly controlled experiments yield more reliable testimony on cause and effect relationships. In other words, how do the variables relate to each other?

Comparison of Alternatives

Suppose that a firm proposes marketing a coffee substitute, dandelion roots. It considers whether to package the product in a black container with white lettering (A), or a yellow container with green lettering (B). In most experiments the chief concern is a comparison of alternatives, not the determination of absolute values.

Any decision involves a tradeoff. We can develop some cost-benefit concepts that help pinpoint these differences, but does that information equip us with the answers to "How high is high?" Or, "How low is low?"

To illustrate, we can reasonably estimate the degree to which sales will rise with each additional dollar spent on advertising (over some definite range of expenditures), but this advertising-sales relationship does not tell us the absolute sales level.

In a test, the researcher will select, let's say, two markets (one a control market) and evaluate performance on different packaging from sales data or attitude surveys. Tests typically assign one experimental treatment to one market. With only one test unit per experimental treatment, we cannot internally generate a measure of experimental error.

On the other hand, experimentation may reveal the reasons why people buy (or do not buy). In experimentation, several market areas are allocated to each package design (see Figure II.2.A) by a randomizing process such as the use of the random numbers table in the Appendix. (Reference to the random numbers table springs up again in Section IV.) In other words, the experiment should be run in random order. This is critical.

If you choose between two markets only, then let someone unconnected to the project flip a coin to allocate test treatments between the two markets. There are always some variables that cannot be controlled, or that are unknown at the time the experiment is initiated, despite all efforts to maintain methodicalness. The partial solution is randomization: it tends to smooth out the influence of those disarrayed variables; it allows time trends to average out; it permits the researcher to forge ahead as though the errors of measurement are independent.

DESIGNS TO EVALUATE PACKAGE COLORS

Experiment		Test
White-on-black (A)	Green-on-yellow (B)	Green-on-yellow (B)
Whitehall, Ohio	Greenville, N.C.	Yellow Springs, Ohio
Whitehall, Penna.	Greenville, Miss.	
Whitefish Bay, Wisc.	Greenville, Texas	

Figure II.2.A: DESIGNS TO EVALUATE PACKAGE COLORS

In the experiment we will evaluate the comparative effects of the two package designs on consumer awareness and attitudes; or we can examine sales for each market area. Because there are at least two markets (actually three in this example) subjected to each package design, we can estimate the degree of variation in performance of each package and from this information develop the experimental error.

One author has pointed out, "The importance of experimental design versus testing lies in the fact that the existence of an experimental error permits the use of a whole system of logical inference about the meaning of data."

To analyze the data, we compare the relative sales of the two package designs by taking the average sales from each group of stores in all markets tested.

We state that average sales per period (A_1) equals the taste of the product (A) and the income level of consumers (R), the price of substitute products (S), family size (T), and other unexplained variables (U).

In other words $A_1 = A + R + S + T + U$, which says that sales per period of the white-on-black package (A) in the first test market, Whitehall, Ohio, (1), derives from product taste (A), consumer income (R), price of other coffee and coffee substitutes (S), family size (T), and other unspecified variables (U).

In an oversimplified form, we can compare the two package designs by subtracting equation B_1 from A_1 to compare package A with package B.

$$A_1 = A + R + S + T + U$$
$$B_1 = B + R + S + T + U$$
$$A_1 - B_1 = A - B + 0 + 0 + 0 + 0 = A - B$$

Which seems to simplify matters considerably except that the difference, $A_1 - B_1$, for the sample, is not necessarily the true difference.

One way to feel more comfortable with this variation is to repeat the experiment several more times, as suggested in Figure II.2.A. Then if we take an average of a large number of results, we may have more confidence in which package is better. Of course, if we begin to generate seemingly inconsistent or widely fluctuating results from test to test, something else may be influencing the outcomes.

Designs for Profits

Although informal experimental design does not conform to strict statistical standards, the idea is to discern which factors influence behavior or are clouding perception of marketplace activity.

Although experimental projects apply to marketing problems, two objectives must be met:

1. The researcher has established a hypothesis that is verifiable in an experimental setting.
2. The researcher can control those conditions pertinent to testing the hypothesis in order to evaluate the performance of various alternatives in such a way that nothing in the creation and conduct of the experiment will favor one alternative over another.

In marketing research the key areas of investigation and experimentation include these key points:

- *Product design*: the form (powder, paste, or liquid deodorant), size (wide or narrow tires), color (brown or pink toothpaste), current trends, size, etc.
- *Package design*: shape (triangular or rectangular—space-using or space-saving), color (extremely important for many products), size (packaged for large families, retired couples, singles), see-through or closed.
- *Pricing experiments*: in-store or simulation (actual experience usually best), price elasticity of demand, discounts, economy sizes, coupons, etc.
- *Promotion*: effects of advertising expenditures on sales, types of media, ad size or length, repetition, color, various emotional or benefits appeals.
- *Sales*: optimum number of sales calls or average number per close, purchase repetition, volume discounts, special services.

A Format for Profit-Testing Experimentation

Much can be learned from experimentation. The degree of confidence the researcher has in the outcome of an experiment depends on how well it is set up. Most experiments will follow this format:

A. Experimental Goals and Factors.
   (1) Statement of purpose for the experiment.
   (2) Choice of dependent variable, the effect.
   (3) Selection of factors to vary, the causes.
   (4) How factors are varied and combined.
B. Design of the Experiment.
   (1) Number of experimental units.
   (2) Order in which the experiment is conducted.
   (3) Method of randomization.
   (4) Model to describe the experiment.
C. Analysis of Data.
   (1) Collection and sorting of data.
   (2) Statistical computations.
   (3) Interpretation of results.

Section I of this handbook mostly covers the material under Part A. Sections IV and V tend to concentrate on Part C type analysis. This section (II) focuses primarily on research design. An experimental design consists of a number of factors:

1. *An Experimental Unit.* The unit may be a group of consumers, or stores, that consist of more or less homogeneous subunits. For example, Stamford, Connecticut and Hamtramck, Michigan do not comprise an experimental unit for testing Kronenbourg beer.

2. *An Experimental Variable.* This is referred to as an independent variable, or experimental treatment. Some items tested include advertising impact, brand name recall, displays, training program, service vs. self-service. As with any design, the experiment itself must not create false signals that favor one experimental variable over others.

3. *Dependent Variable.* We can say that the independent variables are the causes, and the dependent variable is the effect. Examples of the independent variable are number of sales calls on sales or on number of units sold; or brand name recall resulting from repetitive advertising. The objective is to measure the interrelatedness of variables.

Even unearthing a statistical relationship does not guarantee that we have exposed a cause-effect relationship: every time I awake in the morning the sun comes up, and when I close my eyes at night the sun goes down; ergo, I can cause the sun to rise and set. Conclusions as ridiculous as this one, albeit more subtle, spring up when statistics substitute for reason. (Also refer to Sections VI.2 and VI.3.)

4. *Extraneous Forces Encountered.* Probably the basic issue is the detection of experimental factors which interact with environmental variables. These can fuzz up results: i.e., what really causes the observed effect? There are several danger points; some are mentioned.

One problem akin to all types of studies is time. If tomorrow will indeed replicate yesterday, then historical data faithfully predict the future.

Another is generalization, the same problem discussed under test marketing. In the ocean pout test, any researcher must feel uncomfortable with projections predicated on the free distribution of fish fillets to households or to retail establishments. Are those persons who agree to participate in such an experiment typical of the targeted market?

Still another problem on transferability of results is location or type of subjects in the experiment. Doubt always lurks as to whether test respondents are typical, or whether one geographical setting is elected for experimentation simply due to lack of cooperation in the preferred setting.

A fourth type of problem arises when test subjects react to more than one variable (whether intentional or not). Something else to consider in before-and-after tests (discussed later in this subsection) is by how much pretested subjects have been conditioned by the test. Asking people if they have heard of a certain glue, and then asking them again six months later, should produce a higher percentage of *yes* responses the second time, because the name of the glue will now be in their minds, whether at the conscious or the subconscious level. How much of the later response is brought about by effective advertising, and how much by external factors such as the test itself?

Knowing the answers ranks equally with knowing the problems. Below are a few ways around the mentioned difficulties.

a. When you want to generalize about type of store or type of customer, begin with the type of store or customer who will be buying the product.
b. Suppose all groups of people are potential customers. Recall the ocean pout example again. Two or three prices seemed to represent the preferences of more than one-half of the potential buyers of the fish fillets. Evidence suggested market segmentation by price of substitute fish. Pinpoint the characteristics of these groups and conduct further testing among persons, or stores, that tend to reflect preferences of these vaguely distinct groups.
c. Another technique is randomization. You already know about randomizing experimental treatments. Now apply the same method to geographical settings, or persons, or seasons. (See Appendix A as well.)
d. If randomization is not possible, create your own heterogeneous groups of stores, or persons, or places, and then proceed with the experiment.

5. *Internal Validity.* Let's look at some instances and expose the cloven-footed problems.

One is the testing itself. As in most repetitive processes, learning takes place. The learning curve is a well-known management concept. It derives from retesting in experimental designs as well. Improvement of test scores or convergence of ideas tends to occur during successive test encounters.

History is a problem here too, for the impact of variables does change with time. Frequent exposure to the same variables can cause subtle but important changes in results.

Other miscellaneous problems crop up as well. Suppose stock had temporarily run out at one of the test stores; or that the merchandise is displayed carelessly or later disarranged by customers; or the stocker put the wrong price, or no price, on the merchandise. The question of control enters again.

Then too, the issue of whether test subjects are different from others, and whether the sample composition of respondents shifts, may cast doubt on the validity of experimentation conducted over a long period. Statistical problems also can arise; but statistical analysis is reserved mostly for Sections V and VI.

Perhaps all of this sounds discouraging. It need not be, for solutions abound. This handbook will help you improve profits and dampen losses. If there were sure-fire answers, experimentation would be redundant. No one has all the answers, or even many.

The Creator has given us a most engaging game, viz., trying to forecast the future, a game we never tire of playing. I do not encourage you to dispense with hard-earned funds in fruitless searches. Good stewardship does imply prudence. Like the man with the talents, good stewardship means that profitable use of resouces breeds more profits.

Now let's see how others turn experimental design to profitable employment.

The Single-Shot Load Design

This approach may seem rather crude. But one shot in the rifle, well-aimed, that brings down the quarry, is enough. Of course, it has practically no scientific value—but scientists are not always right either.

The experiment omits the base line study. It does not filter out extraneous factors. But it is one way to do a case study.

For example, ContiCommodity Services, Inc., wanted to know why commodity traders change brokers, so they surveyed brokers and traders. Then they published principal reasons in a booklet, available free, and turned it into a promotional vehicle. Scientific? Not really. Profit raising? No doubt, because full-page advertisements in *The Wall Street Journal* offered the booklet, and summarizing survey results suggest they are satisfied with the outcome.

After-Only Design

A similar, simple experimental design gathers responses after subjects are exposed to an experimental variable. Results may not be scientifically valid, but this may be the cheapest way to perform an exploratory operation. An example demonstrates the technique. Comments following the example will show how to improve on it. We will build on the ocean pout experiment discussed in the previous subsection.

Assume that an ad, with coupon, is run in the *Manchester Union Leader* newspaper offering 50 percent off the regular price of ocean pout. Assume, too, that 3,081 persons redeemed coupons over the three-day period. What do those data tell us?

You may conclude that newspaper advertising promises the best vehicle to promote ocean pout; or that demand for ocean pout seems strong in Manchester, New Hampshire; or that the market seems strong, which warrants expanded business operations; or that purchasers in Manchester are bargain hunters; or that we may know nothing more than we already knew.

The after-only technique used in this way is full of holes. Still, if management has some idea of the normal sales level, the experiment is productive. In other words, experience provides management with some base line information, and the experiment is not really being conducted in a total vacuum.

If the experiment is repeated again in a couple of weeks, and coupons redeemed are now 4,629, then we have improved upon the experiment. We may decide that a substantial proportion of coupon redeemers are repeat buyers; therefore, the product does have a viable market in Manchester. Too, learning (or assurance) does occur with ad repetition.

Repetition builds confidence in consumers: the product is acceptable, not a fad; there is stability and reliability; etc. And more people become aware of it. Without follow-up information, of course, we cannot know with certainty how many are actually repeat buyers. Nor do we know whether the product will be as well received in nearby Portland, Maine, or Lowell, Massachusetts. Nor do we know whether the bargain hunters will return and pay the full price for the pout fish fillets. Nor do we know with complete confidence whether newspaper advertising is the best way to promote the ocean pout until further experiments are conducted, using control markets to compare results.

However, as an exploratory study, an after-only survey at least conveys direction. MCA Inc., producers of *Jaws I*, wanted to bring out a sequel, because the first movie was a big money-maker. A sample study, which in one sense may be labeled "after-only," being done after *Jaws I*, was also a "before-only," preceding *Jaws II*. The informally designed survey results suggested that an exciting sequel could pay off, which it did when coupled with promotion targeted to specific audiences.

Two other variations of this design are illustrated in Figures II.2.B and II.2.C. The first, usually distributed at state tourist information centers, does not characterize a well-designed and controlled experiment. Not everyone stops at an information center; not everyone who stops will ask for information; not everyone who registers at the desk receives a card; not everyone returns a survey card; not everyone will even manage to preserve the card and then remember to complete it at the end of the trip.

Dear Traveler:

   The State of Vermont would like to know
something about you and your experience
during this trip to our state.
   **Please save this card until your trip in
Vermont is over** and then complete and
mail. No postage is necessary if mailed in
the United States.

V7   Thank you.

NO POSTAGE
NECESSARY
IF MAILED
IN THE
UNITED STATE

BUSINESS   REPLY   MAIL

FIRST CLASS   PERMIT NO. 1   MONTPELIER, VT. 05602

POSTAGE WILL BE PAID BY ADDRESSEE

**State of Vermont
Agency of Development and
Community Affairs
Montpelier, Vermont 05602**

1. In what state or province do you live? . . . .

2. Please check which of the following states your party visited
on this particular trip:
   Vermont . . . . Maine . . . .
   New Hampshire . . . . Massachusetts . . . .
   Main destination state . . . .
   Car ☐ Bus ☐ Other . . . .
   Approx. miles traveled (total trip) . . . .

3. Dates of trip (in Vt.): . . . .

4. Trip purpose (outdoor recreation, skiing, touring, business,
visit relatives, etc.): . . . .

5. How many persons were in your traveling party? . . . .

6. Please indicate the **number of nights** your party spent at **each
type** of lodging place in Vermont:
   Motel (town . . . .) . . . .
   Hotel (town . . . .) . . . .
   Resort (town . . . .) . . . .
   Campground (State ☐, private ☐) . . . .
   With relatives or friends (town . . . .) . .
   Rented cottage (town . . . .) . .
   Your own seasonal home (town . . . .) . .
   Other . . . . _____
                                              Total Nights   . . . .
   Day trip (no overnights in Vt.)   ☐

7. Please estimate the total amount of money your party spent
in Vermont . . . . $ . . . .
   What part for lodging $ . . . . food $ . . . .

8. Where this card was obtained? . . . .

9. If we may contact you at some later date for additional information about your trip, please give us your name and
address:

10. Comments:

Figure II.2.B: INFORMAL SURVEY OF OUT-OF-STATE TOURISTS

A BRIEF, INFORMAL OPINION SURVEY

Dear Colleague:

Two and a half years have passed since the U.S. Foreign Corrupt Practices Act went into effect in December 1977. The Act makes it unlawful for U.S. companies to corruptly influence foreign officials. It also requires the institution of internal accounting controls to insure that all foreign transactions are executed in accordance with management's specific authorization. The basic purpose of the Act was to sustain international confidence in U.S. business and institutions. However, ambiguities of the Act and the absence of international antibribery treaties led many U.S. businessmen to conclude that the Act put U.S. multinationals at a disadvantage in competing with foreign multinationals.

You will probably agree with some of the following statements and disagree with others regarding the impact of the Act on U.S. multinationals. Please circle the appropriate letter after each statement to indicate your agreement or disagreement (7 = strongly agree, 1 = strongly disagree), and return this form, using the self-addressed envelope enclosed.

1. The Act has achieved its intended purpose.   7 6 5 4 3 2 1
2. The Act has put U.S. multinationals at a disadvantage.   7 6 5 4 3 2 1
3. The Act should be repealed.   7 6 5 4 3 2 1
4. The Act has significantly contributed to the
   unfavorable U.S. balance of payments.   7 6 5 4 3 2 1
5. Bribery, extortion, and payoffs are still the
   facts of life in international transactions.   7 6 5 4 3 2 1

You are strongly urged to add written comments about the Act.

Figure II.2.C: A BRIEF, INFORMAL OPINION SURVEY

The objective of the second survey, in Figure II.2.C, is unclear; but I suspect the researcher was more interested in soliciting comments, possibly related to another project, than in a tabulation of answers to the five questions.

After-only tests are sometimes conducted for name or brand recall. MONY wanted to know how people recognized their new trade style. Groups were tested on the name "MONY" alone, and on MONY coupled with a small subhead, "Mutual of New York."

Similar tests are conducted among magazine readership. If you will refer back to Figure II.1.B, especially Question Nos. 6 and 7, in part it is a type of recognition test; responses can be correlated to other personal characteristics—age, income, sex, etc.—also requested later in the same questionnaire.

Recognition tests are more significant to recall of specific ads that appeared in the magazine (or on television), and the content of the ad. Recall ranges from being aware of the ad's existence to reading and remembering the entire ad.

Before-After Designs

The before-after design, ranked higher than the after-only design, works from base line data. In this approach, the researcher measures the dependent variable before, then again after, exposure to the independent variable. There are two basic approaches to the before-after designs: (a) before-after without a control group; and (b) before-after using a control group.

Without the control group, the procedure first calls for testing the independent variable in the experimental unit. Next introduce the experimental variable, the treatment. Finally, measure the dependent variable after the treatment.

The difference between before and after measurements is attributed to the experimental variable, other things being equal. The results are reliable to the extent that other things remain equal, i.e., the extraneous forces.

Preferably, a before-after with control design, as a technique for monitoring external disturbances, will win your approval. The chief difference is that the control groups' reactions are taken into account.

Let's say that we have two experimental units, in only one of which will the experimental variable be introduced. If sales, the dependent variable, rise in both groups, then we can presume that other factors were at work to cause the sales increase. The before-and-after difference in the experimental market minus the difference in sales of the control market may be attributed to the effect of the experimental treatment.

For example, Ligget & Myers management wanted to reposition L & M cigarettes, as compared with the competition in the "full flavor category." The experimental units were university students at Madison, Wisconsin, the experimental group, and Tucson, Arizona, the control group. Attitude measures were taken in both groups before the introduction of the experimental variable in the Madison group.

L & M's product repositioning was centered on a new blend of tobacco and a new cork filter supported by a massive advertising campaign. Responses from the smokers of both groups were then analyzed to discern the effect of the campaign.

Of course, not everyone smokes, or eats ocean pout, so another marketing research technique needs to be introduced.

II.3: 50 LIFE STYLE ANALYSIS FACTORS FOR QUESTION- NAIRE DESIGNS

The successful researcher must also

(a) take into account changes in the social environment;
(b) perceive major trends when they begin, but discount secondary or minor trends and fads;
(c) anticipate shifts in consumer preferences;
(d) and know something about the customers' life styles.

Life style, a voguish expression not even found in many dictionaries, refers to values, and how people live and relate to the world around them, which led the president of a marketing research firm to state, "Here is where the action is." And this is where we want you to be as well.

Still, the term lacks preciseness of definition. Some newspapers title a section "Life Style." In a recent Sunday newspaper, the "Life Style" section carried articles on the resurgence of tatooing, protection against cockroaches, how to save on electricity consumption while on vacation, mildew protection, antiques, engagements and weddings, etc. In one sense these subjects characterize life styles; but only a few articles seem to fit clearly into this concept as seen from the marketer's viewpoint.

Tripping with the Trends

One article reports on the Conran System of home-built furniture (a trend?); a second on winter jackets and coats (seasonality); a third one on happiness of couples wedded 50 years (the beginnings of a life style analysis); and a fourth one on career uniforms. The last one noted that five distinct trends are evident among the 1.5 million wearers of uniforms, in response to social trends, fashion, federal dye and chemical regulations, a fully integrated workforce, and energy conservation mandates on regulation of building temperatures. The newspaper section contents illustrates definitional incoherence on one hand, but indicates the market value of developing life style information on the other.

For instance, discarding undergarments, a popular fad begun some years ago, has had implications broader than those immediately affecting sales of the foundation garment industry alone.

Ten years later, Sears Roebuck & Co. discerned some important changes. As a result of information gathered and analyzed, the company decreed that the "perfect" size 10 was no longer 35-25-36 but was now 34¼-26-36¼. A manufacturer of torso dummies pinpoints the bra-less, girdle-less trend as the cause for these physical changes among younger women. Together with popularity of dieting, there is more demand now for smaller-sized and reproportioned dresses than a couple of decades ago.

Or consider a Japanese manufacturer of soy sauce. Kikkoman International, Inc., studied the American market thoroughly before setting up an American subsidiary. They particularly focused on life styles. As a result of their extensive studies, they discovered, among other things, that Japanese-Americans, the originally intended market, were so westernized in eating habits that they did not constitute a growing market for the Japanese product. The new market target became the general American population. The firm introduced their product to the revised market segments with a campaign aimed at educating Americans in cooking with soy sauce.

The important thing to notice about this technique is the implicit recognition that humans are unique. While large numbers of people appear to be linked to a particular socioeconomic class, the smaller subgroupings of individuals are more indicative of consumer preferences than these statistical averages which reduce an entire population to one figure.

A good example of the successful use of segmented marketing is the Philip Morris Company's association of various cigarette brands with specific images: the Marlboro man, the Virginia Slims image. Their international expansion has followed the success formula. And they have duplicated that marketing success with Miller's High Life, and even in an unrelated venture, home-building in Mission Viejo, Orange County, California.

Another successful story, in the making, of market segmentation is the production end of the movie industry. Films have been tailored to specific subgroups of individuals mostly by age, with further market refinement derived from life style analysis. At the retail end, those movie exhibitors who caught this trend with specialized bookings aimed toward a narrow local market segment have survived the lean years and are riding the new expansionary trend of this leisure-time activity.

It is true that some people may allow their opinions to be shaped, shorn, and tossed about by the environment, marching in Pavlovian lockstep for a time. But most consumers shape their own environment as much as they are molded by it. And there are some who exercise rather effective control over their environment and sculpt it to their personal needs.

The basic rule is this: There are no human absolutes; and everything is subject to change. Some persons respond early to new trends, some late, and some not at all. Life style analysis attempts to gain deeper insight into how economic and social subgroups behave and think on specific issues directly, or which is peripherally related to the market question being researched.

Knowledge of trends is important in marketing many products and services; but when is a trend a trend? Some are false trends. Or they affect only a small, unrepresentative group of persons. Newspaper stories usually are not good indicators of major trends for they tend to focus on the unusual, the weird, the sensational. A political party of a dozen persons can get national media coverage if they do something outrageous or outlandish. Yet the same media very rarely report on trends in Middle America.

Awareness of a trend does not provide sufficient evidence for a company to act. Turning such information to profitable employment is crucial in strategic planning.

For instance, many men over age 25 believe their hair is thinning, whether it is or not. Since masculinity and virility are associated with a thick mane, a company created "Thicket," a hair cream that makes hair appear thicker. Development, packaging, promotion, and design, were aimed toward that image and belief.

Decision-making depends on basic data trend analysis, which calls for answers to these questions:

- ◎ Is a trend really emerging?
- ◎ If so, how big is it in relation to other trends?
- ◎ Is a counter-trend already in gear?
- ◎ Who (which groups) are involved in the trend?
- ◎ Which groups of people are excluded from the trend?
- ◎ How rapidly, or how slowly, is the trend developing?
- ◎ How soon is the trend anticipated to peak?

For example, what is the commuting-to-work trend? A Roper Organization poll detected that the average white worker travels less than 15 minutes to work; the average black worker travels 25 minutes to work. The shift toward public transportation use and car pooling was only modest, hardly a trend. Only one-fourth of the persons polled said they would switch to good, dependable public transportation if available. In the geographically smaller New England states, commutes are longer than in the larger western states. Still, that information does not fill in the blanks on the seven questions presented above.

Following the Family Life Cycle

Commuters form too broad a group for most product or advertising analysis. Within this broad group life styles will vary substantially due to social class, cultural heritage, racial differences, personality traits, educational level, occupation, family life cycle and so on.

Family life cycle models generally separate family life into five stages for developing market segmentation strategies:

Stage I: Bachelorhood.
Stage II: Honeymoon.
Stage III: Parenthood.
Stage IV: Postparenthood.
Stage V: Family dissolution when one spouse dies.

The growing size and affluence of Stage IV families has drawn the attention of many companies. The Conference Board points out that in the 25 million households headed by a person in the 45-to-65 age group, the husband is at the peak of his earning power, the wife has returned to work, grown children have left home, the couple has the security of generous retirement plans, and household income (as well as uncommitted earnings) significantly exceeds the national average for all age groups. Life style analysis reveals that people in this group are active and leisure-oriented and willing to experiment.

Companies aware of the spending characteristics and incomes at each stage in the family cycle have tailored products and pricing strategies for particular market segments. One advertising executive points out that the "myopic infatuation with the psychological appeal of youth is stupid" in half the cases.

For instance, cosmetic manufacturers have developed facial products for women in the age 45-plus group. Jovan, Inc., enjoyed a happy success with the introduction of their "Wrinkles Away." On the other hand, Pfizer Inc., fizzled with its shampoo conditioner, "New Season," for the over-50 set. And Wilson Sporting Goods Co. began marketing its "Squire" clubs for the middle-aged man.

Life style analysis will reveal that 25 percent of stereo components are sold to Stage IV customers, that they spend the most and buy the biggest recreational vehicles, that they travel 25 percent more than most Americans, that they dine out more often; this underscores the importance of life style analysis in alerting you to new marketing strategies that improve sales and profits.

The demographic characteristics—age, income, sex, education, marital status, occupation, etc.—are fairly accessible from secondary sources, in part (see Section I.1 on the profitable mining of this resource), and easily quantifiable to yield valuable information. Many of these data, available from various government sources, provide the chief starting point for market researchers. Figure II.3.A conveys the wide range and sources of data available at this moment.

POPULATION

POPULATION	Unit	1960	1970	1975	1977	1978
Total, incl. Armed Forces abroad	Mil.	180.7	204.9	213.6	216.9	218.5
Under 5 years old	Mil.	20.3	17.1	15.9	15.2	15.4
5–17 years old	Mil.	44.2	52.5	50.4	49.0	48.0
18 years old and over	Mil.	116.1	135.2	147.3	152.6	155.2
65 years old and over	Mil.	16.7	20.1	22.4	23.5	24.1
Median age	Yr.	29.4	27.9	28.8	29.4	29.7
Male	Mil.	89.3	100.3	104.2	105.7	106.5
Female	Mil.	91.4	104.6	109.3	111.1	112.0
White	Mil.	160.0	179.5	185.6	187.8	188.9
Black	Mil.	19.0	22.8	24.5	25.2	25.6
Percent of total population	Pct.	11	11	11	12	12
Percent in the South	Pct.	60	53	52	54	53
Other races	Mil.	1.6	2.6	3.5	3.9	4.1
Persons of Spanish origin	Mil.	(na)	(na)	11.2	11.3	12.0
Institutional population	Mil.	4.9	5.8	(na)	(na)	(na)
Resident population	Mil.	180.0	203.8	213.0	216.4	218.1
Per square mile	No.	51	57	60	61	62
Urban	Mil.	125.3	149.3	(na)	(na)	(na)
Percent of total residents	Pct.	69.9	73.5	(na)	(na)	(na)
Rural	Mil.	54.1	53.9	(na)	(na)	(na)
Metropolitan areas (279 SMSA's)[1]	Mil.	128	150	156	158	(na)
Percent of total population	Pct.	71.3	73.6	73.1	73.0	(na)
Nonmetropolitan areas[1]	Mil.	52	54	57	59	(na)
Single persons: Male[2]	Pct.	25.3	18.9	20.8	21.9	22.5
Female[2]	Pct.	19.0	13.7	14.6	15.6	16.4
Married persons: Male[2]	Pct.	69.1	75.3	72.8	70.9	70.1
Female[2]	Pct.	65.6	68.5	66.7	65.3	64.2
Divorced persons: Male[2]	Pct.	1.9	2.5	3.7	4.5	4.8
Female[2]	Pct.	2.6	3.9	5.3	6.2	6.7
Households	Mil.	52.8	63.4	71.1	74.1	76.0
One-person households	Pct.	13.1	17.1	19.6	20.9	22.0
Two-person households	Pct.	27.8	28.9	30.6	30.7	30.7
Families	Mil.	45.1	51.6	55.7	56.7	57.2
White	Mil.	40.9	46.0	49.5	50.1	50.5
Husband-wife	Pct.	88.7	88.7	86.9	86.7	85.9
Female head	Pct.	8.7	9.1	10.5	10.9	11.5
Average size (persons)	No.	3.61	3.52	3.36	3.31	3.28
Black and other	Mil.	4.2	5.2	6.3	6.6	6.7
Husband-wife	Pct.	73.6	69.7	63.9	61.9	59.3
Female head	Pct.	22.4	26.7	32.4	33.9	36.0
Average size (persons)	No.	4.39	4.13	3.90	3.78	3.77
Immigrants	Thous.	265	373	386	462	(na)
Rate per 1,000 population	No.	1.5	1.8	1.8	2.1	(na)

(na) Not available. [1] Standard metropolitan statistical areas as defined in Dec. 1978
[2] Percent of total, 18 years old and over, except 1960, 14 years old and over.

EDUCATION

EDUCATION	Unit	1960	1970	1975	1977	1978
School enrollment	Mil.	46.3	60.4	61.0	60.0	58.6
Elementary (kindergarten & grades 1-8)	Mil.	32.4	37.2	33.9	32.4	31.5
Secondary (grades 9-12)	Mil.	10.2	14.7	15.7	15.8	15.5
Elem'y & second'y in private school	Pct.	14.0	10.8	10.1	10.4	10.4
Higher education	Mil.	3.6	7.4	9.7	10.2	9.8
School expenditures, total	$Bil.	24.7	70.4	111.1	131.0	141.2
Elementary and secondary	$Bil.	18.0	45.7	72.2	85.5	90.8
Public	$Bil.	15.9	41.0	65.0	76.8	81.5
Average salary, public school teachers[1]	$Thous.	5.0	8.6	11.7	13.3	14.2
High school graduates, yearly	Mil.	1.9	2.9	3.1	3.2	3.2
College graduates, yearly	Mil.	.4	.8	.9	.9	.9
Adult persons completed high school[2]	Pct.	41	55	63	65	66

EMPLOYMENT AND WELFARE

EMPLOYMENT AND WELFARE	Unit	1960	1970	1975	1977	1978
Civilian labor force, 16 years old & over	Mil.	69.6	82.7	92.6	97.4	100.4
Female labor force	Mil.	22.5	31.2	36.5	40.0	41.9
Married females, husband present	Pct.	54.4	58.8	57.9	56.8	55.6
Employed	Mil.	65.8	78.6	84.8	90.5	94.4
In white-collar occupations	Pct.	43.4	48.3	49.8	49.9	50.0
Unemployed	Mil.	3.9	4.1	7.8	6.9	6.0
Unemployment rate	Pct.	5.5	4.9	8.5	7.0	6.0
White	Pct.	4.9	4.5	7.8	6.2	5.2
Black and other	Pct.	10.2	8.2	13.9	13.1	11.9
Teenagers (16-19 yr. old)	Pct.	14.7	15.3	19.9	17.7	16.3
Married men, wife present	Pct.	3.7	2.6	5.1	3.6	2.8
Weekly earnings in private industry	Dol.	81	120	164	189	204
Manufacturing	Dol.	90	134	191	229	249
Contract construction	Dol.	113	195	266	296	319
Retail trade	Dol.	58	82	109	122	130
Index of productivity[3][4]	1967 = 100	78.6	104.2	112.4	118.2	118.6
Index of compensation per hour[3]	1967 = 100	71.9	123.1	181.2	213.0	232.7
Labor union membership	Mil.	17.0	19.4	[5]20.2	[6]19.6	(na)
Percent of nonfarm employed	Pct.	31.4	27.5	[5]25.8	[6]24.5	(na)
Public social welfare expenditures	$Bil.	52.3	145.9	290.1	362.3	(na)
Federal	$Bil.	25.0	77.3	167.5	219.3	(na)
State and local	$Bil.	27.3	68.5	122.6	143.0	(na)
Social insurance	$Bil.	19.3	54.7	123.0	161.3	(na)
Education	$Bil.	17.6	50.8	80.8	94.6	(na)
Retired worker beneficiaries[7]	Mil.	8.1	13.3	16.6	17.8	18.4
Avg. monthly benefits, 1978 dollars	Dol.	168	201	253	265	263
Public aid recipients: Aged	Mil.	2.3	2.1	[8]2.3	[8]2.1	[8]2.0
In families with dependent children	Mil.	3.1	9.7	11.4	10.8	10.3
Public aid payments[9]	$Bil.	3.3	14.4	30.5	35.4	(na)
To families with dependent children	$Bil.	1.0	4.9	9.2	10.6	10.7
Medical assistance	$Bil.	(x)	5.9	14.2	17.1	(na)

(na) Not available. (x) Not applicable. [1] Elementary and secondary schools only. [2] Persons 25 years old and over.
[3] In private economy. [4] Output per paid hour. [5] 1974 data. [6] 1976 data. [7] Social security.
[8] No longer under public assistance; covered by Federal Supplemental Security Income (SSI) program.
[9] Beginning 1975, includes payments to aged, blind, and disabled under SSI program. See footnote 8 above.

VITAL DATA

VITAL DATA	Unit	1960	1970	1975	1977	1978
Births, live	Mil.	4.26	3.73	3.14	3.33	3.33
Per 1,000 population	Rate.	23.7	18.4	14.8	15.4	15.3
White	Rate.	22.7	17.4	13.8	14.4	(na)
Black and other	Rate.	32.1	25.1	21.2	21.9	(na)
Deaths	Mil.	1.71	1.92	1.89	1.90	1.92
Per 1,000 population	Rate.	9.5	9.5	8.8	8.8	8.8
Infant deaths per 1,000 live births	Rate.	26.0	20.0	16.1	14.1	13.6
White	Rate.	22.9	17.8	14.2	12.3	(na)
Black and other	Rate.	43.2	30.9	24.2	21.7	(na)
Deaths per 100,000 population	Rate.	955	945	889	878	882
Diseases of heart	Rate.	369	362	336	332	(na)
Malignancies	Rate.	149	163	172	179	(na)
Cerebrovascular diseases	Rate.	108	102	91	84	(na)
Accidents	Rate.	52	56	48	48	(na)
Marriages	Thous.	1,523	2,159	2,153	2,178	2,243
Per 1,000 population	Rate.	8.5	10.6	10.1	10.1	10.3
Per 1,000 unmarried women, 15 & over	Rate.	74	77	67	64	(na)
Divorces	Thous.	393	708	1,036	1,091	1,122
Per 1,000 population	Rate.	2.2	3.5	4.9	5.0	5.1
Per 1,000 married women, 15 & over	Rate.	9	15	20	21	(na)

HEALTH

HEALTH	Unit	1960	1970	1975	1977	1978
Life expectancy at birth, male	Yr.	66.6	67.1	68.7	69.3	(na)
Life expectancy at birth, female	Yr.	73.1	74.8	76.5	77.1	(na)
National health expenditures	$Bil.	26.9	74.7	131.5	170.0	192.4
Public, percent of total	Pct.	24.7	36.5	42.3	40.8	40.6
Private consumer expenditures for health	$Bil.	18.0	42.3	68.7	89.1	100.7
Met by private insurance	Pct.	27.8	37.2	45.0	45.5	45.1
Index of medical care prices	1967 = 100	79.1	120.6	168.6	202.4	219.4
Physicians' fees		77.0	121.4	169.4	206.0	223.3
Hospital room rates		57.3	145.4	236.1	299.5	331.6
Physicians, active M.D.'s	Thous.	247	311	366	382	(na)
Patient care, general practice[1]	Pct.	(na)	16.4	12.6	11.8	(na)
Dentists, active[1]	Thous.	85	96	107	113	(na)
Hospitals	Thous.	6.9	7.1	7.2	7.1	(na)
Beds per 1,000 population	No.	9.3	8.0	6.9	6.5	(na)
Average length of stay[2]	Days.	9.3	9.5	8.6	8.3	(na)
Admissions per 1,000 population[2]	No.	136	152	166	168	(na)
Bed disability, days per person: Male	Days.	5.3	5.2	5.4	5.8	(na)
Female	Days.	6.7	6.9	7.6	7.9	(na)
Mentally retarded in public institutions	Thous.	163.7	186.7	159.0	[3]157.1	151.3
Federal food stamps:						
Monthly participation	Mil.	[4].4	4.3	17.1	17.1	16.0
Stamps issued, retail value	$Bil.	[4].1	1.1	7.3	8.3	8.3

(na) Not available. [1] Excludes Federal practitioners. [2] Excludes psychiatric and TB hospitals. [3] 1976 data. [4] 1965 data

Figure II.3.A: RANGE OF LOW-COST DATA AVAILABLE TO THE RESEARCHER

INCOME AND PRICES

	Unit	1960	1970	1975	1977	1978
Gross national product (GNP)	$ Bil.	506	982	1,529	1,887	2,108
Personal consumption expenditures	$ Bil.	325	619	980	1,207	1,340
Gross private domestic investments	$ Bil.	76	141	191	298	346
Net exports of goods and services	$ Bil.	4	4	20	-11	-12
Govt. purchases of goods and services	$ Bil.	100	219	338	394	434
National income	$ Bil.	412	798	1,215	1,515	1,704
Personal income	$ Bil.	400	801	1,256	1,529	1,708
Disposable personal income	$ Bil.	349	686	1,087	1,303	1,452
Personal saving	$ Bil.	17	51	84	67	77
GNP, 1972 dollars	$ Bil.	737	1,075	1,202	1,333	1,386
Per capita	Dol.	4,078	5,248	5,630	6,145	6,341
Median family money income[1]	Dol.	5,620	9,867	13,719	16,009	(na)
White families	Dol.	5,835	10,236	14,268	16,740	(na)
Black and other families	Dol.	3,230	6,516	9,321	10,142	(na)
Median family income, 1977 dollars[1]	Dol.	11,500	15,399	15,447	16,009	(na)
Families with income of $25,000 & over[1]	Pct.	.9	4.6	14.1	22.4	(na)
Families below poverty level[1]	Mil.	3.2	5.3	5.5	5.3	(na)
Percent of all families	Pct.	18.1	10.1	9.7	9.3	(na)
Persons below poverty level[1]	Mil.	39.9	25.4	25.9	24.7	(na)
Percent of all persons	Pct.	22.2	12.6	12.3	11.6	(na)
Consumer price index, all items		98.7	116.3	161.2	181.5	195.4
Food		88.0	114.9	175.4	192.2	211.4
Homeownership cost[2]	1967	86.3	128.5	181.7	204.9	227.2
Rent	-	91.7	110.1	137.3	153.5	164.0
Fuel and utilities	100	95.9	107.6	167.8	202.2	216.0
Transportation		89.6	112.7	150.6	177.2	185.5
Apparel and upkeep		89.6	116.1	142.3	154.2	159.6
Consumer value of the dollar, 1967 = $1	Dol.	1.13	.86	.62	.55	.51
Average retail prices:						
Bread, white, per pound	Cents.	20	24	36	36	36
Hamburger, per pound	Cents.	52	66	88	85	95
Steak, sirloin, per pound	Cents.	109	135	199	192	205
Milk, fresh, ½ gallon (grocery)	Cents.	(na)	57	79	84	86
Producer price index, 1967 = 100	Index.	94.9	110.4	174.9	194.2	209.3

LAW ENFORCEMENT

	Unit	1960	1970	1975	1977	1978
Serious crimes against persons	Thous.	288	739	1,026	1,010	1,062
Per 100,000 inhabitants	Rate.	161	364	482	467	487
Murders, manslaughters[3]	Thous.	9	16	21	19	20
Robberies	Thous.	108	350	465	405	417
Serious crimes against property	Thous.	3,096	7,359	10,230	9,926	10,080
Per 100,000 inhabitants	Rate.	1,726	3,621	4,800	4,588	4,622
Public expenditures for law enforcement	$ Mil.	3,349	8,571	17,249	21,574	(na)
Police protection	$ Mil.	2,030	5,080	9,786	11,865	(na)
Corrections	$ Mil.	722	1,706	3,843	4,934	(na)

(na) Not available. [1]Beginning 1975, figures based on revised methodology. [2]Includes home purchase, mortgage, interest, taxes, insurance, maintenance, and repairs. [3]Nonnegligent manslaughter.

FEDERAL GOVERNMENT

	Unit	1960	1970	1975	1977	1978
Budget receipts	$ Bil.	92.5	193.7	281.0	357.8	402.0
Individual income taxes	$ Bil.	40.7	90.4	122.4	157.6	181.0
Corporation income taxes	$ Bil.	21.5	32.8	40.6	54.9	60.0
Social insurance taxes	$ Bil.	14.7	45.3	86.4	108.7	123.4
Budget outlays	$ Bil.	92.2	196.6	326.2	402.7	450.8
National defense	Pct.	49.0	40.0	26.2	24.2	23.3
Income security	Pct.	19.8	21.9	33.3	34.2	32.4
Health	Pct.	.9	6.7	8.5	9.7	9.7
Surplus (+) or deficit (-)	$ Bil.	+.3	-2.8	-45.1	-45.0	-48.8
Gross debt outstanding	$ Bil.	284.1	370.1	533.2	698.8	771.5
Federal civilian employment (June)	Mil.	2.4	2.9	2.9	2.8	2.9
Voter participation in national elections[1]	Pct.	63	[2]61	[3]56	[4]54	(x)

STATE AND LOCAL GOVERNMENTS

	Unit	1960	1970	1975	1977	1978
General revenue, total[b]	$ Bil.	50.5	130.8	228.2	285.8	(na)
From own taxes	Pct.	71.5	66.4	62.0	61.5	(na)
From Federal Government	Pct.	13.8	16.7	20.6	21.9	(na)
Direct general expenditures, total	$ Bil.	51.9	131.3	230.7	273.0	(na)
Education	Pct.	36.1	40.1	38.1	37.7	(na)
Highways	Pct.	18.2	12.5	9.8	8.5	(na)
Public welfare	Pct.	8.5	11.2	12.2	12.7	(na)
Debt outstanding (end of fiscal year)	$ Bil.	70	144	220	258	(na)
Government employment (Oct.)	Mil.	6.4	10.1	12.1	12.8	12.7

NATIONAL DEFENSE

	Unit	1960	1970	1975	1977	1978
Federal outlays for national defense	$ Bil.	45.2	78.6	85.6	97.5	105.2
Percent of gross national product	Pct.	9.1	8.2	5.9	5.3	4.8
Worldwide military expenditures	$ Bil.	(na)	235	365	421	(na)
Defense-related Fed. civilian employment	Mil.	1.1	1.2	1.0	1.0	1.0
U.S. military personnel on active duty	Mil.	2.5	3.1	2.1	2.1	2.1
In foreign countries	Thous.	633	888	454	460	459
Veterans, living	Mil.	23.8	27.6	29.5	29.8	30.0
On compensation and benefit rolls[a]	Mil.	4.0	4.7	4.9	4.9	4.9
Federal outlays for veterans benefits	$ Bil.	5.4	8.7	16.6	18.0	19.0

ENERGY AND SCIENCE

	Unit	1960	1970	1975	1977	1978
Horsepower of all prime movers	Bil.	11.0	20.4	25.1	26.5	27.4
Consumption of energy (Btu)	Quadril.	44.5	67.1	70.7	76.6	78.0
Per capita (Btu)	Mil.	247	329	332	354	358
Crude oil production, domestic[7]	Bil. bbl.	2.6	3.5	3.1	3.0	3.2
Imports of crude oil & oil products[7]	Bil. bbl.	.7	1.2	2.2	3.2	3.0
Natural gas production, cu. ft	Tril.	13	22	20	20	20
Coal production, short tons	Mil.	434	613	655	697	660
Electric energy production (kWh)	Bil.	842	1,636	2,003	2,212	2,286
Science funds for research and develop.	$ Bil.	13.5	25.9	35.2	42.9	47.3
Federal space program expenditures	$ Bil.	.9	5.5	4.9	6.0	6.5

(na) Not available. (x) Not applicable. [1]Percent of voting age population casting votes for President. [2]1968 data. [3]1972 data. [4]1976 data. [b]Includes intergovernmental. [a]Includes survivors. [7]Barrels of 42 gallons.

BUSINESS AND FINANCE

	Unit	1960	1970	1975	1977	1978
Proprietorships and partnerships, number	Mil.	10.0	10.3	12.0	[1]12.5	(na)
Receipts	$ Bil.	245	331	485	[1]535	(na)
Corporations, number	Mil.	1.1	1.7	2.0	[1]2.1	(na)
Receipts	$ Bil.	849	1,751	3,199	[1]3,606	(na)
Industrial production index (1967=100)	Index.	66	108	118	138	146
Manufacturing output related to capacity	Pct.	80	79	74	82	84
Value added by manufacture	$ Bil.	164	300	442	[1]511	(na)
Average employment in manufacturing	Mil.	17	19	18	[1]19	(na)
Raw steel production, short tons	Mil.	99	132	117	125	137
Manufacturing and trade sales	$ Bil.	730	1,290	2,160	2,701	3,057
Manufacturing and trade inventories	$ Bil.	95	178	285	338	379
Inventory-sales ratio	Ratio.	1.56	1.62	1.58	1.45	1.41
Retail stores, sales	$ Bil.	220	368	585	724	799
Expenditures for new plant and equip.	$ Bil.	36.8	79.7	112.8	135.8	153.8
Manufacturing	$ Bil.	15.1	32.0	48.0	60.2	67.6
Public utilities	$ Bil.	5.2	13.1	20.1	25.8	29.5
Corporate profits after taxes	$ Bil.	25.8	37.0	73.4	102.1	118.2
Corporate capital consumption allowances	$ Bil.	25.3	56.6	89.5	106.0	114.4
Profit ratio to stock equity, mfg. corp.	Pct.	9.2	9.3	11.6	14.2	15.0
Mergers, mfg. and mining concerns	Thous.	.8	1.4	.4	.6	(na)
Industrial and commercial failures	Thous.	15.4	10.7	11.4	7.9	6.6
Current liabilities	$ Bil.	.9	1.9	4.4	3.1	2.4
New construction, value	$ Bil.	55	95	135	174	206
Private	$ Bil.	39	67	94	136	160
Residential, incl. farm	$ Bil.	23	32	46	81	93
New housing units started	Thous.	1,296	1,469	1,171	1,990	2,023
Commercial banks: Assets	$ Bil.	261	582	975	1,177	1,329
Loans, gross	$ Bil.	121	300	513	632	738
Deposits	$ Bil.	231	486	793	947	1,043
Savings and loan assns.: Assets	$ Bil.	72	176	338	459	524
Savings capital	$ Bil.	62	146	286	387	431
Private liquid assets held by public	$ Bil.	387	769	1,289	1,589	1,771
Demand deposits and currency	$ Bil.	134	201	267	303	323
Time deposits	$ Bil.	172	432	788	1,024	1,130
Other liquid assets	$ Bil.	81	136	235	262	319
Consumer credit outstanding	$ Bil.	65	143	223	289	340
Money market rates: Corporate bonds Aaa	Pct.	4.41	8.04	8.83	8.02	8.73
Prime commercial paper, 4-6 mos	Pct.	3.85	7.72	6.33	5.60	7.99
Home mortgages, conventional, new	Pct.	[2]5.97	8.52	9.10	8.95	9.68
NYSE common stock index, mo. avg.[3]	Index.	30	46	46	54	54
Dow Jones industrial (30 stocks), mo. avg., dol. per share	Dol.	618	753	803	895	817
Mortgage debt outstanding	$ Bil.	207	474	802	1,024	1,170
Residential nonfarm	Pct.	78.3	75.5	73.8	75.0	75.4
Credit market debt outstanding	$ Bil.	778	1,595	2,622	3,307	3,795
Life insurance companies, assets	$ Bil.	120	207	289	352	390
Net interest earned on assets	Rate.	4.1	5.3	6.4	6.9	7.3

(na) Not available. [1]1976 data. [2]1961 data. [3]Index base: Dec. 31, 1965 = 50.

Figure II.3.A (continued)

Figure II.3.A (continued)

AGRICULTURE	Unit	1960	1970	1975	1977	1978
Farm population	Mil.	**15.6**	9.7	**8.9**	7.8	**8.0**
Percent of total population	Pct.	**8.7**	4.8	**4.2**	3.6	**3.7**
Farms	Mil.	**4.0**	2.9	**2.8**	2.7	**2.7**
Average size	Acres.	**297**	374	**391**	397	**401**
Gross farm income	$Bil.	**38.9**	58.6	**100.3**	108.5	**126.0**
Government payments	$Bil.	**.7**	3.7	**.8**	1.8	**3.0**
Average income per farm	$Thous.	**2.9**	4.8	**8.8**	7.3	**10.4**
Wheat production, bushels	Bil.	**1.4**	1.4	**2.1**	2.0	**1.8**
Corn production, bushels	Bil.	**3.9**	4.2	**5.8**	6.4	**7.1**
Beef production, pounds	Bil.	**14.7**	21.7	**24.0**	25.3	**24.2**
Agricultural exports	$Bil.	**4.8**	7.3	**21.9**	23.7	**29.4**
COMMUNICATIONS AND TRANSPORTATION						
Postal service revenue	$Bil.	**3.3**	7.7	**11.6**	14.6	**15.8**
Postal service deficit	$Mil.	**597**	165	**988**	688	**379**
Pieces of mail per capita	No.	**355**	415	**419**	427	**445**
Telephone systems, operating revenues	$Bil.	**8.4**	18.2	**31.3**	40.1	**(na)**
Households with telephone service	Pct.	**79**	91	**95**	96	**97**
Commercial broadcast revenues:[1] Radio	$Bil.	**.6**	1.1	**1.7**	2.3	**(na)**
TV	$Bil.	**1.3**	2.8	**4.1**	5.9	**6.9**
Daily newspapers	No.	**1,763**	1,748	**1,756**	1,753	**1,756**
Net paid circulation	Mil.	**58.9**	62.1	**60.7**	61.5	**62.0**
Total highway mileage	Thous.	**3,546**	3,730	**3,838**	3,867	**(na)**
Motor vehicle registrations	Mil.	**74**	108	**133**	142	**149**
New passenger car sales:[2] Domestic	Mil.	**6.1**	7.1	**7.1**	9.1	**9.3**
New passenger car sales:[2] Imports	Mil.	**.5**	1.3	**1.6**	2.1	**2.0**
Intercity passenger-miles by private auto	Pct.	**90.1**	86.6	**86.1**	85.1	**(na)**
Intercity freight[3] moved by railroad	Pct.	**44.7**	39.8	**36.7**	36.1	**(na)**
Operating revenues: Railroads	$Bil.	**10.0**	12.5	**17.4**	21.2	**(na)**
Motor carriers of property	$Bil.	**7.2**	14.6	**22.0**	31.0	**(na)**
Domestic air carriers[4]	$Bil.	**2.1**	7.1	**11.9**	15.7	**17.9**
Revenue passengers: Domestic airlines[4]	Mil.	**56**	153	**189**	222	**254**
Bus lines, intercity	Mil.	**366**	401	**351**	332	**335**
Local transit	Mil.	**7,521**	5,932	**5,643**	5,723	**(na)**
FOREIGN COMMERCE						
Balance on current account	$Bil.	**2.8**	2.3	**18.3**	-14.1	**-13.9**
Exports of goods and services	$Bil.	**28.9**	65.7	**155.7**	184.6	**220.8**
Imports of goods and services	$Bil.	**-23.7**	-60.0	**-132.8**	-194.0	**-229.7**
U.S. assets and investments abroad	$Bil.	**85.6**	165.5	**295.1**	383.0	**450.1**
Foreign assets and investments in U.S	$Bil.	**40.9**	106.8	**220.5**	310.6	**373.3**
U.S. Govt. foreign grants and credits	$Bil.	**4.6**	5.9	**8.7**	6.7	**8.0**
Domestic exports of merchandise	$Bil.	**20.4**	42.6	**106.6**	119.0	**141.2**
Machinery and transport equipment	$Bil.	**7.0**	17.9	**45.7**	50.2	**59.3**
General imports of merchandise	$Bil.	**15.1**	40.0	**96.6**	147.7	**172.0**
Petroleum and products	$Bil.	**1.6**	2.8	**24.8**	41.8	**39.1**

(na) Not available [1]Net revenues [2]Retail sales. Imports exclude domestic models produced in Canada [3]Ton miles.
[4]Certificated route carriers only.

SELECTED DATA — REGIONS AND STATES

Region, State	Land area, 1,000 sq. mi.	Rank	Population, July 1, 1978: Total (mil.)	Per sq. mi.	Average annual percent change, 1970-1978	Population, Apr. 1, 1970: Total (mil.)	Percent: Black	Percent: Urban	Civilian workers, 1978 (1,000): Employed	Unemployed	Personal income, 1978: Per capita (dol.)	Rank
U.S	3,540.0	(x)	**218.1**	62	**.8**	203.2	11.1	73.5	94,373	6,048	**7,810**	(x)
Northeast	163.3	(x)	**49.1**	301	(z)	49.0	8.9	80.4	20,961	1,553	**8,142**	(x)
No. Central	751.8	(x)	**58.3**	77	**.4**	56.6	8.1	71.6	26,044	1,472	**8,005**	(x)
South	873.7	(x)	**70.6**	81	**1.5**	62.8	19.1	64.6	29,891	1,775	**7,076**	(x)
West	1,751.2	(x)	**40.1**	23	**1.8**	34.8	4.8	82.9	17,476	1,248	**8,397**	(x)
Ala	50.7	22	**3.7**	74	**1.0**	3.4	26.2	58.4	1,492	101	**6,247**	47
Alaska	569.6	50	**.4**	1	**3.5**	.3	3.0	48.4	160	20	**10,851**	1
Ariz	113.4	31	**2.4**	21	**3.4**	1.8	3.0	79.6	932	61	**7,374**	30
Ark	51.9	33	**2.2**	42	**1.5**	1.9	18.3	50.0	868	58	**6,183**	49
Calif	156.4	1	**22.3**	143	**1.4**	20.0	7.0	90.9	9,877	755	**8,850**	5
Colo	103.8	28	**2.7**	26	**2.3**	2.2	3.0	78.5	1,221	71	**8,001**	15
Conn	4.9	24	**3.1**	637	**.2**	3.0	6.0	77.4	1,433	79	**8,914**	4
Del	2.0	49	**.6**	294	**.7**	.5	14.3	72.2	252	21	**8,604**	8
D.C	.1	(x)	**.7**	([1])	**-1.4**	.8	71.1	100.0	303	28	**10,022**	(x)
Fla	54.1	8	**8.6**	159	**2.8**	6.8	15.3	80.5	3,444	245	**7,505**	27
Ga	58.1	14	**5.1**	88	**1.2**	4.6	25.9	60.3	2,184	131	**6,700**	37
Hawaii	6.4	40	**.9**	140	**1.8**	.8	1.0	83.1	367	31	**8,380**	11
Idaho	82.7	41	**.9**	11	**2.5**	.7	.3	54.1	382	23	**6,813**	36
Ill	55.7	5	**11.2**	202	**.1**	11.1	12.8	83.0	5,005	323	**8,745**	7
Ind	36.1	12	**5.4**	149	**.4**	5.2	6.9	64.9	2,425	146	**7,696**	23
Iowa	55.9	26	**2.9**	52	**.3**	2.8	1.2	57.2	1,362	57	**7,873**	17
Kans	81.8	32	**2.3**	29	**.5**	2.2	4.8	66.1	1,123	35	**8,001**	15
Ky	39.7	23	**3.5**	88	**1.0**	3.2	7.2	52.3	1,474	82	**6,615**	40
La	44.9	20	**4.0**	88	**1.0**	3.6	29.8	66.1	1,506	113	**6,640**	38
Maine	30.9	38	**1.1**	35	**1.1**	1.0	.3	50.8	444	29	**6,333**	46
Md	9.9	18	**4.1**	419	**.6**	3.9	17.8	76.6	1,918	114	**8,306**	12
Mass	7.8	10	**5.8**	738	**.1**	5.7	3.1	84.6	2,663	173	**8,063**	14
Mich	56.8	7	**9.2**	162	**.4**	8.9	11.2	73.8	3,913	289	**8,442**	10
Minn	79.3	19	**4.0**	51	**.6**	3.8	.9	66.4	1,917	76	**7,847**	18
Miss	47.3	30	**2.4**	51	**1.0**	2.2	36.8	44.5	898	68	**5,736**	50
Mo	69.0	15	**4.9**	70	**.5**	4.7	10.3	70.1	2,148	114	**7,342**	31
Mont	145.6	43	**.8**	5	**1.5**	.7	.3	53.4	348	22	**7,051**	33
Nebr	76.5	35	**1.6**	21	**.6**	1.5	2.7	61.5	748	23	**7,391**	29
Nev	109.9	45	**.7**	6	**3.6**	.5	5.7	80.9	319	15	**9,032**	3
N.H	9.0	42	**.9**	97	**2.0**	.7	.3	56.4	411	16	**7,277**	32
N.J	7.5	9	**7.3**	974	**.2**	7.2	10.8	88.9	3,185	246	**8,818**	6
N. Mex	121.4	37	**1.2**	10	**2.1**	1.0	1.9	69.8	495	30	**6,505**	43
N.Y	47.8	2	**17.7**	371	**-.4**	18.2	11.9	85.6	7,241	603	**8,267**	13
N.C	48.8	11	**5.6**	114	**1.1**	5.1	22.2	45.0	2,562	116	**6,607**	41
N. Dak	69.3	46	**.7**	9	**.6**	.6	.4	44.3	280	14	**7,438**	28
Ohio	41.0	6	**10.7**	262	**.1**	10.7	9.1	75.3	4,675	267	**7,812**	20
Okla	68.8	27	**2.9**	42	**1.4**	2.6	6.7	68.0	1,211	49	**6,951**	34
Oreg	96.2	29	**2.4**	25	**1.9**	2.1	1.3	67.1	1,119	72	**7,839**	19
Pa	45.0	4	**11.8**	261	**-.1**	11.8	8.6	71.5	4,888	364	**7,733**	21
R.I	1.0	39	**.9**	891	**-.2**	.9	2.7	87.1	404	29	**7,526**	26
S.C	30.2	25	**2.9**	97	**1.5**	2.6	30.5	47.6	1,224	74	**6,242**	48
S. Dak	76.0	44	**.7**	9	**.4**	.7	.3	44.6	318	10	**6,841**	35
Tenn	41.3	17	**4.4**	105	**1.3**	3.9	15.8	58.8	1,815	111	**6,489**	44
Tex	262.1	3	**13.0**	50	**1.8**	11.2	12.5	79.7	5,706	288	**7,697**	22
Utah	82.1	36	**1.3**	16	**2.5**	1.1	.6	80.4	519	21	**6,622**	39
Vt	9.3	48	**.5**	53	**1.1**	.4	.2	32.2	222	14	**6,541**	42
Va	39.8	13	**5.1**	129	**1.2**	4.6	18.5	63.1	2,298	130	**7,624**	24
Wash	66.6	21	**3.8**	57	**1.3**	3.4	2.1	72.6	1,634	120	**8,450**	9
W.Va	24.1	34	**1.9**	77	**.8**	1.7	3.9	39.0	674	46	**6,456**	45
Wis	54.5	16	**4.7**	86	**.7**	4.4	2.9	65.9	2,187	118	**7,597**	25
Wyo	97.2	49	**.4**	4	**3.0**	.3	.8	60.5	201	7	**9,096**	2

(x) Not applicable (z) Less than .05 percent [1]11,049

SOURCES OF DATA — **U.S. GOVERNMENT**

Arms Control and Disarmament Agency: World military expenditures.

Bureau of the Census: Population; education (enrollment, school-years completed); family income; law enforcement expenditures; voter participation; State and local govts; mfg. value added and employment; construction; retail sales; imports; exports; land area.

Bureau of Economic Analysis: GNP and national income; business investment and profits; public and private debt; manufacturing and trade sales and inventory; foreign commerce; U.S. foreign aid; personal income.

Bureau of Labor Statistics: Labor force, employment and unemployment, weekly earnings; productivity; compensation, and price indexes; union membership; retail prices.

Dept. of Agriculture: Farms, farm population, production, income, exports; food stamps.

Dept. of Defense: Military personnel.

Dept. of Energy: Energy consumption; oil production and imports, electric energy, natural gas, and coal production.

Fed. Aviation Administration: Air carrier revenues and airline passengers.

Fed. Bureau of Investigation: Crime.

Fed. Communications Commission: Telephone, radio, and TV revenues.

Fed. Deposit Insurance Corp.: Banking.

Fed. Highway Adm.: Highway mileage; vehicle registrations.

Fed. Home Loan Bank Board. Savings and loan associations.

Federal Reserve Board: Industrial production; liquid assets, consumer credit; mortgage debt; money rates, insurance assets.

Fed. Trade Commission: Mergers.

Health Care Financing Administration: Health expenditures.

Immigration and Naturalization Service. Immigrants.

Internal Revenue Service: Business units and receipts.

SOURCES OF DATA — **U.S. GOVT., Con.**

Interstate Commerce Commission: Intercity traffic, transport revenues.

National Center for Education Statistics: School expenditures; graduates.

National Center for Health Statistics: Births, deaths, marriages, divorces; life expectancy, physicians, dentists; bed disability.

National Science Foundation: R&D funds.

Office of Management and Budget: Federal finances.

Office of Personnel Management: Fed. employment.

Postal Service: Postal service finances; mail volume.

Social Security Administration: Social welfare expenditures, retired workers, public aid recipients and payments.

Veterans Administration: Veterans.

NON-GOVERNMENT AGENCIES:

American Bus Association: Intercity bus passengers.

American Council of Life Insurance: Life insurance.

American Hospital Association: Hospitals and beds. (Copyright.)

American Iron and Steel Institute: Steel production. (Copyright.)

American Public Transit Association: Local transit passengers.

American Telephone and Telegraph Company: Households with telephones.

Dun and Bradstreet, Inc.: Business failures.

Editor and Publisher Co., Inc.: Newspapers. (Copyright.)

Motor Vehicle Manufacturers Association: Passenger car retail sales.

National Education Association: Teachers salaries. (Copyright.)

Waring, John A.: Horsepower.

For sale by the Superintendent of Documents, U.S. Government Printing Office, Washington D.C. 20402, or any U.S. Department of Commerce district office. Stock Number 003-024-02138-2

OCTOBER 1979

The elusive, intangible variables—attitudes, interests, life styles—supply the market researcher with a comprehensive and data-rich profile of the potential consumer. Typically, such evidence is gathered from self-administered questionnaires or interviews.

Approaching Open-Ended Questions

One approach is to use open-ended questions such as those developed and exhibited in Figure II.3.B. This type of question can elicit a whole range of responses. Usually the true purpose of the questionnaire is disguised so that the respondent will not second-guess the researcher's intent.

After the survey, these responses are grouped, coded, and analyzed. If the research plan has been carefully designed, it will provide valuable insight into attitudes and life styles of people who, in this instance, dine out, either occasionally or often.

Some questions really try to inspire the respondent to describe himself and then how he perceives his opposite: (10) What kind of people usually dine out? and (17) What do you think of families who rarely eat at restaurants? To complete the profile, the questionnaire will end with standard demographic questions such as age, income, number of children, occupation, etc., in order to assemble a complete profile.

In another example of an open-ended question survey, Figure II.3.C, its purpose is stated. Still, it falls within the scope of an attitude, interest, and opinion survey. Although it was mailed to all recipients of this newsletter-type publication, due to the type of readership the questionnaire produced high-quality, useful information. These kinds of open-ended questions are not recommended for every audience, however.

Identifying the AIOs

AIO research focuses on Activities (A), Interests (I), and Opinions (O). The following summarizes those characteristics on which information is frequently sought in each category.

1. *Activities*. How the consumer (family) spends time:
   (a) work;
   (b) avocation;
   (c) moonlighting;
   (d) television, movies;
   (e) reading;
   (f) other entertainment with family;
   (g) entertainment without family;
   (h) shopping;
   (i) community;
   (j) social events, club membership;
   (k) vacation, leisure, weekend trips;
   (l) church, charitable activities.

OPEN-ENDED QUESTIONS

1. What makes you feel like a useful person?
2. What are the things that make you feel important?
3. How often do you shop for groceries?
4. When you shop, do you ordinarily stick strictly to a shopping list?
5. Do you and your family eat out often for pleasure?
6. When you eat out where do you usually go?
7. What are your favorite kinds and styles of automobile?
8. What kinds of car(s) do you now own?
9. Have you ever bought a product in a supermarket just on impulse?
10. What kind of people usually dine out?
11. If you were entertaining how likely would you be to try a new recipe?
12. How do you feel about buying food products through the mail?
13. How important to you is having wine with dinner?
14. Which magazines have you read in the past month?
15. If you saw a new product advertised in a magazine, how would you feel about trying it?
16. When you eat out how do you choose from the menu?
17. What do you think of families who rarely eat a meal at restaurants?
18. What do you think the average family income is of other people you see eating in restaurants?
19. When you eat in a restaurant, what do you think makes a good waiter or waitress?
20. How do you decide on which restaurant to try?
21. Who usually shops for groceries in your family?
22. Who usually decides when to eat out?
23. How do you feel about preparing meals?
24. In comparison with other women, how well do you think you can cook?
25. When you and your family dine out, how do you usually dress?

Figure II.3.B: OPEN-ENDED QUESTIONS

2. *Interests.* The consumer's (family's) preferences and attitudes:
   (a) family, children;
   (b) neighbors;
   (c) community;
   (d) job;
   (e) hobby;
   (f) study, self-improvement;
   (g) recreation;
   (h) fashion.
3. *Opinions.* The respondent's opinions on political, economic, business, social, news events:
   (a) themselves;
   (b) children;
   (c) neighbors;

WHAT DO YOU THINK?

We would like to know what you believe are the important issues facing the country today. So that Hillsdale College might devise publications and educational courses suited to the crucial issues of the day, may we take a little of your time for the following questionnaire? Your answers will remain strictly confidential; results of this poll will be published anonymously in IMPRIMIS.

1. Please list what you believe to be the top three issues facing the country:

    1._____
    _____
    2._____
    _____
    3._____

2. What three (3) individuals do you most admire?

    1. _____
    2. _____
    3. _____

3. What kinds of publications other than IMPRIMIS would you like to receive?

    ☐ Digest summaries.

    ☐ Hillsdale College seminar speeches published collectively in a book.

    ☐ Regular brief news releases addressing current issues.

    ☐ Quarterly Journal.

    ☐ Annual anthology of Hillsdale College speeches.

    ☐ Other (please specify)_____
    _____

    ☐ No additional publications other than IMPRIMIS necessary.

4. If offered in your area, what types of seminars or educational presentations would you be interested in attending?

    _____

5. Occupation/business title: _____

    Sex: ☐ Male   ☐ Female   Age:_____

    Marital status: ☐ Married   ☐ Single

    Number of children:_____

    Educational background: _____
    _____

    Geographical location: ☐ North   ☐ South   ☐ East   ☐ West
                              ☐ Midwest   ☐ Other_____

6. If you are receiving duplicates of IMPRIMIS, which address(es) do you wish deleted?_____
    _____

7. If you have a regular seasonal address different from your usual address to which you want IMPRIMIS mailed, give that address and effective dates:

    _____
    _____

8. Comments:_____
    _____
    _____
    _____

9. Name and address (optional):_____
    _____

Please return this form in addressed, postage paid envelope that is enclosed.

Thank you.

Figure II.3.C: A SURVEY WITH OPEN-ENDED QUESTIONS

(d) privacy;
(e) inflation and taxes;
(f) politics, politicians;
(g) schools;
(h) future.

Instead of open-ended questions, another method, easier to code, quantify, and analyze, allows for a range of responses from "strongly agree" to "strongly disagree." See the partial questionnaire on automobiles, as illustrated in Figure II.3.D.

DISCOVERING SHADES OF DIFFERENCES

	Agree		Neither Agree nor Disagree		Disagree	
1. I spend a lot of time in my automobile.	+3	+2	+1	0	−1	−2	−3
2. People who drive big cars are lucky because they can afford them.	+3	+2	+1	0	−1	−2	−3
3. We commute a long way to work.	+3	+2	+1	0	−1	−2	−3
4. I believe the government should furnish basic social services.	+3	+2	+1	0	−1	−2	−3
5. I prefer to give casual, informal parties.	+3	+2	+1	0	−1	−2	−3
6. Most families need more than one automobile.	+3	+2	+1	0	−1	−2	−3
7. I need several telephones in my house.	+3	+2	+1	0	−1	−2	−3
8. I prefer brightly colored telephones.	+3	+2	+1	0	−1	−2	−3
9. We live a long way from relatives.	+3	+2	+1	0	−1	−2	−3
10. I prefer to drive a brightly colored automobile.	+3	+2	+1	0	−1	−2	−3
11. I am influential in my neighborhood.	+3	+2	+1	0	−1	−2	−3

Figure II.3.D: DISCOVERING SHADES OF DIFFERENCES

		Agree		Neither Agree nor Disagree		Disagree	
12. People who drive small cars are more patriotic than people who drive big cars.	+3	+2	+1	0	−1	−2	−3
13. People who drive foreign cars put Americans out of work.	+3	+2	+1	0	−1	−2	−3
14. I believe the price of gasoline will double again within five years or less.	+3	+2	+1	0	−1	−2	−3
15. I prefer that neighbors or friends telephone before visiting.	+3	+2	+1	0	−1	−2	−3

Figure II.3.D (continued)

In a complete profile, you will probably want to develop a set of questions that relate to demographic measures (age, income, sex, etc.), to personality factors and traits (authoritarian, tolerant, self-starter, achiever, etc.), and to life style factors (see Figure II.3.E). The life style variables appearing in Figure II.3.E, from the *Journal of Marketing Research*, were organized by Prof. Kathryn Villani. They may furnish helpful guidelines to aid you in putting together your own life style questionnaires.

FIFTY-ONE LIFE STYLE CHARACTERISTICS

A. Cooking

  1. Cooking/Entertaining Self-Confidence—enjoy having guests for dinner, enjoy entertaining
  2. Convenience Cook—desire for convenience in cooking
  3. Creative Cook—enjoyment and skill in cooking fancy meals

B. Household Activities

  4. Home Cleanliness—activities and expectations about house cleaning
  5. Home/Laundry Cleanliness—judge floors by shine, laundry by whiteness
  6. Do Husband's Shirts—do husband's shirts oneself
  7. Planning and Routine—plan shopping and budget, limit shopping trips
  8. Attention to Detail—attend to details in carrying out a task

Figure II.3.E: FIFTY-ONE LIFE STYLE CHARACTERISTICS

C. Family Relationships

9. Spend Time with Children—take time to teach and talk with children, family is close knit group
10. Children Are Center of Attention—consider children in family, household decisions
11. Father Should Be Boss in Family—man (versus woman) should run the family
12. Marriage Should Be a Partnership—neither the man nor the woman should be "boss" in family

D. Leisure

13. Formal Entertainment—go out to dinner, concerts, movies, plays, and formally entertain regularly
14. Reading—read novels, newspapers, and magazines regularly
15. Music—enjoy listening to music
16. Participation in Activities—often visit friends, enjoy activities outside of the home
17. Spend Time Out Every Day—out of house every day
18. Enjoy Doing Nothing—often like to do nothing
19. Self-Indulgence Justified—believe entitled to play hooky once in a while

E. Attitudes Toward Television

20. Television as Primary Entertainment—watch television often; television is a companion, brings enjoyment
21. Watch TV to Relax—watch television to relax and escape problems
22. Watch Television if Nothing Else to Do—watch television because there is nothing else to do at the time
23. Watch Television Selectively—certain about programs liked and watch specific ones, ignore others' opinions about programs selected
24. Watch a Variety of Programs—watch different programs instead of the same ones from week to week
25. Rarely Change the Channel—once the television set is on, the channel is rarely changed
26. TV as Company—like having television on while do other work
27. Like TV Violence—like to watch shows about murder and violence

F. Health

28. Use of Non-Prescription Drugs—believe in use of non-prescription drugs for minor ailments
29. Purchase of Non-Prescription Drugs—believe some brands are more powerful
30. Concern about Nutrition—believe nutrition is important, make family take supplementary vitamins
31. Nutrition Is Instinctive—believe children instinctively know the best foods to eat

G. Appearance

32. Dress for Comfort—usually dress for comfort (versus fashion)
33. Importance of Woman's Appearance—believe woman's appearance is important, tend to dress for fashion
34. Overweight Problem—feel overweight
35. Weight Consciousness—eat carefully and exercise to control weight

Figure II.3.E (continued)

H. Finances

  36. Present Financial Situation—distressed with present financial situation
  37. Financial Future—optimistic about future family income and financial position

I. Mobility

  38. Attitudes Toward Moving—do not mind moving to a new community, have moved often before

J. Risk

  39. Attitudes Toward Risk—not afraid to take a chance

K. Morality

  40. Moral Issues—believe movies should not be censored, marijuana should be legalized
  41. Belief in Work Ethic—believe becoming a success is a matter of hard work, not luck
  42. Religious Practices and Attitudes—attend church and pray regularly, believe abortion should be restricted

L. Buyer Behavior

  43. Attitudes Toward Advertising—believe advertising is expensive, wasteful, and generally misleading
  44. Susceptibility to Advertising—believe advertising cannot sell one anything not wanted
  45. Product Innovativeness/Opinion Leadership—try new food brands before friends and neighbors, like to try new gadgets, products; advise others of new brands and products
  46. Dependent-Influencer—influenced by friends to try new products, desire sympathy of friends, give advice to friends about new products
  47. Price Consciousness—use price-off coupons, check prices and sale advertisements
  48. Price/Quality Believer—believe you get what you pay for
  49. National Brand Preference—believe national brands are better and worth paying more for than private brands
  50. Credit Practices and Attitudes—believe in use of credit cards and charge accounts
  51. Shopping Practices—enjoy shopping, take frequent shopping trips

Figure II.3.E (continued)

Analyzing the Data

Another aspect of consumer behavior is cross-cultural analysis: deciding whether to enter a foreign market; how to approach the market; who is the market target.

There are, of course, distinct marketing dissimilarities that mark the difference between potential success and failure. Aside from these cultural variations, a life style study will turn up particularly profitable interpretations that escape detection of other marketing research techniques used alone.

Finally, there is the question of analysis. After gathering, sorting, and coding this information, how can it be analyzed?

One important way is to just look at it. Ideas have a way of popping out when you become immersed in the data rather than passing it along to someone else for the donkey work, who renders only a summary report for you to read. A more scientific way is regression analysis explained in easy-to-understand language in Section VI.3 of this book. Still, a formal experimental design may best fit your current research requirements.

II.4: IMPLEMENTING FORMAL EXPERIMENTAL DESIGNS THAT GLEAN THE RIGHT DATA

In Section II.2, we examined several ways to design informal experiments. The specific way that data are collected and organized is called the design of the experiment. The chief objective of a good design is to obtain more profitable information at costs generally lower than information gathered by traditional sampling techniques. (Read Section IV to learn how to sample.)

Also, in Section II.2, we discussed the anatomy of an experiment. There are independent (or experimental or explanatory) variables—the causes—which the researcher manipulates: promotion strategies, pricing, packaging, color, product quality, distribution channels.

The dependent variable—the effect—may be physical volume or money value of sales, contribution to profits, brand preference ratings, new product acceptance, attitudes.

The experimental unit—those subjects being observed—can be groups of consumers or potential customers, stores, product lines, sales territories.

Then there are external factors—those variables the researcher does not control: reactions of competitors, seasonality, fads, economic changes, government reports, customer attitudes, prices of substitute products or services, etc.

In this section we will develop some of the more formal experimental designs, formal because the results lend themselves to standard statistical manipulations. Two basic methods of experimental design are (a) blocking, and (b) replication with randomization. A blocking arrangement counterbalances potential sources of random errors so that experimental errors will cancel out. We begin with the Latin Square Design.

Latin Square Design

The Latin Square Design eliminates the before part of before-after experiments. The number of experimental units is a multiple of the number of experimental factors.

Suppose that a company wants to test three variables—promotion, price, and packaging—at three levels. In other words, management wants to determine sales reactions (the dependent variable) to promotion plans I, II, and III, to prices A, B, and C, and to package colors pink, purple, and platinum (all independent or experimental variables). To test every possible combination, 27 treatments are necessary ($3 \times 3 \times 3 = 27$).

The Latin Square Design is a simplified technique. Only nine treatments are applied to the experiment.

Of course, as with any cost shortcut, there is a price. No freebies prevail here either. The price (or risk of error) derives from the unstated assumption that the factors themselves do not interact and influence experimental results. If the factors do not interact, or if the degree of interaction is small, then the easier-to-use Latin Square Design will yield credible results.

An example will demonstrate how to use this technique. Returning to our dandelion root coffee substitute example, from Section II.2, let's say research data are desired on three package designs: a black package with white lettering (B), a yellow package with green lettering (Y), and a red package with black lettering (R). Three retail prices are experimented with: $3, $4, $5. Three promotional plans have been devised: I, II, III. The sales (in units) are recorded in parentheses in each block in Figure II.4.A.

A LATIN SQUARE DESIGN PROMOTION PLAN

	I	II	III
$5	5, I, B (1100)	5, II, Y (1150)	5, III, R (1200)
$4	4, I, Y (1320)	4, II, R (1390)	4, III, B (1220)
$3	3, I, R (1450)	3, II, B (1400)	3, III, Y (1500)

Package color
B = Black
Y = Yellow
R = Red

Figure II.4.A: A LATIN SQUARE DESIGN PROMOTION PLAN

The next step is to determine which combination of price, package, and promotion will produce the best results.

Note: Since we do not have cost data, we cannot determine which will result in the best financial outcome; the solution sought in this example is to maximize the volume of sales. These are the steps to maximize sales:

1. *First*, sum the sales figures for each vertical column, attributed to each promotional plan.
2. *Second*, sum the sales figures horizontally, attributable to each price.
3. *Third*, for each color, black, yellow, and red, sum the sales figures, attributable to package color.

PROMOTION: Σ I　= 3870; Σ II　= ⎡3940⎤; Σ III　= 3920

PRICE:　　　Σ $5 = 3450; Σ $4 = 3930; Σ $3 = ⎡4350⎤

PACKAGE:　　Σ B　= 3720; Σ Y　= 3970; Σ R　= ⎡4040⎤

Examining the highest sales figures for each category, it appears that Promotion Plan II is best, Price $3 is best, and Red package color is best. Putting it together, we can state that the combination that will yield the highest sales figures is: $3,II,R

But we did not test a 3,II,R combination! Now what do we do? For one thing, we have just discovered one of the shortcomings of the Latin Square Design: it's cheaper, but not perfect. In this instance, there are three likely solutions to consider:

(a) We can retest. But this time run the experiment with a 3,II,R combination. Since we are redoing it, why not run the experiment with nine new, untested combinations? Or we can design the experiment so that the three top combinations in this experiment are repeated along with six new ones. If funds and time are available, we can even test all 27 combinations.

(b) Accept the results and put company resources behind the 3,II,R combination. Although we might have found a better combination by further testing, calculations indicate the firm can increase profits with sales resulting from this planning configuration.

(c) A third solution is to forego the additional experimental expenses
　(a) in the risks of choosing, and,
　(b) examine the next best combination.

In this instance, the next best design is a $3,III,Y. Is that a risky choice?

First, we are confident about the $3 price. The highest sales figures are found in the $3 cells.

Second, the total sales computed for promotion plans II and III reveal very little difference, so small that we will consider them identical.

Third, although sales for red packages are significantly higher than for yellow ones, both yellow and red yielded substantially higher results than did the black package. There is a temptation to test a $3,III,R combination as well, or arbitrarily to choose the $3,III,R design.

Fourth, of results recorded in individual cells, the $3,III,Y package produced the highest sales figures, and that may be sufficient evidence to choose the last one.

Essentially the problem centers on color: red or yellow. One solution is to offer both red and yellow packages in the same stores, still using, of course, the $3 price, and promotion plan II or III. Or the two packages can be test-marketed along the lines discussed in Section II.1. If results are not close, as in this illustration, then option (c) above is excluded.

The other problem with the Latin Square Design is that it does not specify the relationship between the dependent variable and the experimental variables. The law of demand tells us that consumers will buy more of the product at lower than at higher prices. But the law of demand assumes everything else remains constant, which seldom happens. Consequently, we cannot measure the factor effect by computing the differences between cells.

But with application of variance analysis, we can determine the significance of these differences. A statistical technique that permits us to measure the importance of the treatment variables, analysis of variance is explained in Section V.4 of this handbook. It is a useful analytical tool.

What other types of experiments utilize the Latin Square Design? Apple producers wanted to know how color affected purchases, so an experiment was designed with red delicious apples in which the apples were segmented into three color grades: (A) highly colored; (B) partly red; (C) combination, about half red. Nine supermarkets in Atlanta, Georgia, participated.

Stores were divided into three groups. Approximately every two weeks the apple color grades were shifted among each group of stores so that each store offered each color grade one time during the six-week test. Rotation equalized the sales effects of non-test variables such as seasonality, characteristics and incomes of customers, price and display space, store location and size, price of substitute produce, etc.

In another experiment a Long Beach, California, newspaper tested color ads versus black and white ads. The experimental units were sales in furniture, jewelry, and variety stores. Color ads far outranked the black and white ads.

The Latin Square Design has also been used by industry associations to test the effect of various promotional programs. Consequently, the technique applies to a wide range of products and services and at any point along the distribution chain.

Randomized Design

Randomization begins before the experiment is designed. This design segments the experimental units. Each grouping constitutes a single trial or replication.

Replication is a technical statistical term that means repetition of the experiment. Its use here refers to the exposure of several test units within a block to the experimental variable.

Randomization means that each experimental unit has an equal chance of receiving a given experimental treatment.

Note: In the Latin Square Design, the numbers of groups and treatments are equal, such as a 3 × 3 Latin Square. This is not a requirement of the randomized block design.

An example will illustrate the technique. Assume the following: ten stores; one product; two prices (independent variables); value of sales (dependent variable).

Let's say that the product is ocean pout again, and we want to know the effect on sales of two experimental prices per pound of fish fillets: $1.39 a pound and $1.89 a pound.

The idea is to assign one price to five of the stores, and the second price to the other five stores, in random order. We can number the stores 1 through 10. Dropping ten numbered, folded pieces of paper into a hat and withdrawing them individually, or using the random numbers table in the Appendix, will produce random order.

Whatever the method chosen, the purpose is to equalize the probability that a store will be assigned one price. Stores numbered 1 through 5 will be assigned the $1.39 price. Stores randomly numbered 6 through 10 will receive the $1.89 price.

The reason we segment the experimental units into blocks is to reduce experimental error. The blocks can represent stores, as in our illustration, or time periods, or seasons, or whatever, to ensure that all experimental variables are exposed to the same set of external forces.

SALES RESULTS OF A RANDOMIZED EXPERIMENT OVER A TWO-WEEK TEST PERIOD

Store No.	$1.39	$1.89	Store No.
1	$309	$122	6
2	217	89	7
3	141	295	8
4	280	296	9
5	264	191	10
Averages	$242.20	$198.60	

Figure II.4.B: SALES RESULTS OF A RANDOMIZED EXPERIMENT OVER A TWO-WEEK TEST PERIOD

In Figure II.4.B, we read the sales figures for each store. At $1.39 per pound, Store No. 1 sold $309 worth of fish fillets, while, at the low end, Store No. 3 sold only $141 worth of the same fish over the same two-week interval.

Among the $1.89 units, Store No. 7 did worst, with only $89 in sales; while Store No. 9 topped the group, with $296 in sales of fish fillets over the same two-week period.

The last figure in each column in the table is the *mean*. It is computed by summing the five sales figures in each column and separately dividing by five, the number of units in each group, to obtain the average sales per store. (See Section V, especially V.2, for more on the population mean.)

In focusing on comparative experiments, we are less interested in the average sales of each group of stores and more interested in the difference between the two population experimental treatment averages. Therefore, the best estimate of the difference between the two population treatment means is the difference between the two sample means. (If you are unfamiliar with, or need to review, sampling methods and problems associated with sampling, please refer to Section IV.)

In other words, the difference in means between our two samples of five stores each is projected more or less to represent results we could have expected if we had experimented with all possible stores (the population).

The difference,

$$\$242.20 - \$198.60 = \$43.60,$$

suggests to us that, based on the experiment, the lower price of $1.39 a pound should generate, on the average, $43.60 more sales per store biweekly. This analysis of the randomized experimental design provides point estimates, or single-valued estimates, of two sample averages and their difference.

Suppose we had exposed 100 stores to each experimental variable (price). As sample sizes increase, we should expect the mean differences to diminish. Why? Because larger numbers tend to approximate the total population. (Refer to Sections IV and V for further explication.)

Consequently, we suspect that since such estimates are vulnerable to sampling errors, we need to subject the data to further statistical analysis.

With confidence intervals (Section V.2) we can specify the intervals within which we can reasonably expect the population means to be located. However, a discussion of confidence intervals and other statistical tools of analysis is reserved for Section V of this reference book of profitable marketing research ideas.

II.5: HOW TO MINE A NATURAL DEPOSIT OF DAZZLING OPINIONS WITH THE DELPHI TECHNIQUE

Some people consider this technique the most powerful one in this book. It must be powerful, because the U.S. military, for some years, treated it as classified information, despite the fact that it had been in use for at least ten years.

Delphi, presented here as another idea-generating profit-raiser, may (or may not) develop futuristic products or services that will better serve the needs of your customers. Already, for many years, Delphi has served a variety of organizations and industries, particularly high-technology ones, and in decision-making areas concerned with long-term policy formulations.

Opinion-Gathering for Profit

Educational institutions, city and state governments, and non-profit organizations have latched onto this technique. It has been applied to problems in the electronics, communications, computer, glass, chemical, retailing, cosmetics, toiletries, aerospace, investment, health care, and many other industries.

An English survey revealed that firms manufacturing glass containers, chemicals, electronics, and plastics, among others, have used the technique. A Canadian firm carried out a three-year Delphi study to forecast the possible market adoption of a number of services. An American corporation employed the technique to predict future changes in department stores. A governmental agency applied Delphi methodology to predict the impact of a new land-use policy. An educational institution adopted it to project course demand and curriculum changes. And a book company has enlisted it to predict top sellers over the next decade.

Although Delphi has been pressed into service to anticipate future world events, new products and product applications, possible inventions and technologies, despite its nomenclature, it is certainly not oracular. We live within the constraints of an unknowable future. Perhaps the Creator designed it this way to shape, sharpen, and stimulate our own personal development and to make us aware that He, not the state, still reigns.

Delphi, really an opinion-gathering mechanism, is designed to secure the best performance of experts when their minds are focused on specific questions or issues or problems. Definitely it is not a brainstorming or think-tank approach to profitable brain-mining. It is a forecasting method based on refinements in group estimation techniques.

Actually, its purpose is to avoid some of the basic problems of face-to-face groups in order to achieve a reliable consensus from a group of knowledgeable people on specific future events (or products) or trends.

The technique may be summarized thus: since one expert may be wrong about the future, averaging the opinions of several experts somehow approaches the true outcome.

Before you argue that the median of ten wrong answers does not produce a single right one, and then cite Socialist and Communist failures (and by the way, the technique is used in the Soviet Union) as examples, let me add that I quite agree with you. In fact, the Delphi experiments conducted with non-experts did not yield good predictive results in those areas requiring basic business or product knowledge.

One essential condition is that Delphi research depends upon persons who are reasonably knowledgeable about the business environment, market, or product. Perhaps one can argue that those who are experts also help to shape future trends (through invention or opinion). Therefore, a convergence of expert opinions is a reflection of tendencies which, already in the making, do eventually emerge.

Certainly Delphi does not substitute for routine decision-making or for short-term market strategy formulation. It is one approach to long-range planning, a method of generating information for establishing priorities, or obtaining solutions to marketing problems, or for evaluating marketing planning, a trend impact analysis.

Another marketing application is subjective probability estimates: what is the likelihood sales will be high, or low, or so-so? Or try this growth-directed idea: attempt to develop a long-range optimal marketing strategy.

Components of Delphi

Three elements stand out in the Delphi process:

1. Anonymity.
2. Controlled feedback.
3. Statistical group response.

• *Anonymity* means that either (a) the group of knowledgeable persons does not know who is participating in the project, or (b) if they do know, in no way are they to communicate with one another. The purpose is not secrecy. In face-to-face discussions there are always some persons who dominate either discussions or opinions, due to personality, position, or knowledge. (Refer back to Sections I.6 and I.7 for more on this issue.) Anonymity eliminates this problem of group dynamics.

• *Controlled feedback* means that in each round of questionnaires, the participants know something of how others have responded. The novelty can provide an environment that motivates participants to respond thoughtfully and continue the experiment. Systematic procedures contribute to a feeling of objectivity both in the experiment design and in its outcomes. Too, the combination of anonymity and controlled feedback allows respondents to change their opinions, whereas in direct group interaction a participant may feel obligated (to his or her ego) to defend even an untenable position.

• *Statistical group response* means that the opinion of every respondent is valued, considered, and entered in the computational summaries. Norman Dalkey says, "I can state from my own experience, and also from the experience of many other practitioners, that the results of a Delphi exercise are subject to greater acceptance on the part of the group than are the consensuses arrived at by more direct means of interaction."

The theory underlying this method is (a) with repetition, responses will converge towards some central set of opinions; and, (b) this convergence of opinions will more closely resemble the true outcome, or response, with repetition.

Nine Steps to the Oracle

Here are the steps followed in a Delphi procedure:

1. The objective(s) (problems and events) of the exercise is clearly defined.
2. From this step, a series of questions is carefully designed to encourage continued participation of respondents in the experiment and to elicit information from them that conforms to the purposes established.
3. A group of knowledgeable people is selected (which may also entail some pretesting) in such a way as to eliminate any direct confrontation and to allow for their opinions to move toward a consensus. A group of 15 to 30 persons seems like a manageable number, large enough to generate some profitable information—although larger groups have been used with success. (Your available time and resources will figure as constraints as well.)
4. Distribute the questionnaire.
5. After the initial responses from the first questionnaire are tabulated, respondents are asked to indicate what additional information they need. They should also indicate what information they have to share to assist other participants in the decision process.
6. Opinions from the group are withheld. Facts tabulated from answers on the questionnaires are provided to the respondents. (If no consistent pattern shows up on the first round, sometimes those figures are withheld. However, such tabular results will precede or accompany each round of questions.)
7. The process (Step 5 and especially 6) is repeated at least once or twice, even oftener if desirable, until sufficient convergence of predictions prevails, or diminishing returns become evident.
8. Interpret, analyze, and adjust extreme responses that may have resulted from inappropriate assumptions or misinterpreted data.

9. Process the end results which should now reflect not only a convergence of opinions but a consensus of assumptions and data interpretation that underlie these projections.

Some Innovative Ideas

Before examining more closely these nine steps, and providing you with *caveats*, let's look at some further examples of its application.

NEXT magazine published a list of 28 stocks likely to be winners in this decade. (Naturally we will not list them here.) As reported in *Computer Career News*, more than a thousand Delphi polls have been conducted in the last decade, including other investment areas such as predictions on the direction of short-term interest rates.

An often-mentioned example, described initially in *Industrial Marketing Management*, the ten-year forecast of electronic components by Corning Glass Works is cited as a successful Delphi experiment.

In another one, 28 respondents cooperated in assessing a proposed revision of the *Oregon Business Review*. One objective of this design was to project the number of subscriptions which would probably result from the new format and promotional plan. The opinions were stated in probabilistic terms, such as, there was an estimated 53 percent chance of obtaining 2,000 to 4,000 subscriptions but only a 2 percent likelihood that subscriptions would exceed 8,000.

Here is a fruitful approach for making sales projections. Skandia Insurance Company some years ago explored the future of computer usage, risks of misuse and malfunction, and possible remedies for these risks. MacMillan Bloedel, Ltd., sponsored a study to assess those factors that would have a significant impact on the demand for newsprint and newspapers over a 30-year interval. AT & T used 210 respondents to examine how government regulation, social changes, existing and new services, labor force, and urban change might affect the communications business.

Nailing It Down

Now let's probe the steps further. The flow chart in Figure II.5.A illustrates the process involved in applying the technique, built on information summarized from the nine steps.

• Step number one has been highlighted on several occasions in this book. Without a clearly defined problem and set of objectives, no market research should be undertaken, or further expenditures made. Since this matter has been discussed adequately earlier in the book, it will not require additional comments here.

• Step number two is to design the first set of questions building upon statements already made in step number 1. Accompanying the questionnaire, adequate background information, complete with a precise statement of assumptions and

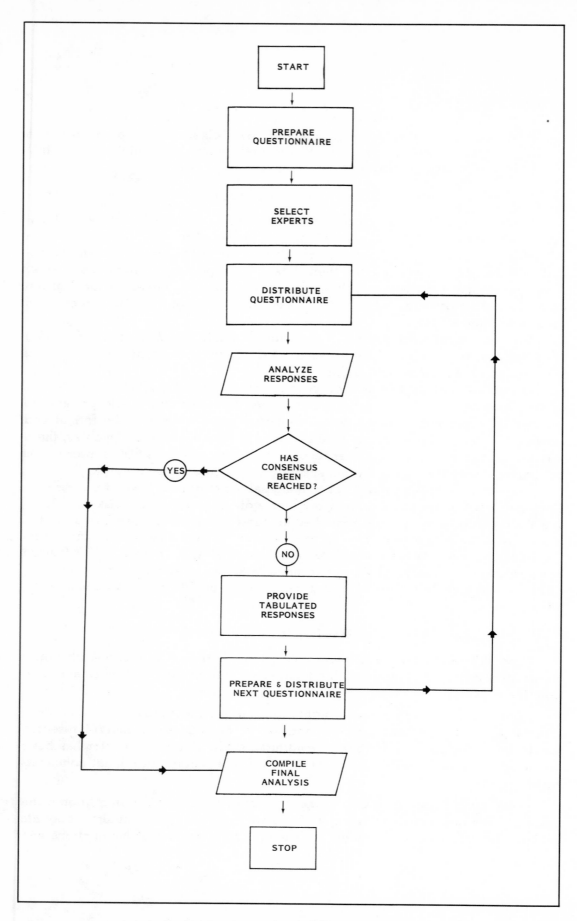

Figure II.5.A: FLOW CHART OF DELPHI TECHNIQUE

conditions, should be included. If additional explanation is needed to back up a particular question, such information should be contained within the questionnaire (or material appended with the mailing). If the issue can be stated in specific terms, each response will consist of the respondent's opinion, his reasoning, and the facts he considered in arriving at that opinion.

Sometimes the issue is handled better with open-ended questions. (Both Sections I.3 and II.2 treat the matter of open-ended or unstructured questions in greater detail.) Some questionnaires are so long that they require half a day to answer, or even to consult with other experts. Others consist of a few questions.

For your purposes, fewer questions, where the respondent can spend two or three minutes of thought on each, are preferable to many questions that demand quick, associative type answers. After all, you want opinion, not fun and games. Leave the latter to the psychologists. If questions are ambiguous, then responses will be ambiguous. My personal preference is a questionnaire restricted to 15 or fewer questions, especially on the first round. Respect other people's time and appreciate their effort to provide you with valid responses.

• In step number three, from a group of knowledgeable persons, select a representative sample, small enough to direct, and large enough to compensate for potential dropouts so that final tabulations will not register the opinions of too few respondents.

Some problems may arise at this point: (a) you may not know many people who are knowledgeable in the subject area; (b) your entire sample may be the entire list of potential participants.

If that occurs, is your list truly a representative sample or only a convenient list of persons? If they are friends, will their opinions differ significantly from yours, or will they be able to offer new insights?

Should you choose individuals entirely within or without the organization? The AT & T study mentioned above consisted of 210 persons from both within and without. If they are all from within, you may have difficulty keeping the respondents apart unless they belong to a large organization, or one widely spread geographically.

• Step number four is obvious.

• Step number five may or may not apply to your marketing problem. This is determined partly by how you have handled step number 3.

• At step number six the sharp criticism begins. The theory underlying the Delphi procedure is to reach a meeting of the minds, a convergence of opinions. The assumption implied is that the true answer is the common one.

• In step number seven, conformity is encouraged through feedback (step number 6). In a sense individuality is penalized. One purpose of the Delphi technique is to avoid those problems created by face-to-face groups in which one or a few persons dominate, and to eliminate the halo and bandwagon effects. Still, those shortcomings are partially neutralized through feedback and the encouragement to reach a consensus.

Consensus seems paramount in Socialist systems, for example. In this country, survival and advancement in a state bureaucracy pivot on blending in with the group. Most educational institutions (even many so-called private ones) operate on the same principle. The same is true of large nonprofit organizations. Even many private (and regulated) enterprises function little differently from bureaucracies. Conformity is the rule, not the exception. A philosophy of not rocking the boat pervades businesses of all sizes. Individuality is discouraged, often severely penalized.

Even among most university professors, some of whom not many years ago marched for something called academic freedom, socialistic conformity is encouraged, if not mandated. Promotion and tenure processes in major universities penalize individuality, despite the cry of academic freedom. These processes call for professors to publish in academic journals. But academic journals are edited by other professors who form their opinions out of the great consensus. Consequently, articles showing any spirit of individuality, free enterprise, or non-welfarist arguments are rejected (usually months after submission, to discourage resubmissions elsewhere).

Although universities are supposed to be the fountainhead of new ideas and research, most of the research money comes from governmental agencies or private foundations allied with the bureaucracy. Money is simply not allocated for research that does not conform to bureaucratic norms. Both academic freedom and individuality in all but a handful of private colleges are myths.

These professors teach students who then are employed by the business sector, despite their prevalent anti-free enterprise bias. They employ others with a similar bent. These students become knowledgeable in their field, and some become Delphi respondents. They have long been conditioned to think uniformly, for conformity is rewarded.

Creative individuals organize their own research organizations because the public ones do not always perform adequately. And the great ideas of tomorrow more often spring from those whose opinions do not converge.

If the technique is that bad, you may wonder why I have even included it in this book. Many organizations do use this methodology, although the exact form of research may follow some modification of the basic technique outlined here. It is popular and has been used with success. Sometimes it produces rather accurate forecasts. There are advantages as well. Perhaps these should be reiterated to conclude this section.

(a) You may have already made some preliminary forecasts—by whatever method. With additional input from Delphi results, you can realign your final forecast and develop a market strategy that suits your company's needs and personality of management.

(b) If you have structured the design well, in some sense it is like having outside directors serve on your board. If they are active, and knowledgeable about your business environment and goals, they are valuable assets in the management of your enterprise. Otherwise, they are as useful, perhaps even as damaging, to your firm as poor Delphi results. Your judgment counts here.

(c) Building on the (b) advantage, you can gain the benefit of the best thinking and best experience to develop a forecast, and outside people can bring in fresh ideas or a new perspective. Some of the best ideas emanate from persons in another field looking at your problem from another angle, for they are not handicapped by the structured knowledge usually passed along in the same profession. In other words, they did not know it couldn't be done that way.

(d) The technique avoids some of the problems coming out of panel discussions. Effective panel discussions depend upon an effective moderator; with Delphi, an effective director of the study can produce superior results.

As with all methods, there is no definitive answer, but perhaps some of the ideas developed in this section will have helped you further toward your profit goals. Now that you have a good grasp of data collection and research design techniques, let's move on to measurements of attitudes, interests, and opinions.

SECTION *III*

ATTITUDE MEASUREMENT

"That which is far off, and exceeding deep, who can find it out?"

Ecclesiastes 7:24

INTRODUCTION

Gordon Kreh, of the Hartford Steam Boiler Inspection and Insurance Company, states: "With just a sales force, you try to persuade the customer to buy what is available, but when you provide a Marketing Department, you try to furnish what the customer wants." And when you try to find out who are your customers, what they want today, probably will want tomorrow, and why or why not they like your product or service, marketing research takes over.

In the market analysis process both customers and market considerations are taken into account. Initially, in Section I, we began research by defining the market structure, and sought to gather information on

- ◎ number of competitors.
- ◎ market share of each competitor.
- ◎ policies and tactics of chief competitors.
- ◎ characteristics of competing products or services.
- ◎ product differentiation.

Then later, in Sections I and II, center stage was held by characteristics of customers and data on buying habits and preferences, such as

- ◎ characteristics of customers.
- ◎ demographics of customers.
- ◎ number of potential buyers.
- ◎ location of buyers.
- ◎ size and frequency of purchases.
- ◎ when buyers buy, including seasonality.
- ◎ brand loyalty.
- ◎ how buyers buy.

Section III is concerned with attitudes and motivation of buyers, the *why* part of the question, which specifies such items as

- ◎ why buyers buy.
- ◎ attitudes and preferences of purchasers.
- ◎ what motivates buyers to purchase initially.

◎ what triggers repeat sales.
◎ brand loyalty, impulse purchases, planned consumption.
◎ changes in buying habits.
◎ buyer resistance.
◎ differential analysis.

Of the several techniques discussed in the following pages, semantic differential ranks highest for all sizes of firms and all types of organizations: retailing, wholesaling, industrial, communications, marketing research, consulting, finance, insurance, and service companies. Therefore, proportionately more space is devoted to that subsection which spells out both a telephone application and the staple scale, five detailed steps, and partial examples of survey questionnaires.

The next method, projective and expressive psychological techniques, is of least importance to management of industrial firms, but of considerable value to consumer-type businesses, service companies, market research organizations, and consulting firms. For retailers and wholesalers it ranks about equal in use with semantic differential techniques. For firms with sales under $200 million, this method ranks second among various attitude measures, but for the largest companies, it ranks third. These techniques deal with word and sentence completion, story completion, and role-playing, *inter alia*.

Ranking and Likert Summated Scales, in the third subsection, are as important as projective techniques for service companies, finance, insurance, utilities, communications, and marketing research firms. The largest firms, those with sales over $200 million, regard Likert Scales on a par with psychological techniques, i.e., in third place below multidimensional scaling.

The following subsection explains how to use several other scales: constant sum scale and five steps to Q-sort, with reference to Thurstone and Guttman's scales, and Kelly's construct. These techniques are only rarely used by industrial firms, but are more widely used by communications and consumer businesses.

The last one, multidimensional scaling, is most popular among the very largest organizations; however, the author notes that not all concerns have adequate marketing research resources for its profitable application, and during the last couple of years it appears that in some instances more sophisticated techniques and analyses are replacing it.

III.1: FIVE LOW-COST STEPS TO SEMANTIC DIFFERENTIAL: KEY MEASUREMENT TOOL

The semantic differential method holds this fundamental advantage: it is easy to use; fast to administer. Performance compares with the more expensive and more complicated scaling techniques, discussed later in this section of the book.

And you can expect the data to register fairly small differences of buyers' attitudes toward your product, or company, just as reliably as with other methods, and even better than some.

Not Just for the Big Boys

If you think this technique works well only for the big budget businesses, here is another pleasant surprise.

A gasoline station owner, whose business included minor auto repairs, wanted to pinpoint why the station played second string to other area competitors, and to discover how to upgrade the firm's image. The complete study embraced 250 customers, on site, and another 250 area residents.

Considering the amount of data gathered, and expensive computer analysis that followed, the study should have cost the owner around $5,000—but it did not. Because the independent market researcher who coordinated the project wanted additional data for his own use, and due to some free student assistance, the actual cost was substantially less. (You can do a similar study on your own for a few hundred dollars and some evening time.)

Several concrete, practical, and inexpensive recommendations surfaced from this analysis. This true story might have had a profitable ending, but the station owner became perturbed because, I suppose, her self-image overreached that perceived by the respondents. Consequently, she refused to implement one single recommendation. (Checking on the business as of yesterday, I can report that it is still struggling, but hardly profitably.)

Predictive Success in Other Cultures

Semantic differential scales can yield attitude scores similar to those obtained by the Likert method (in Section III.4). Therefore, marketing strategists who want to improve predictive success from studies of other cultures, as well as in the domestic market, have made successful use of the semantic differential approach to attitude and image questions.

For example, attitude scaling has spotlighted differences between English Canadians and French Canadians in Quebec Province. Another one: an organization wanted to know how the Japanese and Americans rated various products from different countries, products manufactured not only in the U.S. and Japan but in selected European countries as well.

Some English studies on advertising research plotted the profitable application of the semantic differential method on the best promotional plan to change English attitudes toward using a service. Although it was a tall order, the industry-wide campaign worked. Service sales increased at the retail end, and suppliers' profits rose at the manufacturer's end. Rather than focus on cross-cultural analysis, we will reflect mainly on American experiences and applications.

Do You Love Me?

Exactly what is meant by the term "semantic differential"? Perhaps such a fancy term deserves a fancy definition: "It is the repetitious measurement of a concept compared against a series of descriptive polar-adjectival scales."

On a bi-polar scale, boy asks girl: "Do you love me?" He expects her to say yes or no. But there are shades of meaning. So if the girl says "yes," the boy wants to pinpoint exactly where in this semantic space her true feelings lie.

So he repeats the experiment and asks, "How much?" Which implies that she is to pick a number from 1 to 7, from "very little" to "very much." Picking a Number 4 response presumably is neutral, noncommittal—halfway between very little and very much—a so-so answer.

Of course, if she refuses to play the numbers game, she may opt for "I don't know," or a coy semantical distinction. The computerized brain will answer, "That concept is not in my vocabulary."

Semantic differential is a technique to be used to discover just how much your customers like (or dislike) you (i.e., your company or product), and to provide some information on how quickly your customers may respond to offers of another suitor. If you probe deeply enough, and properly formulate the experiment, they will even tell you what you need to do to avoid separation or divorce.

Some Money-Saving Advantages

The technique offers some distinct advantages for promotion planning, store image assessment, target advertising, new store and layout ideas, product differentiation, use with life style analysis, ascertaining brand or store loyalty, opinion polls, and other areas that may well fit your needs at this moment. Note these money-saving advantages:

1. Quick and clean, it is an efficient method for developing customer, brand, product, company profiles.

2. The data are easily quantifiable and can yield sufficient information for immediate decisions; or the evidence may point toward areas of further research.
3. The experiment can be repeated with the same or different groups. Generally, other things being equal, results are fairly reliable and satisfactory.
4. It can supply information on your competitors' weaknesses and strengths.
5. It does not take long for each respondent to complete—a distinct advantage over other interviewing techniques brought out in Section I. In fact, the quick responses are most desirable, to avoid the standard answers, the ah . . . ummm ones.
6. The technique is adaptable for use with many types of respondents and responses. With it you can zero in on a specific type of customer or specific store or brand attributes, or even use it for broad, macro-type studies.
7. You can develop a deeper profile than with other quick response techniques. With modification of the questionnaire you can even induce the respondent to add adjectives beneficial in later studies. (Other adjectives you may want to file away—permanently.)
8. The method eliminates some of the question-formulation problems mentioned in Section I: ambiguity, unclear statements, overlapping, questions too complicated for inarticulate persons.
9. Although the approach seems to work best directly, it can be adapted for telephone interviewing, and even for mail surveys, the least desirable way to go about it.

Five Steps to Successful Measurement

But we did not promise the world or even a rose garden—only some ideas for profitable recycling. If this technique seems to cover present marketing research needs, let us first see how to do it, and then examine a successful design or two.

STEP 1. Define Your Objectives.

Why do you want to spend money for this study? What do you hope to learn from an analysis of the evidence? Which opportunities exist that will allow you to turn these data to profitable employment? Without purpose, such information becomes profit-absorbing rather than profit-producing. Perhaps one of the following examples fits your requirements as well.

(a) Check ads to determine whether the picture or message in your ad (or proposed copy) is interpreted by respondents as you had intended. For instance, let's say that your business is the sale of cassettes, books, and seminars on how to be and act successful and that your ad copy includes a photo of a model who presumably portrays the posture of a well-dressed, successful, self-reliant, and responsible person. On your questionnaire list those desirable attributes and image concepts along with their respective opposites. Then ask a sample of respondents to rate, on a scale, how they perceive the ad. If they see it less favorably than you, start again (and hire a new model, too).

(b) If you really enjoy games, then undertake objective (a) but for your competitor's advertisements. In this manner you should discover what interests potential clients, what causes them to glance at an ad in the first place, and what motivates them to act. You are practically asking potential customers to write your ad copy. Your advertisements, then, simply reflect what customers say they want to read or hear.

(c) A further refinement of the ideas in (a) and (b) is to employ the semantic differential in comparative studies: yours versus theirs. One company did exactly this to compare their store image against those of nearby competitors. How the store compared with its three chief competitors was the objective. They found out, too.

(d) Or turn the (c) objective around and use the technique for the purpose of learning of your competitors' deficiencies. This is a variation of the time-worn dictum: find a need and fill it. In planning a new store, for example, such valuable information suggests what to do and what to avoid. In fact, this may be the cheapest way to shift the learning curve to your advantage, and reduce learning costs and time.

(e) If you recently opened a new store, office or branch, the semantic differential method easily identifies new customers who visit the establishment during opening weeks. Researchers say that you should not wait too long lest habits and images (especially negative ones) become too well ingrained. Wait just long enough (a few weeks) for some attitudes toward your business to emerge; but do the survey soon enough to correct deficiencies before the (bad) word spreads.

(f) Consumer profile ratings tell us the kind of people who buy a particular product or brand. Some beer and automobile studies are especially well known.

Play a game with yourself. Write all the characteristics that *you* think describe the typical beer drinker (opposed to the typical wine or scotch drinker). Did you not develop a fairly concrete picture of the average beer drinker in your mind's eye with respect to the beer drinker's income, cultural interest, travel and vacation preferences, hobbies, type of entertainment, employment, and other personal factors? Compare that picture with what you think the imported beer drinker is like. Different? Or answer these questions: What kind of persons drive Chevrolets or Volkswagens? Lincolns, Cadillacs, or Jaguars? How do they compare?

People buy or shun certain products or services because of perceived images or aspects attributed to those products. We imagine ourselves, in many instances, to be like (or unlike) those other consumers who are thought to buy (or not buy) the product, or trade at a certain store, or prefer certain lawyers or physicians. Perhaps some persons actually personify products, and, like primitives, believe that qualities inherent (or thought to be, at least) in the product are transferred to the user by its consumption.

Companies often buy equipment only from the most prestigious firms, or bank only with the largest, or deal only with the Big-8 (or 9), because some of that prestige is thought to rub off onto the purchasing company's image.

An interesting example happened some years ago with Avon products in Mexico City. When maids—those who worked in the best residential districts—began exuding the expensive (to them) Avon odor, their bosses stopped buying the products. There are differences. Distinctions extend beyond income and dress.

(g) Although this is a tougher objective to accomplish, you can employ the semantic differential method to determine some or several aspects of the patronage decisions process. You will discover not only why clients buy your products, or trade at your store or shopping center, but, more specifically, how they go about deciding, i.e., the decision-making process itself.

(h) Also, you can use the technique in follow-up studies to verify the results of a previous study. Here's an idea. Do a study while a product, or branch office, or idea, is still in the planning stages; revise according to the outcome of the semantic differential survey. Do a second study after the product is on the market a few weeks; revise your product, package, or plan, if necessary. Then, do a third study several months later; compare the results.

(i) Follow-up studies are particularly beneficial in auditing and revising a promotional plan. That can be tied in with the (h) objective, whether for retail trade, industry-wide promotion, or industrial marketing.

(j) Too, the idea in (h) is a natural for testing package design, copy on the package, color, or other package characteristics. Naturally, the semantic scale in this case is geared to product characteristics, not customer characteristics.

(k) Product differentiation, while often sought, may be a quixotic gambit, or quite ephemeral. Some achieve it. Some think they achieve it. Many do not. As one economist put it: "You can fool some of the people over narrow price differences, but not many over wide price differentials." (Ralph H. Blodgett, if you were curious.) This research technique may confirm whether or not your customers perceive the same degree of differential that you thought had been built into the product and promotion.

STEP 2. Questions and Responses.

When C.E. Osgood first worked out this technique, unmodified adjectives were paired: good-bad, sweet-sour, and so on. Initially, seven responses were used by researchers for fine shades of meaning.

Five responses seem more typical in marketing research: very, slightly, neither, slightly, very. With answers ranging from very good to very bad, these, then, are scored in preparation for quantitative analysis and evaluation. Occasionally, a researcher has employed nine shades of meaning for each pair of adjectival terms. Nine may become cumbersome to handle and evaluate.

However, a problem crops up with the use of an odd number of responses (3, 5, 7, 9). For too many years, and still true today, students in public educational institutions are encouraged to follow a middle course, inappropriately tagged a moderate course. (These are not at all synonymous terms.) "Here is the Left position, and here is the Right position; which do you think is best?" The safe answer, of course (the one resulting in the best grade), is neither and both—nonalignment.

Similar reflexive reaction sometimes shows up in surveys; grouped answers will tend to reflect a middle ground—hardly appropriate for decision-making and policy implementation. To block this occurrence allow only an even number of possible responses, which forces the respondent to take a position, even if only moderately toward one end or the other of the scale.

A second problem in semantic differentials, that has shown up in marketing research, is that many people shy away from absolutes. Philosophically, many so-called moderns (so-called because these ideas are really age-old, not contemporary) have moved away from a concept of the Absolute, and, consistent with prevalent Existentialist thought, have adopted Relativism. "There are no absolute morals; everything is relative."

(Perhaps I should point out that Relativism does lead to political Absolutism, where the state, not God, becomes the source of morality, truth, prosperity, and justice. This pattern of thinking conforms with the middle-of-the-road position mentioned above.)

Therefore, the good-bad pairing needs softening or modification in order to be compatible with prevailing popular philosophies. A modified pair of adjectives may read: fairly good—fairly bad. Not every term, of course, will require a modifier.

A third problem, which springs from the same philosophical base, is the reluctance to express strongly negative opinions about a product, service, or company. The message seems to be "Don't offend, at least not to his face. But stab him in the back at first chance."

Obviously these remarks are not universally valid; but the tendency strongly prevails. If we prepare ourselves to deal with this form of hypocrisy when developing questionnaires, then we can place the burden of interpretation in the researcher's office, not lay it at the respondent's back door.

A technique for circumventing this "very, slightly, neither, slightly, very, good-bad" measurement scale is to bias it leftward, in keeping with actual (not nominal) philosophical bias. The example illustrated in Figure III.1.A, rather than portraying an ideal format, encompasses solutions to these three problems by modifying the semantic differential method from its initial and intended structure.

EXAMPLE OF A MODIFIED SEMANTIC DIFFERENTIAL RESEARCH QUESTIONNAIRE

What do you think of the store?

	Excellent 4	Satis-factory 3	So-So 2	Unsatis-factory 1	
Fast service	____	____	____	____	Slow service
Clean	____	____	____	____	Dirty
Spacious	____	____	____	____	Cluttered
Many brands	____	____	____	____	Few brands
Friendly employees	____	____	____	____	Indifferent employees
Modern	____	____	____	____	Outdated
High quality	____	____	____	____	Low quality
Easy to shop	____	____	____	____	Disorganized
Well stocked	____	____	____	____	Often out of stock
Convenient loca-tion	____	____	____	____	Inconvenient location
Low prices	____	____	____	____	High prices
Helpful employees	____	____	____	____	Discourteous em-ployees
Informative ads	____	____	____	____	Uninformative ads
Known by friends	____	____	____	____	Unknown by friends
Liked by friends	____	____	____	____	Disliked by friends
Good value for money spent	____	____	____	____	Low value for money spent
Many specials	____	____	____	____	Few specials
Honest	____	____	____	____	Dishonest
Better values than other stores	____	____	____	____	Fewer values than other stores
Convenient hours	____	____	____	____	Inconvenient hours

Figure III.1.A: EXAMPLE OF A MODIFIED SEMANTIC DIFFERENTIAL RESEARCH QUESTIONNAIRE

If scores range between excellent and satisfactory, then management is probably on the right track. If my own business scored between satisfactory and so-so, I would consider that a danger signal and take appropriate steps. An even lower score would alarm me. In one respect "so-so" is noncommittal; but who wants to run a so-so company (or product)?

How many adjectival pairs should appear in your survey? My answer is fewer than you now have or contemplate having.

Exclusions prescribe savage scissoring. Severely edit, or let your colleagues do it. Do not overburden or bore your respondents, especially if you survey several stores (products) at the same time.

Of course, the respondent will run through the second and third lists faster because rapid learning occurs during completion of the set of identical questions on the first store or product. Some economies of time accrue here.

Another good idea is to break up copy. This has several advantages:

1. It is easier on the eye.
2. The amount of copy in the questions looks less formidable than if it were set densely.
3. Group headings provide good transitions and direct the respondent's mind toward specific categories of information.
4. It is easier for the interviewer as well to follow.
5. Scoring and analysis may be more appropriate with grouped data when developing plans and solutions.

The partial example exhibited in Figure III.1.B demonstrates another approach. It groups adjectives by categories. Note too, in this illustration, a five-answer response prevails. Two conditions of key importance ought to be kept in mind:

o—➤ Do not expect the same pairs of adjectives to measure every exploratory concept. Product concepts, store concepts, self-image concepts—all possess different qualities and have different meanings in a different context.

o—➤ Suppose you ask respondents to rate ballet, theater and jai alai attendees, and themselves. The ideal self-image is quite sensitive to the social desirability of the adjectives employed. Responses tend to reflect the respondent's interpretation of the social ideal rather than a true self-rating.

Where do all those pairs of adjectives come from? How can you discover whether pairs are truly opposites? Let us begin with the cheapest method and progress to more expensive ones.

(a) Do an informal in-house survey among your own employees (and all the salespeople who walk through the door). Include yourself.
(b) Carefully examine ad copy of your competitors and even of producers of similar, but not directly competitive, products or services.
(c) If you have already done group interviews, rerun those tapes, or reread those transcripts, but this time keep your ear or eye alert for appropriately descriptive words and phrases.
(d) Examine several dozen issues of magazines that relate to your market target or product. Look at ads and articles, editorials, and letters.
(e) Word association games may be played in one of several ways. *One way*: Give interviewees (perhaps students from a local college) a word, and ask them to write or state the opposite word that first flashes into their minds. The word "pretty" may evoke such antonymous responses as ugly, a dog, smart, mean, awful, etc. Of course, choose the most frequently used term. *Another way*: Ask persons to describe in five words or less the opposite of something that you have described (or shown them a picture of); for instance: "What is the opposite of a person who wears gloves while driving her car?" Which may result in such

PARTIAL EXAMPLE OF A SEMANTIC DIFFERENTIAL SURVEY OF A DENTIST'S OFFICE

	Very	Somewhat	Neither	Somewhat	Very	
PHYSICAL CHARACTERISTICS OF THE OFFICE:						
Cheerful	X	X	X	X	X	Depressing
Comfortable	X	X	X	X	X	Uncomfortable
Clean	X	X	X	X	X	Disordered
Attractive decor	X	X	X	X	X	Unattractive decor
Feel relaxed	X	X	X	X	X	Feel uptight
DENTISTS AND PERSONNEL:						
Friendly	X	X	X	X	X	Indifferent
Too many	X	X	X	X	X	Not enough
Modern	X	X	X	X	X	Old fashioned
Feel comfortable with	X	X	X	X	X	Feel uncomfortable with
Seem knowledge-able	X	X	X	X	X	Seem inexperienced
People I can trust	X	X	X	X	X	Not sure I can trust
Talkative	X	X	X	X	X	Quiet
Informative	X	X	X	X	X	Secretive
Courteous	X	X	X	X	X	Discourteous
Answer my questions	X	X	X	X	X	Avoid my questions
YOUR FRIENDS AND THE CLINIC:						
Known to your friends	X	X	X	X	X	Unknown to your friends
Well liked by your friends	X	X	X	X	X	Disliked by your friends
Recommended by your friends	X	X	X	X	X	Not recommended by your friends
Recommended by you to friends	X	X	X	X	X	Not recommended by you to friends
Many friends come here	X	X	X	X	X	Few friends come here

Figure III.1.B: PARTIAL EXAMPLE OF A SEMANTIC DIFFERENTIAL SURVEY OF A DENTIST'S OFFICE

opposing adjectives as "modern" or "free-spirit" or "friendly" or who knows what.

(f) A more expensive approach, running a preliminary survey on your competition, may yield some rich data.

(g) A couple of other ideas appear further along, where adjective-pairs are generated in later stages of the process.

STEP 3. Pretest.

A pretest of the opinion measures may be omitted, but even minimal energies spent in this direction can improve the quality of the research, hence the quality of responses, and from that we can infer that marketing decisions will yield that extra ounce of profit. How does pretesting improve the questionnaire?

- ◎ By eliminating redundancy.
- ◎ By eliminating (and substituting for) muddy concepts and phrases.
- ◎ By eliminating terms or concepts that ordinarily a respondent would not use.
- ◎ By eliminating don't know-type responses.

Redundancy unnecessarily lengthens a questionnaire. It can even create the wrong impressions in the respondent's mind, particularly with industrial accounts. Both redundancy and unclear concepts communicate fuzziness, poor organization, and "Do those guys really know what they're doing?"

What may seem perfectly clear to you may appear otherwise to the respondent. Remember that the respondent has other matters to attend to, other things on his mind, and he will not take the time to sort out what a set of measures really implies.

Some respondents will perceive that some adjectives do not match the intended concept. I know of no way to score 100 percent on this issue. Even an extremely homogeneous group of persons will not totally agree on every scale-concept combination.

As Roger J. Williams proved in his book, *You Are Extra-Ordinary*, each human is unique, even to the point that no two livers are ever precisely alike in size or in physical location within the body.

In pretesting, the survey should allow for an alternate answer—"wouldn't use"—to alert you to these differences and perhaps search for a more universal term.

Similarly, in pretesting, set aside a "don't know" space. Weeding out "wouldn't use" and "don't know" responses reduces the incidence of nonuse and focuses on more familiar concepts. Respondents who do not know, and have no option for expressing this state, are forced into answer fabrication. Too many of these will invalidate results.

An important point is to remember to fit your survey responses to the language, background, and sophistication level of your intended sample of representative consumers.

Also, in the preliminary run, provide spaces so that testees can substitute their own adjectives if they are dissatisfied with yours. The purpose of pretesting is to clean up survey questions rather than to score. The pretest yields still another source of adjective pairs (referred to in Step II (g)).

Generally, respondents will have least difficulty describing humans (themselves and others), and more difficulty as they move from inanimate objects (products, stores) to relational notions (customer-store manager, employee-employer), even among college-educated persons. Abstract ideas and concepts such as freedom, market economy, justice, etc., present extreme difficulty for most respondents to grasp and articulate, and therefore are not suitable areas of empirical investigation.

STEP 4. Administer.

The most frequently asked questions are *to whom?* and *how many?* Section IV on sampling will provide some answers. Your own intelligence and budget limitations provide another part of the answer. If the first 50 persons interviewed say that they believe your product is unsafe, no matter if the next 150 persons feel otherwise, you have an image problem, assuming that the product is indeed safe to use. The issue cannot be ignored.

STEP 5. Analyze.

There are two levels of analysis considered. The easy approach to analysis may accurately enough reflect and summarize survey data. Discussion on an alternative approach to analysis is reserved for Section V.

For the shortcut method, it does not really matter how you score answers. On a seven-step scale, you may score the positive responses $+3$, $+2$, $+1$; the negative ones -1, -2, -3; and assign a zero to the middle answer. Rather than work with negative numbers, simply score responses from $+1$ to $+4$, or to $+5$, or to $+7$, according to the number of possible answers.

For an overall rating, add the scores. Assuming equal weighting, the singular summary statistic pinpoints where respondents have pegged you along the good-bad continuum. Then, if you have grouped responses, an average of each group highlights which set of responses reflects your strong and weak points.

Next, find the average rating, question by question. (Compute the standard deviation, too; Section V tells how, and why.) At this point the data become more interesting and informative.

Now rank all attributes from the best to the worst, according to their respective scores. By ranking them in a table, you can quickly see strengths to bring out in promotional campaigns and problem areas that require resolution.

If you prefer graphic presentation, take a blank survey questionnaire and plot the average score for each pair of adjectives. (If you wish, you can create a scale, using a ruler, that fairly well approximates the actual mean calculated for each response.) Now connect the dots on the page. The resulting vertical line will weave from side to side as it descends the page. This method of presentation is especially effective for comparing your company branch, or product, with three or four competitors. Colored or dashed lines on a graph are more quickly interpreted than numerical data in a table.

Additional Money-Producing Ideas

Several applications of this technique have already been cited. Another two or three may equip you with additional money-producing ideas.

One survey tested words rather than products. In the questionnaires, about 20 products were listed, only two of which were actually produced by the company. Each product had its list of adjectives. The total sample was divided into four subgroups, and a Latin Square Design (explained in Section II.4) was employed to rotate respondent groups systematically.

A great deal of data, which will not be detailed here, was collected from the 175 sample participants. The main purpose of the exercise was to verify the performance of terms such as "new," "improved," "new/improved," etc., in ad copy. Despite their heavy usage, terms implying product newness or innovation still motivate the buyer.

Another impressive application focused on attitude change. The British dry cleaning industry faced a stagnating market and wanted to know how to change habits and increase sales. "The British have their clothes cleaned for Easter and the summer holidays and that's about all."

Although an industry-wide promotional campaign seemed like the best solution, six giants absorbed about 40 percent of the volume of the dry cleaning trade, and the remaining business in the country was scattered among some 2500 independent operators—tough to get them all together. Consequently, seeking cooperation from over 2,000 firms seemed an even more formidable task than to take the British to the cleaners.

ICI, the major chemical supplier, stepped in with some money and leadership. Altogether some U.S. $600,000 was raised for the campaign. Attitude studies pinpointed the negative and positive aspects of public opinion on the matter of more frequent dry cleaning. Advertising was then developed that told people what consumers said were the reasons why clothes should be cleaned more often.

The payoff: The industry grew between 5 percent and 10 percent over the next several years. Of course, Imperial Chemical Industries, Ltd., profited, too.

Still another profitable application is store differentiation. Banks fall into this category; regulated enterprises, too; and some brokerage firms and professional offices.

When price competition is not possible, or undesirable, how does one store or office or airline differentiate itself from competitors? The semantic differential method can dig out competitors' weaknesses.

The payoff potential: A business armed with this information can avoid competition along price differential lines and provide nonprice inducements that attract and retain new and existing clientele.

The Shadow of Optimism

However, there are some disadvantages. All techniques have their limitations, including this one.

1. Survey outcomes do not necessarily prove cause and effect when measurement takes place after the sale. Consumers weigh the effects of an exchange before transactions; i.e., value in exchange derives from anticipated satisfaction or utility. Actual satisfaction or usefulness may diverge considerably from what was anticipated.

2. This method may not distinguish small differences, those dissimilarities at the margin which will mean sale or no sale. If little distinction is perceived between insurance policies of two companies, what is that slight edge that causes the buyer to finally decide on one over the other? This relates back to limitation No. 1. The reason may not be discernible with semantic differentials.

3. Too, there is the problem of the halo effect. A buyer, pleased with an equipment purchase, may buy accessories and supporting materials from the same dealer because the positive relationship from the equipment transaction carries over into supplies and service purchases. Or a negative attitude may arise due to service problems, and future equipment will be bought elsewhere—the negative aspect of the halo effect.

4. Much mention of customer self-image and the product-image link has already appeared. This is not a universally acceptable hypothesis. The customer's self-image may be quite the opposite of the product image, but he wants to measure up socially and buys the product anyway; or he may express individuality by deliberately uncoupling this link; or income and the product price rule all decisions.

5. Do not expect perfect relationships derived from this investigative technique. People are still individuals. They defy measurement by never-changing norms.

6. Generalizations by product grouping (chain saws), or products categorized by country ("made in Taiwan"), are too broad for reliable application across the board. There are electric chain saws and saws with gasoline engines; large, logger types and Saturday afternoon specials; and diverse brands, features and accessories. Taiwan produces some good products, some shoddy ones. Customers soon learn to distinguish by product, not by country of origin.

When to Telephone

Best results for the semantic differential technique emerge from a personal interview approach because the survey is quick and easy, and top-of-the-head responses seem best suited for this type of analysis.

Least dependable outcomes result from a mail survey because respondents take too much time to think over answers. They may tend to favor and report an idealized image rather than rely on their own ideas and preferences.

The telephone has found application with the semantic differential technique. It will not work well in all situations, but here is how one business picked up on the opportunity. (If you need to know more about telephone interviewing, please refer to Section I.4 for some profit-producing hints.)

After preliminaries, securing the cooperation of the respondent, the telephone interviewer says that she (or he) will name a brand of insect spray, and that she will then say a word or phrase:

> If the word I say very strongly describes the product, then you answer "plus 3." If it somewhat describes the product brand, say "plus 2." If the word only slightly describes the product, say "plus 1." But if I say a word or phrase that slightly misdescribes the product, then you will answer, "minus 1." If it somewhat misdescribes, say "minus 2." If it strongly misdescribes the product, say "minus 3." Remember, for each brand of insect spray, if your first impression is to agree with the description, say "plus 3, 2, or 1." If you disagree, say "minus 1, 2, or 3."

That approach may be too complex for some respondents. Unless they pay close attention, they can easily forget whether $+1$ or $+3$ means the best answer. The telephone interviewer may be quite unaware of the confusion.

Since most persons are familiar with A, B, C, D, E and F grades, some alternative using this type of scale may work out. Nevertheless, adopting this telephone method can add up to many responses in a short order (at a lower cost per response), if quantity is desirable and analysis time available.

The Easy Interview with a Staple Scale

The telephone interview variation actually derives from the Staple Scale, introduced by Irving Crespi in 1961. The unipolar scale (a) is believed to overcome some disadvantages of the semantic differential scale, (b) is easier to manage, and (c) produces comparable results at lower costs.

The chief concern, that of using only one adjective rather than a paired set, springs from the difficulty of, and disagreement on, appropriate antonyms. Good-bad, sweet-sour pairs are readily understood at all socio-economic levels.

But, for example, with what do you pair compact? expensive? luxury? unpatriotic? large? Which, in 1961, might have brought out quite different opposites: comfortable, roomy, normal. And divergences of opinions among groups of respondents would be too great to ignore.

Crespi proposed, and utilized, sets of single adjectives related to the object of the survey (product, store, people). He requested interviewees to rate each on a ten-point scale that ranged from $+5$ if the adjective well described the object to a -5 if the adjective did not apply. (No "0" is employed.)

Otherwise, the survey is conducted like semantic differential scaling. Analysis can proceed by calculating the mean for each adjective. Crespi suggested computing scores on a 1-to-100 scale on the basis of the percentage distribution of responses over the scale.

Some further advantages of this approach:

1. Pretesting adjective-pair relationships is eliminated.
2. The alternative technique can be used in personal or mail interviews as well as the telephone application described above.
3. Designs for several product brands can be administered in a few minutes.
4. As with the semantic differential method, an interviewer can be competently trained, easily and inexpensively, in contrast to projective methods.

Still another way to probe personalities of purchasers is by means of projective psychological techniques.

III.2: HOW TO PROJECT PEARLS OF WISDOM FROM A SEA OF PSYCHOLOGICAL TECHNIQUES

You are already acquainted with this approach. One, word association, was introduced in Section III.1. Another you may recognize as a childhood or party game.

These techniques, adapted from psychology, most often are subsumed under the heading "projective psychological techniques." *Projective* implies that a response reflects an aspect of the respondent's personality. At least one psychologist objects to this implication and prefers the label "ego defense dynamism tests."

Numerous tests, or techniques, exist. Market researchers have found that only a few have generated data on perceptions, relationships, imaginations, physical movements, etc. Hence, the term "tests of expression" probably more accurately indicates what finally comes out of these experiments. Nonetheless, we can stay with the term *projective* as a handy reference word to mean many things, however imprecise it may be for the professional psychologists, and get on with the task of examining several possible applications.

Four Tests of Expression

Four categories of projective and expressive techniques seem to prevail among market researchers:

1. association,
2. completion,
3. expression, and
4. construction.

We begin with the one most familiar—word association designs.

In Section III.1, to develop ordinarily understood and agreed-to antonyms, a word association game was suggested. That is one objective. Another end is to develop promotional or advertising copy ideas.

This experimental game can be played with a group of persons to minimize costs, by requiring only one interviewer and only one use of physical facilities. (You may wish to review Sections I.6 and I.7 for a few words on group interviews.)

Each participant of the group receives paper with numbered blank lines. The object is to induce volunteers to write their initial thought; therefore, little time is provided after each spoken word. The group leader calls out a term or word, and each member writes the first word or phrase that comes to mind. (When someone yells "Bingo!" it is time to stop.)

For example, assume you are gathering input on prepared vegetables. A partial list of words may read: (1) Vegetable; (2) Peas; (3) Corn; (4) Canned foods; (5) Fresh vegetables; (6) Vegetarian; (7) Road-side stand; (8) Frozen foods; (9) Fruit; (10) Salad.

And to continue the game, let's assume that one set of corresponding responses reads: (1) Healthy; (2) Goes with carrots; (3) Corn-on-the-cob; (4) Tastes flat; (5) Expensive; (6) Crackpot; (7) Fresh fruit; (8) Convenient; (9) Vitamins; (10) Lose weight.

Three Laws of Successful Marketing

What does this prove? Alone, frankly, not much. In the first place, this is probably a poorly constructed list of words for a test. In the second place, these tests are best developed in consultation with someone who has had psychological training (and such a person may now be employed somewhere in your firm). In the third place, any superficial conclusions drawn from this set of associations need more evidence to justify a budget appropriation.

Perhaps you conclude that packaged vegetables should stress economy, health, full of vitamins, with that road-stand flavor captured by our field-freshness guarantee. If you believe that, then test the idea further. Employ some of the other techniques demonstrated elsewhere in this book. The first three laws of successful marketing are: (1) Test. (2) *Test*! (3) TEST!

A variation of this method requires participants to write (or state) a series of first words that come to mind after hearing a given phrase. For instance, respondents are asked to write the first ten words or ideas that pop into their heads after hearing the phrase "dining out." Typical answers may include these:

1. Special occasion.
2. Family and fun.
3. Expensive.
4. Entertainment.
5. No place to park.
6. Good food.
7. Leave hungry and broke.
8. Fried stuff.
9. Gypsy violins.
10. Long lines.

A restaurant ad that highlights benefits and addresses itself to those problem areas within its control can increase business. To counter objection Nos. 3 and 7, Saccio's Fish Factory (an unlikely name for a restaurant) in San Diego, advertises, "Where you can come away full for a fin." Although the language may seem outmoded, that, plus the rest of its ad copy, has turned into a successful formula. And the restaurant lives up to all of its promises as well.

The Complete Story

Completion techniques represent a more directed version of association tests. The two most popular types are (1) sentence completion, and (2) story completion. Sentence completion typically begins by asking a question or by leaving a sentence hanging for the interviewee to fill in the blank.

    A. What kind of managers prefer computers?
    B. Managers who prefer the use of computers are _____.

Response analysis aims to uncover patterns and marketing ideas.

Story completion offers considerably more structure than sentence completion. With skillful construct of the scene to be played out, the analyst can identify underlying motives and attitudes that may not even surface from indepth interviews.

Suppose that a nursery school wants to discover why they receive a large number of inquiries and visits by parents, but few couples actually enroll their children at the nursery.

Respondents will be told part of a story: A husband and wife have spent the last half-hour talking with the administration and staff of Pink Panther Pre-Schoolers. While driving home in their car, they discuss whether to enroll their four-year-old son in the nursery school. What are they saying to one another? Or the interviewer can end the story by saying: "Sabina said to Austin, her husband, 'The Pink Panther school was nice, but. . .!' "

The advantage is that Sabina and Austin are unknown to respondents. They do not know how Sabina and Austin will react. Too, the respondents are out of the picture and feel freer to talk.

The underlying theory says that the respondents really do project themselves into the picture. Or the story they are asked to create really builds on their own experiences. Many (not all) first novels are autobiographical. It applies here as well.

The Big Picture

Pictures can back up story creation, although they may not be constructed to elicit the specific responses of the verbalized story completion. A picture of a nursery school is shown and the respondent weaves a tale from it.

A common variation is the paired picture. One picture can show a mother staying home with her child; the other mother leads her offspring by the hand into a nursery school. Interviewees then tell a story about each mother.

Psychologists also use a four-picture test. The pictures are arranged in any order desired by the participant, who then spins a yarn after studying them.

Paired pictures, however, do offer many possibilities and can be used for just about any situation that relates to a business problem.

Expressive techniques, too, depend upon the participant's playing a role, much like those in sales training classes, only with different objectives. One possibility is to place the respondent in the role of a salesperson who is trying to sell a product or service to several customers. The customers raise buying objections, and the participant tries to overcome them.

Not everyone responds well to role-playing. In this example given, many persons freeze up. Role-playing requires some acting. Many people may become too embarrassed to respond freely, which leads to a problem with this technique.

The market researcher can never be completely certain how well any group of participants represents the entire market. Persons who volunteer or participate in psychological and expressive technique experiments may turn out to be responsive but unrepresentative of the market segment.

Application of the Three Basic Laws of Successful Marketing

The major criticism of this technique is its expense. Many of the designs require professional assistance and do not readily lend themselves to the do-it-yourself market researcher. Because of the cost, samples tend to be small. With small samples, the possibility of errors creeps in, especially because this technique may appeal only to certain types of persons.

Furthermore, the fact that psychologists use these and many similar tests does not validate their undiscriminating application in marketing research. Most of these psychological techniques have been oversold. As one researcher said, "They are still in the prescientific stage." Many have never been proved empirically, and many have been refuted or contradicted.

The psychological performance tests used in marketing research all have their base in Freudian psychoanalytical techniques. The famous ink-blot tests fall into this category.

Andrew Hacker wrote: "The traditional definitions which spring from liberal theory may perhaps still hold true for those who plan the conditioning of others. But they are gross malaprops for those whose minds are on the receiving end. And this latter group constitutes the vast majority of us." Rousas Rushdoony reminds us too, that "both Marx and Freud were spiritual heirs of Hegel."

William Yoell points out that even if these techniques work for psychologists, evidence is lacking that they will necessarily bring out the right answers for market researchers. The problem centers on the fact that psychologists do not use a single test in isolation. A projective test may be preceded by a series of pretests and confirmed afterward with other analyses.

Of course, a market researcher will construct a questionnaire appropriate to the objective of research. *Important*: A cover letter should accompany the questionnaire. This letter should point out benefits and suggest that cooperative respondents will have an opportunity to air opinions in indepth interviews *for pay*. The follow-up interview, if it employs a projective and expressive psychological technique, will then build on one of the applications discussed earlier in this subsection.

The lesson: Some good information may emanate from the application of projective and expressive techniques, but this should not be the only source of information. Evidence gathered by expressive and projective techniques should be subjected to further validation. There are many additional test techniques available from the nearly three dozen discussed in this book.

Successful companies may spend months, a year, even years, testing a product before it is placed on the market. They are applying the three basic laws of successful marketing: test, test, and test.

Facts derived from those designs discussed in this subsection are idea-sparkers, when idea-sparkers are needed. And the numerous profitable ideas sparked from the application of this technique may well supply you for the rest of your business career.

III.3: PROFIT ADORNMENT WITH RANKING AND LIKERT SCALE SPARKLERS

In order to find some means to quantify data that describe consumer attitudes, the techniques of scale construction have received considerable attention. The semantic differential scale (Section III.1), the most popular method of attitude measurement, is not the only one.

Although many techniques of greater or lesser degrees of sophistication have been developed, a few seem to have achieved more popularity than others in marketing research. These various techniques are interpreted in this and the remaining subsections in Part III. This subsection will deal with two easily implemented ones: (a) Ranking, (b) Likert.

Why Interviewees Respond to Ranking

Ranking is one of the simplest techniques to communicate to respondents. They are asked (for whatever is being tested) which survey items or product attributes are of more importance and which ones are of less importance. The method is easily understood by everyone because, whether consciously or subconsciously, we do this mental exercise often: "I like this product better than that one because . . . ."

However, asking interviewees to rank products, or brands or characteristics, does not even require the *because* part, although such open-ended questions can be added to any questionnaire.

Figure III.3.A illustrates one open-ended practice attached to a ranking survey. The names of four products follow each question with blank space provided for the addition of another name. The respondent is asked to rank each according to preference: 1 for most preferred and 4 for least preferred. Also, if the responding company does not now use a particular brand, then it chooses the preferred one or the one most likely to be used.

The questionnaire may be constructed along different lines. The question may have read: "Which is easiest to use?" Or, "Which are the most and least reliable?"

Then, following each question, a list of product brands appears. The respondent ranks them by the code indicated: 1 through 5 with either 1 or 5 being the best and the opposite number the worst; or A-B-C-D-E-F; or by any other system that is clear and does not distract the respondent from the main purpose of the interview or survey.

ILLUSTRATION OF RANKING

Typewriters

___ Olivetti   ___ Royal   ___ IBM   ___ Smith-Corona   ___ _____

Word Processors

___ Wang   ___ Lanier   ___ IBM   ___ AM   ___ _____

CRTs

___ Hazeltine   ___ Control Data   ___ IBM   ___ Datapoint   ___ _____

Headache Remedies

___ Aspirin   ___ Excedrin   ___ Bufferin   ___ Coffee   ___ _____

Figure III.3.A: ILLUSTRATION OF RANKING

An example of ranking application is Datapro Research Corporation's extensive "Annual Survey of User Opinion of Computer Systems." A sample list of 15,000 names was drawn from *Computerworld's* subscriber list. Each respondent was double-mailed a questionnaire surveying his or her experiences with mainframes, minicomputers, and desktop computer systems. Thirty-five percent responded, which, after discarding statistically invalid answers, resulted in a 31 percent valid response rate.

Among other things, the survey asked users to rank their satisfaction on a scale of 0-to-4, with 4 the best, on various aspects of the particular system; an overall satisfaction rating; and finally, whether the respondent would recommend the system to another user.

The criteria ranked, by manufacturer, appear in Figure III.3.B. (Of course, the reader should refer to the appropriate issue of *Computerworld*, or the research organization in Delran, New Jersey, for published results.) With this information in hand, the list of manufacturers is arrayed with the highest scores heading the list.

QUESTIONNAIRE FOR RANKING COMPUTER SYSTEMS

Survey Item	Computer System				
	A	B	C	D	E

I. (Rate each item, 0 for worst and 4 for best.)

1. Ease of operation
2. Reliability of mainframe
3. Reliability of peripherals
4. Maintenance service:
   a. responsiveness
   b. effectiveness
5. Technical support:
   a. trouble-shooting
   b. education
   c. documentation
6. Manufacturer's software:
   a. operating system
   b. compilers & assemblers
   c. application programs
7. Ease of programming
8. Ease of conversion
9. Overall satisfaction

II. (Answer yes or no.)

Would you recommend this system to another user?
a. Yes
b. No

Figure III.3.B: QUESTIONNAIRE FOR RANKING COMPUTER SYSTEMS

Consumer organizations often rank consumer products according to frequency of repair, convenience, features, durability, guarantees, and other criteria. Maine's Bureau of Consumer Protection employs a version of this technique with the publication of a monthly credit guide, using interest rates under various assumptions as the ranking criterion.

The Maine Bankers Association points out that the presence of too many other variables brings into question the value of single-line summaries. The objection is valid not only for consumer goods and services, industrial products, and computer systems, but for "averages" and other statistical summaries as well.

And, for similar reasons, the reader is urged not to rely on single-point indicators entirely, without additional information or further testing. In the complete computer systems survey mentioned above, users responded to more than 100 questions on the use and operation of equipment. Indepth analysis, not simple ranking, will back up decisions of successful managers.

Ranking is not subject to much statistical manipulation, but some summary statistics are possible: percentage; mode; quartile. However, reliance on some type of rank index, or some type of average, misleads.

Furthermore, ranking only expresses an order of preference. One product ranked 2 and the other 4 does not imply that one is twice as good (or bad) as the other. Differences in perceived qualities may be quite small, in fact.

These are measurements at the margin. Such rankings say little about the overall quality of the product. Therefore, comparison among rankings is not advised. Such data generated from this technique must be handled with care.

How to Judge Products with a Likert's Summated Scale

Like the ranking method, this scale too is an ordinal scale. Therefore, statistical techniques of analysis are limited to positional measures such as median, quartile, and percentile.

Ordinal scales depend on the ability to distinguish between products or brands according to a single direction, from most to least desired; but the least desired product or brand does not mean the same as bad versus good as in semantic differential. The divergence between best and least may be slight or extreme. The scale does not tell us.

With a Likert-type scale, statements are made; and respondents indicate not only whether they agree or disagree with the statement but also by how much they agree or disagree. The degree of differences may be graduated more finely on a 7-step or 9-point scale, or less finely on a 5-point scale.

For example, the Product Development and Management Association, a nonprofit marketers organization, preferred a five-point Likert-type scale for determining which textbooks were rated highest and which lowest. The scale prescribed five ratings:

1. Excellent
2. Good
3. Adequate
4. Poor
5. Very poor

Commonly seen are miniquestionnaires of the type in Figure III.3.C. Sometimes these are not legitimate questionnaires but they serve to create mailing lists, or other purposes, under the guise of a questionnaire. Certainly confidence in results drops since the technique violates basic controls evident in more formal experimental designs. However, a spate of low ratings and negative responses alerts top management to local problems, and may play the role of hidden adversary in subsequent evaluations of local management. But such surveys have little or no value for most marketing research issues.

At Sheraton Hotels & Inns, hospitality is not just another word; it's our reason for existence.

We know if you're not happy with our service and our facilities, you might not come back. We don't want that to happen.

Please let us know how we're doing. Use this easy rating guide and add your comments if you wish.

Many thanks for staying at Sheraton!

Room no. _____ Date _____

Comments _____

_____

_____

_____

Name _____

Address _____

City _____ State _____ Zip _____

Telephone _____

Please print your name and address if we may answer your comments or send you more information on Sheraton Hotels & Inns. Then seal this folder and leave it at the front desk when you leave. Thanks for your help.

Please rate us ↘

	Excellent	Good	Fair	Poor
CHECKING IN				
Reservation	☐	☐	☐	☐
Front Desk	☐	☐	☐	☐
Bellman	☐	☐	☐	☐
YOUR ROOM				
Cleanliness	☐	☐	☐	☐
TV/Radio	☐	☐	☐	☐
Bath	☐	☐	☐	☐
Bed/Furnishings	☐	☐	☐	☐
RESTAURANT / LOUNGE				
Name	☐	☐	☐	☐
Food	☐	☐	☐	☐
Beverages	☐	☐	☐	☐
Service	☐	☐	☐	☐
GENERAL				
Swimming Pool	☐	☐	☐	☐
Parking	☐	☐	☐	☐
Room Service	☐	☐	☐	☐

Figure III.3.C: AN INFORMAL SURVEY

On the other hand, the conference questionnaire in Figure III.3.D was sent to *all* 2,000 conferees for future planning aid. As a marketing research tool, even for a nonprofit association, it signals to conference planners not only how well they managed the last one but also possible constraints to future growth. The "marketing" objective, in this instance, is volume rather than profits.

Typically, the questionnaire is constructed so that the respondent may check off an answer:

1. Agree very strongly
2. Agree fairly strongly
3. Agree
4. Undecided
5. Disagree
6. Disagree fairly strongly
7. Disagree very strongly
X. Do not know

The directions need not be repeated for each question. The respondent can refer to the scale as he or she goes down a list of statements. Illustrated in Figure III.3.E are partial results from a survey based on a five-point scale.

Of course, there are many types of applications for this technique. In one instance the researchers gauged attitudes toward advertising. The questionnaire proceeded with a series of statements that alternated between positive and negative ones concerning advertising.

In another application the processor measured attitudes toward types of cereal. Still another one graded job satisfaction.

In a Worcester County survey of small and medium-sized businesses, the researcher combined ranking, scaling, and other techniques to determine the attractiveness (or unattractiveness) of the business environment in Worcester County and the possible mobility of established businesses. Answers to the 44-question survey in Figure III.3.F provide a wealth of data and insights into growth potentials.

1980 CONFERENCE EVALUATION

We hope you enjoyed your 1980 conference experience in San Diego. Let us know how you rate the conference by filling out this questionnaire. Then, re-fold the questionnaire and drop it in the mail. Your feedback will help us plan a more successful conference next year.

By the way, it's not too early to begin planning for the Fifty-sixth Annual WEA Conference, July 2-6, 1981, at the Hyatt Regency Hotel, San Francisco. See you there!

1. Please check the years you have attended WEA conferences.
   1980, San Diego _____   1978, Hawaiian Islands _____   1976, San Francisco _____
   1979, Las Vegas _____   1977, Anaheim _____   1975, San Diego _____

2. Did your firm or organization pay your 1980 registration fee? Yes ___ No ___
   What percentage of your conference travel and housing expenses did your firm or organization pay? (Exclude expenses for non-economist spouse/guest.)
   Zero _____   1-25% _____   26-50% _____   .51-75% _____   76-100% _____

3. On which days were you at the 1980 conference?
   June 15 _____   June 16 _____   June 17 _____   June 18 _____   June 19 _____

4. Did you bring a spouse/adult guest? Yes _____ No _____

5. Did you bring children? Yes _____ No _____

6. HOUSING: Please rate the Sheraton Harbor Island Hotel/Sheraton Inn guest rooms and hotel services.
   Excellent _____   Good _____   Fair _____   Poor _____
   Comments:

7. MEETING FACILITIES: Please rate the meeting facilities at the Sheraton Harbor Island Hotel.
   Excellent _____   Good _____   Fair _____   Poor _____
   Comments:

8. CONFERENCE PROGRAM: How would you rate the over-all conference program?
   Excellent _____   Good _____   Fair _____   Poor _____
   Comments and/or suggestions for improvement:

9. EXECUTIVE STAFF PERFORMANCE: How would you rate the performance of the WEA Executive Staff?
   Excellent _____   Good _____   Fair _____   Poor _____
   Comments and/or suggestions for improvement:

Figure III.3.D: AN AFTER-ONLY QUESTIONNAIRE FROM A NONPROFIT ASSOCIATION

10. Please rate the events below which you attended.
Historic San Diego Tour: Excellent ____ Good ____ Fair ____ Poor ____
No-Host Cocktail Party (Monday, June 16): Excellent ____ Good ____ Fair ____ Poor ____
Wild Animal Park Tour: Excellent ____ Good ____ Fair ____ Poor ____
WEA Presidential/Awards Luncheon: Excellent ____ Good ____ Fair ____ Poor ____
No-Host Cocktail Party (Tuesday, June 17): Excellent ____ Good ____ Fair ____ Poor ____
Harbor Cruise: Excellent ____ Good ____ Fair ____ Poor ____
Tijuana Tour: Excellent ____ Good ____ Fair ____ Poor ____

11. OVER-ALL CONFERENCE RATING: Excellent ____ Good ____ Fair ____ Poor ____
Comments and/or suggestions for improvements:

BUSINESS REPLY MAIL
First Class Permit No. 4337, Long Beach, California

POSTAGE WILL BE PAID BY ADDRESSEE

WESTERN ECONOMIC ASSOCIATION
Executive Office
Department of Economics
California State University
Long Beach, California 90840

No Postage Stamp Necessary If Mailed in the United States

716 — 065

WESTERN ECONOMIC ASSOCIATION
Department of Economics
California State University
Long Beach, Calif. 90840

716-065

1980 WEA CONFERENCE EVALUATION

Figure III.3.D (continued)

Media Update
continued

PRELIMINARY FINDINGS

The December issue of **Interface** contained a survey inquiring as to the "true condition" of school media centers in Connecticut. The following represents a preliminary tabulation of questions concerning critical issues. Results are based on the 81 surveys returned to date by Connecticut media personnel.

	Strongly Agree	Agree	Not Sure	Disagree	Strongly Disagree
16. Information skills should be part of any state competency testing program	59%	33%	7%	<1%	<1%
17. The state should mandate staffing ratios for media specialists and their support staff	50%	33%	9%	5%	1%
18. The state should mandate per pupil expenditures for school media programs	42%	32%	16%	9%	1%
19. A formal program of information skills should be required in each school district	38%	44%	9%	5%	4%
20. The state should mandate minimum school media resources for Connecticut schools.	49%	40%	5%	5%	1%

The school media center is an instructional area of the school and should be vitally linked to the rest of the instructional program. Because the role and success of the school media program is related to its function in the school, survey questions concerning the media program and the school curriculum are important. The responses to curriculum related questions are as follows:

9. The media center staff (certified) should be involved in curriculum development   97% yes   39% no
Are you personally involved in curriculum development?   47% yes   53% no

11. My media center adequately supports the school goals, objectives, and curriculum   76% yes
15% no   9% not sure

Figure III.3.E: PARTIAL EXAMPLE OF RESULTS OF A SUMMATED SCALE

WORCESTER COUNTY BUSINESS
COMMUNITY SURVEY

Where appropriate please circle the *number* next to your response. Otherwise write in your response. If a question does not apply to your business please omit it and continue.

1. What is the nature of your business? _____

2. What is your S.I.C. (If known) _____

3. In what town is your firm located? _____
   _(zip)

4. How many years has your business been in its present location? _____

5. How many full-time employees do you currently have? _____

6. How many seasonal employees do you have? _____

7. What is your approximate total annual sales volume? _____

8. Is the market for your business *primarily:*
   1. Regional
   2. National
   3. International

9. Approximately what percentage of your annual sales are made within Worcester County?
   1. 0-20%   2. 21-40%   3. 41-60%   4. 61-80%   5. 81-100%

10. Compared to 5 years ago, has your business grown in sales volume?
    1. Yes   2. No

    10a. If yes, by how much?   1. 0-50%   3. 100-200%
                                        2. 50-100%   4. over 200%

11. Looking ahead 5 years from now, do you feel your business will grow in volume?
    1. Yes   2. No

    11a. If yes, by how much?   1. 0-50%   3. 100-200%
                                        2. 50-100%   4. over 200%

12. Overall, how would you rate the competitive position of your own business?
    1. Excellent   3. Only Fair
    2. Good   4. Poor

13. Do you plan to expand in your present location in the near future?
    1. Yes   2. No

14. For banking services does your business use:
    1. Banks in Worcester County.   2. Non-local banks.   3. Both

15. If planning expansion, how do you plan to finance it? _____

16. Which of the following development agencies are you familiar with? (circle the number of each)
    1. SBA   (Small Business Administration)
    2. EDA   (Economic Development Administration)
    3. UDAG (Urban Development Action Grant)

Figure III.3.F: A 44-QUESTION BUSINESS COMMUNITY SURVEY

4. CARD (Community Action Revitalization District)
5. MCRC (Massachusetts Capital Resource Corporation)
6. MIFA (Massachusetts Industrial Finance Corporation)
7. CETA (Comprehensive Employment and Training Programs)
8. CDC (Grants to Community Development Corporations)
9. FHMA (Farmers Home Mortgage Administration)

17. Are you planning to develop new products or services in the near future?

    1. Yes   2. No

18. Do you have any plans for diversification in the near future?

    1. Yes   2. No

19. Overall, how would you rate *general* business conditions in Worcester County?

    1. Excellent   3. Only Fair
    2. Good   4. Poor

20. As far as your type of business is concerned, how would you rate Worcester County as a business location compared to:

CONDITIONS IN WORCESTER COUNTY ARE:

	Much Better	Somewhat Better	The Same	Somewhat Worse	Much Worse	No Opinion
a. the rest of Massachusetts	1	2	3	4	5	6
b. New Hampshire	1	2	3	4	5	6
c. Connecticut	1	2	3	4	5	6
d. Vermont	1	2	3	4	5	6
e. Rhode Island	1	2	3	4	5	6
f. the northeast	1	2	3	4	5	6
g. the nation	1	2	3	4	5	6
h. the international market	1	2	3	4	5	6

21. Looking ahead 5 years from now, do you feel general business conditions in Worcester County will:

    1. Improve greatly   3. Stay the same   4. Decline somewhat
    2. Improve somewhat   5. Decline greatly

22. If you had an unlimited choice of business locations, would you stay in Worcester County or would you move elsewhere?

    1. Stay   2. Move
    22a.   If "move," where would you move? _____

23. Which areas of business do you see expanding in Worcester County over the next 5 years?

_____

24. Which areas of business do you see contracting? _____

25. At present what do you see as the two or three major advantages of doing business in Worcester County?

_____

_____

Figure III.3.F (continued)

26. What do you see as the two or three most serious problems of the Worcester County economy?

   _____

   _____

27. Were you to consider a major expansion of your firm here, what do you see as the major obstacles? (circle all that apply)
    1. Labor availability
    2. Labor cost
    3. Markets
    4. Financing
    5. Vendors
    6. Personal taxes
    7. Business taxes
    8. Real Estate
    9. Transportation
    10. Utilities
    11. Union problems
    12. Environmental regulations
    13. other (specify) _____

28. Please rate each of the following:

	Excellent	Good	Only Fair	Poor
a. the quality of public schools in general in your area	1	2	3	4
b. the quality of vocational education in your area to meet your needs	1	2	3	4
c. Worcester County as a location to attract executives	1	2	3	4
d. the availability of quality trained people for your business	1	2	3	4
e. the availability of employees in general in your area	1	2	3	4
f. responsiveness of community colleges to employment needs	1	2	3	4

29. How useful are each of the following in your company's hiring of new employees?

	Very Useful	Somewhat Useful	Not Useful	Do Not Use
a. urban job center program	1	2	3	4
b. direct training reimbursements	1	2	3	4
c. "targeted jobs" tax credit program	1	2	3	4
d. government sponsored skills training programs such as CETA	1	2	3	4
e. DES (Division of Employment Security)	1	2	3	4

Figure III.3.F (continued)

30. In your opinion has the performance of the DES as a government "employment agency" improved, worsened or stayed the same?

    1. Improved   3. Stayed the same
    2. Worsened   4. No experience

31. How much do you spend on product advertising annually? _____

32. Which of the following sources do   In approximate percentage terms how do
    you use for advertising?   you allocate your advertising costs?
    (check all that apply)

    a. Radio   _____   _____
    b. TV   _____   _____
    c. Local daily
        newspapers   _____   _____
    d. Local weekly
        newspapers   _____   _____
    e. Magazines   _____   _____
    f. Direct mail   _____   _____
    g. Collateral
        material   _____   _____
    h. Trade papers   _____   _____
    i. Trade shows   _____   _____

33. In what city or town is your advertising agency headquarters located? _____

34. How satisfied are you with the results of your advertising?

    1. Very satisfied   3. Somewhat dissatisfied
    2. Somewhat satisfied   4. Very dissatisfied

    If dissatisfied, for what reasons? _____
    _____

35. Looking ahead 5 years, at what level do you think the inflation rate will be?

                    _____ 0-5%   _____ 10-15%
                    _____ 5-10%   _____ 15-20%

36. How will inflation affect your business? Please explain your response.

    1. Help
    2. Hurt
    3. No effect

37. Do you presently have any problem with solid waste disposal in your business?

    1. Yes   2. No
    37a.   If No: Do you anticipate a problem with solid waste disposal in your business in the near
                       future?
                       1. Yes   2. No

38. Do you presently have any problem with hazardous waste disposal in your business?

    1. Yes   2. No
    38a.   If No: Do you anticipate a problem with hazardous waste disposal in your business in the
                       near future?
                       1. Yes   2. No

Figure III.3.F (continued)

39. Do you agree or disagree with the following: There should be stronger legislation for the protection of the environment, even if it meant less economic growth.

    1. Agree strongly
    2. Agree mildly
    3. Disagree mildly
    4. Disagree strongly

40. From your perspective please rate the *current* attitude of each of the following institutions *toward* business growth.

	Highly Favorable	Somewhat Favorable	Neutral	Somewhat Unfavorable	Highly Unfavorable
a. the federal government	1	2	3	4	5
b. the Massachusetts state government	1	2	3	4	5
c. local government in your area	1	2	3	4	5
d. lending institutions in your area	1	2	3	4	5

41. Now rate the same institutions in terms of whether you feel each is becoming more favorable or less favorable toward business growth.

	More	Less	No change
a. the federal government	1	2	3
b. the Massachusetts state government	1	2	3
c. local government in your area	1	2	3
d. lending institutions in your area	1	2	3

42. Different administrations can have different orientations toward business and personal taxes at the state level. How would you rate the tax climate in Massachusetts during each of the following administrations?

	Sargent Administration	Dukakis Administration	King Administration
Personal Taxes	1. Very favorable 2. Somewhat favorable 3. Neutral 4. Somewhat unfavorable 5. Very unfavorable	1. Very favorable 2. Somewhat favorable 3. Neutral 4. Somewhat unfavorable 5. Very unfavorable	1. Very favorable 2. Somewhat favorable 3. Neutral 4. Somewhat unfavorable 5. Very unfavorable
Business Taxes	1. Very favorable 2. Somewhat favorable 3. Neutral 4. Somewhat unfavorable 5. Very unfavorable	1. Very favorable 2. Somewhat favorable 3. Neutral 4. Somewhat unfavorable 5. Very unfavorable	1. Very favorable 2. Somewhat favorable 3. Neutral 4. Somewhat unfavorable 5. Very unfavorable

43. What kind of effect will the classification of property for taxes have on your business?

    1. positive
    2. negative
    3. no effect
    4. too early to tell

Figure III.3.F (continued)

44. Please rate the quality of the following public services in your area:

	Excellent	Good	Only Fair	Poor
a. police	1	2	3	4
b. fire	1	2	3	4
c. postal service	1	2	3	4
d. sanitation	1	2	3	4
e. water supply	1	2	3	4
f. telephone system	1	2	3	4
g. electricity	1	2	3	4
h. gas	1	2	3	4

THANK YOU VERY MUCH FOR YOUR TIME.
PLEASE FEEL FREE TO ADD ANY ADDITIONAL COMMENTS YOU MAY HAVE.

Figure III.3.F (continued)

Five Steps to Better Decisions

Now let's run through the steps necessary to create a Likert-type scale that can produce profitable information for better decision-making.

STEP 1. Assemble.

Assemble a sizable number of statements relevant to the attitude being examined. These statements must meet at least two criteria:

(a) Each statement should reflect a favorable or unfavorable position on the attitude in question.
(b) Not all statements assembled will be used. Keep the ones relevant to the attitude being studied; i.e., each should reflect equally important attitudinal aspects; discard the others.

How many statements should be gathered? Start with, say, 100 to 150 statements that seem to be related to the attitude.

Where can you get these statements for the scale design? You and your research team can make them up; it may require some overtime and active imaginations. Those unstructured responses resulting from personal and group interviews will supply ideas. Application of some techniques already discussed in this book may convey some resource ideas: Sections I.2, I.3, I.6, I.7, II.2, II.5, III.2.

STEP 2: Select.

Select statements consistent with purposes of the survey. (They may be pretested at this point in the preselection process.)

Each statement should be ratable to reflect favorable or unfavorable positions from "strongly agree" to "strongly disagree." Choose an odd number of positions, typically 5 or 7, so that the middle point represents a neutral position. You can include a "don't know" in the pretest, but in the actual survey, the middle position serves both doubtfuls and don't knows.

STEP 3. Pretest.

Pretest survey statements with a representative sample, a group of persons who fairly represent the group that will finally receive the test. This allows an opportunity to debug the survey.

If a small sample is not available for pretesting, use company employees and management to complete the survey. Leave space for comments, too.

An example of a survey in ready-to-go format appears in Figure III.3.G. In this one, H.C. Barksdale and W.R. Darden wanted to reveal consumer attitudes toward advertising and marketing tactics and government regulation. (If you are interested in the actual survey results, you should refer to the appropriate issue of the *Journal of Marketing*.)

In this example, 67 statements were pretested; 40 survived for the survey. The pretest, conducted in three cities, comprised a sample of 160 adults. This particular survey was mailed to 785 households. Of 376 returns, 345 were complete and usable. Demographic information (not illustrated) was also requested: age, sex, family size, occupation, geographic location, city size, political preference, home ownership.

COMPLETE EXAMPLE OF A LIKERT-TYPE QUESTIONNAIRE					
	Level of Agreement				
Statements	Strongly Agree	Agree	Uncertain	Disagree	Strongly Disagree
Philosophy of business:					
1. Most manufacturers operate on the philosophy that the "consumer" is always right.					
2. Despite what is frequently said, "let the buyer beware" is the guiding philosophy of most manufacturers.					
3. Competition ensures that consumers pay fair prices.					

Figure III.3.G: COMPLETE EXAMPLE OF A LIKERT-TYPE QUESTIONNAIRE

	Statements	Level of Agreement				
		Strongly Agree	Agree	Uncertain	Disagree	Strongly Disagree
4.	Manufacturers seldom shirk their responsibility to the consumer.					
5.	Most manufacturers are more interested in making profits than in serving consumers.					
Product Quality:						
6.	In general, manufacturers make an effort to design products to fit the needs of consumers.					
7.	Over the past several years, the quality of most products has not improved.					
8.	From the consumer's point of view, style changes are not as important as improvements in product quality.					
9.	Manufacturers do not deliberately design products that will wear out as quickly as possible.					
10.	Manufacturers often withhold important product improvements from the market in order to protect their own interests.					
11.	The wide variety of competing products makes intelligent buying decisions more difficult.					
12.	For most types of products, the differences among competing brands are insignificant and unimportant to consumers.					
Consumer Responsibilities:						
13.	The problems of consumers are less serious now than in the past.					

Figure III.3.G (continued)

		Level of Agreement				
	Statements	Strongly Agree	Agree	Uncertain	Disagree	Strongly Disagree
14.	The information needed to become a well-informed consumer is readily available to most people.					
15.	The average consumer is willing to pay higher prices for products that will cause less environmental pollution.					
16.	The problems of the consumer are relatively unimportant when compared with the other questions and issues faced by the average family.					
17.	Many of the mistakes that consumers make in buying products are the result of their own carelessness or ignorance.					
18.	Consumers often try to take advantage of manufacturers and dealers by making claims that are not justified.					
19.	For most types of products, consumers do not find it worthwhile to shop around to find the best buy.					
20.	Concern for the environment does not influence the product choices made by most consumers.					
Advertising:						
21.	Most product advertising is believable.					
22.	Manufacturers' advertisements are reliable sources of information about the quality and performance of products.					
23.	Generally, advertised products are more dependable than unadvertised ones.					

Figure III.3.G (continued)

Statements	Level of Agreement				
	Strongly Agree	Agree	Uncertain	Disagree	Strongly Disagree
24. Manufacturers' advertisements usually present a true picture of the products advertised.					
Other Marketing Activities:					
25. Generally speaking, the products required by the average family are easily available at convenient places.					
26. In general, the quality of repair and maintenance service provided by manufacturers and dealers is getting better.					
27. Generally, product guarantees are backed by the manufacturers who make them.					
28. The games and contests that manufacturers sponsor to encourage people to buy their products are usually dishonest.					
29. The American marketing system operates more efficiently than those of other countries.					
Consumerism:					
30. Manufacturers seem to be more sensitive to consumer complaints now than they were in the past.					
31. When consumers have problems with products they have purchased, it is usually easy to get them corrected.					
32. Most business firms make a sincere effort to adjust consumer complaints fairly.					

Figure III.3.G (continued)

	Statements	Level of Agreement				
		Strongly Agree	Agree	Uncertain	Disagree	Strongly Disagree
33.	From the consumer's viewpoint, the procedures followed by most manufacturers in handling complaints and settling grievances of consumers are not satisfactory.					
34.	Consumerism or the consumer crusade has not been an important factor in changing business practices and procedures.					
35.	Ralph Nader and the work that he has done on behalf of consumers has been an important force in changing the practices of business.					
36.	The exploitation of consumers by business firms deserves more attention than it receives.					
Government Regulation:						
37.	The government should test competing brands of products and make the results of these tests available to consumers.					
38.	The government should set minimum standards of quality for all products sold to consumers.					
39.	The government should exercise more responsibility for regulating the advertising, sales and marketing activities of manufacturers.					
40.	A Federal Department of Consumer Protection is not needed to protect and promote the interests of consumers.					

Figure III.3.G (continued)

STEP 4: Score.

Score the results. Actual numbers (if you score with a numbering system) do not have to appear directly on the survey material. But you should score consistently.

Let's say you have decided on five possible answers and will number them 1 through 5. A simple 1-2-3-4-5 from left to right will not work when you try to apply analysis in Step 5. If you decide that the highest number will represent the "strongly agree" responses and the lowest number the "strongly disagree" responses, each statement must be coded according to its positive or negative position. Compare these two statements:

(a) New Orleans is one of the most interesting cities to visit in the U.S.
(b) It is not safe to walk alone at night in New Orleans.

If you want high scores to reflect a favorable attitude, then for statement (a), "strongly agree" merits a 5 but "strongly disagree" a 1. But for statement (b), "strongly agree" receives a 1 value, while "strongly disagree" reflects a favorable response, a 5 value. Each individual item is then scored.

Another application took 200 housewives on an imaginary shopping trip. They were asked to pretend they were shopping for two products: instant potatoes and dry beans.

Each housewife was presented with a list of attributes, identical for each product, and for each attribute indicated which bit of information was most or least important in deciding which product brand to buy. The objective of this exercise was to learn how housewives decide which brand to buy among the many available on the shelf.

STEP 5: Analyze.

Analysis is the next step. Analysis of individual items will indicate whether you are on the right track. It is fairly easy to pick out the high scores and the low scores for individual items.

Beyond this instant evaluation, you can divide the scores into *quartiles*. (Reference to Section V can help you out here.) Eliminate the middle quartile since those statements really fail to take a solid position, favorable or unfavorable. The middle, noncommittal response may be chosen for any of several reasons:

(a) Person is an indecisive type.
(b) Person did not understand the statement.
(c) Person lacked information or experience to provide a response for a particular statement.
(d) Person refuses, for some unknown reason, to take a position.

Remaining are the high scores and low scores in the high and low quartiles. For each quartile, determine the average score. Then locate those statements that differ from these averages by the greatest amount. These are the most discriminating. The remaining statements, then, form the Likert scale.

Note: This function also applies to Steps 2 and 3 as well. After pretesting a sample of respondents, eliminate those statements that are too far away from the middle range of scores, and use the remaining statements on the full-fledged survey.

This type of scale was used to measure attitudes toward advertising. The respondent read a number of advertisements (or slogans) and then evaluated them along three lines, indicating whether they were (a) informative, (b) persuasive, or (c) a reminder. Analysis followed by product groups.

Some distinct advantages spring up with the Likert summated scale.

1. It is easy to construct and easy to administer.
2. Because the instructions are easily and readily understood, interviewers require less expensive training, or experience; and the format is easily adapted for self-administration via mail surveys.
3. It is a practical device when management wants to undertake a program involving change, improvement, or experimentation with new ideas in which consumer attitudes play an important role.
4. This technique is practical in combination with before-and-after studies (Section II.2) to measure attitudes or evaluate whether the effort (whatever was being measured) produced the results desired.
5. The survey may also include statements that do not directly bear on the attitude studied. It can be subjected to profile analysis (refer to Section III.1).
6. The Likert scale, easier to construct and administer than the Thurstone or Guttman scales, and, in fact, faster to structure, brings costs down.

III.4: FIVE STEPS TO Q-SORT AND OTHER SCALES OF SUCCESS

An attempt to scale the steep wall to success and profits without proper tools and safety equipment can, with one false step, meet with the tragic but swift plunge to failure, causing severe injuries, even death, to a previously healthy organization.

Even with the best tools of research and analysis, the wall remains steep; but, by comparison with the task confronting the ill-equipped manager, the prepared market researcher will seemingly glide upward on steps of onyx.

Building Profits with Marketing Research

The well-equipped manager not only knows which tools to apply but is well enough acquainted with all available implements to know which ones to avoid in any given set of circumstances. Whether a manager is diving for pearls of marketing wisdom, mining alluvial deposits for "diamondiferous" profits, or scaling the treasure mountain of new markets, marketing research helps to produce a more abundant outcome.

Numerous scales have in fact been developed for applications in psychology; very few have been adapted for marketing research. In the last subsection, Thurstone's Differential Scale was mentioned. Discussion of Thurstone's Law of Comparative Judgment, omitted from this book, is used by some businesses in marketing research. However, it is less practical for most small and medium-sized businesses, more complex to develop and administer, and certainly more expensive for one-time applications. Repeated use of the same scale, however, would lower costs. Consequently, Likert-type scales tend to dominate for reasons already cited in the previous subsection. Two techniques are illustrated below: (A) the low-cost, easy-to-use Constant Sum scale; and, (B) the more expensive Q-Sort method.

A. Building a Promotional Campaign from a Constant Sum Scale

You have probably put this scale into action in instances other than marketing research. The respondent quickly gets the hang of it. Easy to apply and inexpensive to administer, it can, in fact, be self-administered; ergo, appropriate for a mail survey.

If I were to ask how you use your time during a 24-hour period, you would subdivide your day into categories of main activities and allocate a percentage to each. It must total 100 percent, of course—the full 24 hours.

Rather than call these entries percentages, let's refer to them as points, and ask a respondent to assign 100 points, in any manner, among a dozen attributes, to indicate how important each was in deciding the acquisition (purchase or lease) of a new computer system.

____ Price
____ Dependability
____ Service
____ Technical consultation
____ Prestigious name
____ Appearance of peripherals
____ Quality
____ Current technology
____ Availability
____ Speed
____ Expandability
____ Bells and whistles
_100_ TOTAL

In dividing the 100 points among these items, the respondent is ranking them, assigning more or less importance to each, or even no importance to some.

This rank-order format, extended, can include a number of product brands according to characteristics, or the respondent can rank a number of computer companies on a similar scale, as in Figure III.4.A. The resulting values, averaged cross-sectionally, produce an approximate interval scale.

Recall that the Likert scale is an ordinal scale. The Constant Sum scale is an interval scale. An interval scale displays the characteristics of a constant unit of measurement, such as the pound markings on the bathroom scales.

As a plus benefit, an interval scale permits additional statistical computations: arithmetic mean, standard deviation, correlation coefficients, t-test, F-test, *inter alia* (discussed in Sections V and VI of this book).

Figure III.4.A illustrates how this method helps to determine the relative importance of each significant reason in the purchase decision process. Armed with information from an analysis of the outcome of such a survey, a dealer, distributor, importer, or manufacturer can launch a potent promotion campaign.

You may find it easier to work with smaller numbers, say 10, if the number of elements is fewer, or 20. Any number can be readily converted into percentages. To avoid fractions, the number of allocable points should be great enough to permit divisibility, but preferably not so many that the respondent gets caught up in keeping track of the number of points, involving repeated erasures, and

---

EXAMPLE OF A CONSTANT SUM SCALE APPROACH

INSTRUCTIONS: Assign a total of 100 points in any manner among any or all of the following 22 reasons to indicate how important each were in deciding a new car purchase.

◆◆◆◆◆◆◆◆◆◆◆◆◆◆◆◆◆◆◆◆◆◆◆◆◆◆◆◆◆◆◆◆◆◆◆

What reason would you say was most important to you in selecting the particular make of car you bought rather than some other make?

_____	a.	advice of friends and relatives?
_____	b.	operating economy?
_____	c.	experience with this make?
_____	d.	manufacturer's reputation?
_____	e.	power and pick up?
_____	f.	size and weight?
_____	g.	exterior styling?
_____	h.	interior styling?
_____	i.	maneuverability in city traffic?
_____	j.	interior roominess?
_____	k.	riding comfort?
_____	l.	maneuverability on highway?
_____	m.	quality of workmanship?
_____	n.	safety features?
_____	o.	immediate availability of style and color?
_____	p.	dealer location?
_____	q.	dealer reputation and service?
_____	r.	length and coverage of warranty?
_____	s.	price or deal offered?
_____	t.	value for the money?
_____	u.	future trade-in value?
_____	v.	unrelated factors such as government restrictions or local personal property taxes?
_____	w.	other?
100	x.	TOTAL

Figure III.4.A: EXAMPLE OF A CONSTANT SUM SCALE APPROACH

ends by not concentrating on the purpose of the survey—or, worse yet, not even finishing and returning it.

B. Building Blocks of the Q-Sort Technique

The Q-Sort technique is not recommended for every firm or for every market research problem.

In the first place, it is expensive to operate. The technique requires that each item or attribute appear on separate cards. It depends upon the more costly personal or group interviews. Its analysis derives from more sophisticated statistical techniques, with sufficient computer time and capacity to analyze all but the smallest samples.

Nevertheless, for certain types of research problems, the Q-Sort, or some modification of it, may deliver the big-money answers.

In this technique each participant sorts out or separates into piles those characteristics (printed on the cards) which correspond to the respondent's attitudes, along an eleven-point spectrum. Then the participants are grouped, according to selected characteristics. The idea is to discover whether persons with similar profiles express similar attitudes.

Of course, you will immediately recognize this as a behavioralist approach. Behavioralists seek similarities among persons in order to segment the consumer population into large groups that can be linked to specific products or types of products through manipulation. Humans resist this aggregation and express individuality in diverse and imaginative ways.

However, if your objectives are to uncover what buyers or potential users like or dislike about your product, and you utilize this information to make legitimate improvements in product and service, this is an ethical application of information derived from this or similar techniques.

Let's work through the basic steps of the Q-Sort to better understand how this technique hangs together, and how results are analyzed.

• Step I. After careful identification of the problem and a complete statement of goals this research should accomplish, select the criteria on which statements are to be sorted.

Typically these criteria will lie along the good-bad continuum and will be expressed in such opposites as most nutritive—least nutritive; natural flavor—artificial flavor; best liked—least liked; most economical—least economical; etc. Decide on the number of brands. Researchers often will prefer that respondents rate the ideal brand, their current brand, and the brand of interest to the researcher. Perhaps you wish to rate the most competitive brand as well.

• Step II. Decide on the list of product characteristics or attributes that are to be sorted. As pointed out in Section III.3 and elsewhere, this step may well involve extensive research and careful pretesting. Further, about 100 items is an appropriate number to use in order to validate the analysis of results that follow the survey.

Creating a list of 100 items may take some time and imagination. It is like playing the childhood game of seeing who can draw up the longest list of uses of a brick within an allotted time span. (And today, some people will pay to play versions of that same game in something referred to as "creativity development" seminars.)

• Step III. Assemble a sample of volunteers that you hope represents a large segment of the market. (Sampling problems are discussed in Section IV of this book.) You may choose to interview persons separately or in groups. (Refer to Sections I.3 and I.6 for more on problems and solutions in interviewing.)

• Step IV. Instruct the volunteers to separate the cards into 11 piles, which describe the various reactions of the respondent to the attributes indicated on each card, and for each brand.

However, to use more sophisticated statistical techniques, it is better to have a normal, or bell-shaped, distribution. One way to achieve this neatly balanced distribution is to instruct the interviewees to place a specific number of cards in each pile. This may force the results, even to the point of creating some distortions, but you will have a normal distribution. Figure III.4.B illustrates this layout.

	(1)	(2)	(3)	(4)	(5)	(6)	(7)	(8)	(9)	(10)	(11)
	Most pleasing to the taste					Most neutral about these items					Least pleasing to the taste
No. of cards per group	2	4	8	12	14	20	14	12	8	4	2

AN EXAMPLE OF Q-SORT TECHNIQUE

Total Number of Cards = 100

Figure III.4.B: AN EXAMPLE OF Q-SORT TECHNIQUE

• Step V. Score the items placed in each group and then analyze with correlation techniques (Section VI.2); i.e., you can correlate each respondent's scores with those of every other subject, and then conduct factor analyses on the intercorrelations.

Building Profits from Other Scales

Too, there are other scales. One that holds promise is Kelly's Personal Construct scale. As with other scales, this one also came out of applied psychology.

As it achieves further reliability in market research through repeated testing, this technique can contribute significantly to consumer attitudes toward products. It explicitly recognizes that individuals take purposeful action to gain control and direction over their lives. It also recognizes that with changing circumstances decisions change; i.e., nothing is forever.

The Guttman Scalogram Analysis has received wider acceptance, but it is still rejected by many marketing researchers because of weaknesses in predicting product or advertising acceptance in some situations. Too, it costs more and is complex to administer. Results are more difficult to analyze than with the Likert scale, or Constant Sum scale, for example.

III.5: MULTIDIMENSIONAL SCALING: FROM AMETHYST TO ZIRCON

As humanists tardily recognize both the uniqueness and the complexities with which the Creator has endowed us, research techniques follow along this continuum of awakening. Research methods advance from the one-dimensional horizons of insects to the two-dimensional horizons of certain animals, and, subsequently, to the multidimensional economic, social, and spiritual space of persons. (Since it implies limitations, "space" is perhaps an inappropriate word.)

Research and analytical problems, and costs too, rise to the point that organizations with smaller budgets necessarily rely less, or not at all, on marketing research, and entirely on luck or intuition of personal judgment or tying long-term contracts.

Certainly, where top management is close to the market, and to operational and production strengths and weaknesses, individual and group judgments substitute for a great deal of marketing research—but not completely. A portion of the budget should be allocated to learning and earning even more of your firm's market, whether research depends upon the most rudimentary investigations or builds on the more complex, more costly, Q-Sort or multidimensional scaling techniques.

Inequality of Relationships

Numerous possible applications of nonmetric (i.e., inequality of relationships) multidimensional scaling for generating information on marketing problems crop up; e.g., new product analysis, product-life cycle, advertising effectiveness, product positioning, market segmentation analysis, brand-switching analysis, product satisfaction, store image studies, test marketing—a partial list.

In addition to the fact that results are more difficult and more expensive to analyze, statistical measurement problems spring up, too. Because researchers today continue to experiment with, improve, and expand applications of this technique, an introductory explanation follows.

The scaling methods explained in preceding subsections are founded on *uni*-dimensional scales. The Likert, Guttman, and Thurstone scales are scaled along a one-dimensional continuum; i.e., a single attitude dimension is assumed, which is rated somewhere between good and bad.

The semantic differential scale, discussed at the beginning of this section on data measurement, relies on several relevant dimensions. The researcher already knows what these attitude dimensions are because he has applied them in the research project.

On the other hand, *multi*dimensional scaling characterizes consumers' perceptions and preferences as points defined in multidimensional space. In this application neither the researcher nor the respondent has previously identified the number or nature of these perceptions and preferences. Actually, multidimensional scaling is not a single technique. It represents an accumulation of researcher experience, the respondents' judgments of similarity or dissimilarity of product attributes, and an available computer program to compute all possible combinations.

Improving a Product Image

Nonmetric multidimensional scaling requires only a rank order of perceived differences among products. Although this approach requires only ordinal input, ratio output may be generated from it.

Metric multidimensional scaling requires ratio-scaled measures of the differences perceived among products. Nonmetric techniques are the most popular.

One application of this technique is in before-and-after studies on product positioning. Product position refers to images held by consumers for a group of competing products. Through advertising, a company can try to improve a product image, which, in turn, should reposition the product to advantage, vis-a-vis similar products of competitors. Multidimensional scaling must therefore be used in test evaluations both before and after the campaign.

From among a group of products, respondents choose pairs of brands that seem *very similar, similar, dissimilar,* or *very dissimilar.* Suppose there were 18 brands. Respondents pair and rank the most similar ones, then next most similar, and so on. How many possible pairs are there? The answer, 153 (for 18 brands), is found by this formula:

$$X = \frac{(N-1)N}{2}$$

Where N equals the number of brands tested, so that

$$X = \frac{(18-1)\,18}{2} = 153$$

Even with only 100 respondents in the sample, you can readily appreciate that the large number of responses are best sorted, ranked, and analyzed with a computerized procedure (algorithm) that arranges items in one or more dimensions.

Notice, too, by experimenting with different numbers of brands, how the problem multiplies as the number of brands increase. With four brands, there are only six pairs to worry about; with eight brands, a doubling, the number of pairs more than quadruples, to 28; and with 40 brands, the number of possible pairs jumps to 780.

For sake of example, let's assume eight product brands, a combination of 28 pairs. These 28 pairs are listed on cards.

    ◎ *First*, the respondent begins by separating the 28 pairs into two piles: similar and dissimilar.

    ◎ *Second*, s/he further subdivides each pile into two or more categories: very similar and similar; very dissimilar and dissimilar. S/he continues this process step by step, working toward a solution.

    ◎ *Third*, s/he ranks each subset by choosing the most similar, then the next most similar pair, until s/he has completed an examination of each pile.

On what basis does the respondent pair the brands? Each brand may have many characteristics and combinations of features. New cars and computer systems are good examples. But the respondent decides on his or her own why some brands are similar and why others seem dissimilar. Afterwards, it is the researcher's responsibility to interpret results derived from experiences, intuition, observation, and imagination.

Uncovering Attitudes toward the Competition

Sometimes the respondent is asked to describe an ideal brand. For example, a pharmaceutical company wanted to learn why physicians prescribe some brands more often than others, and some brands not at all.

The characteristics measured were *high* versus *low* potencies, and *few* versus *many* side effects. An ideal brand was perceived as one with medium potency and few side effects.

Those brands rating nearest the ideal brand were interpreted as being most desirable, while brands with potency extremes (either high or low), with many potential side effects, were evaluated as least prescribed.

If the sample of respondents is representative of the larger market of physicians, say, a national market, then brands most like the idealized one should be best sellers. The policy implication here is that the successful introduction of a new brand should appear quite similar to the ideal one, viz., medium potency and few side effects.

In another study, a wholesaler wanted to uncover the attitudes of regional distributors (their customers) toward it. Because exploratory research produced only vague answers, nonmetric multidimensional scaling was engaged to penetrate the minds and hearts of the purchasing agents. The respondents, i.e, the purchasing agents, paired this wholesale firm and competitors according to similarities and dissimilarities, and also ranked the firms in terms of preference.

In a much larger and longer study, DuPont investigated market segments for 45 products over a five-year interval. Similarly, computer users were surveyed on a number of operational items, listed in Figure III.5.A, ranking various brands according to experience of knowledge of the equipment.

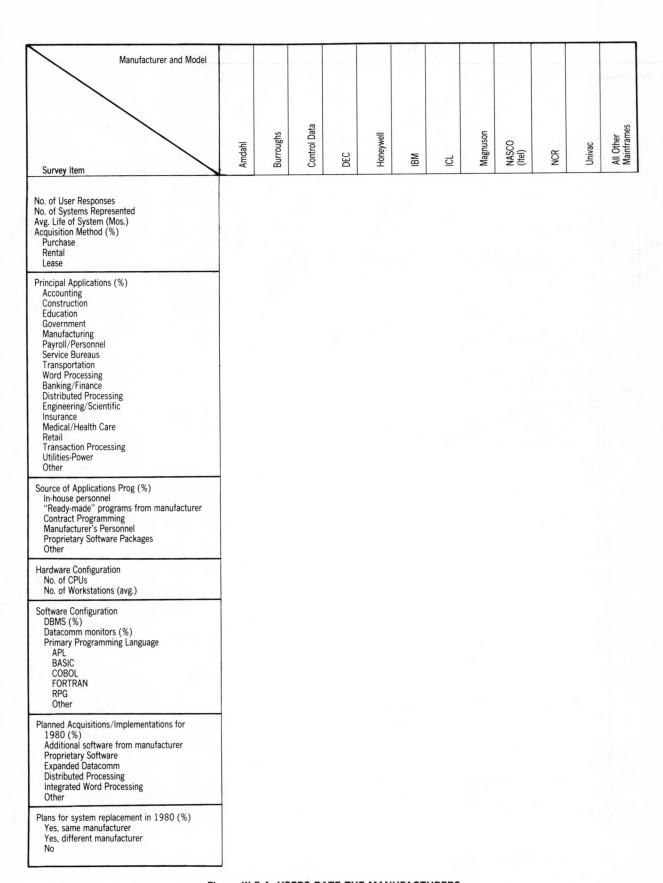

Manufacturer and Model / Survey Item	Amdahl	Burroughs	Control Data	DEC	Honeywell	IBM	ICL	Magnuson	NASCO (Itel)	NCR	Univac	All Other Mainframes
No. of User Responses												
No. of Systems Represented												
Avg. Life of System (Mos.)												
Acquisition Method (%)												
Purchase												
Rental												
Lease												
Principal Applications (%)												
Accounting												
Construction												
Education												
Government												
Manufacturing												
Payroll/Personnel												
Service Bureaus												
Transportation												
Word Processing												
Banking/Finance												
Distributed Processing												
Engineering/Scientific												
Insurance												
Medical/Health Care												
Retail												
Transaction Processing												
Utilities-Power												
Other												
Source of Applications Prog (%)												
In-house personnel												
"Ready-made" programs from manufacturer												
Contract Programming												
Manufacturer's Personnel												
Proprietary Software Packages												
Other												
Hardware Configuration												
No. of CPUs												
No. of Workstations (avg.)												
Software Configuration												
DBMS (%)												
Datacomm monitors (%)												
Primary Programming Language												
APL												
BASIC												
COBOL												
FORTRAN												
RPG												
Other												
Planned Acquisitions/Implementations for 1980 (%)												
Additional software from manufacturer												
Proprietary Software												
Expanded Datacomm												
Distributed Processing												
Integrated Word Processing												
Other												
Plans for system replacement in 1980 (%)												
Yes, same manufacturer												
Yes, different manufacturer												
No												

Figure III.5.A: USERS RATE THE MANUFACTURERS

Manufacturer and Model / Survey Item	Amdahl	Burroughs	Control Data	DEC	Honeywell	IBM	ICL	Magnuson	NASCO (Itel)	NCR	Univac	All Other Mainframes
Significant Problems (%)												
System proposed by vendor was too small												
Delivery and/or installation of equipment was late												
Delivery of required software was late												
System costs exceeded expected total												
Vendor did not provide all promised software or support												
Program/data compatibility not what vendor promised												
Terminals/peripherals compatibility not what vendor promised												
Vendor enhancements/changes to hardware/software hard to keep up with												
Equipment excessively noisy												
Power/Cooling requirements excessive												
Other												
Significant Advantages (%)												
Users happy with response time												
System easy to expand/reconfigure												
System costs less than expected												
Programs/data compatible, as vendor promised												
Terminals/peripherals compatible, as vendor promised												
System is power/energy efficient												
Productivity aids help us keep programming costs down												
Database language effective												
Delivery and/or installation of equipment was ahead of schedule												
Delivery and/or installation of software was ahead of schedule												
Other												
System Ratings (4.0-0.0)												
Ease of operation												
Reliability of Mainframe												
Reliability of Peripherals												
Maintenance service												
Responsiveness												
Effectiveness												
Technical support:												
Trouble-shooting												
Education												
Documentation												
Manufacturer's software												
Operating system												
Compilers & Assemblers												
Applications Programs												
Ease of programming												
Ease of conversion												
Overall satisfaction												
Would you recommend system to another user? (%)												
Yes												
No												

Figure III.5.A (continued)

One Last Example

Let's consider one last example. Suppose we are analyzing five brands of guava paste. Attributes rated may include spreadability, flavor, price (which you will notice now moves us away from two-dimensional considerations). These data are employed to generate two multidimensional scales: (1) one expresses pair relationships; (2) the other expresses attribute ratings.

Next we want to know which attribute is *most important* in determining the product's market position. Comparison of the scales will tell a fairly clear story. Significant correlations between scales will aid in axis labeling of the product comparison scale.

The purpose of the analysis is to convey some insights into how customers perceive your company's brand in relation to the competition, and which attributes the customer apparently thinks are important. And if the venture appears profitable, you are armed with information to improve your product and plan promotional activity to make yours the number-one seller.

The first three sections have covered the essentials of research design and collection of data on competitors, markets, and opinions of consumers and potential consumers. But the task does not end here. Data have little commercial value until they are analyzed and interpreted. Therefore, the next three sections of this book are devoted to this tedious but important endeavor.

SECTION *IV*

SAMPLING PROCEDURES

"I returned, and saw under the sun, that the race is not to the swift, nor the battle to the strong, neither yet bread to the wise, nor yet riches to men of understanding, nor yet favour to men of skill; but time and chance happeneth to them all."

Ecclesiastes 9:11

INTRODUCTION

From the human viewpoint, randomness plays a dominant role in our lives. The fact that chance and time underlie the outcomes of our personal and business decisions moves us to reduce risk, or at least shift it to someone else, and to compress or rearrange time to our liking.

The truth is that risk, the chance of failure as well as the chance of outrageous success, is everpresent in all undertakings. No act of man or state can wipe out these risks.

All we can ever succeed in achieving is to spread risks around so that each participant (firm or individual) in the risk pool shares a small part of the burden, which is essentially the principle of insurance; or, by plan, accident, or legislation we strive, too, to shift risks, particularly the burden of failure, onto someone else's shoulders. Some willingly accept risk—for a price: the speculators. Others prefer to function in a low-risk environment.

Time, like risk, follows us right into the bathroom; and the ravages of time sooner or later are reflected in the bathroom mirror. Like risk, we cannot really dissolve time, but we can rearrange it—again, for a price. Savings and borrowings represent shifting around . . . not of time, but of the *use* of time. But in the end, the price of risk and time must be paid, by someone.

Marketing research has, as one end, the reduction of risk, and, more subtly, rearrangement of time. This is particularly evident in sampling procedures, where the tradeoff plants a wedge between pertinent information, necesssary for risk reduction, and time (costs) required to get enough of it to achieve the desired ends. And sampling becomes the intermediary in this tradeoff. Sampling is a technique to get just enough quality information at costs below returns to investment, which translates into a policy of figuring out samples that are big enough, but not too big.

Therefore, the sampling techniques brought to light in the following pages aim to accomplish two ends: (a) size—neither too small nor too large; and (b) representativeness. The second issue occupies more time and skill than the first one because of the heterogeneity of buyers. The problem is unlike finding a sample bite of candy representative of the entire box, for if the ingredients are well mixed, the samplers adequately tell the story of every like piece in the box.

Blessed with distinctness and heterogeneity, individuals and their whimsical desires have confounded a whole army of statisticians whose task has been to discover some efficient method for mixing up batches of humans and then taking a thin slice of opinions expected to reflect the whole sweet mixture.

The techniques explicated in the first four subsections of this section on sampling procedures demonstrate, in a practical manner, where to go and how to find the smallest number of persons who reflect the ideas and preferences of the largest number of customers.

Some techniques are better suited to one set of circumstances than to another. Finding the best or most likely one hinges on at least a cursory understanding of how each of these techniques solves distinct problems. But satisfactory outcomes derived from the techniques presented in Sections I, II, and III depend on an appropriate application of sampling procedures.

By far, businesses of all sizes, small to giant, depend upon simple random sampling procedures discussed in the first subsection. These practical techniques require no advanced degree in anything, just a little time to study how and when to implement the ideas found in the following pages.

None of these techniques require any complicated investment in time or application costs, but understanding and implementing such simple techniques as throwing all the names in a hat, done at the right time and under the right circumstances, will mean the difference between sample results that increase risks and sample results that decrease risks. The line between profits and bankruptcy, often quite thin, is widened by the careful planner and thorough manager.

The sampling procedures in the first four subsections are presented in their decreasing order of importance to most business concerns. Although medium-sized firms, according to one survey, typically prefer judgmental sampling procedures over quota sampling, both small and large businesses prefer the opposite, i.e., quota sampling over judgmental. The differences hinge on your needs.

For instance, quota sampling is used least by industrial concerns because it does not fit business needs, whereas consumer and utility companies depend heavily on it. Cluster sampling seems to be least popular among all types of firms. Simple random sampling and stratified sampling, according to the survey, rank tops for all types of organizations.

The other critical issue is size of the sample, because that together with your budget determines how much marketing research takes place or whether there will be a project at all. The formulas demonstrated should provide profitable guidelines for planned endeavors.

The last subsection deals with two items. The first part of the subsection tells how to code the information in a survey prior to entering the data for analysis. The remainder of the subsection focuses on a data-organizing technique, cross-tabulation—popular, practical, and easy to apply. Finally, the section ends by telling you how to wring more out of data, that extra squeeze that lowers cost per unit of information and produces the additional bit or byte of information that propels you into profit-dom.

IV.1: THE GOLDEN TOUCH OF SIMPLE RANDOM SAMPLING

Possibly the safest marketing approach is to know individually each present and potential customer well enough to box in potential, untapped markets. Firms with a direct sales force, in one sense, do this—but in a rather inconsistent and altogether statistically unreliable way.

But this source is only part of our treasure trove of marketing information. What techniques must we rely on when we have many actual and potential customers widely scattered geographically?

Four Critical Elements

It is not always possible to know enough about each customer or potential customer; at least four principal barriers stand between the researcher and complete, reliable information.

1. *Cost*. Because data collection is not cost-free, cost-conscious firms specifically allocate funds for this task. If it costs $100 per survey unit (say, each customer) to gather information on that person or item, and only $10,000 can be allocated to the process, data from a limited number of elements enter into marketing calculations. The sample must be carefully chosen. The objective is to obtain the maximum amount of data with the minimum amount of costs.

2. *Time*. Given enough time, almost everyone can accomplish or learn about anything. One author joked that he would even undertake to write a book on brain surgery, self-taught, given enough time and financial resources. But it is the timely combination of labor and natural resources that converts raw ideas and information into hard profits.

And timing is critical in getting a jump on competitors. Scheduling a new product to come out by year-end limits time available for market research and the quantity and depth of data accumulated.

3. *Risk*. Several kinds of risk lie in wait ready to pounce on the unsuspecting researcher. If information-gathering takes too long or is accumulated too soon, then the information becomes too well known, too stale, or outdated. Ask a present class of college students what kind of entertainment or clothes they prefer, then base product development to sell to this shifting market some five years later. The sales outcome is totally unpredictable in the absence of other information. There is the risk of timing. Changing events, moods, even habits,

alter with time and color interpretation of data. Competition may spoil the market or survey results.

And, too, the longer we take to collect evidence and the more of it we require, as things become more universally known, the more competitive the market becomes, and the lower the potential profits. Higher profits result from the ability of management to differentiate substantially its products based either on uniqueness or on market information.

4. *Method*. Methods of information collection and interpretation are stressed throughout this idea book because, in dealing with an uncertain, even unknowable, future, improperly applied techniques of sampling, analyzing, and interpreting data can severely distort results and possibly render the whole output of information invalid—a costly waste of time and money. With any method some bias is present; the objective is to minimize that bias.

A Representative Sample

Therefore, we must strive to blast away these barriers to a profit-producing market data mine. How we organize the process has, in large measure, been pre-determined.

If we interview, or measure, the entire population, or entire universe, this implies that the elements (people or items of merchandise) must be few enough in number to permit examination of each one individually. *Population* refers to the total market concerned.

The universe may be finite, in which case we know the number of elements involved. For example, if the potential market is U.S. Senators, then the population is finite—a total of 100. If we want to define characteristics pertinent to all past, present, and future senators, then the market population is infinite.

In either situation, it may not be feasible to deal with the entire population. Therefore, we must study a representative sample of senators, and then project findings onto the entire population of senators. Cost, time, risk and methodology will indicate the sample size of senators.

However, from a sample too small, or insufficiently representative, we can easily draw erroneous conclusions from the misleading data. Usually a larger sample is preferred to a smaller one—unless, of course one senator is typical of the entire population of senators; then a sample of one, or a small sample, is justifiable.

No magic number prevails when we deal with humans, each one purposively acting to fulfill individual objectives, despite the best efforts of statisticians to make it otherwise. But a sample of 5 to 10 percent for smaller and medium-sized populations provides a starting point for generating acceptable estimates. Nevertheless, Section IV.5 explicates a technique for estimating sample size.

Dealing with millions of elements, of course, necessitates a substantially smaller but well-chosen sample. Recognize, of course, that not all samples lead to the same estimates of the entire population.

Simple Random Sampling

One technique, simple random sampling, easy to understand and apply, serves as a good approximation to other, more complex, sampling methods.

An important underlying assumption overshadows this technique: it is assumed that each and every element of the population has an equal chance of being chosen.

If, for a week, you stood in front of the grain elevator at Butler, Ohio, and asked everyone who passed what s/he thought of *The Ohio Farmer*, your survey results would not be useful; neither would this be a simple random sample.

Restricted location, time of year, and likelihood that not every interviewee reads the magazine means that not every element of the population of readers has an equal chance of selection. The following example of a finite population illustrates three methods for selecting a simple random sample.

Assume that the universe consists of seven salespersons: Aaron, Bathsheba, Charity, David, Ezra, Faith, and Gallio. We want to select a sample of two persons to represent the entire population.

The sample must be chosen in such a manner that each salesperson has an equal chance of being tagged. Because we are dealing with small numbers, Figure IV.1.A enumerates all the sample possibilities.

There are 21 possible combinations. Actually there are 42 combinations (7 $\times$ 6 = 42). Since AB and BA, for example, represent the same two individuals, no practical reason exists to count them twice.

> *Note*: The reason that there are only 42 and not 49 samples is that no combinations such as AA or BB exist; ergo, each of the seven persons can enter into only six distinct combinations, or 6 $\times$ 7.

The samples derive from a simple random sampling method. The question arises as to how to select a representative sample that reasonably characterizes the rest of the population.

Selection from All Possible Samples

A simple way to choose a sample is the fishbowl method:

1. Write each sample number on a scrap paper and slip it into capsules of uniform size and quality.
2. Place the sealed capsules in a bowl; mix thoroughly.
3. Draw one capsule.

The pair of salespersons indicated on the paper in the capsule will be the sample.

Of course, even with this technique the possibility of biases exists. Reaching in the bowl and drawing out one capsule suggests a degree of selectivity—including processes that occur at the subconscious level. The depth, shape, and size of the bowl, or the position of the capsules within the bowl, will probably in-

ALL POSSIBLE SAMPLES OF TWO FROM A FINITE POPULATION OF SEVEN

Sample	Persons	Sample	Persons	Sample	Persons	Sample	Persons	Sample	Persons	Sample	Persons
1	A B	7	B C	12	C D	16	D E	19	E F	21	F G
2	A C	8	B D	13	C E	17	D F	20	E G		
3	A D	9	B E	14	C F	18	D G				
4	A E	10	B F	15	C G						
5	A F	11	B G								
6	A G										

Figure IV.1.A: ALL POSSIBLE SAMPLES OF TWO FROM A FINITE POPULATION OF SEVEN

fluence sample selection. If the sample pairs were written on pieces of paper, variations in paper sizes, how they were folded, etc., could influence the sample chosen.

Selection of Individual Elements

For most practical occasions, the foregoing method is impractical. Another system is to select each element of the sample individually.

1. Place each salesperson's name in a separate capsule and mix the capsules thoroughly in a bowl.
2. Select one capsule from among the seven.
3. Again thoroughly mix the remaining six capsules.
4. Select the second capsule from among the six.

Obviously, in dealing with large numbers the superiority of the second method prevails; however, in either situation, we end up with a sample presumed to reflect the chief characteristics of most or all of the other salespersons.

Tables of Random Numbers

But in struggling with large numbers, neither of the above methods seems very efficient. Imagine drawing a sample of 12,000 elements from a finite population of 1,000,000! That's a lot of fishing!

A table of random numbers equips us with a viable alternative. Such tables are frequently used in sampling. Tables are readily available—including the one in Appendix A of this handbook.

Our simple illustration of seven salespersons will demonstrate the application of a random numbers table.

1. Begin by numbering the seven salespersons in the sample: A-1, B-2, C-3, D-4, E-5, F-6, G-7.
2. Next, choose two random numbers from Appendix A. (You may simply open the book to the table, close your eyes, and take a stab in the dark. The digit you pick numbers the first element of the sample. Then, the number above that one—or below, or left or right—numbers the second element in the sample.) Let's say that before opening the book to the table we agree to select from Row 24, Column 2, picking consecutive numbers to the right.
3. Step 3 is to find the digit corresponding to Row 24, Column 2, which is "2" in the table. Therefore, Bathsheba is the first person of the sample. Moving to the right we encounter a zero. No element is numbered 0, so we continue to the next digit to the right, an "8." Neither do we have an eighth element. Further to the right we encounter a "4," so David is the second person of the sample. The sample queried will consist of Bathsheba and David.

Here is how the same method works with larger numbers. Suppose that you want to sample retail lumber outlets. With 75 in the population, you decide to sample 20 percent, or a total of 15 stores.

Number the stores (in any order), from 1 through 75. Pair two sets of columns from the random numbers table, say columns 7 and 11, and 18 and 19. Start down columns 7 and 11, continue down 18 and 19, if necessary, until you have 15 viable numbers. The sample will now consist of stores numbered: 53, 74, 55, 69, 59, 31, 35, 54, 06, 08, 30, 44, 61, 29, 52.

Using the Data

After gathering sample data, it is necessary to put it in more usable form, that is, analysis, interpretation, presentation. To illustrate several of the chief concepts, refer to data in Figure IV.1.B, which describes the distribution of workers' hourly wages ranging from $1.50 to $16.49 per hour.

To better handle the data, 15 levels of hourly wages are indicated rather than to record individual hourly wages of each of the 3,000 workers in the population. The middle-of-the-range figure is employed in the calculations, i.e., $2, $3, $4, . . . $16. Notice the third column entry which shows preparation before reference to a random numbers table.

The first three important summaries discussed measure central tendency: (a) mode, (b) median, and (c) arithmetic mean. They are kinds of averages. The one selected is naturally that one most appropriate to the situation.

The Mode (MO)

The mode, or modal value, conveys the idea of the most popular value in the frequency distribution. A sample with one mode is unimodal. More than one mode may spring up, just as more than one dress fashion may prevail in any given season.

In the accompanying table, what is the most frequently paid hourly wage? A careful examination reveals that there are two points of maximum density: hourly wages around $5.00 ($4.50–$5.49), and again around $8.00 ($7.50–$8.49). This is a bimodal distribution, because two modes, or popular wage rates, exist.

More specifically, the mode can be determined by the following formula:

$$\text{Mode} = \text{lower limit of modal class} + \frac{f_m - f_1}{2(f_m) - (f_1 + f_2)} \, i$$

f_m = number of frequencies in modal class interval.
f_1 = number of frequencies in preceding class interval.
f_2 = number of frequencies in following class interval.
i = size of modal class.

$$\text{Mode} = \$4.50 + \frac{480 - 280}{2(480) - (310 + 280)} \, \$1 = \$5.04$$

The mode, then, is $5.04, one of the two most typical values in this bimodal distribution. This measure is most useful in highly skewed or nonnormal distribution because it highlights the point(s) of heaviest concentration(s).

DISTRIBUTION OF HOURLY WAGES, AND THREE SAMPLES

Hourly Wages	Number of Workers f	Cumulative Numbers For Random Selection		Sample # 1 Tallies	f	Sample # 2 Tallies	f	Sample # 3 Tallies	f
$ 1.50 2.49	15	0	15	卌 II	7	卌 II	7	卌	5
2.50 3.49	345	16	360	IIII	4	IIII	4	IIII	4
3.50 4.49	280	361	640	卌 III	8	卌 卌	10	卌 III	8
4.50 5.49	480	641	1120	卌 III	8	II	2	卌	5
5.50 6.49	310	1121	1430	卌 III	8	卌	5	IIII	4
6.50 7.49	305	1431	1735	卌	5	卌 卌 II	12	卌 IIII	9
7.50 8.49	480	1736	2215	卌 I	6	III	3	II	2
8.50 9.49	275	2216	2490		0	II	2	II	2
9.50 10.49	185	2491	2675	III	3	II	2	III	4
10.50 11.49	155	2676	2830	I	1	I	1	I	1
11.50 12.49	65	2831	2895					III	3
12.50 13.49	40	2896	2935					II	2
13.50 14.49	30	2936	2965					I	1
14.50 15.49	25	2966	2990						
15.50 16.49	10	2991	3000						
	3000				50		50		50

$$\bar{X} = \frac{20,705}{3,000} = \$6.90$$

Figure IV.1.B: DISTRIBUTION OF HOURLY WAGES, AND THREE SAMPLES

The mode requires only nominal data. Recall the discussion of nominal scales, the least restrictive of scales, in Section III. In this example, the mode is that value which appears most frequently. In a relative frequency distribution, the mode is the class with the highest frequency.

A distribution can have several peaks, called multimodal. Such information may be useful where there are fairly direct and known relationships between, say, hourly wages and the type and quantity of certain products consumed. (That possibility arises in the ocean pout example in Section II.1.)

The Median (MD)

Another kind of average, the median, is the midpoint in a frequency distribution. If there is only one element in each category, such as 1, 2, 3, 4, 5, then the midpoint, 3, is easily located.

In our example of 3,000 workers, we need to cumulate data. Adding the number of workers, we discover that the one-half point, or 1500 workers, lies in the $6.50—$7.49 class. This is the median class.

Exactly where the median worker's wage lies in this class cannot be ascertained. However, we can estimate the median by the following formula.

$$\text{Md} = \text{Lower class limit} + \left(\text{class interval} \times \frac{\text{required number}}{\text{class frequency}}\right)$$

The lower limit of the median class is $6.50. The class interval is $1.00. Through $6.49, the distribution accounts for 1430 workers. Therefore, we require 70 additional workers from the next class to add up to 1500.

The portion in parentheses in the above formula relates to that portion of the next class times the difference among classes, or (70/305 $\times$ $1.00).

$$\text{Md} = \$6.50 + (\$1.00 \times \frac{70}{305}) = \$6.50 + \$0.23 = \$6.73$$

By an estimating technique we have discovered another average, the median, to be $6.73 per hour.

The median requires only ordinal data, referred to in Sections III.1, III.3, III.4. The median is a ranking technique. Values of 50 percent of observations fall below the median, and 50 percent lie above the median. Being average, in this sense, means that the value falls precisely at mid-range.

An example: The Newspaper Fund surveyed journalism school graduates and discovered that the median salary range for 14,600 newly hired graduates, for the year of the survey, was $151—$170 weekly. In this instance, the median, rather than representing a single figure, consists of a range, a convenient method for dealing with a large sample.

The Arithmetic Mean (X)

Usually when someone refers to the term "average," s/he is thinking of the arithmetic mean. But, like all averages, it is a statistical convenience. There is no average person, with an average taste, who measures up to all the other average statistics. God created individuals, each distinctly different. The concept of mass man is a figment of a Socialist's imagination. While such an erroneous concept may be convenient for government control, it is suicidal for marketing decision-making.

If half of the consumers in a given market area eat white bread and the other half eat dark (rye) bread, the average color is gray—hardly valuable information for marketing.

Or a restaurant management who discovers that tea drinkers prefer iced tea in summer and hot tea in winter will hardly promote lukewarm tea as a year-round beverage. And here should lie the remains of a normalized statistic.

Roger J. Williams writes, "Statistical man has little to do with you or me or any other real person. But the blame should not be cast on statistics. Rightly used by experts who understand their limitations they are a boon to humanity. But in dealing with people they should be used with care!" With precaution we proceed.

The mean of any set of values is simply the summation of those values divided by the number of items. To find the *arithmetic mean* of a population, here is the formula:

$$\overline{X} = \frac{\Sigma x_i}{N} \text{ or } \mu = \frac{\Sigma x}{N}$$

Which reads that the arithmetic mean of a given population is equal to the sum of (Σ) values of the elements (let $i = 1,2,\ldots N$) divided by the number of (N) elements in the population

By the same token, to find the *mean of a sample*, which is a subset of a population:

$$\overline{x} = \frac{\Sigma x}{n}$$

Or to find the *mean of a distribution*, we need to determine the frequency (f) with which each class appears in the distribution, so that:

$$\overline{x} = \frac{\Sigma fx}{n},$$

where Σfx represents the sum of the products obtained by multiplying each class (x) by its class frequency (f).

For example, in Figure IV.1.B, to find the mean of the population we multiply each class (hourly wages) times the class frequency (number of workers) and sum these products (20,705), which is then divided by the number of workers (3,000), resulting in a population mean ($\overline{X}$) of $6.90, the average hourly wage.

To find a sample mean (of a sample consisting of 50 elements), we first need to select the sample by using a random numbers table, for example. This results in sample frequencies registered under "tallies" of Sample #1.

The sample frequency is multiplied by its class value. The sum of these products (317) is divided by the number of elements in the sample (50). This gives us a sample mean ($6.34 for Sample #1).

Choosing different columns from the random numbers table produces two other samples with different sample means: $6.80 for Sample #2, and $7.54 for Sample #3.

Notice that the three samples produce rather divergent results. Sample #1 and #3 means vary significantly greater from the population mean.

We conclude, therefore, that although two samples are identical, they will yield different results; and neither one will necessarily be close to the population mean. This illustrates (a) the necessity of having a good sample; and (b) the importance of treating no results as absolutes.

If we take all possible samples, using every possible combination, and then average all sample means, the result will equal the population mean.

If we average the three sample means—$6.34, $6.80, and $7.54—a new mean of $6.89 emerges, which just happens to coincide rather well with the population mean. (It may not always work out so well.)

Another interesting aspect of this illustration is that if we plot the distribution in a graph (hourly wages on the horizontal axis and number of workers on the vertical axis), the shape of the sample curves tends to approximate (not necessarily overlap) the shape of the population. The importance of this information will become clearer in Section V.1, with the discussion on standard error of the mean.

Averages are employed in many ways. For example, the Employee Relocation Council surveyed its 530 corporate members and learned that council members transfer an average 282 employees per year. Although costs for employee transfers average $13,000 at Whirlpool Corporation, they average $23,000 for Exxon Corporation. Without further data on range costs, administrative level of employee, and definition of costs, these averages remain incomparable and supply us with only a limited amount of useful data.

Ratio Estimates

Ratio estimates consist of a ratio of quantities (both numerator and denominator vary from sample to sample) illustrated in Figure IV.1.C.

RATIO ESTIMATES

	Sales of		
Store	Brand X	Total Product Class	
I	8	24	
II	2	15	
III	15	25	50/120 = 0.4167
IV	15	36	
V	10	20	
	50	120	

Figure IV.1.C: RATIO ESTIMATES

Suppose the population encompasses five quick-service stores which sell both Brand X and competing brands. Sales of Brand X and the total sales of Brand X plus competing brands appear in the two columns of the table. For all five stores together, the ratio of Brand X sales to total product sales is $50/120 = 0.4167$, or about 42 percent.

However, note that in considering all possible samples in Figure IV.1.D, the averages of all ten possible brand shares do not equate, contrary to the preceding discovery.

RATIO ESTIMATES OF VARIOUS SAMPLE POSSIBILITIES

| Possible Sample | Sample Total of | | Sample Brand Share |
	Product X	Class	
I, II	10	39	$10/39 = 0.2564$
I, III	23	49	$23/49 = 0.4694$
I, IV	23	60	$23/60 = 0.3833$
I, V	18	44	$18/44 = 0.4091$
II, III	17	40	$17/40 = 0.4250$
II, IV	17	51	$17/51 = 0.3333$
II, V	12	35	$12/35 = 0.3429$
III, IV	30	61	$30/61 = 0.4918$
III, V	25	45	$25/45 = 0.5556$
IV, V	25	56	$25/56 = 0.4464$
			Average $= 0.4113$

Figure IV.1.D: RATIO ESTIMATES OF VARIOUS SAMPLE POSSIBILITIES

Ratio estimates of the sample average out to 0.4113. This is an example of a biased estimate; the example above, fully carried out, would have produced an unbiased result. Nevertheless, the concept is useful.

Interquartile Range

If pricing and marketing strategy center on a middle group target, another procedure to determine this market target easily is the interquartile range. Because the quartile deviation focuses on the middle 50 percent, it is necessary to calculate the first and third quartiles.

The first quartile (Q_1) relates to the lower 25 percent of the distribution. The third quartile (Q_3) relates to the highest 25 percent of the distribution. Therefore, the second quartile (Q_2) must encompass the middle 50 percent.

To explain these calculations, refer again to Figure IV.1.A, the distribution of 3,000 workers' hourly wages.

In a straightforward distribution, finding the first quartile means marking off the lowest 25 percent. However, in Figure IV.1.B, the lowest 25 percent (i.e., $3,000 \div 4 = 750$) lies within a class. The technique now is to estimate where the 25 percent level falls within a particular wage class. (The method, while not as accurate as sin, does impart a reasonable approximation.)

Although the subscripts in the formula below pertain to the first quartile, the formula is the same for finding each quartile.

$$Q_1 = L_1 + \frac{\frac{n}{4} - CF_1}{f} \text{ (i)}$$

Q = the quartile boundary indicated by the subscript (1, 2, or 3).
L = the lower limit of the class within which the quartile falls.
n = the total number of frequencies.
CF = the cumulative frequency for all classes below the class containing the quartile being calculated.
f = the total number of frequencies in the class containing the quartile being calculated.
i = the width of the class in which the quartile being calculated falls.

To illustrate the application of the formula for the first quartile, we observe that n/4 equals an even 750. The next step is to ascertain within which hourly wage class the 750th worker falls.

Adding together the number of workers, we learn that 640 (CF_1) workers of the universe earn less than \$4.50 per hour. The first quartile, then, must lie in the next class of \$4.50—\$5.49, so that the lower limit (L_1) of the class is \$4.50, and the total number of workers of this last class, 480, represents the frequency (f) of that class.

Finally, we note that the width of the class (i) is \$1.00. Substituting in the formula results in this:

$$Q_1 = \$4.50 + \frac{\frac{3000}{4} - 640_1}{480} (\$1.00) = \$4.50 + \$0.23 = \$4.73$$

The hourly wage that roughly corresponds to the boundary of the first quartile, then, is \$4.73. By the same process we can also demarcate the third quartile (Q_3).

$$Q_3 = \$8.50 + \frac{\frac{3}{4}(3000) - 2215}{275} (\$1.00) = \$8.50 + \$0.13 = \$8.63$$

The interquartile range, the distance between Q_1 and Q_3, encompasses the 50 percent middle group: \$8.63—\$4.73. If the distribution were symmetrical, then the distance between Q_2 and Q_3 would equal the distance between Q_2 and Q_1, which it does not in this example.

The semi-interquartile range (or quartile deviation):

$$\text{SIR} = \frac{Q_3 - Q_1}{2}$$

Or, in this distribution, the SIR is $1.95. In a symmetrical distribution, adding or subtracting the SIR to or from Q_2, the results correspond to Q_3 or Q_1, respectively. Solving for Q_2 yields $6.73. With this information we can peg whether the distribution is positively or negatively skewed.

If $Q_2 - Q_1 > Q_3 - Q_2$, then the distribution is negatively skewed.
If $Q_2 - Q_1 < Q_3 - Q_2$, then the distribution is positively skewed.

In this example, $6.73 - 4.73$ is greater than $8.63 - 6.73$. Hence, the distribution is negatively skewed, which tells us that the median plus and minus the semi-interquartile range does *not* embody the central 50 percent of the distribution.

Skewness suggests imbalance. A small part of the distribution, that is, extreme cases, pulls the averages either higher or lower. If these figures are diagrammed, the extreme values pull the mean right or left.

A negatively skewed distribution means that some extreme values to the left of the mean are lowering the mean's value. A positively skewed distribution raises the mean. (Also see Section V.3.)

For instance, *Drug Topics* magazine surveyed the workweek and salaries of pharmacists. The survey revealed that 20 percent of the pharmacists work 40 hours or less per week; about 33 percent work 50 hours or more. Furthermore, more than one-half of them earn between $15,000 and $25,000 annually, and 12 percent earn $35,000 or more.

The distribution of hours worked suggests that it is positively skewed, pulling the average upward. The interquartile range seems to embrace the $15,000 to $25,000 group.

Some Shortcuts

At this point we may note some other effects of skewing on the arithmetic mean, median, and mode. In a perfectly symmetrical single mode distribution, the mean, median, and mode are coincident. They equal each other.

In a negatively skewed, asymmetrical distribution, the mean being pulled by a few, but very low-value, observations, will be the lowest of the median and mode. (The distribution in Figure IV.1.B is only very slightly skewed, and the mean is not sufficiently negatively affected.)

In a positively skewed distribution, the mean will be the highest of the three central measures.

We also observe that in a moderately skewed, single-mode distribution, the median tends to fall about one-third of the distance between the mean and the mode. Accordingly, if we know any two of the measures, the third can be estimated quickly by any of these shortcut formulas:

Formula I: $M_d = \dfrac{Mo - \overline{X}}{3} + \overline{X}$

Formula II: $Mo = \overline{X} + 3\,(Md - \overline{X})$

Formula III: $\overline{X} = \dfrac{3\,Md - Mo}{2}$

Some Pros and Cons and Uses

Finally, we can summarize some advantages and disadvantages of these various measures. The mean has the distinct advantage of being the most commonly used and understood measurement. It is used extensively in sampling and forecasting, and is easily manipulated algebraically. On the other hand, it loses its value in extremely skewed data, where a few high or low extreme values can significantly raise or lower the mean and obscure the results.

Of course, the mean may be modified by eliminating extreme values and deriving a new mean from remaining observations. A modified mean is appropriate under certain conditions.

Another way of dealing with extreme values is the geometric mean, an accurate method of averaging ratios, percentages, indices, and relatives. Another alternative for special situations is the harmonic mean of numbers—n divided by the sum of the reciprocals of the n numbers:

$$n \div \Sigma\, 1/x.$$

Consequently, the median, not affected by extreme high and low values, ranks highly as a popular middle measure of highlighting the typical purchaser or user. It also has the advantage of applicability, where classes are of unequal value, or where distributions are open ended. A drawback is that it cannot be manipulated algebraically.

Similarly, the mode is not influenced by extreme values. It can also be used with open-ended distributions, even where class intervals are of unequal value. It, too, cannot be manipulated algebraically.

The semi-interquartile range can be utilized with open-ended distributions, and, like the mode, is not influenced by extreme values (a disadvantage).

However, measures finer than quartiles may be replaced by deciles, which divide the distribution into 10 equal parts; and percentiles, which divide the distribution into 100 equal parts.

The formula and procedures are similar to those used in finding quartiles except that instead of n/4 in the basic formula, for deciles n/10 substitutes, and for percentiles n/100 applies.

Averages have a variety of applications. For example, Data Probe, Inc., a New York research firm, studied the readers of *Prevention*, a health magazine.

Data Probe calculated that the average *Prevention* household spends $206.70 annually on vitamins, dietary supplements, and health foods. With readership in excess of two million, the potential market for these items among the readership exceeds $400 million a year.

Consequently, this information represents a strong sales clout to advertisers and potential advertisers who spent about $9 million annually, at the time of the survey, to reach that market.

To pinpoint exactly which age, income, and geographical groups spend the lion's share of this some $400 million, further sampling refinement is required. For example, it is known that 70 percent of the readers are over age 50. With a process known as stratification, or cross-stratification, more can be learned about these readers.

IV.2: SIMPLIFIED STRATIFIED SAMPLING FOR PROFITABLE RESULTS

To adjust for some shortcomings of simple random sampling, a technique known as stratified sampling, widely used in marketing research, reduces both sampling costs and errors. This sterling approach focuses directly on those groups which most significantly relate to the profit variables under analysis.

Stratified sampling depends on at least a basic acquaintance with population characteristics and their relationships to the measured variables. It is not a recommended approach when nothing is known about the market.

For instance, in a study of commodity speculators, if the researcher suspects significant differences between male and female speculators, or among age or income groups, then stratified sampling is appropriate.

An example of applied stratified sampling is subgrouping a radio audience by age categories. Because the lyrics of a song titled *Short People* were controversial, several radio stations banned it to avoid losing radio audience.

Radio station WFIL of Philadelphia researched listener reactions. Management concluded that 50 percent of all persons between ages 35 and 44 strongly objected to the song, and that 38.5 percent of all women ages 25 to 34 said they would switch stations rather than listen to the song; but less than 30 percent of men of the same age group reacted negatively.

Listening audience, for this survey, was stratified by age and sex. The population could have been stratified by income group, job categories, location, etc.; but the cost of finer stratification would not have produced details of any greater significance in this instance, for the answer sought was whether to play the song —a yes/no decision.

Market segmentation, especially important to radio advertising, presumes that specific market segments can be identified and serviced. Stratified sampling is an important technique for identifying these segments. Although advertising may be directed to a smaller number of persons in any given market segment, return per advertising dollar spent should be higher due to apparent market homogeneity.

Steps to Stratified Sampling

The procedure is not complicated. You can learn the basics of it in a few minutes. Just follow these time-saving steps to stratified sampling.

STEP 1: Stratify the Universe into Subgroups.

There are three basic questions to consider here:

◎ How should the population be stratified?
◎ How many strata should there be?
◎ How should each stratum boundary be identified?

As a general rule, to lower sampling costs, the elements within each stratum ought to be as nearly similar as possible. The reason for this should become apparent.

If a subgroup of people whose incomes are very nearly alike is sampled, a fairly small sample will characterize the entire subgroup. If incomes vary widely, a larger sample is necessary to account for as many different incomes as reasonable.

Too, it is desirable to establish strata that will maximize differences in stratum means for the principal variables in the survey.

Typically, populations are stratified on demographic characteristics such as income, age, sex and density. For institutional surveys, a measure of size represents the norm: dollar value of sales, number of employees, net worth, etc.

Likewise, there are cost restraints. Beyond a certain point additional stratification may not yield sufficiently beneficial information to justify additional costs of stratification; i.e., marginal outcomes are less productive than incremental costs of obtaining these results.

Also, there is nearly always unexplained variability within a set of observations. Even with the finer tuning of additional stratification it is not likely that this data noise will disappear: sampling techniques are not perfect; other factors as well, not accounted for, produce this residual effect.

Stratum boundaries are decided on whether stratification is based on qualitative or quantitative variables. Qualitative subdivisions hinge largely on judgments, which means familiarity with the market, product, etc. For quantitative variables, definite rules exist; one method is explained at the end of this subsection.

STEP 2: Sample Each Stratum Independently of Other Strata.

The objective of sampling is to obtain the maximum amount of useful information at the least cost.

Sometimes we know in advance the cost of each observation. In this case a fixed budget predetermines a sample size. To illustrate, if the survey budget is $5400, and the cost per sample item is $20 each, then the sample size is limited to 270 elements.

But assume there are four strata. How large will each sample be from each stratum?

One method depends on an equal random sample (employing concepts learned in the previous subsection). However, such a technique can produce rather lopsided outcomes. Two other possibilities are (1) a proportional sample, and (2) a nonproportional sample.

Assume that a research project focusing on sales of butter involves sampling various kinds of grocery stores, from supermarkets to convenience neighborhood stores, to determine stocking and display practices, advertising specials and expenditures, number of employees, and number and varieties of close substitutes.

The stores surveyed can be stratified according to dollar volume of sales in the manner illustrated in Figure IV.2.A. How many stores shall enter into each sample?

STRATIFICATION BY DOLLAR VOLUME OF SALES			
Annual Sales	No. of Stores	Percent of Total	No. in Sample
Over $5 million	1200	6.67 %	18
From $2.5 up to $5 million	4000	22.22	60
From $1 up to $2.5 million	6800	37.78	102
Under $1 million	6000	33.33	90
	18,000	100.00 %	270

Figure IV.2.A: STRATIFICATION BY DOLLAR VOLUME OF SALES

Proportional Sampling

Proportional sampling means that the number of elements in each stratum sample must be in the same proportion as in the entire population.

To continue with the foregoing example, total sample size is restricted to 270 stores because of budget constraints. There are 18,000 stores in the entire population, which have been stratified into four groupings of unequal size.

Sample size equals 1.5 percent of the total population:

$$\frac{270}{18,000} = 1.5\%$$

The method, then, is to multiply the number of stores in each stratum by 0.015 to determine the number of stores in each sample. (Results appear in Figure IV.2.A.)

The categories with the larger number of stores are most heavily represented in their respective strata samples. To select specific stores in each stratum, recourse to random numbers, discussed in Section IV.1, may economically solve the problem of selection. (A random numbers table in Appendix A has been generated for your convenience.)

Weighting of sample statistics for each stratum helps to derive a solitary figure indicative of the market population. For example, one of the variables mentioned in the proposed survey on butter sales was advertising expenditures. Each subgroup of stores can be weighted by the average amount spent on advertising (as a percent of sales). Then, each sample is weighted according to the scheme illustrated in Figure IV.2.B.

WEIGHTED VALUES FOR EACH SAMPLE			
Annual Sales	Number in Sample	Percent of Sales Spent on Advertising	Weighted Values
Over $5 million	18	9	162
$2.5 up to $5 MM	60	6	360
$1 up to $2.5 MM	102	8	816
Under $1 million	90	3	270
	270		1608

Figure IV.2.B: WEIGHTED VALUES FOR EACH SAMPLE

In the table, the very largest stores spent an average 9 cents of every sales dollar on advertising, while the stores with the lowest dollar volume spent an average 3 cents of their sales dollars on advertising.

Multiplying each weight (advertising expenditures) times the number of stores in each sample yields weighted values totaling 1608.

The arithmetic mean of advertising expenditures (1608 ÷ 270) for *all* stores in the population registers around 6 cents of every sales dollar (actually 5.96).

If the population size is manageable, another proportioning method arises, namely, ranking of all elements by some criterion. In this illustration, stores are ranked from largest to smallest based upon annual sales. The next step is to decide upon the number of stratum.

Suppose that the population is divided into six strata. With a total of 18,000 stores, and dividing by 6, each stratum will comprise 3,000 stores.

After ranking the 18,000 stores, the cutoff point for each interval will be in multiples of 3,000. Still working with a total sample of 270 stores, each sample will now consist of 45 stores (45 × 6 = 270).

If required, the results can be weighted again in the manner described above. However, one difficulty with this method is the disproportionate size of stores, which rank from multimillion dollar operations to small country stores selling gasoline and a limited line of groceries.

Nonproportional Stratified Sample

To offset divergences in size and volume, a nonproportional stratified sample gives greatest weight to the largest stores and least importance to the smallest.

In proportional sampling, only *one* large store is sampled for each *five* small stores, biasing results in favor of the smaller units. Quite possibly, the 1200 largest stores sell more than all the 12,800 stores in the under 2.5 million categories together. Consequently, greater weight should be given to high volume stores in the total sampling process.

Although the mathematics of this process will be outlined in Section V, the principle of nonproportional sampling is known as optimum allocation.

Nonproportional sampling may mean, for example, sampling 100 of the largest stores, 60 of the second category, and 40 each in the lowest volume categories, for a total sample of 240.

If the stores in each stratum are sufficiently similar, then a smaller sample will closely approximate the entire stratum. Too, with concentration of larger stores in more populous areas, sampling costs will probably be less. On the other side, a larger sample can be obtained for the same cost.

Nonproportional sampling, therefore, offers the advantages of (1) allowing for more representative stores in the total sample (in terms of volume), and (2) lowering per-interview costs. Further, after reviewing Section V, it will be observed that probably the sampling error will be smaller with stratified sampling than with simple random sampling.

Cross-Stratification

Stratification may take place with respect to only one characteristic. But cross-stratification takes into account two or more characteristics, a further refinement of the stratification process.

For instance, in the foregoing butter example stores may have been sampled with respect not only to sales but also to type of operation, location, medium income of customers, etc.

Therefore, part of each sample is allocated to supermarkets in the southwestern section of the geographical region, which cater to clients with median incomes of $15,000 or more.

Cross-stratification frequently crops up in market surveys. It provides the means to keener insight into important profit characteristics of the population being sampled.

Strata Boundaries

How should strata boundaries be determined? One method of determination is the cumulative square root of frequency rule, or the $C\sqrt{f}$ rule.

Application of the rule is easiest explained with an example. The data in Figure IV.2.C represent 20 classes of the relationships of college book to total book sales expressed as a percentage. The f column is the frequency of each class.

The third column is found in this manner: 19.77 is the square root of 391; 38.62 is the square root of 391 plus the square root of 355; that is, the last column records cumulative results.

AN APPLICATION OF THE C$\sqrt{f}$ RULE

College Texts Total Books	f	C$\sqrt{f}$
%		
0 up to 5	391	19.77
5 up to 10	355	38.62
10 up to 15	299	55.91
15 up to 20	260	72.03
20 up to 25	204	86.31
25 up to 30	109	96.75
30 up to 35	61	104.56
35 up to 40	57	112.11
40 up to 50	43	118.67
50 up to 55	33	124.42
55 up to 60	28	129.71
60 up to 65	22	134.40
65 up to 70	14	138.14
70 up to 75	9	141.14
75 up to 80	4	143.14
80 up to 85	4	145.14
85 up to 90	3	146.87
90 up to 95	1	147.87
95 up to 100	1	148.87

Figure IV.2.C: AN APPLICATION OF THE C$\sqrt{f}$ RULE

Let us assume that we prefer seven strata. Dividing 148.87 by 7 results in the following divisions: 21.27, 42.53, 63.80, 85.07, 106.34, 127.60, and, of course, the highest limit of 148.87

Looking at the table in Figure IV.2.C, we discover that none of these points exactly correspond to the C$\sqrt{f}$ column. Taking the nearest figures results in the Figure IV.2.D boundaries.

STRATA BOUNDARIES

	STRATUM						
	1	2	3	4	5	6	7
Boundaries	0-5%	5-10%	10-15%	15-20%	20-25%	30-35%	60-100%
Interval on C$\sqrt{f}$	19.77	18.85	17.29	30.40	18.25	25.51	19.16

Figure IV.2.D: STRATA BOUNDARIES

The rather unequal 4th and 6th intervals, 30.40 and 25.51, can be improved upon only with a finer categorization of the population. We also observe that this is a highly skewed distribution with the mode on the lower end. Another technique used in stratified sampling, quota sampling, is popular in market research surveys.

IV.3: HOW TO CASH IN ON NONPROBABILITY SAMPLING

So far we have examined probability sampling methods. But a substantial amount of nonprobability sampling crops up because of convenience, or because it is sometimes less expensive or less time-consuming.

The three following types of nonprobability sampling provide expressway means of cashing in on old-fashioned profits. Actually, any sampling procedure that does not allow the selection of any element in a population is a nonprobability sampling method.

Quota Sampling

An offshoot of stratified sampling, quota sampling, derives its name from the quota, or number of interviewees, which each interviewer must fill for a given stratum or subgroup of a population. There are three basic steps in quota sampling.

STEP 1: Subdivide Population.

First, the researcher subdivides the population in a manner akin to stratification. Subgroups are called cells. The basis for stratification is called controls.

Controls can be based on age, income, residence, marital status, ethnic group, political party, etc. If there are several controls and several subgroups, the number of required cells will become enormous.

Suppose, for instance, that buying habits of federal food stamp recipients in Puerto Rico are surveyed. It is estimated that 75 percent of the population receives food stamps directly from the government, according to available governmental statistics.

Let's say that four controls enter into the sampling process, along with several subdivisions for each control:

Age: Under 25, 25-39, 40-59, over 60 (4 subdivisions)

Civil Status: Married, not married (2 subdivisions)

Number of Children: 0, 1-2, 3-4, 5 or more (4 subdivisons)

Residence: rural, town, city (3 subdivisions)

How many cells are needed? $4 \times 2 \times 4 \times 3 = 96$

For the sake of simplicity, assume that we confine our interest to two controls with three subdivisions: (a) ages—under 30, and 30 or over; and (b) number of children—0-1, 2-4, over 4. Figure IV.3.A summarizes the data.

TWO CONTROLS WITH THREE SUBDIVISIONS

No. of Children	Cell No.	Under 30	Cell No.	Over 29	Totals
0 - 1	1	16%	4	11%	27%
2 - 4	2	25	5	8	33
Over 4	3	37	6	3	40
		78%		22%	100%

Figure IV.3.A: TWO CONTROLS WITH THREE SUBDIVISIONS

In the population to be sampled, of heads of households under age 30, 37 percent have more than 4 children. For the entire population, 40 percent of the families have more than 4 children. But only 3 percent of the younger families, under age 30, have more than 4 children. The data seem to suggest that age and family size go hand in hand.

STEP 2: Sample Each Cell.

Next, the researcher must decide how to sample each cell. Proportional sampling, taking the same proportion from each cell, may be one method. Assuming that a sample size of 900 persons is desired, the data in Figure IV.3.B summarize the number of observations assigned to each cell.

SAMPLE SIZE OF EACH CELL

Cell Number	Percent	No. in Sample
1	16	144
2	25	225
3	37	333
4	11	99
5	8	72
6	3	27
	100	900

Figure IV.3.B: SAMPLE SIZE OF EACH CELL

STEP 3: Assign Quotas.

Finally, the researcher will assign a quota to field interviewers. Each interviewer is required to interview a certain number of persons in either one or more than one categories, but more likely in several subgroups.

Naturally, the interviewer will finish his or her job in the shortest time and most convenient way possible, which means that s/he will be interviewing those persons most accessible and most cooperative.

Consequently, rather biased results may arise, since the respondents (i.e., the persons interviewed) have not been randomly selected. If a potential respondent has a disagreeable appearance, odor, or attitude, or if a vicious dog scares off the interviewer, s/he will, no doubt, move on to pleasanter situations.

Similarly, interviewers must be chosen for their reliability. A researcher will want to feel confident that the data were not fudged, hedged, or invented conveniently in a nearby bar or restaurant.

There is another difficulty with this method, and with others as well. The quota may be based on out-of-date, inaccurate, or otherwise inadequate information. In this example, quotas are established on census data taken several years earlier. With migration onto and off the island, coupled with a high birth rate, sample estimates are indeed biased.

Judgmental Sampling

Judgmental sampling, sometimes known as purposive sampling, another method of nonprobability sampling, is claimed by its supporters to have several merits:

(a) it is less expensive,
(b) it is more convenient,
(c) it is less time-consuming, and
(d) it is as good as probability sampling.

Essentially, the method depends upon the expert judgment of the researcher, a specialist, who selects what seems to be the best sample for the study.

Although the researcher selects the area or subpopulation, that segment of the population still may be stratified according to pertinent criteria; and other randomizing techniques may be used in sampling. But judgmental sampling by itself is considered nonrandom, which precludes the use of various statistical measures that coexist with probability sampling.

One company used a judgmental sampling technique to discover why new products fail. Surveys were conducted on competitors for products similar to or related to those produced by the company.

Although such responses are difficult to quantify for statistical manipulation, the critical issues can be sorted out to peg strengths and weaknesses of competitors. These results are then placed in a tabular format, along the lines of Figure IV.3.C, for comparative analysis. Output from this survey then becomes input in strategic planning.

NEW-PRODUCT FAILURE OF THE COMPETITION
(for similar or related product)

Reason for Failure or Poor Performance	Firm A	B	C	D
Technical Problems				
Timing Too Late				
Timing Too Early				
Did Not Understand Customers' Requirements				
Defensive Actions by Competitors				
Misdirected Selling & Promotion Effort				
Government Regulation				
Other External Factors (Union, Suits, etc.)				
Price Competition				

Figure IV.3.C: NEW PRODUCT FAILURE OF THE COMPETITION

Convenience Sampling

Convenience sampling, also known as chunk sampling or incidental sampling, means that the elements in the sample are

(a) accessible,
(b) convenient, easy to measure,
(c) cooperative, or
(d) articulate.

Consumer panels are considered convenience sampling. (Consumer panels were discussed in Section I on "Data Collection.")

Test marketing (Section II.1) of a new product in a limited area is a form of convenience sampling. For example, a toy manufacturer invited a number of parents to lend them their children for a few hours of play with some new toys. Observing the children through one-way mirrors, the researchers came up with redesigns for some of their toys. It was observed that the tots pulled a particular toy around; ergo, the designers put wheels on the toys to conform with the children's assessment of the toy's purpose.

Perhaps you have often seen interviewers, frequently women, standing in enclosed shopping centers with clipboards—a type of "man-in-the-street" survey that may be more properly tagged "people-in-the-shopping mall" survey.

Although such sampling methods are not statistically sound, many researchers like them not only because of lower costs and convenience but also because they produce more usable information per interview dollar spent. However, if this approach does not suit your needs, the next ones may.

IV.4: THE RICH VEIN OF CLUSTER AND AREA SAMPLING

Underlying sampling decisions is availability of information on the population being surveyed. But some lists of potential respondents simply are not available; or, if confidential, not obtainable; or simply too costly to compile. Grouping together sample elements or respondents in clusters, known as cluster sampling, is a popular technique when dealing with human populations.

Clearly, problems arise with grouped elements. Clustering tends to produce homogeneous groups, not an entirely desirable situation when sampling heterogeneous populations. A simple example will point out these consequences and solutions.

The Concept of Clustering

Suppose we are dealing with four kinds of fruits:

1. actinidia kolomitka (a sweet, greenish-yellow berry),
2. buffalo berry (a very sour red or yellow berry),
3. carambola (a very sour yellow fruit), and
4. date (a sweet fruit).

If there were a maximum degree of similarity of sweetness or sourness in a four-cluster universe, each cluster of four elements would appear as follows:

Cluster Number	Elements
1	ADAD
2	DADA
3	BCBC
4	CBCB

At the other extreme, the minimum degree of similarity of elements within the cluster would be:

Cluster Number	Elements
1	ABCD
2	BCDA
3	CDAB
4	DABC

Consequently, construction of clusters must be recognized for their effect on survey results. This becomes more apparent in the illustration on area sampling discussed later in this subsection.

One-Stage Cluster Sampling

To continue with the above fruit example, suppose that we decide to sample one cluster. Selection of a single sample produces two results:

1. All elements within the sample cluster are automatically included.
2. All elements in the other clusters are automatically excluded.

With simple one-stage cluster sampling, simple random sampling is not possible because not all elements of the universe have an equal chance of being selected in the sample.

Systematic Sampling

One cluster sampling technique, systematic sampling, is most easily explained with an illustration. American Commodities Exchange, Inc., of Atlanta desired to survey potential funds investors among registered chiropractors. Although state registration records supplied a ready-made list of chiropractors, no means prevailed to isolate, readily or cheaply, who among them were likely commodity speculators or investors.

There were 420 names on the list; management agreed upon a sample of 70. Hence, they organized the list into six clusters.

Drawing numbers out of a hat determined the number of the first name. From that first number each cluster was constructed in multiples of 6 until each group comprised 70 candidates. (See Figure IV.4.A.)

AN ILLUSTRATION OF SYSTEMATIC SAMPLING		
Cluster Number	Indentification Numbers of Chiropractors from List	
I	2,8,14,20,26,32,38,44	416
II	5,11,17,23,29,35,41,47	419
III	1,7,13,19,25,31,37,43	415
IV	4,10,16,22,28,34,40,46	418
V	3,9,15,21,27,33,39,45	417
VI	6,12,18,24,30,36,42,48	420

Figure IV.4.A: AN ILLUSTRATION OF SYSTEMATIC SAMPLING

Then, from these six clusters, one or two clusters for sampling were picked at random. Instead of composing six individual clusters in detail, as in Figure IV.4.A, and then assigning numbers to all chiropractors in the directory, the sample can be chosen systematically in this manner:

STEP I: Ascertain the total number of elements (persons) in the population.

STEP II: Divide the figure from Step I by the desired sample size. The resulting figure is called the sample interval.

STEP III: Select a number randomly from 1 through the sample interval determined in Step II above. The randomly chosen number marks the number of the first person in the cluster.

STEP IV: Adding the number chosen in Step III to the sample interval in Step II, and adding the sample interval to each successive sum, will identify the numbers of the persons to be sampled in the resulting cluster. That is, referring to the chiropractor example, randomly selecting a 5 means that every 6th (from 6 clusters) chiropractor, beginning with person number 5, will be selected in the sample of 70.

Systematic sampling at least avoids some of the problems earlier mentioned. It is a cheaper method. It is easy to apply. It provides data on a cross-section of elements in a manner superior to simple random sampling.

Two-Stage Sampling

A technique of subsampling with equal sized units, two-stage sampling, is a two-step process:

(a) First select a sample called the primary units.
(b) Then select a sample from each chosen primary unit.

An American paint manufacturer, who had been selling into the Central American market through distributors, wanted to determine whether the rather limited market could be expanded sufficiently to justify local paint manufacturing and to explore establishing new distribution channels.

Applying the judgmental sampling technique (discussed above in Section IV.3), market researchers decided to target the Costa Rican market. (At the time of the survey the Central American market was not integrated, and subsequent disintegration justified the selection.)

Further, it was decided to survey only urbanized areas since these seemed to represent the bulk of present and potential paint sales; the rural market was too scattered; and survey costs dictated sampling constraints.

The urban zones chosen for the survey were: (a) the capital city, San Jose; (b) a smaller city, Cartago; and (c) a small town, Liberia. San Jose was subdivided into four zones, Cartago into two, and Liberia was undivided. Each zone represented a cluster of inhabitants roughly similar in incomes and social characteristics.

American manufacturers channeled their exported paint through local distributors who creamed, rather than penetrated, the market; that is, marketing was passive, primarily to small paint contractors (frequently one- and two-man operations).

Since this was not a do-it-yourself market, paint contractors secured the business, usually selected the paint, and normally established fairly close relationships with one or two distributors according to discounts and credit offered.

The American manufacturer wanted to learn who the residential buyers were, how often they painted (interior and exterior), and who chose a particular paint brand and why.

The next step in the survey was to select a proportional sample from each cluster, a sample thought fairly to represent each subgroup. Because of impreciseness in data, difficulty in training interviewers, and lack of street names and numbers in some instances, pragmatically the survey proceeded on a quota basis.

Although the data did not well lend itself to statistical manipulation, the survey was economically efficient in the volume and type of information generated. Subsequently, the American firm built a paint manufacturing plant in Central America.

Area Sampling

Area sampling is similar to the Central American paint company cluster sampling cameo. Mainly, area sampling is cluster sampling achieved on a geographic basis, although some variations in sampling techniques will serve to differentiate the two.

One-Stage Sampling

The easiest way to understand area sampling quickly is to begin with a city map. City maps are sliced up in many distinct ways—wards, precincts, income groups, census tracts, or the block as a commonly used basic unit.

The next step is to enumerate the basic unit. Then, select areas, using a simple random, stratification, or systematic technique (previously discussed), but in such a way that each unit, called a primary unit, has an equal chance of being selected. (Even primary units may be subdivided into elementary units, such as school districts subgrouped by blocks.)

Interviewing may follow for *all* residents of the selected unit; or systematic sampling of the unit will further cut surveying costs. Sampling of the unit is justifiable if it appears that considerable homogeneity prevails among residents of a particular primary unit.

Area sampling does have the advantage of being cheaper than random sampling because all respondents are situated within a concentrated area, which reduces travel and interview time. On the other hand, the biggest disadvantage is that the sampling error is larger with area sampling than with probability sampling (discussed at the beginning of this section). Sample sizes can, of course, be increased to reduce the magnitude of errors. But the sample should include enough of the entire population to embrace important market differences.

Two-Stage Sampling

Area sampling can be subjected to further refinement with a two-stage sampling process. Still working with the city map, suppose there are 60 elementary units. Within each elementary unit, or subgrouping, there are 12 residents. And we desire a 5 percent sampling, or 36 residents in the sample. That is, the objective is to interview 1 out of every 20 residents. How should they be selected?

One way: Select 12 elementary units or 1 out of every 5. Then subsample each elementary unit at the rate of 1 for every 4 residents.

$$(\frac{60}{5} \times \frac{12}{4}) = 36$$

Another way: Reverse the above. Sample 1 elementary unit out of every 4; then subsample 1 resident out of every 5.

The only problem with this last possibility lies in discovering how to sample that 4/10ths of a person within each elementary unit. Which suggests that any combination of divisors ought to aim to maintain residents whole and hearty.

Three-Plus-Stage Sampling

Since no rule limits area sampling to two stages, a need may arise for three- or four-stage sampling. Sticking with the city sample, let's expand the survey to several cities (as in the Central American paint market example).

From these cities select a sample of cities. Now divide the chosen cities into primary units. Next, choose subsamples of primary units in each of the sampled cities. Then, after breaking down primary units into elementary units, sample these units. The work begins when residents in these elementary units are sub-subsampled. Which leads us to that troublesome issue of sample size.

IV.5: THE SILVER LINING OF SELECTING SAMPLE SIZE

How large should the sample be? Theoretically, if one person characterizes the preferences of large numbers of the entire market population, then a sample of one is sufficient.

Of course, no segment of buyers is strictly homogeneous. And no amount of statistical wizardry can change the point made at the Tower of Babel, viz., our individuality.

A Small Sample Size Problem

To a limited extent, the diversity of individual preferences is at least acknowledged, if not entirely accounted for, with statistical measures of dispersion (Section V.1) and variance analysis (Section V.4).

On the other hand, a central tendency of certain preferences and ideas (see Sections IV.1, V.2, VI.3 for further refinements) can exist among categories of buyers for limited periods. Riding these central tendencies and trends for a long enough time can truly turn averages into the "golden mean" of Section V.2.

If you recall from Section I.8, several figures illustrated SAMI/SARDI reports from an independent marketing research organization. The company proudly points out that their SARDI sample is large and consists of over 5500 stores in 39 market areas. A table (reproduced in Figure IV.5.A) presents their summary of the problem with very small samples, especially with the desire for accuracy at the 90 percent confidence level.

Although the best sample, in terms of informational accuracy, is the entire population, the cost and logistics of data collection on a very large population are impractical. The objective is to lower risks by obtaining the best and most information that will not erode the rate of return. Both risks and information cloud returns on investment.

But even storm clouds of losses have silver linings, we are told. The researcher is obligated to strike a reasonable balance between the costs of risks and the costs of additional information. Therefore, we begin with a low-cost technique to limit sample size.

An Inexpensive Approach

This technique, to determine sample size, offers some appealing advantages:

- It is simple to understand and use.
- It is nonmathematical.
- It appeals to the practical mind.

TABLE
The Problem With Very Small Samples

Assume: Chain "A" has 30 stores in the market and 3, accounting for 10% of the ACV, do not carry Brand "X".

How close can a small sample of stores ever come to measuring the true 90% distribution?

If Sample Is	Closest % Is	Difference From 90%	Point Change If One Store Drops
3	100%	10%	33%
4	100	10	25
5	80 or 100	10	20
6	83	7	17
7	86	4	14
8	88	2	12.5
9	89	1	11
10	90	0	10

In the large SARDI sample, the typical Key Account is reported on the basis of 22 stores, thereby minimizing this problem. SARDI, like SAMI, is designed to produce accurate individual market trended data.

Figure IV.5.A: SAMPLE SIZE ILLUSTRATION

The method is simply this: continue increasing the sample size, meanwhile measuring results as data are accumulated, until the evidence sought tends to stabilize.

Suppose we want to know the typical annual expenditures for playing records and cassettes for a 20-to-30 age group. As a growing sample of results is analyzed, the cumulated sample value will fluctuate, possibly at first within a wide band of values. As information on more respondents is gathered, at some point the fluctuations of typical annual expenditures will dampen within a narrower range until a tendency emerges.

When results seem to point toward a fairly definite but narrow range of expenditures, then assume that additional samples of the population will add no further information of sufficient value to offset the additional cost of collecting it. The sample size has now been determined during the cumulative analysis of the data.

Because of some undesirable limitations, this simple method is not always reliable, so apply it with considerable caution. Preferably it should not be used alone, without additional measures, due to this unreliability.

One limitation is that data stability alone does not prove that the sample characterizes the entire population. In part, this is offset by knowing the market and securing a good sample to begin with, according to techniques already presented in Sections IV.1, IV.2, IV.3, and IV.4.

Another limitation is that the criterion of minimizations of fluctuation itself may be misleading and arbitrary. It may lead the researcher to terminate sampling too soon. In instances where the researcher is quite knowledgeable about the market, and merely seeks verification, this technique seems adequate. Otherwise, lean toward a more traditional approach.

Another Approach

Because some of this material draws upon concepts that will not appear until Section V, some readers may feel more comfortable reading ahead, then returning to this subsection. The technique presented here will be the sampling distribution of a proportion for a simple random sample.

For a population of a finite size, a sampling distribution of the proportion is "the relative frequency distribution of the sample proportions (p) of all possible samples of size n taken from a population of size N."

To transform that definition into a practical, prize-winning method, suppose that you want to know what percentage of customers repeatedly return to your pizzeria. This procedure requires three steps:

1. Select a confidence error.
2. State the allowable error.
3. Survey a sample to estimate the population proportion.

The confidence coefficient means how accurately you want results to turn out. Say that you have specified that 95 percent of the time you expect correct results. Also, say that you specify that the error in estimating the population (your customers) should not exceed 3 percent (p $\pm$ 0.03).

So, for the next several days your cashiers ask customers whether they have been in your pizzeria previously. From that informal survey, assume that 30 percent are repeat customers, the *estimate of the population proportion*.

Here is the formula to use in determining sample size of a population:

$$s_p = \sqrt{\frac{p(1-p)}{n}}$$

s_p = standard error the sample.
p   = the sample proportion, the highest probable value for p.
$(1-p)$ = nonrepeat customers.
n   = the sample size, the unknown, taken from a population N.

In order to calculate s_p, divide the allowable error (E), 0.03 (or 3%) by the z-value of a normal curve. At a 95 percent confidence level, results must reflect that at least 95 percent of the observation results are accounted for within the normal distribution of the curve, and that 5 percent of the observations fall outside. (The explanations in Section V, especially V.3, will clear up any questions.)

From Appendix B, the relevant z-value is 1.96. Therefore, the standard error of a sample, of still unknown size, is this:

$$s_p = \frac{0.03}{1.96} = 0.015$$

Since the mini-survey turned up a proportion of 30 percent with the above formula, we can determine n, the projected sample size:

$$0.015 = \sqrt{\frac{0.30\,(0.70)}{n}}$$

$$n = \sqrt{\frac{0.21}{0.015}} = 30.55$$

$$n = 934$$

Which seems like quite a few interviewees.

Suppose that tabulated results reveal that actually 36 percent are repeat customers. You, the pizzeria owner, can say: "I am 95 percent confident that the proportion of pizza eaters who return to buy my pizza at the Oak Field Shopping Mall location is somewhere between 33 and 39 percent" (because $p = 0.36 \pm 0.03$).

The following *shortcut formula* approximates the desired sample size:

$$n = \frac{p\,(1-p)z^2}{E^2}$$

n = the sample size taken from a population N.
p = the sample proportion; estimated proportion of repeat customers.
z = z-value from Appendix B.
E = the allowable error.

Substituting the same values from the above cameo, here is how the sample size turns out:

$$n = \frac{0.30\,(1 - 0.30)\,1.96^2}{0.03^2} = 897$$

We can also doublecheck on sample size, based on the newest figures, to decide whether the sample should, in fact, be smaller or larger. Since we have learned that repeat customers account for about 36 percent of total trade, the sample size should have been as follows:

$$n = \frac{0.36(1 - 0.36)\,1.96^2}{0.03^2} = 983$$

Perhaps data from another 100 interviewees will increase confidence in the survey results.

Statistical Precision

The larger the sample size the more confidence the researcher will have in its outcome. But there are three points to remember:

1. No data are ever wholly accurate.
2. No results are forever.
3. No information is free.

However, if information can be converted into sales dollars and profits at an advantageous rate of exchange, the effort is worthwhile.

Another approach builds on the standard deviation of a pretest sample. (Standard deviation is explained in Section V. Especially refer to V.1 and V.2.) Let's work through this approach by the numbers.

STEP I: Specify the amount of allowable error.

STEP II: Select an acceptable confidence level.

STEP III: Estimate the standard deviation from a pretest sample of the target population. Overestimate the standard deviation in order not to underestimate the needed sample size. (Section V.1 explains the meaning and calculation of the standard deviation.)

STEP IV: Solve for n, the sample size, with the following formula:

$$n = \frac{s^2 z^2}{E^2}$$

E = allowable error.
Z = z-value from Appendix B for the appropriate confidence level.
s = standard deviation of the sample.
n = sample size (number of respondents).

Suppose that you now wish to learn the average income of customers who visit your pizzerias. Say that an error of $500 is acceptable (E = 500). But you want to be 95 percent certain that results from your survey fall within the acceptable error level (at 95% confidence level, z = 1.96 from Appendix B).

The standard deviation of the sample(s) is used to estimate the standard deviation of the target market, your customers. From the initial survey, the standard deviation turns out to be 4600, which you interpret as 5,000 to be on the safe side of guesstimates. Therefore, you arrive at the needed sample size this way:

$$n = \frac{(5000)^2 \ (1.96)^2}{(500)^2} = 385$$

Had we used 4600 instead of the estimated standard deviation of 5,000, the required sample size would have been 325 respondents instead of 385.

An alternative formula for finding n, the sample size, is as follows:

$$E = z \frac{s}{\sqrt{n}}$$

This formula will yield the same figures: 385 respondents for a standard deviation of 5,000, or 325 for 4600.

Should you decide that 385 is too large a sample, or too costly to administer, a smaller sample will suffice—

(a) if you are satisfied with a larger error, and/or
(b) if you are satisfied with a lower level of confidence.

For instance, the z-value from Appendix B, for a 90 percent confidence level, is 1.65. Hence, a smaller sample will satisfy the revised criterion.

$$n = \frac{(5000)^2 \ (1.65)^2}{(500)^2} = 273$$

And if a 90 percent confidence level plus an allowable error of 1,000, instead of 500, is permissible, it brings the projected sample size down to bite-size proportions:

$$n = \frac{(5000)^2 \ (1.65)^2}{(1000)^2} = 69$$

Accuracy, information, and risk reduction cost money, time, and other resources; and accepting high-risk opportunities increases the chance of loss—once again illustrating that the free-lunch utopia never has and never will exist in reality.

IV.6: RUBIFICATION WITH TABULATION AND CROSS-TABULATION

Collected data must be edited and coded for quantitative measurement and analysis. This process can become expensive, absorbing as much as 20 or 30 percent of the total research budget.

But these costs can be controlled: hence, the need to spend adequate time in construction of the questionnaire and sample—all of which must meet your company goals and marketing objectives of the research undertaking in order to yield the highest return at the lowest cost.

Therefore, reduction of editing and coding costs begins with decisions on the method of analysis of data, and which tabulations are required.

Codification

Coding is easiest with multiple choice type answers. In the various scaling examples in Section III, some answers were precoded along a scale ranging from $+3$ to -3, with or without the intermediate zero. Others employed only positive numbers, no negative values. In other words, each possible answer receives a numerical value.

"Don't know" answers, or unanswered questions, can cause considerable problems. When a respondent answers "don't know," what may the answer really mean?

(a) The question is confusing.
(b) The respondent may not know the circumstances surrounding the issue or problem, or whatever.
(c) The respondent does not want to answer the question.
(d) The question seems unimportant to the respondent.
(e) The response requires too much time, research, checking, recall, or thought—more than the respondent wishes to expend.
(f) The respondent really does not know (or understand).

If there is no place for a "don't know" answer in the questionnaire, the respondent may be forced to misstate his or her opinion, or leave the question unmarked, or place an "X" between two answers. These you will want to interpret, assign a value to, and use; or you may want to disregard and toss out possibly *all* responses from a particular respondent. In the end, these types of answers will reduce the size of a usable sample.

Open-end questions require a different approach for coding. Coding is done *after* rather than before the survey. The method: read all answers—possibly by question or category—to get a feel or sense of the types of answers, and then, with this information available, decide on the categories. After a coded value is assigned to each category, the questionnaires are again reviewed and answers categorized prior to tabulation.

Tabulation

Tabulation means counting the number of responses that fit into each category and then presenting data in summarized format. Tabulation may proceed by hand, or with hand calculators; or the mass of data and complexity of analysis may require substantial computer time. Data may be key-punched into tab cards, inputted directly, read by optical scanner, or entered from OCR printed responses.

The purpose of tabulation is to put data in a form employable for analysis and to calculate summary or descriptive statistics as explained in Sections IV, V, and VI. Several examples of tabulated data appear throughout this book—especially in Section IV, the examples of one-way frequency distributions.

NUMBER OF HOURS SPENT PER MONTH BY SMALL MANUFACTURERS ON BUREAUCRATIC PAPERWORK

Size of Business (by annual sales)	Absolute Frequency	Cumulative Number	Relative Frequency (%)	Cumulative Frequency (%)
Less than $1 million	37	37	10.57	10.57
$1 million to $4.9 million	53	90	15.14	25.71
$5 million to $9.9 million	91	181	26.00	51.71
$10 million to $14.9 million	84	265	24.00	75.71
$15 million to $20 million	85	350	24.29	100.00
TOTAL	350		100.00	

Measures of Central Tendency		Measures of Dispersion	
Mode:	$6.3 million	Interquartile Range:	10
Median:	$9.7 million	Standard Deviation:	5.89
Mean:	$9.6 million	Variance:	34.71

Figure IV.6.A: NUMBER OF HOURS SPENT PER MONTH BY SMALL MANUFACTURERS ON BUREAUCRATIC PAPERWORK

After data are tabulated for each variable in a one-way frequency distribution, the data reduction process continues by calculating measures of central tendency (Sections IV.1 and V.2), and measures of dispersion (Sections IV.1, V.1, and V.4).

A one-way frequency distribution, Figure IV.6.A, is a simple tabulation for a single variable. For several variables we employ cross-tabulation, explained next. The frequency distribution by sales is expressed in different forms as shown in the table.

The absolute frequency represents the number of hours per month spent in bureaucratic paperwork for each class size of business.

The relative frequency is the percentage of hours spent in each class for the firms in the sample.

The cumulative frequency is the cumulated percentage of hours per month spent by that particular class as well as all smaller classes of firms by sales volume.

Also in the table in Figure IV.6.A, you will find summary statistics on the measures of central tendency—mode, median, and mean—and on selected measures of dispersion—interquartile range, standard deviation, and variance. All of these measures are explained, with examples, elsewhere in this book. (Also, see the frequency table in Figure VI.1.H.)

Cross-Tabulation

The problem of tabulation and presentation of data multiplies as we increase the number of variables above one. Simple tabulation of one-way frequency distributions provides useful information when we want to look at only one variable at a time.

With cross-tabulation, we can examine two or more variables at the same time. Its purpose is to convey a broad view of the data and to assemble the figures into a manageable format.

Through cross-tabulation, and subsequent analysis, new relationships turn up, because the technique does not derive from linear assumptions as do many other analytical methods. For comparative purposes, data are expressed as percentages, basis 100, to allow for comparisons among different sample sizes.

How to Analyze Sale Territories

Let's say that we want to analyze Bible sales of deluxe-bound editions, and begin with an analysis of sales of the top salespersons from each region.

Salesperson	Sales per Week	Percent
John	30	12
James	40	16
Paul	90	36
Ruth	60	24
Sarah	30	12
TOTAL	250	100

Paul seems to be a real go-getter, although John and Sarah may protest that it's the territory, not superior sales ability, that makes the difference. Perhaps we ought to segment the data by customer age for further insight. An analysis of internal company records (also refer to information in Section I.2 on this important source of data) reveals the following:

Customer Age	John	James	Paul	Ruth	Sarah
Under 25	55%	25%	15%	40%	57%
25 to 39	7	5	5	30	17
40 to 54	8	5	10	5	6
55 to 69	25	35	60	25	15
Over 69	5	30	10	0	5
TOTAL	100%	100%	100%	100%	100%

We have now developed new insights into the activities of these star performers. Paul concentrates on older buyers, while John, Ruth, and Sarah focus on the younger trade. Except for Ruth, no one has made many sales in the middle group. Can John and Sarah do better if they concentrate more on the over-age-55 group?

James seems to have good balance among three age brackets. Is the problem James, or the territory, or does the mix seem about right given the population composition in his area? Can Ruth outperform Paul if she spreads her wings more in the direction of older customers?

VOLUME OF SALES BY REGION AND AGE GROUP						
Region	Age Level					
(Star Salesperson)	Under 25	25-39	40-54	55-69	Over 69	TOTAL
East & N.E. (Sarah)	240	10	40	280	130	700
Southeast (Ruth)	1100	400	400	1400	400	3700
Midwest (Paul)	390	80	280	1920	230	2900
Southwest (James)	340	50	130	500	380	1400
West (John)	680	50	90	410	70	1300
TOTAL	2750	590	940	4510	1210	10,000

Figure IV.6.B: VOLUME OF SALES BY REGION AND AGE GROUP

How to Highlight Differences

The key element of analysis here is cross-tabulation between two (or more) variables. Let's begin with some raw data for all deluxe-bound Bible sales in each region and then demonstrate how to highlight the results.

In Figure IV.6.B, we have tabulated raw sales data by region, and by age group, but (a) the data are difficult to decipher in this format; and (b) we cannot tell whether the data result from chance occurrence.

First, we can compute conditional probabilities, or contingencies, as in Figure IV.6.C. These column percents appearing in the table represent the conditional probability of a region, given each age bracket. What we want to determine first is where the big sales are. (Of course, much of this is already apparent because of simplification of data in the example.)

To interpret the table, ask this question: What is the probability (or chance) that a 50-year-old person from New England will purchase a deluxe edition of the Holy Bible? From data in Figure IV.6.B, we project there is a chance of 40 sales out of 940, or a 4.3 percent probability that a 50-year-old person in New England will buy a deluxe-bound edition of the Bible. The latter figure, 4.3 percent, is recorded in the table in Figure IV.6.C.

COLUMN PERCENTS (Region Given Age Level)					
			Age Level		
Region	Under 25	25–39	40–54	55–69	Over 69
East	8.7	1.7	4.3	6.2	10.7
Southeast	40.0	67.8	42.6	31.0	33.1
Midwest	14.2	13.5	29.7	42.6	19.0
Southwest	12.4	8.5	13.8	11.1	31.4
West	24.7	8.5	9.6	9.1	5.8
TOTAL	100.0	100.0	100.0	100.0	100.0

Figure IV.6.C: COLUMN PERCENTS (Region Given Age Level)

How does that compare with a 50-year-old person living in southeastern United States? From the tables we surmise there is a 42.6 percent chance of sales with a 50-year-old person in the Southeast, compared with an only 4.3 percent chance for a person of the same age in the east-northeast corridor.

An example of application is advertising aimed at a specific market target. For magazine ads read by the 40-54 age group, prospects wax better in the Southeast and Midwest than in either eastern or western extremes of the country. Actually, in undertaking such a study, we should like to know more about incomes and sex of buyers, at the very least, and religion and occupations, if available.

The table in Figure IV.6.D is constructed similarly. What are sales by age bracket given the region? The table tells us which age groups are the most active buyers in which regions. In the East, the 25-to-55 age bracket is a poor market target. This age group, in fact, represents a poor market in most regions but with the best chance of sales occurring in the Southeast. On the West Coast, the youngest age class seems to represent the biggest spenders.

	ROW PERCENTS (Age Level Given Region)					
		Age Level				TOTALS
Region	Under 25	25–39	40–54	55–69	Over 69	
East	34.3	1.4	5.7	40.0	18.6	100.0
Southeast	29.7	10.8	10.8	37.8	10.8	100.0
Midwest	13.4	2.8	9.7	66.2	7.9	100.0
Southwest	24.3	3.6	9.3	35.7	27.1	100.0
West	52.3	3.8	6.9	31.5	5.4	100.0

Figure IV.6.D: ROW PERCENTS (Age Level Given Region)

Even so, the data are not conclusive. We should also like to know something about the population composition in each region, and perhaps marital status and number of children. And, are West Coast sales to young people high because young people there buy more expensive Bibles, or are they high because John, our star West Coast salesman, likes to sell mostly to young people? Which is cause? Which is effect?

To check for statistical significance, we recommend the chi-square test, demonstrated in Section V.3, to discern whether there is a significant relationship between the variables. (Also, compare this with the analysis of variance in Section V.4.) Preferably there will be five segments of at least one variable. (Also, computerized versions of cross-tabulations appear in Figures VI.1.F and VI.1.G.)

SECTION *V*

DATA ANALYSIS

"Who is as the wise man? And who knoweth the interpretation of a thing? A man's wisdom maketh his face to shine, and the boldness of his face shall be changed."

Ecclesiastes 8:1

INTRODUCTION

Any experience we have in life is better than having none at all, for it provides at least a vague notion of what life means. But the value and accuracy of our brief exposures depend, too, on our ability to interpret, analyze, and then project those experiences onto the whole fabric of life, or at least onto that market segment that interests us.

Who is as the wise man? He who can interpret and understand, for "wisdom makes his face to shine." And how his face shines and countenance changes when the boldness of his actions turns correctly analyzed data into a rewarding cash flow!

At best, we must always deal with partial data that hide profits far better than potential losses. The market value of that data hinges, in part, on an ability to analyze it and incorporate it into profit-making decisions.

Sampling techniques are statistical techniques. As such, they depend upon statistical tests and interpretations that correspond to these various methods. Prior to these analytical steps a great deal of time and expense has gone into the market research process.

In the earliest stages, management made certain marketing decisions. Information needs were then defined, the literature reviewed, and the research sources identified. At some point during these early stages the research problem was stated, restated, and finalized, and the hypothesis formulated.

Then, the variables were identified—the cause-effect relationships that were to be subjected to sampling and tests. The research project was carefully designed and an adequate research budget approved. Marketing success usually hangs on one word: *test*.

Testing provides the means to cut costs and reduce risks, but no testing, or market research project, is free of cost, as we have already learned. It costs money to design the research. It costs money to collect the data. It costs money to sort, label, and classify the information gathered from whatever source. It costs money to analyze the data. It costs money to evaluate it. It costs money to present the evidence and to move the organization toward specific courses of action.

At this point in the process, we are at the analysis stage. Data analysis is dull stuff for the practical, action-oriented person. Volumes have been written on numerous methods of managing and interpreting data, often so esoteric that only statisticians find such reading interesting or even comprehensible.

The measures and tests presented in the following pages are the most common and widely used ones—a bare-bones level of information. No special talents are needed to perform a practical analysis of the research data.

Data are beneficial only when they assist in the transformation of ideas into dollars. This section has been written with time and profits in mind, so that the material goes right to the heart of analysis in each instance. Additional analytical techniques and evaluative methods are discussed in Section VI as well.

V.1: THE SECRET OF AVOIDING THE SHORTCUT TRAP TO SHORTCUT ANALYSIS

In Section IV.1, various measures of central tendency served to locate point(s) of concentration. Nothing was written, however, on data distribution—whether all data congregated around the point of concentration (mean, median, mode, etc.), or whether data were widely dispersed with some points located quite far from the center. But so what?

What difference does it make whether data are spread out or not? Dispersion measures provide some handle on how reliably central tendency measures gauge concentration.

For example, we read that countries like Kuwait and Abu Dhabi have the highest per capita income in the world. Per capita income is an average usually derived by dividing total personal income by the number of inhabitants.

But do the per capita income figures mean the same thing as in Switzerland, or the United States, which ranks slightly lower but where incomes tend not to have a concentration of either high or low extremes? Obviously not!

Of many possible ways of denoting dispersion of data, three important ones stand out: range, standard deviation, and coefficient of variation.

Sample Range

The simplest, crudest indicator of concentration, the sample *range*, unfortunately does not provide a very useful index of variation; but it does have applications. The range is the difference between the highest and the lowest values. Its value depends exclusively on two figures: the high (H), and low (L) measures. The range does not indicate anything about data concentration or dispersion between the highest and lowest points in a distribution.

For ungrouped measurements, the formula for the range (R) is:

$$R = H - L$$

For example, if the following figures represent the number of hot dogs 7 boys can eat in 30 minutes, ungrouped data—12, 24, 19, 3, 15, 16, 17—the range is:

$$R = 24 - 3 = 21$$

If the 3-hot-dog lad drops out from the data, then the range, still dependent upon two numbers, the extremes, descends sharply to:

$$R = 24 - 12 = 12$$

which points out a further weakness of the measure.

For grouped data organized in a frequency distribution, the range is calculated essentially in the same way; namely, the difference between the upper boundary of the highest class with any frequencies and the lower limit of the lowest class with any frequencies.

In popular parlance, the range is sometimes spoken of as the middle range: what most people do or buy, or the majority of the elements.

There is, however, an indicator that highlights the middle half of all elements: the interquartile range. (Also, see Section IV.1.) With this index, one-fourth of the elements lie below the middle half, and one-fourth of the elements above the middle half. The interquartile range encompasses the central 50 percent of the distribution.

Standard Deviation

When they are graphed, frequency distributions display almost any shape. But for all frequency distributions, of any shape or size, all the items lie within its range; none are left out. And exactly 50 percent of the observations lie within the interquartile range. Nevertheless, the shape of the distribution determines what proportion of observations fall within one standard deviation. What does that mean?

First of all, recall that we are dealing with dimensions that reflect how data are dispersed around the mean. The standard deviation is possibly the most useful measurement of dispersion. Statisticians prefer the standard deviation to explain how scattered, or bunched up, data are around the mean.

When we calculate the standard deviation below, notice that it is small when the values of a data set are concentrated close to the average. To illustrate, the standard deviation for a class of fourth graders should be quite small, with respect to age, because most fourth graders tend to be about the same age.

Therefore, each student's age will fall very close to the average age for the entire class, the sample. The same will be true for the entire population of fourth graders. On the other hand, a large standard deviation signals that data are scattered widely about the mean.

Comparing per capita incomes in Kuwait and Switzerland, we anticipate a larger standard deviation for the Kuwait data than for the Swiss data. That is, even if average incomes were identical in both countries, the distribution of incomes is not; and dispersions of income, gauged by the standard deviation, will be quite different for each country.

Let us say that for two sets of data the average value for each is 8,000. Assume, also, that the standard deviation (i.e., dispersion from the mean) is 500 for one set of data and 5,000 for the second set.

We may assert that two-thirds of the data lie within one standard deviation of the mean. If that is the case (as in a normalized distribution), we expect that for the first set of data about two-thirds of the observations will fall within a rather narrow range—between 7500 and 8500.

For the second set of data, one standard deviation means that two-thirds of the data embrace a very wide range—between 3,000 and 13,000—not very useful for pinpointing a specific or narrow market target.

The first step is to understand the mathematics that underlie the calculation of this measure of dispersion, the standard deviation. The next step is to apply it to a specific marketing problem.

The basic formula for finding the *standard deviation of a population*, is simply the square root of the average squared deviations from the mean:

$$\sigma = \sqrt{\frac{\Sigma(x-\mu)^2}{N}}$$

σ	=	(Greek letter, lower case, sigma) standard deviation.
Σ	=	(Greek letter, upper case, sigma) sum of.
x	=	each element of the data set.
μ	=	(Greek letter, lower case, mu) mean of a population.
$(x-\mu)^2$	=	the squared difference between each element and the mean of the population.
N	=	total number of elements, or observations, in a population.

Most of the time, however, we will work with samples rather than with an entire population because sampling (Section IV) is a cheaper form of data-gathering (Section I). Adjusted results of sample survey often are sufficiently reliable for most marketing problem applications. The formula for the standard deviation of a sample is:

$$s = \sqrt{\frac{\Sigma(x - \bar{x})^2}{(n - 1)}}$$

s	= sample standard deviation.
$(x - \bar{x})^2$	= the difference, squared, between the value of each element and the mean (average) of the sample.
$(n - 1)$	= the number of elements of observations in the sample, minus 1*.

For instance, calculate the standard deviation in the sample consumption in Figure V.1.A of five gentlemen (no lady smokers of this cigar were discovered) who say they smoke from 1 to 5 imported Hoyo de Nicaragua cigars daily.

According to the computations, the average person sampled smoked three cigars daily. Later we will estimate how closely x = 3 (the sample average) corresponds to the population mean, μ, of all smokers of Hoyo cigars, using s = 1.58 (the sample standard deviation) as an estimate of σ, the standard deviation of the population.

Shortcut Formula

Working with fractions or decimals, or a large quantity of data, may prove cumbersome in applying the above formula. The following time-saving formula,**

---

*Mathematicians and statisticians tell us that the standard deviation of a sample would be understated if we divided by n instead of (n — 1), especially with small samples. The easiest course to follow is to assume the correctness of this observation and go on about our business of making profitable marketing decisions.

**It may not appear to be a time-saver in this simple example but you will quickly appreciate its convenience in more complex situations.

SAMPLE OF CIGAR SMOKERS

Gentlemen	x	$(x-\bar{x})$	$(x-\bar{x})^2$
Paul F.	5	-2	4
Teddy R.	4	-1	1
Warren H.	3	0	0
Anastasio S.	2	$+1$	1
Chester A.	1	$+2$	4
	$n = 5$	$\Sigma x = 15$	$\Sigma(x-\bar{x})^2 = 10$

x = number of cigars smoked daily by each person.

$\bar{x}$ = (mean) average number of cigars smoked by all persons in the sample.

$$\bar{x} = \frac{\Sigma x}{n} = \frac{15}{5} = 3$$

s = the standard deviation of the sample:

$$s = \sqrt{\frac{\Sigma(x-\bar{x})^2}{n-1}} = \sqrt{\frac{10}{(5-1)}} = 1.58$$

Figure V.1.A: SAMPLE OF CIGAR SMOKERS

to find the standard deviation of a sample, may be a good one to asterisk for your own personal future reference. This formula eliminates the tedious steps of determining actual deviations from the mean, its chief advantage.

$$s = \sqrt{\frac{n(\Sigma x^2) - (\Sigma x)^2}{n(n-1)}}$$

Again substituting values from Figure V.1.A, we have:

x	x^2
5	25
4	16
3	9
2	4
1	1
15	55

$$s = \sqrt{\frac{5(55) - (15)^2}{5(5-1)}}$$

$$= \sqrt{\frac{275 - 225}{20}}$$

$$= \sqrt{2.5} = 1.58$$

And in the event that you prefer a shortcut method to find the standard deviation of a population, σ, try this formula:

$$\sigma = \sqrt{\frac{N(\Sigma x^2) - (\Sigma x)^2}{N^2}}$$

Suppose that a particular office is surveyed to discover how much each employee spends for lunch. Brown-baggers are assigned a value of *0*, unless they spent for extras or for a drink either from a machine or in a nearby restaurant. Others record what they actually spent. The Σ x equals 51.45 and the Σ x^2 is 167.50. The standard deviation of the population of 70 (**N**) is:

$$\sigma = \sqrt{\frac{70\,(167.50) - (51.45)^2}{(70)^2}} = \sqrt{\frac{11725 - 2647.10}{4900}} = 1.36$$

Which suggests wide expenditure variations among some employees.

Grouped Data

However, data in the foregoing lunch expenditure example, instead of being calculated individually, are grouped by classes. Just as we did with the frequency distributions illustrated in Section IV of this book, we can adapt the preceding formulas to determine the standard deviations of grouped data.

For a population:

$$\sigma = \sqrt{\frac{\Sigma(x - \mu)^2 \cdot f}{N}}$$

where *x* represents the class mark and *f* the frequencies, or number of times the value of *x* crops up in the data.

For a sample:

$$s = \sqrt{\frac{\Sigma(x - \bar{x})^2 \cdot f}{n - 1}}$$

where the *xs* represents class marks and *f* the frequencies.

For example, posit that a local radio station desires to estimate the time (in hours) that commuters from a suburban area spend in their cars each day going to and from work. Survey results are summarized in Figure V.1.B.

From the survey data we learn that the average motorist spends nearly 1½ hours commuting to and from work daily. Further, with a standard deviation of slightly more than ¾ of an hour, we can safely suggest that about two-thirds of all commuters from the surveyed area spend between ¾ and ¼ hours daily in their vehicles. (This interpretation of the standard deviation will be explained later in this section.)

Shortcut Method

Obviously this process can involve a considerable amount of computation when organizing a large quantity of numbers with many digits. By coding the class marks, a change of scale facilitates calculations.

Instead of the class marks in Figure V.1.B, because all class intervals are equal, we can assign consecutive numbers to each class mark beginning with *0*, somewhere around the midpoint of the distribution.

APPLICATION OF STANDARD DEVIATION

Class Marks x	Frequencies f	$(x - \bar{x})$	$(x - \bar{x})^2$	$(x - \bar{x})^2 \cdot f$
0.25	7	−1.223	1.496	10.472
0.75	12	−0.723	0.523	6.276
1.25	22	−0.223	0.050	1.100
1.75	19	+0.277	0.077	1.463
2.25	8	+0.777	0.604	4.832
2.75	1	+1.277	1.631	1.631
3.25	4	+1.777	3.158	12.632
3.75	1	+2.277	5.185	5.185
TOTAL				43.591

$$\bar{x} = \frac{\Sigma x \cdot f}{n} = \frac{109}{74} = 1.473$$

$$s = \sqrt{\frac{\Sigma(x - \bar{x})^2 \cdot f}{n - 1}} = \sqrt{\frac{43.591}{73}} = \sqrt{0.597} = 0.773$$

Figure V.1.B: APPLICATION OF STANDARD DEVIATION

Now, a coded class mark, designated *u* in Figure V.1.C, replaces the former *x*. Thus we eliminate some bothersome computations in finding the mean and standard deviation of the sample.

EXAMPLE OF A CODED CLASS MARK

x	u	f	uf	$u^2 f$
0.25	−3	7	−21	63
0.75	−2	12	−24	48
1.25	−1	22	−22	22
1.75	0	19	0	0
2.25	+1	8	8	8
2.75	+2	1	2	4
3.25	+3	4	12	36
3.75	+4	1	4	16
		74	−41	197

Figure V.1.C: EXAMPLE OF A CODED CLASS MARK

With these simplifications, calculations can now be performed without aid of a calculator. The last column, u^2f, is simply the uf column times the u column. However, to use these revised figures requires modified formulas.

To find the mean:

$$\bar{x} = x_0 + \frac{\Sigma u\,f}{n}\,i$$

x_0 = original value of the class mark now assigned a 0 value.
u = coded class marks.
f = frequencies of each class.
n = number of items.
i = class interval.

Substituting values, we should come up with the same answers, we hope.

$$\bar{x} = x_0 + \frac{\Sigma uf}{n}\,i = 1.75 + \frac{(-41)}{74}\,0.50 = 1.473 \text{ hours.}$$

So far, so good. With so much confidence, let's replicate our good fortune with figures and experiment with a shortcut formula to determine the standard deviation of this sample.

$$s = i\sqrt{\frac{n(\Sigma u^2f) - (\Sigma uf)^2}{n\,(n-1)}}$$

Substituting values, we have:

$$s = 0.50\sqrt{\frac{74\,(197) - (-41)^2}{74\,(74-1)}} = 0.50\,\sqrt{2.387} = 0.773$$

Note: If you do not come out with the same answer, recheck until the source of error shows up.

Trap No. 1

At this juncture there may exist a tendency to seek a shortcut even for the shortcuts to reduce time spent on calculations. It is a temptation to conclude that since a measure of dispersion registers deviations from the mean, that difference $(x - \bar{x})$ should not only be accurate as sin but should eliminate the need to square all those results.

Return to Figure V.1.A and add the results in the $(x - \bar{x})$ column; the sum is zero, as it always will be. Some differences are positive, others negative, and the unfortunate sum is zero. That is why these figures are squared, to eliminate the negative signs.

Trap No. 2

Beware of others' statistical proofs. Data can be manipulated statistically to prove most anything.* By the same token, a user of statistics has a moral obligation to inform, not mislead.

---

*An entertaining and enlightening book on this subject is *How to Lie with Statistics,* Darrell Huff. NY: W.W. Norton & Company, Inc., 1954.

Unfortunately, what once was considered standard business ethics has deteriorated to "situational ethics"—which is a fancy label for excusing one's actions and obligations. Moral principles are absolutes. Either an action is right, or it is not. And no shading of meaning or statistical play on words can justify a mal-intent.

			TRIALS						
AUTO	I	II	III	IV	V	$\bar{X}$	Md	MR
A	28.7	30.5	31.0	29.1	27.0	29.3	31.0	29.0
B	32.3	32.4	30.3	32.1	27.9	31.0	30.3	30.2
C	34.0	29.9	29.3	28.0	29.8	30.2	29.3	31.0

FIVE TRIALS WITH THREE PRODUCTS

Figure V.1.D: FIVE TRIALS WITH THREE PRODUCTS

For example, data in Figure V.1.D represent five trials each on three closely competing automobiles by an "independent" research company. Each trial run represents the distance, in miles, that each car travels on one gallon of gasoline. Which car gets the most miles per gallon (MPG)?

Actually, the test shows that all three cars get the "best" gasoline mileage. Anyone can prove that any of the tested automobiles is the most economical on gasoline, depending on which "average" is touted.

The manufacturer of car A, preferring the median (the center point of a set of data), can claim that tests prove A cars get better MPG than competitive B and C cars.

Touting the mean, the manufacturer of B automobiles can state that actual tests demonstrate that B cars go farther on a gallon of gasoline than do competitors'.

Not wanting to be left out of this game of oneupmanship, analysts from the manufacturer of C cars shop around, manipulating data, searching for proof positive that C cars outdistance A and B cars. The solution? Use the mid-range. The mid-range (MR) is the mean of the smallest and largest values of a sample. Naturally, producer C makes a stand against his competitors in this verbal contest.

Standard Units

One application of the standard deviation is to compare otherwise disparate data.

An illustration: A large corporation with diversified activities evaluated the sales performance of various managers prior to shifting personnel. The firm owned both a fast-food chain and a number of convenience stores retailing a limited line of groceries.

As an example, suppose top management compared the performances of two unit managers—Joe Zitkus, a restaurant manager, and Mark Gerk, a retail store manager.

During one accounting period, Zitkus did $80,000 worth of business and Gerk $150,000. At first blush it appears that Gerk may replace Zitkus to bring up dollar volume in a unit.

It's an apples and oranges type problem. Sales from these distinct businesses are not readily comparable unless they are expressed in a common term—fruit for apples and oranges, standard deviation for Zitkus and Gerk.

Mean sales for all fast food units during this period came to $56,000, with a standard deviation of $8,000. Mean sales for all convenience food stores amounted to $120,000, with a standard deviation of $15,000. Obviously, both managers are above average in their respective divisions, but is Gerk nearly twice the manager of Zitkus?

$$\text{Zitkus} = \frac{80,000 - 56,000}{8,000} = 3 \text{ standard deviations}$$

$$\text{Gerk} = \frac{150,000 - 120,000}{15,000} = 2 \text{ standard deviations}$$

With three standard deviations above the mean of his division, Zitkus is the stronger competitor. By measuring performances in standard units (Z), we can readily discern how much better (or worse) each is, compared with the average (mean) of like stores in the division.

$$z = \frac{x - \bar{x}}{s}$$

Although there are further uses of the z calculation (see any elementary statistics book), these discussions are considered beyond the scope of this profit manual. But refer to the brief discussion on z-values and example in Section V.3.

Another Application

Previously, we garnered one piece of significant information, viz., that with any frequency distribution precisely 50 percent of *all* items lie within the distribution's interquartile range; but the number of items that fall within, say, one standard deviation of the mean depends upon the shape of the distribution.

Statisticians have come up with some useful generalities that make further use of the concept of standard deviation. With rare exceptions, such as the V-shaped distribution, for example, at least 50 percent of all items of a distribution will lie within one standard deviation (1σ) of the mean.

The most useful generalizations apply to what is known as a "normal," or bell-shaped, or Gaussian distribution,* where extreme items balance each other, and the mass of data lie in the middle.

*In a Gaussian distribution (Karl Gauss), the curve is symmetrical and bell-shaped. The mean equally divides the distribution so that 50% of the items fall above and 50% below the mean, and the mean, mode, and median are equal. The tails of the curve never quite touch the horizontal axis but move toward it (asymptotically).

Students frequently refer to "curving the grade," which distribution means, they hope, that regardless of how poorly they do on an exam, at least 70 percent of the class will do acceptably well. A so-called normal distribution would call for 10% As, 20% Bs, 40% Cs, 20% Ds, and 10% Fs.

Unfortunately, most distributions found in marketing research problems are skewed. (See Sections IV.1 and V.3 for further discussion of skewness.) Fortunately, distributions can be normalized so that the following rules apply to an analysis of data. (Refer to any elementary textbook* on statistics; also, see Section V.2 on confidence intervals.)

For "normal" distributions we know that about two-thirds of all items lie within one standard deviation of the mean. Approximately 95 percent of the items fall within two standard deviations (2σ). Except for isolated instances, all items lie within three standard deviations (3σ).

For your future reference, here are some additional generalizations on various shapes of distributions:**

(a) If the distribution is shaped like a rectangle, say, twice the distance horizontally as the vertical height, then 57 percent of the items fall within 1 σ of the mean and 100% within 2σ. Thus, if $\mu = 205$, and $\sigma = 20$, in this type of distribution all items are encompassed in the range 165 to 245 ($2\sigma = 40$).

(b) If the distribution is shaped like a triangle, or sharply pointed pyramid, starting from the origin, then 64 percent of all items lie within 1σ and 96 percent within 2σ.

Chebyshev's theorem has a few interesting observations worthy of our attention:

◎ The theorem states that for any set of data at least 75 percent of the items must lie within 2σ of the mean.
◎ Further, at least 88.8 percent of the items must fall within 3σ.
◎ And 96 percent of the items of a distribution must come within 5σ of the mean.

Accordingly, if two populations exhibit an identical mean of $\mu = 850$, but one has a standard deviation of $\sigma = 40$, and the second has a standard deviation of $\sigma = 16$, then we can say with a fair degree of certainty, according to Chebyshew's Theorem, that for the first distribution at least 75 percent of the data lie in the range 770 to 930; but for the second distribution, at least 96 percent of the data lie within an identical range. In the second distribution, the data are more concentrated around the mean.

---

*E.g., John E. Freund and Frank J. Williams. *Elementary Businesss Statistics: The Modern Approach.* Englewood Cliffs, N.J.: Prentice-Hall, Inc., 1964; or Simpson, Pirenian, Crenshaw, and Riner, *Mathematics of Finance*, 4th ed., Englewood Cliffs, N. J.: Prentice-Hall, Inc., 1969.

**If you plot a frequency distribution on a graph, a certain pattern or shape results. To plot a distribution, the frequency density is measured on the vertical axis and the class marks (X) on the horizontal axis. That is, the higher a point on a vertical axis, the greater is the number of elements representing a particular class; the farther to the right from the origin on the horizontal axis, the higher the value of the Xs.

The purpose, of course, is to identify some of the characteristics common to large segments of the population in order to gear our marketing campaign toward the larger numbers.

- ◎ This is especially important in marketing standardized products, techniques, or services.
- ◎ It also helps us to better estimate the success or failure of our marketing program if we can make some valid generalizations on population characteristics.
- ◎ These tools aid in summarizing, analyzing, and gleaning likely facts from relatively small samples of data (see Section IV on sampling techniques), and then in generalizing about large numbers of actual or potential customers.

Mean Deviation

Earlier we observed that most marketing data are skewed. Because of this problem, some researchers prefer to use a mean or average deviation, instead of a standard deviation. The mean deviation is particularly preferred when there is extreme skewness, or such odd-shaped ones as *J* or *U* distributions.

$$\text{M.D.} = \frac{\Sigma |x - \bar{x}|}{n}$$

M.D.　　　　= mean (or average) deviation.
Σ　　　　= sum of.
$|x - \bar{x}|$　= absolute value of the difference between the value of an item and the mean of the distribution (i.e., the $|\ |$ designation means to ignore signs).
n　　　　= the number of items in the distribution.

For a simple application of the mean deviation, refer again to the data in Figure V.1.A. If we ignore the plus and minus signs in the (x − x) column, and add them, it will total 6. There are five persons in this sample. Ergo:

$$\text{M.D.} = \frac{\Sigma(x - \bar{x})}{n} = \frac{6}{5} = 1.33$$

Applying the mean deviation to the population, we now conclude that there is less dispersion than previously thought among Hoyo cigar smokers.

For grouped data, we can adapt the foregoing formula to evolve the next one:

$$\text{M.D.} = \frac{\Sigma f |\mu|}{n},$$

where f equals the number of items in each class mark, and, using the coding system explained in a shortcut method earlier in this section, the absolute value of $|\mu|$ now substitutes to bring us right to the money.

We have learned that in a normal distribution, 57.5 percent of the items fall within *one mean deviation*. Therefore, we may conclude that 57.5 percent of Hoyo smokers burn up between 1.67 and 4.33 cigars daily. (We won't worry about how they managed the fractional part of the cigar unless some were snuffed out and re-ignited the following day. Ugh!)

Or, perhaps it sounds more logical to report that 57.5 percent of the time Hoyo smokers light up between 1.67 and 4.33 cigars daily. (Still stuck with the fractions!)

Coefficient of Variation

If we have two or more sets of dissimilar, or not readily comparable, data, we need to compare their *relative dispersions*, similar to examples above relating to *z* values.

Although the standard deviation is a useful gauge, one disadvantage is that it is based on units of measurement, like the mean deviation and range discussed above . . . which, too, are *absolute* measures of dispersion.

However, if we express the standard deviation as a percentage of the mean (see Section IV.1 for further explanation of the mean), we can develop a *coefficient of variation*, or *relative variation* (attributed to Karl Pearson), to ascertain which set of data is more or less variable.

$$CV = \frac{s}{\bar{x}} (100)$$

In this formulation *s* is the standard deviation of a sample and $\bar{x}$ the mean of a sample. For population deviation substitute σ for *s* (standard deviation) and μ for *x* (mean).

That is, the value of the CV (coefficient of variation) is computed as a ratio between two values and expressed as a percentage. With this formulation we determine within what percent of the true total our estimate is likely to be correct.

For example, let's compare price volatility of two commodities—corn and hogs—within a given period. Say that corn has a mean price of 250 (cents per bushel) with a standard deviation of 40, and that hogs exhibit a mean price of 41 (cents per pound) with a standard deviation of 14. In terms of cents, which commodity, corn or hogs, experiences greater volatility?

Measuring absolute values, we conclude that corn prices are more variable than hog prices. Employing a relative measure, such as the coefficient of variation, we determine that the coefficient of variation for corn is 16 percent, and for hogs 34 percent.

A relative measure is the proper basis for comparing changes in cents per bushel with changes in cents per pound. Furthermore, we discover that the price of hogs is 2⅛ times more variable than the price of corn (0.34 ÷ 0.16 = 2.125).

But the values compared need *not* be measured in the same units (such as cents). The coefficient of variation can just as well compare cents and tons, or sales revenue and production, or value of each sale with number of sales, because the result is always expressed as a percent.

There are, of course, other relative measures, but since the mean and the standard deviation are the most commonly employed concepts, the coefficient of variation is a useful technique for comparing distributions stated in different units.

V.2: SEARCH FOR THE GOLDEN MEAN OF THE POPULATION

This subsection deals with some problems associated with the nagging question: Just how good is a sample? Does the sample mean fairly represent the population mean? Or are we off base?

After all, if the sample is not characteristic of the entire target market, then erroneous marketing decision-making and marketing management policies can cause errors so costly that the business owner or marketing manager may well wish s/he had never become involved in marketing research techniques.

Statistics are not the *sine qua non*; there are *caveats*, as well as little tricks and shortcuts that make them work better, or more easily, than fortuitous decisions. These methods produce sufficiently reliable results enough of the time to induce large enterprises to invest substantial sums in marketing research and analysis.

This subsection illustrates a couple of those cost-saving techniques which aid in statistical interpretation of those data gathered from the application of techniques explained in Sections I, II, and III above. Also, the reader may wish to refer to Section IV.5 for more on determining sample size. This depends on an understanding of the standard error of the mean, estimated error of the mean, and confidence intervals—all explained below.

Standard Error of the Mean

How closely does the mean of a single sample match the mean of an unknown, and likely unknowable, population?

In dealing with samples, we have calculated measures of dispersion of the sample mean, such as the standard deviation. But if we take several samples and then array the various sample means, we can calculate the standard deviation of the sample means, known as the standard error of the mean.

The standard error of the mean computations allow us to answer the question above, if we start with an unrealistic assumption that the standard deviation of the population is known. Under this assumption we can determine the standard error of the mean for *all* possible sample means from a given population. Let's begin with the formula.

$$\sigma_{\bar{x}} = \frac{\sigma}{\sqrt{n}}$$

$\sigma_{\bar{x}}$ = standard error of the mean.
σ^x = standard deviation of the population.
n = number of observations in the sample.

To illustrate, suppose that the standard deviation of monthly wages of Born-Again Christians is $130, and that 100 wages were randomly chosen from the estimated population.

An interesting observation is this: the pattern of the sample means will exhibit the characteristics of a "normal" distribution, even though the population from which the samples are drawn is skewed.

A normal distribution plots as a symmetrical, bell-shaped curve, as a continuous distribution in a graph. The mean, mode, and median equate; they evenly bisect the distribution. The tails of the curve approach, but do not intersect, the horizontal axis.

A skewed distribution is asymmetrical. (Further discussion on distribution characteristics appears in Section V.1, and on skewness in Sections IV.1 and V.3.)

Therefore, employing the information on distribution characteristics from Section V.1, we can fairly safely assume that approximately 68 percent of all sample means of samples of size 400, randomly chosen from the Born-Again population, will fall within the population mean $\mu + 1\sigma_x$ (plus or minus one standard error of the mean).

We can also estimate that roughly 95 percent of all possible means of sample sizes of 400, randomly chosen, will fall within $\mu + 2\sigma_x$ (plus or minus two standard errors of the mean).

Finally, we can presume that practically all possible means will fall within $\mu + 3\sigma_x$ (plus or minus three standard errors of the mean). Unfortunately, we began with an unlikely assumption, namely, that the standard deviation of the population is known.

Estimated Standard Error of the Mean

On a more practical level, the standard deviation of the population (σ) is unknown for solutions to marketing research problems. An estimate must be derived. The following formula helps to develop this estimate:

$$s_{\bar{x}} = \frac{s}{\sqrt{n}}$$

$s_{\bar{x}}$ = estimated standard error of the mean when the sample represents less than 5 percent of the population but still a fairly large sample size.

s = standard error of the sample.

n = number of sample observations.

But when the samples represent 5 percent or more of the population, computations are adjusted downward, as in the following formula:

$$s_{\bar{x}} = \frac{s}{\sqrt{n}} \cdot \sqrt{\frac{(N - n)}{N}}$$

N, of course, is the number of items in the entire population. The significance of the other symbols remains the same as above.

Returning again to our previous example, assume now that the standard deviation of the population (σ) of Born-Again Christians is unknown but that the standard deviation of a random sample is $110. The estimated standard error of the mean will be:

$$s_{\bar{x}} = \frac{\$110}{\sqrt{100}} = \$11$$

Given what we already know about characteristics of distributions, we can estimate the mean of the population with a 95 percent confidence interval.

Assume that the sample mean is $1200:

$$\$1200 \pm 2\left(\frac{\$110}{\sqrt{100}}\right) = \$1200 \pm 2(\$11) = \$1200 \pm \$22$$

Because, in a normal distribution, 95 percent of all observations tend to fall within 95 percent of the mean, we can now state with 95 percent confidence that the mean of the population will lie between $1178 and $1222.

In other words, the degree of confidence associated with this interval indicates the percentage of such intervals that would include the population mean, *if* a large number of random samples were analyzed.

Confidence Intervals

To further explain the concept of confidence intervals, let's construct an interval estimate of the population mean.

The population mean (μ) is unknown. The standard deviation of the population (σ) is known and was presumed to be $130 in the example above. The sample size (n) remains 100 observations.

To construct a 95 percent confidence interval, we are saying that there is a 95 percent chance the sample mean will fall within 2σ of the population mean, and a 95 percent probability the population mean lies within two standard errors (σ) of the sample mean.

Still assuming the sample mean ($\bar{x}$) of $1200, the population mean (μ) will probably lie between:

$$\$1200 - 2\frac{\$130}{\sqrt{100}} \text{ and } \$1200 + 2\frac{\$130}{\sqrt{100}}.$$

The sample mean will probably lie between:

$$\mu - 2\frac{\$130}{\sqrt{100}} \text{ and } \mu + 2\frac{\$130}{\sqrt{100}}$$

Unfortunately, there are no free lunches. This freebie, too, exacts a tribute. The cost is hidden in the weasel phrase "95 percent confidence interval."

It is not possible to manufacture something out of nothing. This applies both to products and to figures. We can be confident of these estimates *only if* a large number of samples is drawn.

Not every sample mean will necessarily fall within two standard errors of the population mean. But the computations do suggest that 95 percent of such observations about the population mean are correct *if* a 95 percent confidence interval prevails.

In addition, a confidence interval that embodies practically all possibilities will fall within three standard errors of the mean. On the other hand, be aware that at even this degree of confidence there are isolated observations that fall outside of the interval estimate—the occasional exceptions.

A variation of this technique can provide us with an estimate of the sample size needed to achieve an acceptable tolerance level. The steps are:

First,   decide on an acceptable confidence level.

Second,   estimate the standard deviation of monthly wages of the target population.

Third,   solve for n in the formula, the required sample size.

Similarly, we can construct confidence intervals for percentages because the same rules apply for proportions as in the above case. For proportions, the basic formula is now modified to read:

$$s_{\bar{x}} = \sqrt{\frac{p(1-p)}{n-1}}$$

$s_{\bar{x}}$ = estimated standard error of a percentage.
p = sample proportion.
$(1-p)$ = remaining part of the sample proportion where $1 = 100\%$ of the sample.
n = number of sample observations.

Let's say that the same Born-Again Christian families were surveyed to determine in how many families wives held employment outside of the home (p) and how many did not $(1-p)$.

In a sample of 135 families, 31 percent of the wives were employed 30 or more hours weekly (p); 69 percent $(1-p)$ did not work outside of the home. Substituting values in the formula, the estimated standard error is:

$$s_{\bar{x}} = \sqrt{\frac{0.31(1-0.31)}{134}} = \sqrt{0.001596} = 0.04 = 4\%$$

From these data and estimates, we can state, with a 95 percent degree of confidence, that:

$$p \pm 2\,s_x = 31\% \pm 2\,(4\%),$$

which is the true percentage of working wives in the population. That is, the true percentage of employed wives is estimated to fall between 23 and 39 percent of Born-Again families.

Costs permitting, we may further reduce the probable error by increasing the sample size and encompass virtually all possibilities within a wider interval. (To determine the sample size required, refer to the mathematical illustration in Section IV.5.)

Within three standard errors of the sample proportion, practically all working wives of the targeted population will come within:

$$p \pm 3s_x = 31\% \pm 3(4\%),$$

the interval, 19 percent to 43 percent.

Generally, when *p* values fall outside of the 30 to 70 percent range, the sample size should be at least 100.

The nearer *p* is to 50 percent, the greater the standard deviation. In the foregoing illustrations, the projected results fall within a fairly broad range. Therefore, take note: proportions are not very precise measurements.

A Question of Review

For purposes of review at this point, Figure V.2.A summarizes differences between true values and estimations of what the true value is likely to be. Generally, Greek letters represent true values, Roman letters approximations. Since a researcher never really knows the true parameters (Greek letters) of the market, s/he must guess at what they are.

And for further review, Figure V.2.B summarizes various statistics applicable to four scale measurements, the appropriate tests of significance (referred to in the next subsection), and some examples of their use with reference to specific sections in this book. This tabulation will provide a handy reference before applying various statistical techniques to data collection and marketing research design.

SUMMARY OF TERMS FOR TRUE VALUES AND ESTIMATES

	True Value	Estimate
Mean	μ	$\bar{x} = \dfrac{\Sigma x}{n}$
Standard Deviation of Mean	$\sigma_{\bar{x}} = \dfrac{\sigma}{\sqrt{n}}$	$s_x = \dfrac{s}{\sqrt{n}}$
Standard Deviation of Population	$\sigma = \sqrt{\sigma^2}$	$s = \sqrt{s^2}$
Proportion	θ	$p = \dfrac{\text{No. successes}}{n}$
Variance	σ^2	$s^2 = \dfrac{\Sigma(x - \bar{x})^2}{n - 1}$

Figure V.2.A: SUMMARY OF TERMS FOR TRUE VALUES AND ESTIMATES

MEASUREMENT SCALES AND APPLICABLE STATISTICAL ANALYSIS

Scale	Applicable Statistics	Determi-nation of	Tests of Significance	Examples	Some Section References
NOMINAL	Number of cases MODE Percentage Contingency Correlation	equality	Chi-square	Multiple Choice Binary Cross-tabulation	V.3 IV.1 IV.5
ORDINAL	Median Percentiles Order Correlation	greater or lesser	Sign test Run test Two-way analysis of variance	Likert Scale Guttman's Scalogram Semantic Differential Q-Sort Ranking	III.3 III.4 III.1 III.4 III.3, V.4
INTERVAL	Mean Average Deviation Standard Deviation Rank-order correlation Product-moment correlation Regression Factor Analysis	equality of intervals or differences	t-test f-test	Thurstone Scale Semantic Differential (Bi-polar Adjective Scale)	V.2, III.4, V.3 III.1, V.4 V.1 VI.2 VI.3
RATIO	Geometric Mean Harmonic Mean Coefficient of Variation	equality of ratios	Percent variation Coefficient of variation	Multidimensional Scaling Constant Sum Scale Delphi Procedure	III.5 IV.5 III.4, V.4 II.5, V.1

Figure V.2.B: **MEASUREMENT SCALES AND APPLICABLE STATISTICAL ANALYSIS**

V.3: HOW TO GRADE YOUR TREASURES WITH STATISTICAL TESTS OF SIGNIFICANCE

To what extent do sampling variations throw results off track? How much risk will you absorb with market projections? How can you statistically control that risk?

Tests of significance highlight whether differences observed between two groups of data represent true differences of the entire market or whether the differences result from chance variations in the sampling process itself.

Some important analytical, profit-making tools surface in this subsection and the next. Most of these are quite easy to master without prior training in statistics. They provide profitable ways of mining more information out of a limited amount of data already gathered, or about to be gathered. Thus, they represent cost-reducing research tools of analysis.

If you feel a little uncomfortable with a couple of these concepts, or want to explore some in greater depth, a book on elementary business statistics is a practical addition to your business library. However, for most applications additional study will not be necessary. You can profitably apply the ideas here to your particular marketing questions.

Degrees of Freedom

"Degrees of freedom" is a concept easier to use than to explain. In fact, you have already used it in this book. With sample data it is necessary to determine the number of variables that you are free to vary.

For instance, in Section V.1, the denominator for the standard deviation of a sample was given as $(n - 1)$; and a footnote recommended $(n - 1)$ instead of n, especially when dealing in small samples.

The $(n - 1)$ is called the number of degrees of freedom. For large samples, as the sample size approaches the total market, $(n - 1)$ becomes less important and n alone is sufficient.

In a random block design (Section II.4), for a two-treatment analysis, the degrees of freedom associated with the estimated standard deviation are $2(n - 1)$. As always, n stands for the number of observations, or items, or persons.

Computation of the error degrees of freedom is necessary when referring to convenient statistical tables, such as with the F-test in Section V.4. These referential statistical tables are usually found in the appendices of elementary statistical books; some appear at the end of this book as well for problem-solving.

Later in this subsection, the chi-square test relies on determination of the number of degrees of freedom as one of the procedural steps. In the examples (here and in Section IV.5), the number of degrees of freedom for rows is the number of rows minus one. For columns, it is the number of columns minus one.

In order to use the chi-square table in the Appendix, we need to know the degrees of freedom. In this instance, the number of degrees of freedom will be the number of columns minus one times the number of rows minus one.

To apply an analysis of variance (Section V.4), we will make considerable use of degrees of freedom:

(1) first, to determine sample variance;
(2) then, to calculate the interaction degrees of freedom;
(3) later, to estimate variance; and
(4) last, to use the table in computing the variance ratio.

Total degrees of freedom (d.f.), in the analysis of variance example in Section V.4, is the number of rows times the number of columns, minus one.

▶ Total d.f. $= (R \times C) \times 1$

Degrees of freedom for either rows or columns will be calculated as the number of rows (columns) minus one:

▶ Row d.f. $= R - 1$
▶ Column d.f. $= C - 1$

The interaction degrees of freedom (also explicated in Section V.4) is:

▶ Interaction d.f. $=$ Total d.f. $-$ (Row d.f. $-$ Column d.f.)

These examples at least indicate some instances in which the degrees of freedom concept is employed, and comprise the chief examples in this book.

Z-Values

How can we compare the standard deviations from two sets of data? One method is to transform each standard deviation into a standard measure termed a z-value. The z-value for a given value in a sample is:

$$z = \frac{x - \bar{x}}{s}$$

x $=$ the value of a given observation in the sample.
$\bar{x}$ $=$ the sample mean.
s $=$ the sample standard deviation.

These z-values have been calculated for different levels of significance. A table of selected z-values appears in Appendix B.

Let's say that we have two sets of data: one for hourly employees in the shop, the other for management. The average shop worker draws $275 ($\bar{x}$) per week, straight time; the standard deviation is $45 (s). The average weekly salary for management works out to $425, with a standard deviation of $270.

Specifically, you want to compare your own salary of $640 a week to a certain shop supervisor's of $320 per week. Obviously, yours is twice his, but the comparison lacks meaning because data are drawn from two dissimilar populations.

Let's convert these data into z-values to make them comparable.

$$z_s = \frac{370 - 275}{45} = 1.0 \text{ standard deviations}$$

$$z_m = \frac{640 - 425}{270} = 0.80 \text{ standard deviations}$$

Converted to standard measures, the shop supervisor receives a higher wage within his group than you do within yours. Your salary is 0.80 standard deviations above the mean, while his is 1.0 standard deviations above the mean of his group.

The shop supervisor's salary is surpassed by a smaller percent of shop workers. Your salary is surpassed by a larger percent of individuals within your group. By referring to the table in Appendix B, we can fairly accurately determine those percents.

Under a normal curve (i.e., one with a perfectly symmetrical distribution), between the mean and a z-value of 1.0, lies 34.13 percent of the total. The total area is 1.0. The area under the curve between the mean of $425 and your wage of $640, represented by a z-value of 0.8, is 28.81 percent.

These percents were found by reading down the left vertical column to the closest z-value, and then across to the figure representing the proportion under one side of a normal curve.

Since 50 percent of the shop employees earn over $275 a week, and 34.13 percent earn between $275 and $320, then 15.87 percent (50.00 − 34.13 = 15.87%) earn more than the shop supervisor.

In your case, 50 percent of management earn over $425 weekly, and 28.81 percent receive between $425 and $640. Therefore, 21.19 percent earn more than you do. (You may want to review the example in Section V.1.)

The z-statistic is also used for the interval estimate of the mean for samples of 30 or more observations.

Formula 1: $\bar{x} + z\sigma_x$ = upper point of the interval

Formula 2: $\bar{x} - z\sigma_x$ = lower point of the interval

$\bar{x}$ = sample mean.

z = number of standard errors for the desired confidence level.

σ_x = the size of the standard error.

At a 95 percent confidence level, the z-value (taken from the table in Appendix B) is 1.96. (Also, refer to the discussion on confidence intervals and standard errors of the mean in Section V.2.)

For sample sizes of less than 30, the t-distribution substitutes. Since both the t-statistic and the z-statistic are calculated and applied in the same manner, an explanation will follow with reference to the t-statistic without repeating the procedure here for the z-statistic.

T-Values

When the sample size drops below 30 observations, the normal curve no longer describes accurately the distribution of the sample means. Another set of curves, called t-curves, substitute for z-values. But this brings us back to the degree of freedom concept, $(n - 1)$.

Before working through a brief example, take a look at the t-distribution table in Appendix C. The t-values describe the distribution of a deviation of a sample from a population value, divided by the standard error.

Values in the horizontal heading are probabilities. They refer to the sum of the two-tailed areas, under the curve, which lie outside the points $\pm t$.

Two-tailed is like saying that every stick has two ends, i.e., the lowest and highest extremes of the distribution. For a single-tailed area, that is, only one set of extreme data, divide the probability by two, so that 0.05 becomes 0.025. In the left-hand vertical heading of the table, degrees of freedom $(n - 1)$ are registered.

To use the table, say that sample size, n, equals 12. Therefore, degrees of freedom equal 11 $(12 - 1)$. At a 95 percent probability level, 5 percent of the area under the curve lies in the two tails—the extremes—outside of the interval $t = \pm 2.20$. The last row indicates corresponding areas under the normal curve.

> *Note*: At the 0.05 level, all the t-values are greater than 2. Therefore, we can reject values under 2—even without reference to the table—and accept those over 2.

Index of Significance. Let's call the t-value an *index of significance* to indicate whether a difference in a mean is significant or not.

$$t_{(n - 1)} = \frac{\bar{x} - \mu}{\frac{s}{\sqrt{n}}}$$

t_{n-1} = index of significance with $(n - 1)$ d.f.
$\bar{x}$ = the sample mean.
μ = the standard of comparison.
$s/\sqrt{n}$ = uncertainty: how well the sample mean does or does not represent the mean of the population.

When uncertainty decreases, the index rises. When the difference between the sample mean and the standard increases, the index rises.

At the 0.05 significance level, a t-value over 2 will be significant, which implies that the population represented by the sample differs from the standard with respect to average behavior. Those values less than 2 generally are not significant.

Suppose we have the following data:

μ = 57.5 (purchases of the typical consumer per month).
$\bar{x}$ = 70.1 (average monthly purchases of a sample of nurses).
n = 25 (number of nurses in the sample).
s = 35 (standard deviation of the sample).

Do nurses (or at least those in our sample) consume more of the product per month than the rest of the population, or is the difference in average consumption attributable to the small sample size?

$$t_{(25 - 1)} = \frac{70.1 - 57.5}{\frac{35}{\sqrt{25}}} = 1.8 < 2.06$$

From the calculations we conclude, despite the fairly large divergence in mean values, that the difference is not significant. There is a good chance that the difference is due to the small sample size.

Working from a small sample alone, here are the steps to take in calculating the predicted range for the population mean based on sample data:

STEP I.   Calculate the sample mean and the standard deviation.

STEP II.   Determine the degrees of freedom from the sample size.

STEP III.   Decide on how certain you want to be (the probability).

STEP IV.   From the table in the Appendix, locate the appropriate t-value, given degrees of freedom and the level of confidence.

STEP V.   Compute the predicted range for the population mean, from the sample mean and standard deviation, with the following formula:

$$\text{Predicted Range for Population Mean} = \bar{x} \pm \frac{s_x}{\sqrt{n}} t$$

Results from the application of this formula will be the upper and lower limits of typical consumption for the population.

Coefficient of Skewness

Skewness has been referred to and defined in Sections IV.1 and IV.2. In brief, a frequency distribution with no skewness is perfectly symmetrical. The coefficient of skewness is zero.

If there are some big numbers pulling the average up, so that the mean exceeds the median or mode, then the distribution is positively skewed. At the other extreme, if the weight of the smaller value of the observations pulls the mean below the median and the mode, the distribution is negatively skewed.

To measure the amount and direction of skewness, the formula is:

$$Sk = \frac{3(\bar{x} - Md)}{s}$$

Sk = coefficient of skewness
$\bar{x}$ = sample mean.
Md = sample median.
s = sample standard deviation.

The coefficients will range between plus and minus three. The higher the absolute value of the coefficient, the greater the skewness.

Say that the coefficient is + 0.28. The distribution is slightly, positively skewed, not too far away from a normal or symmetrical distribution.

A coefficient of − 0.17 is very slightly negatively skewed, which signifies that the mean is less than the mode or median. (These concepts of central tendency—mean, median, mode—are explained in Section IV.1.) Graphed, the curve will not be a perfect bell-shaped one, but will stretch out slightly on the left in a negatively skewed distribution. (The tail is on the right in a positively skewed distribution.)

If the coefficient is −2.82, the distribution will be very negatively skewed, with a long tail on the left. The tail will be considerably longer than a distribution with a coefficient of −1.05, for example.

Chi-Square Test

If you will refer back to the figure in Section IV.5, under the heading "cross-tabulation," you learned there how to cross-tabulate data and calculate conditional probabilities, but not how to check for statistical significance. We will employ the same data again in the following example.

The chi-square (χ^2) test is suggested because:

◎ It can be used even with nominal measurements.
◎ It presumes to compare two unrelated variables.
◎ It is the most frequently used test with a two-way cross tabulation.
◎ It yields an index that spotlights the difference of actual results from the theoretical results, had the variables been independent.
◎ It is easy to use when the index calculated is compared with a table value such as the one on the Appendix.

The table in Figure V.3.A contains the same basic raw data as the one in Figure IV.5.B, except that we have added row and column probabilities in the margins and the probability of being in any given cell in parentheses.

The probability of being in any given row is the row total (Bible sales by region) divided by sales for all regions (10,000) expressed as a decimal. Thus, for the eastern region, 700/10,000 = 0.07. That is, there is a 7 percent chance of sales originating in the East.

RELATION OF AGE LEVEL AND REGION AND EXPECTED CELL SIZES (in parentheses)

Region	Under 25	25-39	40-54	55-69	over 69	TOTAL	Row PROBABILITY
East	240 (193)	10 (41)	40 (66)	280 (316)	130 (85)	700	0.07
Southeast	1100 (1018)	400 (218)	400 (348)	1400 (1669)	400 (448)	3700	0.37
Midwest	390 (798)	80 (171)	280 (273)	1920 (1308)	230 (351)	2900	0.29
Southwest	340 (385)	50 (83)	130 (132)	500 (631)	380 (169)	1400	0.14
West	680 (358)	50 (77)	90 (122)	410 (586)	70 (158)	1300	0.13
TOTAL	2750	590	940	4510	1210	10,000	
Column Probability	0.275	0.059	0.094	0.451	0.121		1.00

Figure V.3.A: RELATION OF AGE LEVEL AND REGION AND EXPECTED CELL SIZES

The column probability is total sales for that column divided by total sales for the country. Therefore, there is a 27.5 percent chance (2750 ÷ 10,000 = 0.275) that sales will originate in the under-age-25 bracket.

What we next want to project is the probability that sales will derive from any particular cell, such as the under-age-25 group on the East Coast.

Here is one method:

Multiply the column total by the row total and divide by grand total sales:

(i) For the cell, under age 25, eastern region: (2750 × 700) ÷ 10,000 = 193.

(ii) For the cell, under age 25, Southeast: (2750 × 3700) ÷ 10,000 = 1018.

With this information computed we next construct an index to measure the difference between actual and expected sales in each cell.

$$\text{Index} = \overset{r}{\Sigma}\,\overset{c}{\Sigma}\ \frac{(f_a - f_e)^2}{f_e}$$

$\overset{r}{\Sigma}$ = sum of rows.

$\overset{c}{\Sigma}$ = sum of columns.

f_a = actual number of sales recorded in each cell.

f_e = probable sales for each cell.

The formula states that the index is the sum of the squared differences for all cells (rows and columns) expressed as a percent of expected sales in each cell.

First, we will calculate, then evaluate, the index.

$$\text{Index} = \frac{(240 - 193)^2}{193} + \frac{(10 - 41)^2}{41} + \frac{(40 - 66)^2}{66} + \frac{(280 - 316)^2}{316}$$

$$+ \frac{(130 - 85)^2}{85} + \frac{(1100 - 1018)^2}{1018} + \frac{(400 - 218)^2}{218} + \frac{(400 - 348)^2}{348}$$

$$+ \frac{(1400 - 1669)^2}{1669} + \frac{(400 - 448)^2}{448} + \frac{(390 - 798)^2}{798} + \frac{(80 - 171)^2}{171}$$

$$+ \frac{(280 - 273)^2}{273} + \frac{(1920 - 1308)^2}{1308} + \frac{230 - 351)^2}{351} + \frac{(340 - 385)^2}{385}$$

$$+ \frac{(50 - 83)^2}{83} + \frac{(130 - 132)^2}{132} + \frac{(500 - 631)^2}{631} + \frac{(380 - 169)^2}{169}$$

$$+ \frac{(680 - 358)^2}{358} + \frac{(50 - 77)^2}{77} + \frac{(90 - 122)^2}{122} + \frac{(410 - 586)^2}{53}$$

$$+ \frac{(70 - 158)^2}{158}$$

$= 11.45 + 23.44 + 10.24 + 4.10 + 23.82 + 6.61 + 15.19 + 7.77$
$+ 43.36 + 5.14 + 208.60 + 48.43 + 0.18 + 286.35 + 41.71 + 5.26$
$+ 13.12 + 0.03 + 27.20 + 263.44 + 289.62 + 9.47 + 8.39 + 52.86$
$+ 49.01$
$= 1454.79$

The easiest way to evaluate this index is by comparison with a chi-square table like the one reproduced in Appendix D. In order to use the table we need to determine the number of degrees of freedom (d.f.), which is:

$$\text{d.f.} = (C - 1)\,(R - 1) = (5 - 1)\,(5 - 1) = 4 \times 4 = 16$$

Along the horizontal heading of the table appear the probabilities of chi-square occurring due to sampling variation. Degrees of freedom appear in the vertical column.

After determination of the degrees of freedom (16 in this case), look up the corresponding probability value. This will be the probability that differences between actual and expected values arise due to sampling variation.

Test of Independence. At a 0.05 level of significance, the critical value of chi-square, according to the table, is 26.30, the test of independence. The probability of rejecting a true sample when it is actually representative of the market is the level of significance, designated by the lower case Greek letter alpha, α. How much risk you want to assume with a given set of data of rejecting a true hypothesis determines the chosen level of significance.

Typically, 0.05 and 0.01 alphas are employed. You can even select a level of significance as small as 0.001, which, in this case, yields a chi-square value of 39.3. A 0.05 level of significance corresponds to a confidence coefficient of 0.95, which is another way of saying that you are 95 percent certain that expected values correspond to actual values.

Since the index number exceeds the chi-square from the table, 1454.8 > 26.3, we can reject the idea that the variables are not related at the 0.05 level of significance.

But we can conclude that both variables, region and age level, are very definitely related, and we can take another but serious look at the conditional probability tables, Figures IV.5.C, and IV.5.D.

Two further tests of significance are explained in the next subsection: analysis of variance and the F-test.

V.4: TWELVE FORMULAS FOR KEEPING SALES ON TARGET AND REDUCING RISKS

Experimenting with consumers' individual preferences, tastes, habits, and perceived needs introduces risks not prevalent in strictly controlled laboratory tests.

Of course, neither lab nor people experiments produce perfect results; but experiments probing minds of purchasers will never wring out all or even a major component of business risks because

(a) buyers change their minds;
(b) the test and purchase environments change with time;
(c) other environmental variables (actions of competitors, for example) influence responses and results;
(d) no pair of test objects will be exactly alike.

In earlier parts of this book, these types of problems, concerning uncontrolled variations in comparative studies, were dealt with by

(1) establishing a control group, or
(2) randomization.

Before-and-after studies, paired groups, replications of the experiment, and similar techniques have proven useful devices for ironing out these differences during the experiment itself. After the data are gathered, however, an analysis of variance and covariance is a means of describing the variability of a distribution of results.

Measure of Variability

In Sections IV.1 and V.2, we examined some measures of central location to describe tendencies of a majority of likely buyers out of a population of buyers. In Section V.1, we described the spread, or dispersion, or variability, of a distribution. Variance is another measure of variability.

The purpose of an analysis of variance is to test for significant differences among average responses due to controlled variables.

Recall from discussions in Sections IV and V that the standard deviation is the square root of the variance. The mean describes the central tendency of a group of data, or a group of consumers, i.e., the average. Standard deviation tells us whether the data are clustered around the center (lots of buyers thinking along similar lines) or whether the data are scattered all over the spectrum (no typical buyers).

Variance measures the spread of a group of data by averaging the squared deviations from the mean. The analysis of variance is a test of means among two or more sets of data.

Sample Variance

For reference purposes, let's begin with the basic formulas. (Various formulas are also summarized in Figure V.2.A) For *sample variance*, the formula is:

$$s^2 = \frac{\Sigma (x - \bar{x})^2}{(n - 1)}$$

s^2 = sample variance; the square root of the above is the sample standard deviation referred to in Section V.1.

Σ = sum of (upper-case Greek sigma).

x = value of each observation in the group of data.

$\bar{x}$ = the mean (or average) of the sample.

$(n - 1)$ = the number of observations in the sample, minus 1. (See the footnote in Section V.1 for explanation why $(n - 1)$ rather than n alone is used.)

Shortcut Formula

Here's a shortcut formula, especially valuable when not dealing with whole numbers:

$$s^2 = \frac{n (\Sigma x^2) - (\Sigma x)^2}{n (n - 1)}$$

All letters mean the same as in the previous formula.

Population Variance

To determine population variance, the formula preferred is:

$$\sigma^2 = \frac{\Sigma(x - \mu)^2}{N}$$

σ^2 = population variance (lower-case Greek sigma).

Σ = sum of (upper-case Greek sigma).

x = value of each observation.

μ = population mean (lower-case Greek mu)

N = total number of elements in the population. (If N represents people, then substitute the word *people* for elements.)

Probability Distribution

The variance of a probability distribution is the value *expected* for the squared deviation from the mean. Probability means the chance or likelihood that actual sales will measure up to anticipated sales. The formula is:

$$\sigma^2 = \Sigma(x - \mu)^2 \cdot f(x)$$

σ^2 = variance of the probability distribution.

Σ = sum of.

x   = the numerical value of the experiment.

μ = the mean of the probability distribution.

$(x - \mu)^2$ = deviation from the mean, squared.

f   = frequency or probability of number of times a given value of x will occur.

If this last formula is unclear, an example later in this subsection should clear up any questions.

Variance Ratio

The *variance ratio*, also known as the F-ratio, is the ratio of the two sample variances. Obviously, if both samples are drawn from the same market population and their variances tend to equal each other, the variance ratio will approach one, but probably will not equal it due to random error.

$$F = \frac{s_a^2}{s_b^2}$$

F   = variance ratio.

s_a^2 = variance of the first sample (a).

s_b^2 = variance of the second sample (b).

It is possible to construct a distribution of variance ratios which shows the probabilities that different ratio values arise. The example used later in this subsection will explain an application of the variance ratio.

Perhaps you should at least be aware that certain assumptions and preconditions underlie an analysis of variance:

1. (a). The researcher must be able to define the group of buyers;
   (b). S/he must be able to identify subgroups of the market;
   (c). Test data are randomly generated from normally distributed populations.
2. The chance variation in one observation is not affected by the chance variation in another.
3. Sources of variation must be additive, not multiplicative.
4. The data must be discrete, not continuous, and must have a constant standard deviation (homoscedastic).

Some examples will demonstrate the power and value of an analysis of variance. A firm that sells investments by telephone, the Mutual Security Investment Co., wanted to develop a structured sales presentation that could be read by less experienced salespersons. The presentation must be sufficiently effective to at least cover costs of expensive sales leads and telephone services during the initial learning period.

Two sales presentations were tested by the company's two top salespeople. During the experiment, each salesperson telephoned the same number of randomly selected leads in five cities, a different city each day. At the end of the test period, actual sales generated (checks received) were tabulated by number of new accounts and dollar value of each account.

Results in Figure V.4.A appear for the number, not the value, of sales. The number seems to be the relevant figure in this case, to evaluate sales performance during the training period.

						COMPARATIVE RESULTS OF TWO SALES PRESENTATIONS			
	Norwalk	Lancaster	Springfield	Marion	Greenville	Total Sales	Mean Sales	s^2
Ronald	3	4	5	6	7	25	5	2.5
Ed	1	2	3	4	5	15	3	2.5

Figure V.4.A: **COMPARATIVE RESULTS OF TWO SALES PRESENTATIONS**

The first thing we notice is that Ron's average sales exceed Ed's. Does this mean that one sales presentation is superior to the other?

An important characteristic of a data set is that values are usually different. Statistical analysis focuses on discovering how alike, or unalike, these figures really are.

One method of compressing data into one or two figures is the computation of middle values, such as the means shown in Figure V.4.A. But the means tell us nothing about that other important characteristic: how data are dispersed or bunched around the middle.

Therefore, analysis of variance suggests that the differences in our illustration derive from experimental errors rather than from the degree of effectiveness of the sales presentations. Now let's treat the analysis in more depth.

Say that a producer wants to experiment with three promotional approaches in four cities to promote the acceptance and sale of carambolas. The sales results shown in Figure V.4.B are by city and by marketing plan.

The first step is to calculate the means by rows, by columns, and the grand mean. To compute it by rows, add sales data for each row and divide by 4 (cities). It turns out that average sales for each promotional plan are identical, i.e., 100 units of sales in each instance.

To compute column means, add together sales for each city and divide by 3 (plans). To compute the grand mean, add up all sales and divide by 12 (4 columns by 3 rows), which also happens to work out to 100 units.

Promotion Plans	(1)	(2)	(3)	(4)	Row Means	Row Variations
SALES OF CARAMBOLAS IN FOUR CITIES BY PROMOTION PLAN						
A	50	70	160	120	100	0
B	20	170	170	40	100	0
C	80	60	180	80	100	0
Column Means	50	100	170	80	100	

Figure V.4.B: SALES OF CARAMBOLAS IN FOUR CITIES BY PROMOTION PLAN

Variation

Because analysis of variance focuses on the significant differences within one set of data rather than on significant differences between two sets of data, as in chi-square analysis (Section V.3), we need to introduce a concept called *variation*. Its formula is:

$$\text{Total Variation} = \Sigma(x - \bar{x})^2$$

Variation is computed by summing (Σ) the square of the deviation of each item in the set of data from the grand mean, where x represents the value of each item, and $\bar{x}$ the mean of all items.

Referring again to data in Figure V.4.B, the grand mean is 100 ($\bar{x}$); therefore, total variation is:

$$TV = (50 - 100)^2 + (70 - 100)^2 + (160 - 100)^2 + (120 - 100)^2 +$$
$$(20 - 100)^2 + \ldots + (80 - 100)^2 = 36,000$$

The purpose behind these calculations is to discover whether sales in different cities arise from different promotions or are due to sampling variations. And whether differences in sales have resulted from differences in geography or are due to sampling variations. In other words, did sales differences occur by chance? Or did our promotion and choice of cities cause the difference?

Row Variation

The next steps are to account for this variation, for we know that total variation must equal the sum of the components of variation.

So we begin by computing the variation attributable to the rows, the promotional activities.

$$\text{Row Variation} = C \, [\Sigma(\text{Row mean} - \text{Total mean})^2]$$

C = number of columns.
Σ = sum of.

Row and total means appear in Figure IV.4.B.

$$RV = 4 \, [(100 - 100)^2 + (100 - 100)^2 + (100 - 100)^2] = 0$$

Now that seemed like an unproductive exercise—a lot of work for nothing. How can we interpret a zero? The zero row variation means there is no variation due to different promotional efforts. That may be a big blow for someone's ego. Out of 36,000 units of variation, none are attributable to promotion.

Column Variation

Remembering that total variation must be accounted for somewhere, does this mean we can abandon the entire 36,000 to geography, and then later analyze the demographics of each locale for more detail on who is buying the carambolas?

$$\text{Column Variation} = R\,[\Sigma(\text{Column mean} - \text{Total mean})^2]$$

R = number of rows.
Σ = sum of.

Column and total means appear in Figure V.4.B.

$$CV = 3[\,(50 - 100)^2 + (100 - 100)^2 + (170 - 100)^2 + (80 - 100)^2\,]$$
$$= 3(2500 + 0 + 4900 + 400) = 23{,}400$$

Now what happened? Oh well, at least we are getting closer to accounting for total variation, although we're not quite there yet.

Interaction Variation

Therefore, we must have a third component of total variation which is unaccounted for either by geography or promotion. We can call this residual variation *interaction variation*.

$$\text{Interaction Variation} = TV - (RV + CV)$$

TV = total variation.
RV = row variation.
CV = column variation.

$$IV = 36{,}000 - (0 + 23{,}400) = 12{,}600$$

Interaction variation means a chance arises that variation emerges from the interaction of row treatments with column treatments. In other words, a special combination of cities and promotion brought out the carambola lovers. And City No. 3 seems to be where the action is.

Because row variation is less than the interaction variation (much less in this case), we really cannot attach much importance to the different promotion plans. On the other hand, the column variation exceeds interaction variation, which suggests that at least part of the variation may derive from the location where this exotic tropical fruit is sold.

Degrees of Freedom

So we must dig deeper and proceed to the next step: determine the degrees of freedom (d.f.) associated with total, row, and column variations. (Section IV.3 has more to say on degrees of freedom.)

Total d.f. $= (R \times C) - 1 = (3 \times 4) - 1 = 11$
Row d.f. $= R - 1 = 3 - 1 = 2$
Column d.f. $= C - 1 = 4 - 1 = 3$

Interaction d.f. $=$ Total d.f. $-$ (Row d.f. $+$ Column d.f.)
$= 11 - (2 + 3) = 6$

SUMMARY DATA FOR ANALYSIS OF VARIANCE

Source of Variation	Variation	Degrees of Freedom	Estimated Variance	F Value
TOTAL	36,000	11	————	
Rows	0	2	0	
Columns	23,400	3	7,800	1.86
Interaction	12,600	6	2,100	

Figure V.4.C: SUMMARY DATA FOR ANALYSIS OF VARIANCE

Like interaction variation, all degrees of freedom must be accounted for. The residual is subsumed under the label, interaction degrees of freedom, and in this cameo amounts to 6. (By the way, these computations are summarized in Figure V.4.C.)

Estimated Variance

We can use the above calculations to estimate variance. What we want to know, and are leading up to, is the effect of geography (cities) and promotion on total variance. We need to find out what is occurring between cities and between promotion plans.

$$\text{Estimated Variance} = \frac{\text{Variation}}{\text{Degrees of freedom}}$$

Once again, let's take the calculations by row, by column, and for interaction.

$$EV_r = \frac{0}{2} = 2$$

$$EV_c = \frac{23,400}{3} = 7,800$$

$$EV_i = \frac{12,600}{6} = 2,100$$

The F-Test

Now we are ready for the variance ratio, the F-test, mentioned earlier in this subsection (as well as in Section V.3). To compute the ratio, divide the estimated variance of the row or column by the interaction estimated variance. Since row value is zero, we are not concerned with it; but we can look at the F-ratio for column datum.

$$F_{c/i} = \frac{EV_c \,(d.f._c)}{EV_i \,(d.f._i)}$$

EV_c and EV_i are estimated variances from Figure V.4.C for columns and interaction respectively; $d.f._c$ and $d.f._i$ are degrees of freedom for columns and interaction respectively.

$$F_{c/i} = \frac{23,400 \,(3\ d.f.)}{12,600 \,(6\ d.f.)} = 1.86 \frac{(3\ d.f.)}{(6\ d.f.)}$$

Next, go to Appendix E, the Table of Critical F-Values, to determine the minimum value of F when there are three degrees of freedom in the numerator and six degrees of freedom in the denominator. The critical F value, at 95 percent confidence level, is 4.76.

From this we conclude that observed variation in sales of carambolas is not attributed to the different locations of the experiment. Why?

Notice that the F-value is smaller than 4.76: $1.86 < 4.76$. This fails to meet the minimum value associated with statistical significance. If the F-value were equal to, or greater than, 4.76, then 95 times out of 100 we could attribute sales to column treatments.

For F-values lower than the critical value of 4.76 (only when there are three degrees of freedom in the numerator and six in the denominator), a hit would have to be attributed to chance, 95 times out of 100.

Assuming lack of any statistical bias, precision is measured by the variance of the estimate: the smaller the variance, the more precise the estimate.

Typically, analysis of variance is practical only when no more than three factors are involved. Otherwise, regression analysis (Section VI.3) becomes a practical substitute.

Probability Distribution

One last example promised is the variance of a probability distribution, which is defined as the value we expect for the squared deviation from the mean; its formula appears near the beginning of this subsection.

Suppose that your company offers three types of pens for office application. What is the probability of making no sale, or a sale of type I, II, or III pens, or some combination of types I, II, and III, or a sale of all three types at once? (Incidentally, this same approach has many marketing applications. For example, what is the probability of receiving 220 direct mail responses with a mailout of 1500?)

When your sales representative approaches a customer, s/he will receive either a yes or a no answer. A no answer, naturally, means a sale of zero pens. A yes answer, however, may mean a sale out of a possible combination of seven yes answers (quantity aside) for one, two, or all three types of pens.

```
        100  120
000     020  103  123
        003  023
```

In other words, although a definite no answer means just one thing, a yes answer can comprise any one of the seven combinations shown above.

Three possible yeses can produce a sale of only one type of pen; another three possible yeses can result in a sale combination of any two types of pens; still another possibility can yield a sale of all three types of pens. These possible yes answers (x) are summarized in Figure V.4.D.

		VARIANCE OF A PROBABILITY DISTRIBUTION		
Number of Yeses (x)	Probability (out of 8) (f (x))	$(X-\mu)$	$(x-\mu)^2$	$(x-\mu)^2 \cdot f(x)$
0	1/8	−1.50	2.25	0.28125
1	3/8	−0.50	0.25	0.09375
2	3/8	+ 0.50	0.25	0.09375
3	1/8	+ 1.50	2.25	0.28125
				$\sigma^2 = 0.75$

Figure V.4.D: VARIANCE OF A PROBABILITY DISTRIBUTION

What is the probability, or chance, of any one of these combinations occurring? There is a 1 in 8 possibility that either a big NO or a big YES will pop up. But there is a 3 in 8 possibility that either one type or a combination of two types will be sold.

Since the mean (μ) is 1.50 (first column multiplied by the second column, and summed), the deviation from the mean (x − μ) is readily computed (third column) as well as its squares, $(x - \mu)^2$, in the fourth column. The values appearing in the last column result from the multiplication of each squared deviation from the mean, $(x - \mu)^2$, times the corresponding probability (second column).

Summing these values yields the variance of the probability distribution. The square root of the variance is the standard deviation of the distribution. Both are measures of dispersion. When they are small, chances are fairly good that sales will be close to the mean. When these values are large, it's anyone's guess how sales will turn out.

Analysis of variance is another tool in the bag of profitable ideas for marketing experimentation. From the cursory examination of applications, we can see how this set of tools helps to determine the significance of marketing results and to separate the effect of different variables in a marketing experiment. Analysis of variance compares the mean response of different subgroups of test units to determine whether the difference between means is small enough to be attributed to chance or large enough to be attributed to various experimental treatments.

SECTION *VI*

THE COMPUTER AND OTHER TECHNIQUES

"For he knoweth not that which shall be: for who can tell him when it shall be?"

Ecclesiastes 8:7

INTRODUCTION

It can be statistically proven that a greater proportion of persons will die who are under the care of a physician than those who are not. Consequently, carrying such statistical proofs of cause and effect into the policy arena implies staying away from physicians. Which is probably a fairly safe policy if you are healthy, but not if you are ill.

Assuming that such a cause and effect is a tenable conclusion does not allow us to conclude that persons who are not under physician's care will live either longer or better. Neither does the opposite conclusion hold. "For he knows not that which shall be."

The existence of relationships simply means that two or more phenomena occur at such intervals (not necessarily simultaneously) that causal links may be present. Then again, causal relationships may not exist, as in the exaggerated example above, despite the simultaneous or sequential occurrence of events.

Because statistical manipulation will not necessarily prove cause and effect, erroneous policies arising from statistically sound but otherwise inaccurate analysis will lead to profits by chance, or derive from other, unobserved factors, rather than from sound decision-making. Public policy-makers are notorious for wrong decisions based on unquestioning faith in statistical relationships. With costs of mistakes passed on to taxpayers, they are sluggish to respond with corrective measures.

Private policy-makers, too, make the same type of errors for similar reasons, but with personal and company survival on the chopping block, they respond more quickly to cut losses.

The point is this: the analytical techniques presented in the preceding section, and in this one, are powerful tools of analysis that can contribute to profitable decision-making as long as intuition and basic familiarity with the market are not tossed aside. Surface relationships, which are easy to derive because the data are cheaply available, and which very nicely fit a linear regression model, may provide catnip for the cat; but the successful manager seeks underlying reasons, the real causes.

You may be saying, "Well, that's obvious." Indeed it is, but let me provide two illustrations—and these are only two out of thousands—where lag or other causal forces have led to incorrect conclusions.

One is inflation. Most people believe that higher prices cause inflation. Actually, higher prices may be only one of several effects of inflation. Further, it is possible to have inflation (increase of the money supply) without any perceptible price rise; and some prices may even fall for a brief period. Incorrect interpretation of correlations have led to costly public policies.

Another conclusion is that people make babies. Here, the nine-month lag between apparent cause and effect is well documented. Therefore, if this is true, we must conclude that a laboratory reproduction of skin and bones and all the artificial organs is all that is necessary to reproduce people, when we arrive at that state of technology.

Not everyone agrees with that conclusion. The insertion of motors and electronic circuitry will transform the laboratory creation into an automaton, but without a spirit present we have no human being. And a discussion of the spirit gets us out of the bedroom or laboratory and into theology. As one scientist put it, speaking of the scientific community, "It's like climbing a steep, unknown mountain, only to discover when you've reached the top that the theologians have been there for centuries."

Whether you agree with the conclusions from these two examples is not at issue. How you use the research and analytical tools in this book is the point of this discussion. With computer application to marketing research problems, tons of printouts, while available, are not the object. Correlation, regression, and trend series analysis will help you see around many corners; but the decision as to which corners are the relevant ones still lies with you. Whether profits or losses arise, you, not the research technique, still carry bottom-line responsibility, "for who can tell you when it shall be?"

VI.1: THE COMPUTER, WORTH ITS WEIGHT IN GOLD*

Computer applications in business predominately have supported finance and accounting functions. By contrast, marketing applications have been more limited, often unimaginatively restricted to a narrow range of routine processing, or, in some companies, given low priorities on computer usage.

Still, the highest return, in terms of asset growth, arises from the profitable use of marketing research techniques developed in this book. Do not overlook marketing applications of small computers when pressing for asset growth.

Asset Growth

Figure VI.1.A summarizes possible asset growth and asset protection opportunities for four basic business functions: marketing, research and development, production, and accounting. Notice from the table that asset growth is highest (with four pluses) in marketing, but lowest (with one plus) in accounting.

RETURNS FROM SMALL COMPUTER APPLICATIONS IN VARIOUS BUSINESS FUNCTIONS			
FUNCTION	ASSETS UNDER FUNCTION'S CONTROL	ASSET GROWTH	ASSET PROTECTION
1. Marketing	Customers and Prospects	+ + + +	+
2. R & D	Ideas and Equipment	+ + +	+ +
3. Production	Machines and Material	+ +	+ + +
4. Accounting	Flow of Funds	+	+ + + +

Figure VI.1.A: **RETURNS FROM SMALL COMPUTER APPLICATIONS IN VARIOUS BUSINESS FUNCTIONS**

On the other hand, computerized applications provide greatest asset protection in the accounting function but least in marketing. Therefore, application of your micro- or mini-computer to marketing research problems has the potential of providing your organization substantial customer and prospect growth.

---

*Some of the ideas presented in this subsection draw on materials assembled and organized by Paul Zorfass, Vice President, Waters Business Systems, Inc., of Framingham, Massachusetts.

It is a cost-saving method in those repetitive, routine areas found in all functional activities, whether accounting, sales, or inventory control, and those uses of the computer are not minimized. Asset growth from marketing applications, however, is a frequently overlooked high-profit potential use for many concerns.

Of course, neither computer nor systems analyst makes decisions and takes action, but each forms part of the organization's information system to support marketing decisions and actions taken by you and your managers.

Consequently, sufficient computer time should be alloted to marketing research, because the use of computers can

- ◎ increase effective use of informal information gathered;
- ◎ facilitate handling and absorption of large volumes of data;
- ◎ raise the quality of decisions made because of more thoroughly analyzed and timely information;
- ◎ free up human time and energy poured into routine matters for goal-seeking and judgmental tasks;
- ◎ provide an audit trail.

Development of a System

Additionally, the computer can aid in the formalization and stabilization of a system. Because a computer does not think, instructions to it must be very precise with no steps deleted in the logic flow of ideas and processes that make up a marketing research project. The output of a computer depends on

- ◎ which data are entered;
- ◎ how they are entered;
- ◎ instructions given to the machine-beast.

For instance, the computer cannot provide data on sales trends, product use by customer, or potential sales by customer even though data from routine handling of sales and service reports and billing may have been entered previously in the machine's memory. The history file must be structured with the right building blocks of data and properly constructed sales statistics in order to benefit the market researcher immediately. Some data may not have been accumulated or stored for subsequent analysis or entered in a format most efficient to the researcher.

Illustrated in Figure VI.1.B, the 12-step approach to a typical marketing research undertaking provides a logical flow from start to end plus provision for subsequent evaluation. These steps have been developed and reinforced at various points throughout this book and are appropriately summarized here.

• *First*: Unless the marketing research problem is adequately defined and the objectives made crystal clear, a lot of money can be wasted in later, unproductive steps. At this point, too, information sources are developed; consulting Section I of this book will help during this initial stage (Steps A and B in Figure VI.1.B).

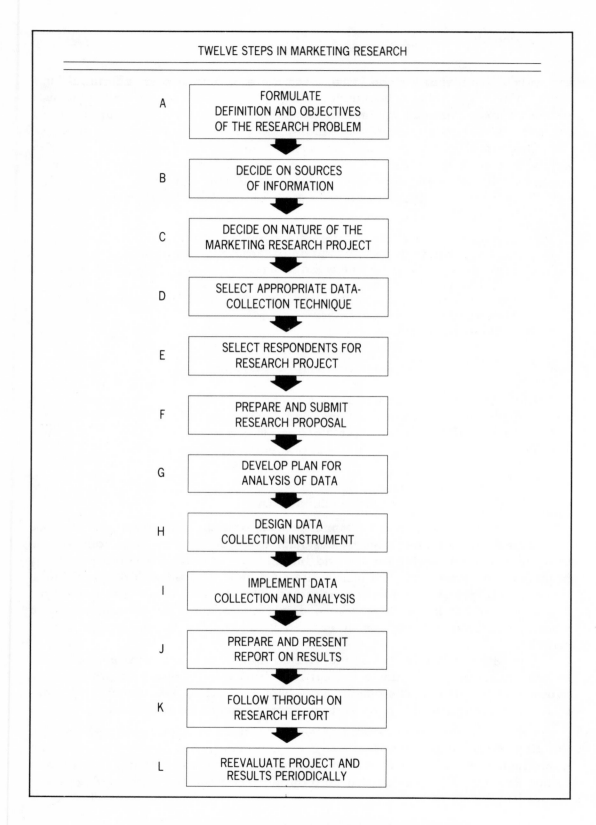

TWELVE STEPS IN MARKETING RESEARCH

A · FORMULATE DEFINITION AND OBJECTIVES OF THE RESEARCH PROBLEM

B · DECIDE ON SOURCES OF INFORMATION

C · DECIDE ON NATURE OF THE MARKETING RESEARCH PROJECT

D · SELECT APPROPRIATE DATA-COLLECTION TECHNIQUE

E · SELECT RESPONDENTS FOR RESEARCH PROJECT

F · PREPARE AND SUBMIT RESEARCH PROPOSAL

G · DEVELOP PLAN FOR ANALYSIS OF DATA

H · DESIGN DATA COLLECTION INSTRUMENT

I · IMPLEMENT DATA COLLECTION AND ANALYSIS

J · PREPARE AND PRESENT REPORT ON RESULTS

K · FOLLOW THROUGH ON RESEARCH EFFORT

L · REEVALUATE PROJECT AND RESULTS PERIODICALLY

Figure VI.1.B: TWELVE STEPS IN MARKETING RESEARCH

• *Second*: Steps C through F are linked to the planning process: How will the data be collected? Who are the potential respondents? How will they be selected? Answers to many of these important questions appear in this book. Also, do not overlook the very important matter of preparing a written research proposal—logically organized with objectives and steps to those objectives clearly stated.

• *Third*: Execution and presentation of the proposal (Steps G through J) means not only carrying through the project according to plan but also analyzing it and then presenting the results of the analysis in a manner that invites action, for without action nothing happens. Miles of computer printouts seldom generate much enthusiasm for decision-makers and action-takers in a company, although your computer supplies house will be happy. The final report must be analyzed and interpreted by whoever stands between the computer and the decision-maker.

• *Fourth*: Last are the follow-up stages (K and L). Research done produces nothing but research done—hardly a productive activity in itself for pinpointing and selling to new customers. In addition, there should be periodic reevaluation of the effort to develop further insight into costs and benefits. These periodic reevaluations may occur over several months, even years, after the initial research is completed.

Application of computer technology can occur at several phases during this process. To develop a systems approach, consider that a sales and marketing information base relies on receiving information before the data can be digested and used in a profitable manner. The details of a systems approach are diagrammed in Figure VI.1.C.

Starting at the top of the diagram we can summarize some of the highlights pertinent to each box in Figure VI.1.C.

1. Analysis of customer/prospect company:
   a. complete market data base on both customers and potential customers.
   b. a needs analysis of potential customers—e.g., demographics, equipment usage, rate of materials used per employee, etc.
   c. development of sales potential factors.
2. Inquiries/leads:
   a. complete inquiry history.
   b. process and time for lead qualification.
   c. accurate lead distribution to sales force.
   d. product mix response.
   e. evaluation of effectiveness of advertising and sales promotion.
3. Systematic account tracking—service:
   a. improved utilization of field engineers.
   b. training and support related to customers' needs, equipment installation, service call time.
   c. maintenance of customer loyalty with service.
   d. increased service income.

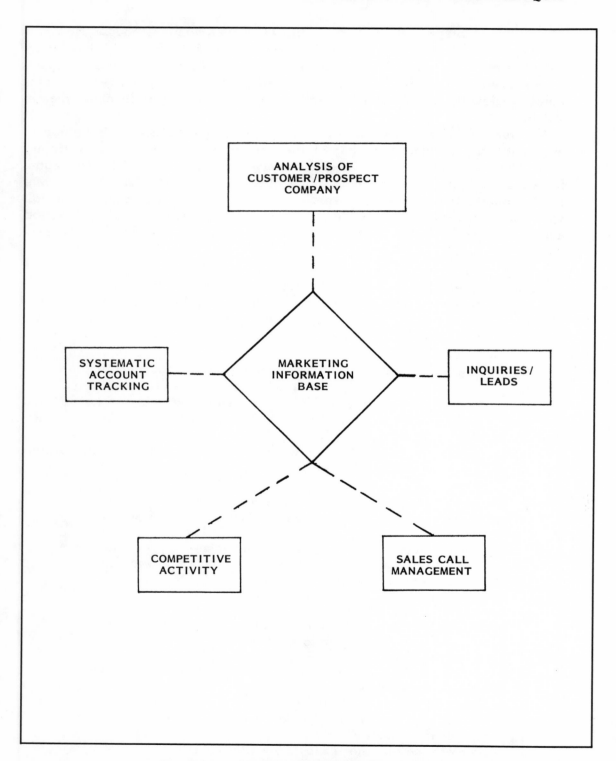

Figure VI.1.C: DIAGRAM OF A SYSTEMS APPROACH

4. Analyze competitive activity:
   a. product.
   b. service.
   c. industry and/or by market segment.
   d. account by account.
   e. steps to neutralize competition.
5. Sales call account management:
   a. automated account book.
   b. sales time organizer.
   c. territory coverage and realignment.
   d. training programs.
   e. sales and trend forecasting.
   f. key factors such as priorities, contract date, probability of close and how soon.

Of course, if the data base is not in a format comprehensible to management and sales personnel, the printouts become round file fodder.

A systematic approach to marketing is illustrated in Figure VI.1.D. The computer can be used to generate a sales action report highlighting sales effectiveness, improved sales forecasts, and better sales personnel productivity. The computer can also be used in systems that do far more than track customers or screen potential customers.

A systematic approach to Marketing.

The Waters Business Systems, Inc. Marketing Pipeline is a systematic method of developing prospects from the world at large into customers. It is a multi-stage process that emphasizes maximum productivity and communication at minimum cost.

How the Pipeline helps planning and profitability.

The Marketing Pipeline provides you with greater control in two important areas: profitability and planning.

It helps you to:
- Identify and individually track all of your customers and prospects
- Categorize prospects according to purchase probability
- Develop prospects into customers using the most cost-effective methods
- Analyze your marketing and sales efforts
- Reduce your ratio of sales cost to sales volume

Plus, it provides you with the necessary information to:
- Predict and plan for changes in sales volume (both cyclical and long term)
- Evaluate and rapidly penetrate new areas for market growth
- Increase your marketing effectiveness

™MARKETING PIPELINE is a trademark of Waters Business Systems, Inc. (WBS)

Figure VI.1.D: A SYSTEMATIC APPROACH TO MARKETING
(Courtesy of Waters Business System, Inc., Framingham, Massachusetts 01701.)

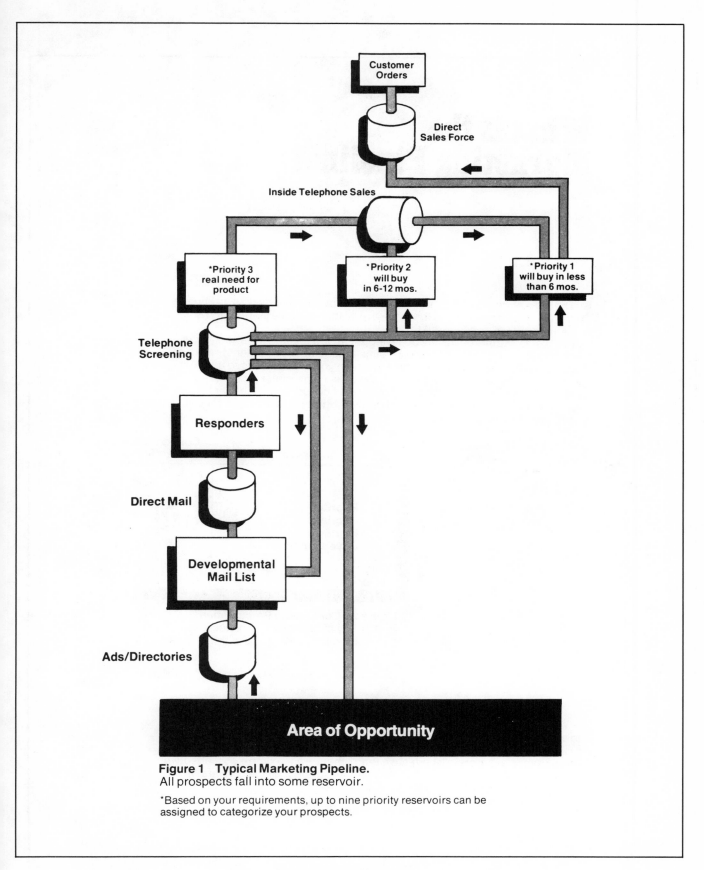

Figure 1 Typical Marketing Pipeline.
All prospects fall into some reservoir.

*Based on your requirements, up to nine priority reservoirs can be assigned to categorize your prospects.

Figure VI.1.D (continued)

What is the Marketing Pipeline?

The Marketing Pipeline. through which all your prospects flow, originates in the world at large, passes through several intermediate stages, and ends in customer orders (see Figure 1).

Prospects at different levels of development are located in various reservoirs along the Pipeline. Each reservoir is a stage of development toward a sale and is defined by the time frame in which you expect to close its prospects to orders. As shown in Figure 2, the closer a prospect is to the order reservoir, the higher the probability of a sale. The further a reservoir is from an order, the lower the probability of converting its prospects to a sale, and the larger the size of the reservoir.

Reservoir	Conversion Probability*
Priority 1	32%
Priority 2	10%
Priority 3	5%
Developmental List	.05%

Figure 2   Conversion Probabilities
Probability of converting prospects in a particular reservoir to a sale within the next 6 months

*Combined average of several companies' actual figures.

Your efforts to develop the prospect is the "pump" that moves him closer to an order. For example, a pump can be an advertising campaign, a direct mail program, a telephone call, or a sales call. Between specific reservoirs, some pumps are more cost effective than others. To maximize cost effectiveness, the cost of each pump must be commensurate with the conversion probability and size of the reservoir it addresses.

Figure VI.1.D (continued)

How the Pipeline helps you develop customers economically.

Figure 3 shows a compilation of several companies' actual costs and success ratios for various pumps. Not every pump will be applicable in all situations. Also, depending upon your industry and the effectiveness of your sales and marketing programs, your results may vary from the figures shown. The important factor, however, is the relative comparison between cost per contact and success ratio for various pumps available to you.

Reservoir	Pump	$/Contact	Success Ratio
High Priority Prospects	Direct Sales	80.00	32%
Low Priority Prospects	Inside Telephone Sales	12.00	10%
Responders	Telephone* Screening	3.00	36%
Developmental List	Direct Mail	.40	1.5%
Area of Opportunity	Advertising	.03	.6%

Figure 3   Pump Costs and Their Success Ratios
The Success Ratio of a pump is defined as the probability of its moving a prospect from a specific reservoir to at least the next higher reservoir (e.g., from Developmental Mail List to Responders).

*This pump is specifically designed to qualify and prioritize prospects into various reservoirs.

Clearly the success ratio and the conversion probability for prospect reservoirs are strongly interdependent (see Figure 2). Therefore, using a direct field sales representative to make cold calls on someone who has never heard of you or your product (a prospect in the Developmental Mail List) is the most expensive and least productive method of interfacing with that prospect. On the other hand, it is likely to be the most cost-effective way to close a sale with a prospect who is funded and ready to buy.

Figure VI.1.D (continued)

Why a computer is necessary.

Tracking prospects from reservoir to reservoir is a massive information handling job. For instance, a typical Developmental Mail List reservoir might contain anywhere from 1,000 to 80,000 prospects. It is too difficult and too expensive to control the Pipeline using manual methods. However, with WBS Marketing System computer software you can track and report Marketing Pipeline information easily and economically.

Mail List

You can mail to any segment of your mail list. Labels are printed automatically for both direct mail programs and for response literature. All responses are logged by prospect. Non-responders are periodically cleaned from the mail list.

Fulfillments

Response literature, samples, or premiums can be quickly assembled. All necessary information appears on computer generated mailing labels.

Telephone Screening

All prospects who have asked for further information but have not been assigned to a priority reservoir can be listed for telephone screening. Priority assignments and other pertinent information are retained by the computer for review by marketing and sales personnel.

Sales Action Reports

Sales call reports are maintained on the computer for easy access by the sales representative, the sales manager, or a new sales rep. Should you desire to realign sales territories, prospects can be transferred automatically.

Telephone and field sales reps communicate by adding commentary to the prospect's record as he is developed toward an order. The computer becomes the major communications vehicle. It stores all prospect data.

Customer Lists

You can maintain customer lists for all your products as well as for your competitors' products. The lists can be used to analyze market segments, sell disposables, and project market share.

Management Reports

A wide variety of management reports can track your sales costs, point out where the pipeline needs strengthening, or help predict changes in sales volume.

These are only a few examples of how the Pipeline concept and the WBS Marketing System combine to give you a more productive marketing approach.

How WBS can help you.

WBS is a team of marketing and computer specialists committed to helping clients realize the full benefit of the Marketing Pipeline concept and the computer programs which support it. Our service consists of both marketing consulting and computer software rental.

For further details, call (617) 879-2503.

Waters Business Systems, Inc.

47 New York Avenue, Framingham, Massachusetts 01701

M31   1278

Figure VI.1.D (continued)

Donkey Work

Computers serve market researchers well in the processing and analysis of large quantities of data—and effort that requires hours of repetitious labor and computations. The analytical techniques explained in Sections IV, V and VI can be done by hand with the aid of a professional calculator as illustrated in the various examples.

Or the computer can process, sort, and analyze to produce printouts such as those illustrated in Figures VI.1.E, VI.1.F, VI.1.G, and VI.1.H. The first two exhibited are simple cross-tabulations: Figure VI.1.E cross-tabulates sex and family income; Figure VI.1.F, productivity by company. Cross-tabulations are explained in Section IV.6. Notice, too, the use of chi-square and degrees of freedom (Section V.3).

The illustration in Figure VI.1.G is a frequency table. Note the appearance of several terms explained in this book: mean, mode, and median (Section IV.1); skewness (Sections IV.1, V.3); standard deviation (Section V.1); standard error (Section V.2); range (Section IV.1); and variance (Section V.4).

The printout in Figure VI.1.H tabulates results of a sample of 20 observations. The linear model (refer to remaining portion of Section VI, especially VI.3) relates operating expenses and value added of these firms. Note the provision for values of the intercept and linear coefficients (Section VI.3), as well as several other concepts discussed elsewhere in this book, such as confidence level (Sections V.2,3,4); least squares (Section VI.3); standard error of the mean (Section V.2); F-values (Section V.4); R-values (Sections VI.2,3); as well as others previously mentioned. (Also, refer to Figure VI.3.C for scatter diagrams and regression analysis.) In other words, most computer applications in marketing research have centered around statistical analysis.

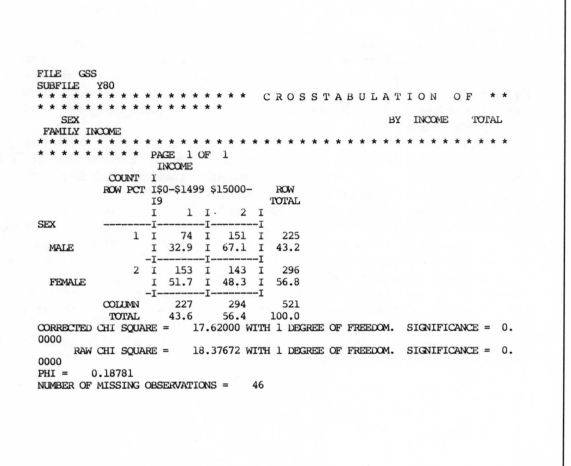

```
FILE    GSS
SUBFILE  Y80
* * * * * * * * * * * * * * * *   C R O S S T A B U L A T I O N   O F   * *
* * * * * * * * * * * * * *
   SEX                                              BY  INCOME   TOTAL
 FAMILY INCOME
* * * * * * * * * * * * * * * * * * * * * * * * * * * * * * * * * * * * * * *
* * * * * * * *  PAGE  1 OF  1
                 INCOME
           COUNT  I
           ROW PCT I$0-$1499 $15000-     ROW
                 I9                      TOTAL
                 I    1  I.    2  I
SEX        --------I---------I---------I
             1  I    74  I   151  I    225
   MALE         I  32.9  I  67.1  I   43.2
                -I---------I---------I
             2  I   153  I   143  I    296
   FEMALE       I  51.7  I  48.3  I   56.8
                -I---------I---------I
           COLUMN    227      294      521
           TOTAL    43.6     56.4    100.0
CORRECTED CHI SQUARE =    17.62000 WITH 1 DEGREE OF FREEDOM.  SIGNIFICANCE =  0.
0000
     RAW CHI SQUARE =     18.37672 WITH 1 DEGREE OF FREEDOM.  SIGNIFICANCE =  0.
0000
PHI =    0.18781
NUMBER OF MISSING OBSERVATIONS =     46
```

Figure VI.1.E: **CROSS-TABULATION OF SEX AND FAMILY INCOME**

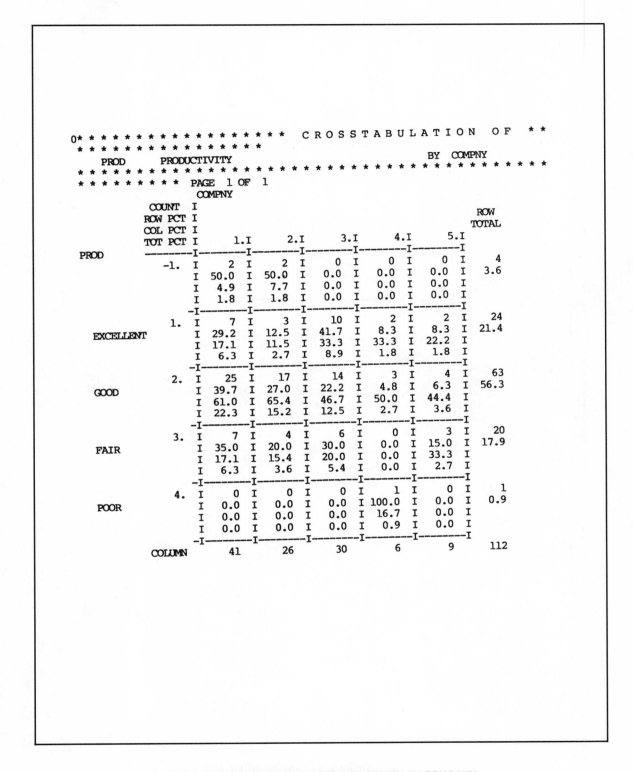

Figure VI.1.F: CROSS-TABULATION OF PRODUCTIVITY BY COMPANY

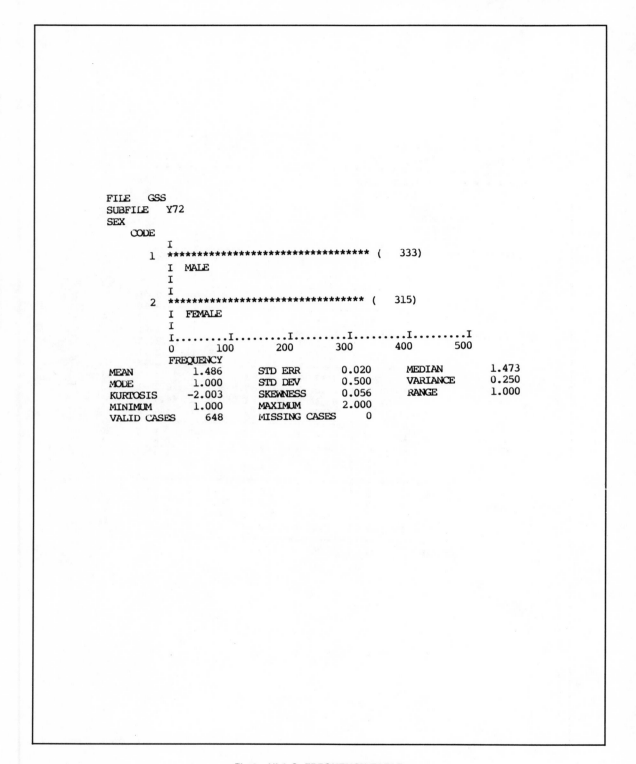

```
FILE    GSS
SUBFILE  Y72
SEX
   CODE
        I
     1  ******************************** (    333)
        I  MALE
        I
        I
     2  ******************************* (    315)
        I  FEMALE
        I
        I........I........I........I........I........I
        0      100      200      300      400      500
        FREQUENCY
MEAN          1.486    STD ERR      0.020    MEDIAN     1.473
MODE          1.000    STD DEV      0.500    VARIANCE   0.250
KURTOSIS     -2.003    SKEWNESS     0.056    RANGE      1.000
MINIMUM       1.000    MAXIMUM      2.000
VALID CASES    648     MISSING CASES    0
```

Figure VI.1.G: FREQUENCY TABLE

```
                                    STATISTICAL ANALYSIS SYSTEM                     22:37 FRIDAY, NOVEMBER 9, 1979    1
                                  GENERAL LINEAR MODELS PROCEDURE

DEPENDENT VARIABLE: Y
GENERAL FORM OF ESTIMABLE FUNCTIONS
EFFECT        COEFFICIENTS
INTERCEPT     L1
X1            L2
X2            L3


                                    STATISTICAL ANALYSIS SYSTEM                     22:37 FRIDAY, NOVEMBER 9, 1973    2
                                  GENERAL LINEAR MODELS PROCEDURE

DEPENDENT VARIABLE: Y
TYPE I ESTIMABLE FUNCTIONS FOR: X1
EFFECT        COEFFICIENTS
INTERCEPT     0
X1            L2
X2            1.0519*L2


                                    STATISTICAL ANALYSIS SYSTEM                     22:37 FRIDAY, NOVEMBER 9, 1979    3
                                  GENERAL LINEAR MODELS PROCEDURE

DEPENDENT VARIABLE: Y
TYPE 1 ESTIMABLE FUNCTIONS FOR: X2
EFFECT        COEFFICIENTS
INTERCEPT     0
X1            0
X2            L3


                                    STATISTICAL ANALYSIS SYSTEM                     22:37 FRIDAY, NOVEMBER 9, 1979    4
                                  GENERAL LINEAR MODELS PROCEDURE

DEPENDENT VARIABLE: Y
TYPE II ESTIMABLE FUNCTIONS FOR: X1
EFFECT        COEFFICIENTS
INTERCEPT     0
X1            L2
```

Figure VI.1.H: STATISTICAL ANALYSIS SYSTEM: GENERAL LINEAR MODULES PROCEDURE

```
                                    STATISTICAL ANALYSIS SYSTEM                    22:37 FRIDAY, NOVEMBER 9, 1979    5
                                 GENERAL LINEAR MODELS PROCEDURE

DEPENDENT VARIABLE: Y
TYPE II ESTIMABLE FUNCTIONS FOR: X2
EFFECT       COEFFICIENTS
INTERCEPT    0
X1           0
X2           L3


                                    STATISTICAL ANALYSIS SYSTEM                    22:37 FRIDAY, NOVEMBER 9, 1979    6
                                 GENERAL LINEAR MODELS PROCEDURE

DEPENDENT VARIABLE: Y
TYPE III ESTIMABLE FUNCTIONS FOR: X1
EFFECT       COEFFICIENTS
INTERCEPT    0
X1           L2
X2           0


                                    STATISTICAL ANALYSIS SYSTEM                    22:37 FRIDAY, NOVEMBER 9, 1979    7
                                 GENERAL LINEAR MODELS PROCEDURE

DEPENDENT VARIABLE: Y
TYPE III ESTIMABLE FUNCTIONS FOR: X2
EFFECT       COEFFICIENTS
INTERCEPT    0
X1           0
X2           L3


                                    STATISTICAL ANALYSIS SYSTEM                    22:37 FRIDAY, NOVEMBER 9, 1979    8
                                 GENERAL LINEAR MODELS PROCEDURE

DEPENDENT VARIABLE: Y
TYPE IV ESTIMABLE FUNCTIONS FOR: X1
EFFECT       COEFFICIENTS
INTERCEPT    0
X1           L2
X2           0
```

Figure VI.1.H (continued)

378

Other Applications

Nevertheless, statistical analysis does not represent the total potential of computer applications. Section I.1 mentioned computer data bases. As more information from secondary sources is put on tapes, previously published data will become an even more valuable resource for the market researcher as information searches are done faster and more economically.

Another data base system, particularly beneficial to the small concern seeking export markets, is the Worldwide Information and Trade System (WITS). Available through the Industry and Trade Administration of the U.S. Department of Commerce, WITS provides on-line information on your own terminal,* or hard copy reports through one of the U.S. Commerce Department's district offices if you do not have a computer terminal, on such things as these:

◎ An up-to-date file of information of U.S. companies who have filled out Commerce forms indicating interest in exporting and a list of goods and services available.

◎ Specific "hot" trade leads from buyers and agents or distributors in foreign countries.

◎ Selected foreign market information, and listings of promotional opportunities abroad.

Some typical questions that WITS can help answer:

◎ Where are the best markets abroad for my product?

◎ What are the import demand and business outlook in those markets?

◎ Who specifically may want, or can buy or distribute, many products?

◎ What is known about these potential customers?

◎ What upcoming promotional events can I show my product in?

◎ Who can give me more information or assistance on marketing my product abroad?

Considering the low cost of this service, management of small and medium-sized businesses should not overlook it as a source of marketing information.

On a different and more expensive level are on-line services offered by various private organizations to present and potential international traders. For instance, Business International Corporation provides immediate computer access to a wide selection of demographic, economic, and labor data on 70 countries, including trend projections, imports and exports, exchange and interest rates. Access to this data base is available through an arrangement with an international time-sharing network.

---

*On-line means that data are available through your own terminal or a portable one via telephone hook-up.

At the domestic level, an on-line service offered by Selling Areas-Marketing, Inc. (refer to Section I.8) is SOLO, SAMI on-line operations, "to analyze marketing data instantly for decision-making in the consumer packaged goods industry." The system is fully integrated, which means that SOLO can make different data bases compatible. And it is *interactive*, which means that questions and answers are completed in abbreviated English. Illustration (A) in Figure VI.1.I demonstrates an inquiry-answer routine. The computer's answers are preceded by the symbol >.

SOLO analysis, derived from SAMI data, rapidly locates and processes data such as the impact of pricing policies, promotion, coupon redemption, media, distribution and household penetration in one or several markets.

One convenient feature is the Interactive Language Program (ILP), which stores a program containing a series of SOLO commands. Once you have created an ILP, like the one in illustration (B) of Figure VI.1.I, instead of repeating the steps each time the same type of analytical information is derived, a coded command of a few characters will cause the ILP to execute the whole program of SOLO commands.

Additionally, SOLO provides a complete package of statistical routines: moving averages, correlation and regression analysis, lead/lag, exponential smoothing, curve fitting, etc. As explained in this book, such routines apply to sales analysis, price elasticity studies, project planning and control, simulation/risk analysis, budgeting, brand planning and forecasting.

Looking Ahead

All the marketing research techniques in this book are forward looking. All aim to develop information that may lead to some clues about tomorrow's secrets. The Delphi technique (Section II.5) opinion-gathering process can be expedited with the use of on-line terminals to a computer. Experts can communicate directly and rapidly via the computer as a form of cybernetic arbitration.

Later in this section regression and time series analysis provide the basics on trend lines for sales forecasting or any other projections that can be derived from historical data and relationships.

Although simple applications of these techniques can be done with a hand calculator, as the number of variables and complexity of data output grow, computer usage becomes not only a cheaper but the only really practical approach for multiple regression analysis, linear programming, simulation, Markov processes, conjoint measurement, factor analysis, canonical analysis, discriminant analysis, and other similarly sophisticated techniques employed by market research departments with sufficient qualified personnel, funds and computer time availability.

Even for organizations that have only the smallest computers, canned programs are available at low cost and can furnish a fairly large amount and variety of statistical summary data and information. These refer to the analytical stage in the marketing research process.

(A)

> **RUN MDI**

FOR WHICH SAMPIER (S):   > **FANTASTK**

ERROR: FANTASTK*

FOR WHICH SAMIPER (S)**:   > **145*****

FOR WHICH SAMIMKT (S):   > **ALL**

DO YOU WANT INDEX TO MEASURE BRAND TO
   MARKET? > **YES**

FOR WHICH BRAND (S):   > **FANTASTK**

WHICH UNIT OF MEASURE DO YOU WANT TO USE?
   1)   DOLLARS   2)   PINTS   3)   UNITS   > **2**

   * Computer notes user error. FANTASTK is not a SAMI period.
   ** Computer repeats question.
   *** Answer is now correct.

(B)

ILP COMMAND: > **RUN MDI**

FOR WHICH SAMIPER(S): > **147**

FOR WHICH SAMIMKT(S): > **ALL**

DO YOU WANT INDEX TO MEASURE
BRAND TO
MARKET? > **YES**

FOR WHICH BRAND(S): > **BRAND B**

WHICH UNIT OF MEASURE DO YOU WANT
TO USE?

1) DOLLARS2)PINTS3)UNITS > **2**

BRAND B	
SAMIPER	147
SAMIMKT	MDI
ATLANTA	107
BALT/WASH	100
BIRMINGHAM/MONTGOM	112
BOSTON/PROVIDENCE	92
BUFFALO	64
CHARLOTTE	95
CHICAGO	98
CINCI/DAYTON/COLUM	61
CLEVELAND	52
DALLAS/FT.WORTH	139
DENVER	61
DETROIT	102
HOUSTON	114
INDIANAPOLIS	53

Figure VI.1.I: SOLO ON-LINE COMPUTER SERVICE

For example, here are a few of the programs available even for micro-computers that will perform essential statistical analysis after data are gathered and inputted:

1. Time series analysis (Section VI.4).
2. Seasonal indices, moving averages, trend lines (Section VI.4).
3. Multiple linear regression analysis (Section VI.3).
4. Correlation analysis (Section VI.2).
5. Analysis of variance and F-ratio (Section V.4).
6. Chi-square analysis (Section V.3).
7. T-test; degree of freedom (Section V.3).
8. Confidence intervals; population mean (Section V.2).
9. Standard deviation; variance; range (Section V.1).
10. Frequency distribution (Sections IV.5, IV.1).
11. Skewness (Section IV.1).
12. Mean, and other descriptive statistics (Sections V.1 and IV.1).
13. Random sampling (Section IV.1).
14. Graphics: histogram, trend line, etc.

These are not all of the available programs for small computers. Several high-powered statistical programs are not mentioned. But notice that the above list covers all the techniques presented in the analytical portions of this book, Sections IV, V, and VI.

Some of these mass-produced programs are available for as little as $30; but do not expect a micro-computer and a cheap program to handle thousands of entries and a dozen variables. That costs more money.

Information is not free. More information, more costs. Also, we should add a 15th item to the above list. These are data sources (usually requiring high-powered equipment and personnel): census data, statistical packages, and information on manufacturers classified by SIC, or number of employees, or geographical location, or by product lines, or even by narrow, carefully defined, segments—are all available, for a price, of course, to use during the data-gathering stage of research (Section I).

VI.2: HOW CORRELATION ANALYSIS HELPS YOU PICK WINNING PRODUCTS

Here is a method to forecast product sales over the near term. Correlation and regression analysis can be used to establish sales quotas in various regions, areas, or territories. The techniques explained in this subsection and the next one can help you measure the relative success of your organization.

Correlation analysis has also been applied in stratified sampling problems to learn whether purchases of a particular product are more closely linked to the buyer's age or occupation or to some other critical factor. Also, it has been used with consumers' panels, and with scaling measurements.

Several correlations are undertaken between product rating by various respondents and personality characteristics of the respondent to nail down which factors seem most closely related to those ratings each respondent assigned to the product.

How effective are various advertising messages on product sales? The cause-and-effect relationships may be discoverable through correlation analysis.

Getting It Straight

With these techniques, you can now pinpoint the relationships between two or more variables instead of dealing with only one characteristic at a time. In this subsection you will be introduced to correlation analysis, which is the measurement of the extent of relationships among variables. In the next subsection you will learn the basics of regression analysis, the derivation of such numerical relationships.

Of course, the mere knowledge that relationships exist is not enough to put much money in your pocket, except by chance. (Money is lost by chance, as well.) There may be a relationship between stock market prices and the hemline of women's apparel, but how close is that relationship? The correlation coefficient, or correlation index, indicates whether a good fit exists between the dependent and independent variables.

If the index, or coefficient, is zero, no relationship exists. The higher the absolute value of the index, the better the correlation. Index values range from plus one to minus one.

Positive correlation means that when dress hemlines go up, stock prices go up—both moving in the same direction. Negative correlation means that when dress hemlines go up, stock prices go down—moving in opposite directions.

Two other terms already mentioned are

(a) the dependent variable, the one being estimated, and
(b) the independent variables, the ones used to estimate the value of the dependent variable.

The purchase of dog food (dependent variable) depends on the number of dogs born, net (births minus deaths), each year, and family incomes (the independent variables).

Naturally enough, the quantity and value of processed dog food purchased each year depends on a great many other factors: prices of steaks and roasts (assuming the dog gets the bones); city versus country dogs; status of the animal within the family; family size and composition; type of dog; whether dog eats inside or outside of house; number of family members working; age of family members (possibly age of the dog, too); etc.

It is not possible to know and list all variables, let alone gather any amount of reasonably accurate information on them. By the time we gathered it all, it would be outdated anyway.

The purpose of correlation and regression analysis is to pinpoint the most significant variables, those which are key factors in the buying-decision process. If we can localize a variable that accounts for 70 percent of the buying decision, why squander time and money trying to determine the 500 variables that account for the other 30 percent?

That one inexpensive indicator may be enough to keep us on the trendline as long as we acknowledge and accept the risks that attend a simple analysis and recognize that other factors are lurking nearby.

Overuse of the single indicator approach often makes the philosopher's stone seem more like the Blarney stone. Inevitably the moon's nocturnal glow will be correlated with a multitude of sins and profits: murders, alcoholism, ocean tides, planting times, high and low energy periods, sales of automobiles, and prices of corn—to cite a few examples among a list that would fill pages.

Commodity speculators too are sometimes moonstruck; and one found a close correlation between purchase and sell times of corn futures and moon phases.* If you are aware that this is not a cause and effect relationship, any two variables may be paired. If it works, why not use it? Just remember that nothing, except God, is forever, and relationships change at the most inconvenient and unprofitable times.

Quite often correlation techniques are employed in sampling and cross-tabulation procedures, discussed in Section IV, and in the analytical process, such as analysis of variance, presented in Section V.

With these methods we can test the validity of assumptions of independence between two variables (or between two time periods) as in simple correlation, or

---

*This example and others are cited in Robert Vichas. *Getting Rich in Commodities, Currencies, or Coins*. New Rochelle, N.Y.: Arlington House Publishers, 1975.

between more than two variables as in multiple correlation. Relationships between variables may be linear (a straight line), or they may be curvilinear (a curve, one in which the slope of the line (or curve) is not constant).

Simple Linear Correlation

Correlation analysis assumes that both dependent and independent variables are random variables. But regression analysis presumes fixed values for the independent variables, i.e., those variables chosen to predict future events such as dog food sales, or other business activities.

The correlation index, r, registers the relationship between two measures, x and y. Its formula is:

$$r_{xy} = \frac{\Sigma[(Y_i - \bar{Y})(X_i - \bar{X})]}{\sqrt{[\Sigma(Y_i - \bar{Y})^2][\Sigma(X_i - \bar{X})^2]}}$$

r_{xy} = correlation index, or correlation coefficient, for x and y.
Σ = sum of.
i   = designation for each observation in the sample.
Y   = dependent variable.
X   = independent variable.
$\bar{Y}$ and $\bar{X}$ = means, for each set of data.

Let's work our way through a rather simple example to understand how to set up a problem using correlation analysis and then how to interpret the meaning of the *r* coefficient. All data appear in Figure VI.2.A.

The issue is this: a cosmetic manufacturer wants to learn whether individual incomes of single women are good predictors of the amount this group of consumers will spend on cosmetics each month. Two samples are taken: Johnstown and Georgetown. Each sample is small (for illustrative purposes), consisting of seven women in each.

The size of the sample brings out an important point. At least three conditions must be met for correlation and regression analysis to be appropriate:

1. The sample size and number of valid observations (or respondents) must exceed the number of variables.
2. The variables are continuous (rather than discrete values).
3. More than one variable is measured for each respondent or observation.

In our example we have seven respondents in each sample (enough to qualify). The data are continuous. Each respondent is queried on monthly cosmetic expenditures and average monthly income over recent months.

Notice that in each sample, the mean income for each group is an identical $990 monthly. Mean expenditures for cosmetics of the Johnstown group are $47 monthly and for the Georgetown gang, $52 monthly, hardly a significant difference.

The $\bar{Y}$ and $\bar{X}$ symbols represent the averages of two sets of data. The fourth columns in the table record the difference between monthly purchases of cos-

MONTHLY COSMETIC PURCHASES AND INCOMES OF SINGLE WOMEN

Person	Monthly Cosmetic Purchases (Y)	Recent Monthly Income (X)	$(Y_i - \bar{Y})$	$(Y_i - \bar{Y})^2$	$(X_i - \bar{X})$	$(X_i - \bar{X})^2$	$(Y_i - \bar{Y})(X_i - \bar{X})$
		JOHNSTOWN					
i = 1	$Y_1 = \$25$	$X_1 = \$800$	−22	484	−190	36,100	4180
i = 2	$Y_2 = 37$	$X_2 = 650$	−10	100	−340	115,600	3400
i = 3	$Y_3 = 95$	$X_3 = 1200$	48	2304	210	44,100	10,080
i = 4	$Y_4 = 70$	$X_4 = 780$	23	529	−210	44,100	−4830
i = 5	$Y_5 = 45$	$X_5 = 1500$	−2	4	510	260,100	−1020
i = 6	$Y_6 = 45$	$X_6 = 1100$	−2	4	110	12,100	−220
i = 7	$Y_7 = 12$	$X_7 = 900$	−35	1225	−90	8,100	3150
Averages:	$\bar{Y} = \$47$	$\bar{X} = \$990$		4650		520,200	14,740
				$\Sigma(Y_i - \bar{Y})^2$		$\Sigma(X_i - \bar{X})^2$	$\Sigma[(Y_i - \bar{Y})(X_i - \bar{X})]$

$r_{xy} = 0.30$

Person	Monthly Cosmetic Purchases (Y)	Recent Monthly Income (X)	$(Y_i - \bar{Y})$	$(Y_i - \bar{Y})^2$	$(X_i - \bar{X})$	$(X_i - \bar{X})^2$	$(Y_i - \bar{Y})(X_i - \bar{X})$
		GEORGETOWN					
i = 1	$Y_1 = \$15$	$X_1 = \$1050$	−37	1369	60	3,600	−2220
i = 2	$Y_2 = 70$	$X_2 = 900$	18	324	−90	8,100	−1620
i = 3	$Y_3 = 14$	$X_3 = 630$	−38	1444	−360	129,600	13,680
i = 4	$Y_4 = 10$	$X_4 = 850$	−42	1764	−140	19,600	5,880
i = 5	$Y_5 = 90$	$X_5 = 1400$	38	1444	410	168,100	15,580
i = 6	$Y_6 = 80$	$X_6 = 1000$	28	784	10	100	280
i = 7	$Y_7 = 85$	$X_7 = 1100$	33	1089	110	12,100	3,630
Averages:	$\bar{Y} = \$52$	$\bar{X} = \$990$		8218		341,200	35,210
				$\Sigma(Y_i - \bar{Y})^2$		$\Sigma(X_i - \bar{X})^2$	$\Sigma[(Y_i - \bar{Y})(X_i - \bar{X})]$

$r_{xy} = 0.66$

Figure VI.2.A: MONTHLY COSMETIC PURCHASES AND INCOMES OF SINGLE WOMEN

metics for each single woman in the sample and the mean for her group. The sixth columns show the results of the same computation but for individual monthly salaries. These values are multiplied. The product, by individual, shows up in the last column to the right.

The products are summed and substitute in the numerator of the formula. Hence, the numerator is the sum of the products of the deviations of the Y-variable and the X-variable, for each sample, from the mean values of Y and X.

The fifth columns in the tables of Figure VI.2.A contain the sum of the squared deviations from the mean of cosmetic purchases for each group: $\Sigma (Y_i - \overline{Y})^2 = 4650_j$ and 8218_g.

The seventh columns display the sum of the squared deviations from the mean for personal gross income: $520,200_j$ and $341,200_g$.

The square root of the sums of these two columns comprises the denominator of the formula used to calculate the correlation coefficient. The denominator takes into account the range of variability in the measures.

Substituting values into the formula, we have:

$$r_j = \frac{14,740}{\sqrt{4650} \cdot \sqrt{520,200}} = \frac{14,740}{(68.19)(721.25)} = 0.30$$

$$r_g = \frac{35,210}{\sqrt{8218} \cdot \sqrt{341,200}} = \frac{35,210}{(90.65)(584.12)} = 0.66$$

To evaluate the *r* coefficient, remember that the closer to zero, the less likely the variables are to be related. At zero they are no kin at all. (Reference here is to the absolute values; i.e., the value of the coefficient without regard to its sign, whether negative or positive.)

Typically, the coefficients will be some decimal other than zero and will range between the limits $+1$ and -1. Should you ever come up with a $+1$ (not likely), this denotes a perfect linear relationship between two sets of measures. If you represent this relationship in graph form, the line will be upward sloping, from southwest to northeast in the graph. Each time one variable increases, the other will also rise by the same proportion.

A coefficient of -1 also denotes a perfect linear relationship; but in a graph this line slopes downward from left to right. This means that as one measure rises, the other falls in direct proportion.

Now that you understand the significance of the extreme values, you will have less difficulty interpreting the intermediate values of the coefficient, those which you will most frequently encounter.

In our cosmetic purchases examples, both measures are positively correlated. Both indicate a tendency for cosmetic purchases to rise as incomes rise, although the Georgetown coefficient is a little more than twice that of the Johnstown group. This suggests that other factors must be at work. However, we need to know how high is high, or how low is low.

Some Guidelines

Although no answer is absolute, these key guidelines will prove helpful:

- To state that a strong, or high, relationship exists between variables implies a correlation coefficient of at least 0.80.
- A fairly good relationship exists if the absolute value of the coefficient ranges between 0.60 and 0.80.
- A range of values between 0.40 and 0.60 suggests only a moderately significant link between measures.
- For values below 0.40, we are on fairly shaky ground for making any strong assertions about the data.

There may be a weak link between these low values, but the relationship is fragile. Personally, I would not bet my money on any decision based on low coefficients.

The Georgetown group, $r_{xy} = 0.66$, is at the lower end of the acceptable range. We judge that links between measures are in the moderately strong to good range.

But the coefficient for the Johnstown group, $r_{xy} = 0.30$, suggests we ought to examine other factors. For one thing, the samples are too small. For another, single women do not form a homogeneous group. Social environments in Johnstown and Georgetown are distinct. Nevertheless, we know more about our target market than before.

R-Values

Now let's take the analysis another step toward certainty. These samples are small. They may not truly represent the local markets for cosmetics in either urban area. Therefore, any predictions about trends or relationships are rather chancy. Despite this *caveat*, there is something more we can do to remove some of the "iffiness" contained in a correlation coefficient of 0.66—one that is neither high nor low. Reference will be made to the table of r-values in Appendix F.

Here is the five-step procedure for verifying the validity of the correlation coefficient.

STEP I: Decide on the degree of certainty.

STEP II: Find the r-value, in a table of r-test coefficients, that corresponds to the sample size and desired degree of certainty.

STEP III: Evaluate the correlation coefficient. If r_{xy} < r-test value, then the correlation coefficient is not valid; proceed to Step IV. If r_{xy} > r-test value, then the coefficient is valid at the confidence level; omit Step IV and go to Step V.

STEP IV: If r_{xy} is less than the r-test value, at the degree of certainty se-
               lected in Step I, then move left or right across the rows of the
               table until you find an r-value close to the coefficient of the
               sample. Then, at the top of the table, read the degree of certain-
               ty indicated in the heading.

STEP V: Decide whether to accept the results and advance with the proj-
               ect or return for more research and testing.

For the Georgetown group, $r_{xy} = 0.66$, in the r-value in Appendix F, find 7,
the number of observations in the sample, and move your finger to the right
across the table.

The r-value corresponding to the correlation coefficient is at the 90 percent
level of confidence. That means there is 1 chance out of 10 that the relationship
is not valid, and a 90 percent chance that it is valid.

If your cutoff point is a 95 percent degree of certainty, the r-value of 0.755,
which corresponds to the 95 percent level, exceeds the value of the correlation
coefficient, 0.66; and the relationship is rejected. Back to testing.

If you want to know how to derive values in the r-test table in Appendix F,
you can develop your own from a t-distribution table (Appendix C) and the following formula:

$$\text{r-value} = \sqrt{\frac{t^2}{(t^2 + \text{d.f.})}}$$

t   = t-value for each degree of freedom from a t-distribution table.
d.f. = degrees of freedom.

This formula may come in handy if an r-test table for the values you want is
not readily available for comparison.

For example, for the t-value of a two-tailed distribution, with 5 degrees of
freedom, $t = 2.015$. Plugging in values, we have:

$$\text{r-value} = \sqrt{\frac{(2.015)^2}{(2.015^2 + 5)}} = \sqrt{\frac{4.060}{9.060}}$$

$$= \sqrt{0.448} = 0.669$$

Summing Up

Each step in the analytical process was demonstrated here—obviously a la-
borious task for large samples if done by hand. Actually, for situations where
you are linking only two variables and the number of observations is not too
large, the cheapest and most efficient tool for data analysis is the professional
hand calculator, preferably a programmable type.

Even at the low end of the price range ($50 – $100), these calculators are equipped to provide the correlation coefficient, slope, intercept, mean, standard deviation, and variance, and similar, easy-to-use functions for simple correlation and regression computations discussed here and in the next subsection.

But for more variables than two, and large amounts of data input, a computer is more practical and time saving. Since programs for correlation and regression analysis are readily and cheaply available, not much technological sophistication—but just a little patience and practice—is needed to solve many of your marketing problems. In fact, for your firm's requirements, nearly all of the applications described in this book can be done on the less expensive micro- or mini-computers.

VI.3: EIGHT STEPS TO PREDICTING TOMORROW'S SALES WITH REGRESSION ANALYSIS

How can you profitably apply linear regression analysis to your business?

Use linear regression to predict future sales from various advertising budgets. Or predict sales from personal incomes, population changes, or some other global observation available from sources listed in Section I.1. Or develop a trend line to project prices of your raw materials, securities, or costs of government regulations.

Use the technique to project future demand for your product or service, or as a basis for predicting real estate values five years hence. You can even apply the technique to an analysis of the efficiency of your competitors' operations before you finalize a marketing strategy.

Use it to determine the best height to display merchandise in your display center, trade show, or store. Or develop brand loyalty scores for durable goods with such predictors as satisfaction with, and age of, originally purchased equipment, optimism (or pessimism) regarding future business conditions, type of business or industry, sales level of purchasers, etc.

Use it to determine the impact of the message on direct mail response. Or further analyze data developed through the application of one of the research methods already explained in this book.

Scatter Diagram

Just what is linear regression? It is important to understand what it is, and does, in order not to be misled into believing it provides the ultimate answer to sales, profits, and endless acquisitions. Perhaps an easy technique for understanding what it is, and what it can do for you, is to return to the preceding subsection (on correlation analysis) and build on what we know.

In correlation analysis, we want to discover the degree of relationship between two variables and to summarize all the relationships of the sample compressed into a single index, the correlation coefficient. Such relationships are difficult to define through simply staring at data in the tables in Figure VI.2.A.

Another way to present the data is to construct a picture, a graphic presentation known as a scatter diagram. The Johnstown data appear in Figure VI.3.A, the Georgetown data in Figure VI.3.B, in the form of a scatter diagram.

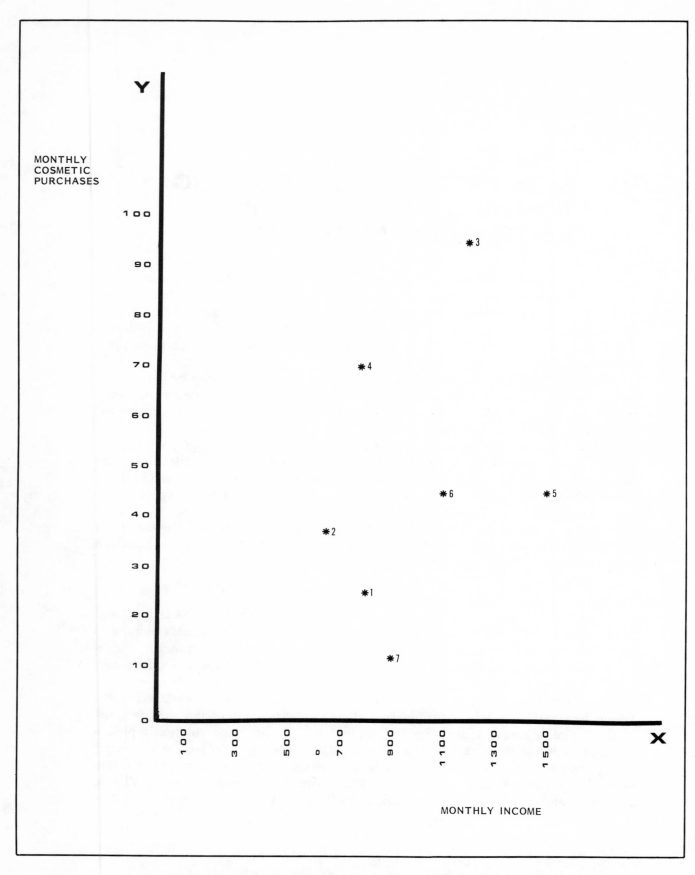

Figure VI.3.A: SCATTER DIAGRAM FOR JOHNSTOWN DATA ON COSMETIC PURCHASES AND
MONTHLY INCOMES

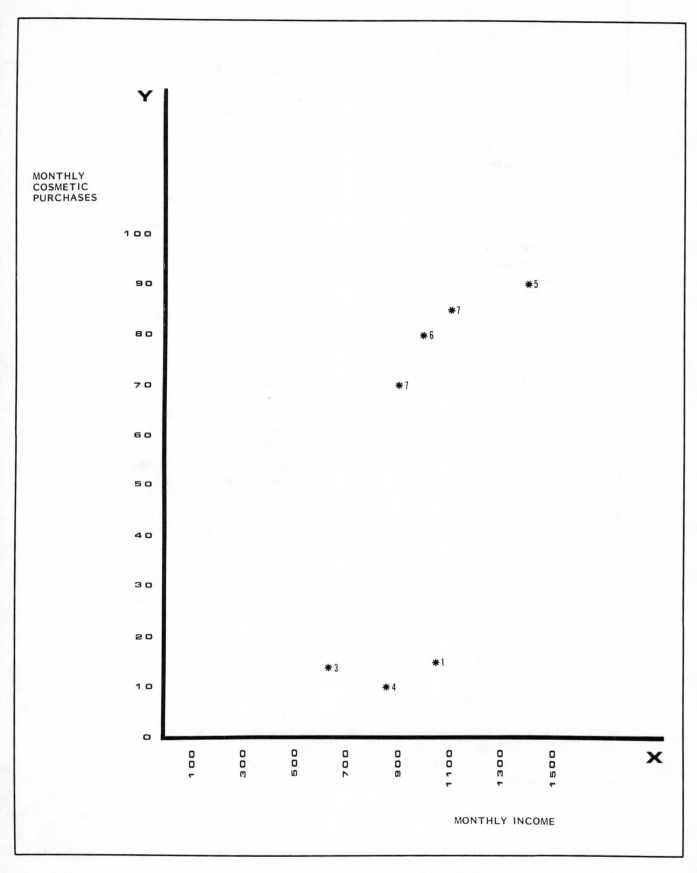

Figure VI.3.B: SCATTER DIAGRAM FOR GEORGETOWN DATA ON COSMETIC PURCHASES AND
MONTHLY INCOME

What do the scatter diagrams show us? That the data are scattered. The results are widely dispersed. Therefore, relationships may not be immediately apparent. Such is not always the case. The scatter diagram tends to highlight whatever relationships exist or do not exist.

To construct a scatter diagram, record values for the dependent variable up the vertical axis, starting from the origin of the graph (point 0), the Y axis (Y = monthly cosmetic purchases).

Record independent variable values along the horizontal axis (X = monthly personal incomes). Each dot or point in the graph is a visual, summary statement of the monthly income and corresponding monthly purchases for each respondent of the sample.

Figure VI.3.C demonstrates how a computer can be programmed to process data on dependent and independent variables and then plot the correlation results in a scatter diagram. In this printout example there are 20 observations and two sets of data correlated.

Correlation between independent and dependent variables refer to the columns of data headed "IND 1" and "DEP," and "IND 2" correlated with "DEP." The two scatter diagrams correspond to these two sets of data, respectively.

Each scatter diagram should embrace 20 reference points. The bottom one does. The top one does not, because several points of correlation coincide. Points of coincidence are indicated by the numbers in the upper diagram.

For reference, notice that the correlation coefficient (already explained) has been calculated by the computer; in addition, the regression equation and r-squared values (explained next in this subsection), and an analysis of variance (V.4), also appear on the printout. These data, of course, do not refer to the examples being developed within the textual material, but are exhibited to illustrate computer usage in solving the same types of problem we are working through by the longhand method.

If the dots fall into a fairly consistent pattern, you can fairly easily guess where the center values should lie. If the pattern is tightly clustered, then lay a straightedge along where you think the line (that is, the average values) should fall and draw it in (with pencil). The eyeball, or graphic, method may yield quite adequate evidence.

Next, pick a point along the line you have just drawn and read values off the horizontal and vertical axes. From this line, you can predict what cosmetic sales are likely to be at each income figure.

If incomes are good predictors, and *if* original data are fairly representative of the entire market, and *if* you have taken reasonable care in drawing the line, presumably you can develop data through cluster analysis in, say, the San Francisco Bay area, and predict what cosmetic sales should be in each neighborhood. You can check on your salespeople with this same approach.

While you are doing that, however, do not forget all the "if's" the analysis begins with. Take it easy on promotions and firings until you have developed a solid case with at least a 95 percent degree of certainty. Other factors present may create statistical noise in the data.

```
-- SET C1
COLUMN          C1
COUNT           20
             1.              2.              3.              4.    .    .    .

-- SET C2
COLUMN          C2
COUNT           20
        2.71800         1.48800         0.45900         0.31400   .    .    .

-- SET C3
COLUMN          C3
COUNT           20
        1.40800         0.47400         0.29100         0.12500   .    .    .

-- SET C4
COLUMN          C4
COUNT           20
        1.71800         0.94300         0.16900         0.18800   .    .    .

-- NAME C1='IDNO',C2='IND1',C3='IND2',C4='DEP'

-- PRIN C1,C2,C3,C4
COLUMN       IDNO            IND1            IND2             DEP
COUNT          20              20              20              20
ROW
  1           1.          2.71800         1.40800         1.71800
  2           2.          1.48800         0.47400         0.94300
  3           3.          0.45900         0.29100         0.16900
  4           4.          0.31400         0.12500         0.18800
  5           5.          0.80800         0.96200         0.70200
  6           6.          0.44900         0.23400         0.35100
  7           7.          0.59500         0.65400         0.47100
  8           8.          0.28500         0.50000         0.27500
  9           9.          0.58800         0.21600         0.53500
 10          10.          0.62900         0.49600         0.46500
 11          11.          0.56300         0.20500         0.45900
 12          12.          0.43500         0.39200         0.37200
 13          13.          0.61500         0.17700         0.50900
 14          14.          0.56300         0.30800         0.45800
 15          15.          0.93600         0.49000         0.78900
 16          16.          0.51500         1.01000         0.46500
 17          17.          0.39000         0.54900         0.36800
 18          18.          0.47600         0.39700         0.46000
 19          19.          0.29600         0.21700         0.24300
 20          20.          0.53000         1.19600         0.48600
```

Figure VI.3.C: THREE EXAMPLES OF COMPUTER PRINTOUT SCATTER DIAGRAMS

```
-- REGR C4 2 C2 C3 C5 C6

THE REGRESSION EQUATION IS
Y =  0.0893 + 0.568 X1 +0.0895 X2


                                        ST. DEV.     T-RATIO =
          COLUMN      COEFFICIENT       OF COEF.     COEF/S.D.
          --           0.08930          0.03078         2.90
X1        IND1         0.5676           0.0382         14.87
X2        IND2         0.0895           0.0580          1.54

THE ST. DEV. OF Y ABOUT REGRESSION LINE IS
S =     0.07440
WITH ( 20- 3) =  17 DEGREES OF FREEDOM

R-SQUARED = 95.7 PERCENT
R-SQUARED = 95.2 PERCENT, ADJUSTED FOR D.F.

ANALYSIS OF VARIANCE

 DUE TO       DF          SS        MS=SS/DF
 REGRESSION    2      2.080977     1.040488
 RESIDUAL     17      0.094096     0.005535
 TOTAL        19      2.175072

FURTHER ANALYSIS OF VARIANCE
SS EXPLAINED BY EACH VARIABLE WHEN ENTERED IN THE ORDER GIVEN

 DUE TO       DF          SS
 REGRESSION    2      2.080977
 IND1          1      2.067820
 IND2          1      0.013157

          X1                 Y      PRED. Y    ST.DEV.
ROW       IND1             DEP      VALUE      PRED. Y     RESIDUAL    ST.RES.
 1        2.72           1.7180     1.7579     0.0659      -0.0399      -1.15 X
 2        1.49           0.9430     0.9762     0.0362      -0.0332      -0.51
 3        0.46           0.1690     0.3758     0.0198      -0.2068      -2.86R
 4        0.31           0.1880     0.2787     0.0249      -0.0907      -1.29
 5        0.81           0.7020     0.6340     0.0288       0.0680       0.99
 6        0.45           0.3810     0.3651     0.0213       0.0159       0.22
 7        0.59           0.4710     0.4855     0.0196      -0.0145      -0.20
 8        0.28           0.2750     0.2958     0.0222      -0.0208      -0.29
 9        0.59           0.5350     0.4423     0.0228       0.0927       1.31
10        0.63           0.4650     0.4907     0.0167      -0.0257      -0.35
11        0.56           0.4590     0.4272     0.0229       0.0318       0.45
12        0.43           0.3720     0.3713     0.0184       0.0007       0.01
13        0.61           0.5090     0.4542     0.0247       0.0548       0.78
14        0.56           0.4580     0.4364     0.0195       0.0216       0.30
15        0.94           0.7890     0.6644     0.0197       0.1246       1.74
16        0.51           0.4650     0.4720     0.0368      -0.0070      -0.11
17        0.39           0.3680     0.3598     0.0208       0.0082       0.12
18        0.48           0.4600     0.3950     0.0180       0.0650       0.90
19        0.30           0.2430     0.2767     0.0223      -0.0337      -0.48
20        0.53           0.4860     0.4971     0.0462      -0.0111      -0.19 X

R DENOTES AN OBS. WITH A LARGE ST. RES.
X DENOTES AN OBS. WHOSE X VALUE GIVES IT LARGE INFLUENCE.


(X-PRIME X)INVERSE

                  0              1            2
   0       0.171193
   1      -0.060360       0.263221
   2      -0.155308      -0.231656     0.608556
```

Figure VI.3.C (continued)

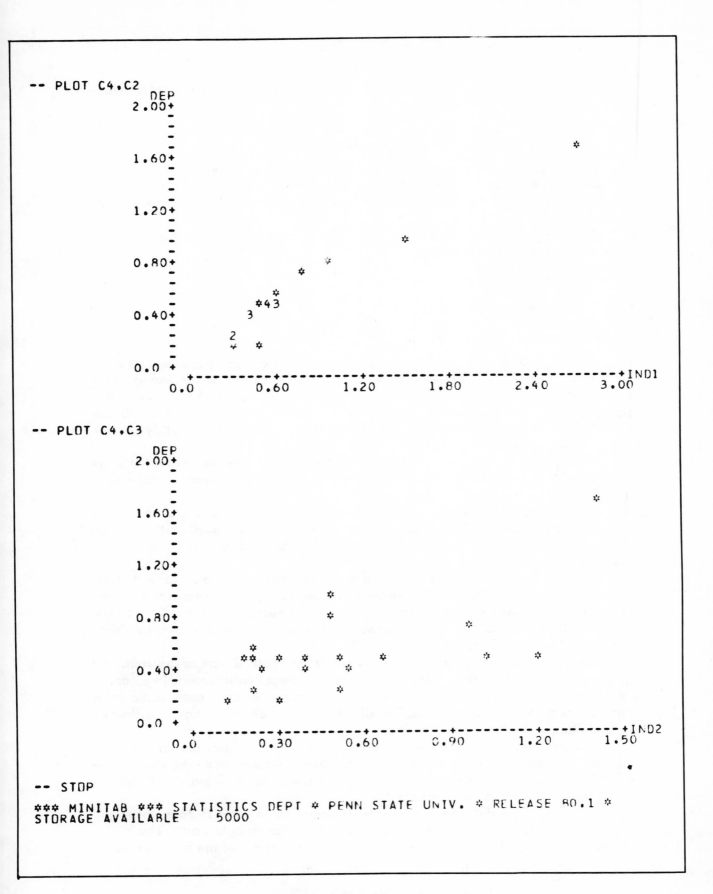

Figure VI.3.C (continued)

A Linear Equation

If you are satisfied with an eyeball technique, even when data are dispersed, as they are in Figures VI.3.A and VI.3.B, here is a shortcut approach that may provide exactly the kind and level of information needed for those key decisions.

A linear regression can be defined with the general equation for a straight line, which is what linear means.

$$Y = a + bX$$

Y = dependent variable.
a = vertical intercept.
b = slope of the line.
X = independent variable.

The **Y** and **X** values are represented along a vertical and horizontal axis, respectively. If you have drawn a line correctly, and extend it far enough in a southwesterly direction, it will eventually cross the vertical axis. The value at that point of interception is the "a" part of the formula. For instance, if a = 30, the line drawn will pass through the vertical axis at the point where monthly cosmetic purchases equal $30.

But suppose the line does not intercept the vertical axis but crosses at some point on the horizontal axis? No problem—as a well-known product manufacturer tells it.

The graphs we normally work with represent only one-fourth of the entire plane. Draw a cross: $\frac{NW \mid NE}{SW \mid SE}$. The graph we are using is the northeast quadrant. Along both vertical and horizontal axes of the northeast quadrant all values are expressed as positive ones.

Now draw a line that descends through the horizontal axis. Extend it far enough, crossing a portion of the southeast plane, and it will eventually intercept the vertical axis. At the point of interception of the vertical axis, the **X**-value (incomes) will be zero, and **Y** = a, because in the above formula the term bX drops out when **X** equals "0" (b(0) = 0).

Below the horizontal axis, all values along the vertical axis in the southeast quadrant are negative ones. Hence, do not let a negative intercept (−a) cause any anxiety—at least not mathematically—although it surely upsets some sales projections for low-income levels. Usually the a-value has no policy significance in marketing.

Now for the "b." As long as you know any two points, they can be connected with a straight line, in complete confidence. Suppose you know only one point, the value of the intercept (a)? That, and the slope, will get you a straight line. Slope is the tilt, or slant, of the line.

The slope of a flat line, like the horizontal axis, is zero. It does not slope. For the vertical axis, there is no value, since it heads straight north. Think of a hill on a highway. A 12 percent grade expresses the slope of the highway. A 12 percent grade means that for every 100 feet you travel forward (horizontally), you are also traveling 12 feet upward (vertically).

Therefore, slope is the change in the vertical distance divided by the change in the horizontal distance. For a straight line, a slope is always constant. Consequently, you can predict the value of X for any value of Y once you have described the point of intercept and slant of the line, i.e., the linear equation.

Suppose that "b" turns out to be negative? Don't worry about it. That means the line is negatively sloped, rather than positively sloped.

A positively sloped line runs from southwest to northeast in the graph. A negatively sloped line runs from northwest to southwest, which is interpreted to mean that higher incomes result in fewer cosmetic purchases.

For a more practical approach, think of the "b" as a coefficient which tells us the effect on Y for each change in X. If the b-coefficient were $+0.05$, then we would say that for every $100 change in income (X), the corresponding change in cosmetic expenditures would be $5 (Y). A b-coefficient of $+2.5$ reports that for every $100 change in X, a $250 change in Y results. But if the b-coefficient were -0.25, every change in X would produce a $25 change in Y in the opposite direction, i.e., downward.

Shortcut. Back to the promised shortcut: After drawing the line in the scatter diagram, locate two Y and X values by reading off the values on the vertical and horizontal coordinates. Pick any point. Try X = $1,000. The corresponding Y value seems fairly close to $49 worth of cosmetics. Our first equation, then:

$$49 = a + b\,(1{,}000) \qquad (1)$$

To solve for "a" and "b," we need a second equation. So try X = $500. That appears to yield about $34 worth of cosmetics. Hence, our second equation:

$$34 = a + b\,(500) \qquad (2)$$

Now the easy part. Subtract equation (2) from equation (1):

$$
\begin{aligned}
49 &= a + 1000b \qquad (1) \\
\text{Minus:} \quad 34 &= a + 500b \qquad (2) \\
\hline
15 &= 0 + 500b
\end{aligned}
$$

And solve for the slope, b:

$$b = 15/500 = 0.03$$

Now substitute the value of the slope back into either equation to determine the intercept, a:

$$49 = a + 0.03\,(1000)$$
$$a = 49 - 30 = 19$$

Voila! And you have your linear equation. The regression of **Y** on **X** is:

$$Y = 19 + 0.03X$$

For any value of X, monthly income, finding Y, predicted cosmetic purchases, presents no problem; and a $100 change in income should produce a $3 change in cosmetic purchases.

But use reason. The equation does not. According to it, a single woman with zero monthly income will still spend $19 a month on cosmetics. Some may. Nevertheless, below some subsistence level, food and rent will probably take priority over cosmetics. At the other end, extending the line out into forever, the equation suggests that a woman earning $10,000 monthly will spend $319 a month on cosmetics. Will she?

Least Squares Method

The answer is, she probably will not. We developed a predictive equation from Figure VI.3.A, the Johnstown data. Did we not already decide, in Section VI.2, that the correlation coefficient was so low that we ought to pin our predictions and decisions on something more reliable? Yes, we did. Well?

Regression analysis is profitable to undertake if the sample studies demonstrate a high correlation index. An r_{xy} of 0.30 for Johnstown does not provide strong evidence of a close or reliable relationship between monthly incomes and cosmetic purchases by single women.

Because the relationship seems somewhat clearer for the Georgetown women, $r_{xy} = 0.66$, at least at the 90 percent confidence level, we are less reluctant to employ regression analysis. The remaining discussion will center on data in the scatter diagram of Figure VI.3.B.

For first glance decisions, the two methods for establishing the linear equation, described above, have the advantages of being fast, simple, and cheap. The disadvantage is inaccuracy, especially when dispersed and when extreme values are present. Hence, the least squares method to pin down those regression coefficients is the mathematical substitute.

If you already have the computer program, run it through, for it provides the faster means of obtaining data analysis and summaries (Figure VI.3.C). The long method below simply tells us what the computer is up to.

Two conditions must be met to arrive at the correct regression coefficients:

1. The sum of the differences between the actual values of the dependent variable (Y), based on the observations in the sample, must equal the expected values of the dependent variable (Y*) based on the regression line. That is, the vertical deviations from the regression line must equal zero.
2. The sum of the squares of the deviations from the regression line must be less than that of any other linear equation.

• *Step I*: The data we will need to determine the equation by the least squares method is tabulated in Figure VI.3.D: Calculate the data for Σ Y, Σ X, X_i^2, Σ X^2, $X_i Y_i$ and Σ XY.

DATA FOR LINEAR REGRESSION COMPUTATIONS BY THE LEAST SQUARES METHOD

Person	Monthly Cosmetic Purchases (Y_i)	Recent Monthly Income (X_i)	X_i^2	X_iY_i	Y_i^2
$i = 1$	$Y_1 = \$15$	$X_1 = \$1050$	1,102,500	15,750	225
$i = 2$	$Y_2 = 70$	$X_2 = 900$	810,000	63,000	4900
$i = 3$	$Y_3 = 14$	$X_3 = 630$	396,900	8,820	196
$i = 4$	$Y_4 = 10$	$X_4 = 850$	722,500	8,500	100
$i = 5$	$Y_5 = 90$	$X_5 = 1400$	1,960,000	126,000	8100
$i = 6$	$Y_6 = 80$	$X_6 = 1000$	1,000,000	80,000	6400
$i = 7$	$Y_7 = 85$	$X_7 = 1100$	1,210,000	93,500	7225
$N = 7$	$\Sigma Y = 364$	$\Sigma X = 6930$	$\Sigma X^2 = 7,201,900$	$\Sigma XY = 395,570$	$\Sigma Y^2 = 27,146$
	$\bar{Y} = \$52$	$\bar{X} = \$990$			

Figure VI.3.D: DATA FOR LINEAR REGRESSION COMPUTATIONS BY THE LEAST SQUARES METHOD

• *Step II*: Substitute values from the table in the following formula to estimate the coefficient, b.

$$b = \frac{n\,(\Sigma X_i\, Y_i) - (\Sigma\, X_i)\,(\Sigma\, Y_i)}{n\,[\Sigma\,(X_i^2)] - (\Sigma\, X_i^2)^2}$$

b = coefficient, or slope, of the regression line.
n = number of observations in the sample.
Σ = sum of.
X_i = independent variables (income) for the ith observation.
Y_i = dependent variable (purchases) for the ith observation.

• *Step III*: Solve for b, the coefficient estimate.

$$b = \frac{7\,(395{,}570) - (6930)\,(364)}{7\,(7{,}201{,}900) - (6930)^2} = 0.1032$$

• *Step IV*: Determine the mean value for **X** and **Y** and substitute them, along with the b-coefficient estimate from Step III, in the following equation to estimate the vertical intercept.

$$a = \overline{Y} - b\overline{X}$$

• *Step V*: Solve the above equation for the a-coefficient estimate.

$$a = 52 - (0.1032)\,(990) = -50.168$$

• *Step VI*: Based on the coefficient estimated from Steps III and V, complete the equation of the regression line.

$$Y^* = -50.168 + 0.103\, X$$

Both **X** and **Y** have the same meaning except that we now employ **Y*** to stand for projected (rather than actual) values, based on a regression line that describes the best fit of the sample data. Values derived are theoretical ones rather than actual ones. Actual data can only originate from specific observations; the regression line expresses a tendency.

• *Step VII*: Fit a line based on this estimated equation to the scatter diagram of the data (Figure VI.3.E). (The actual drawing of the line may be omitted, but the equation identifies the shape of the line and is now available for sales projections.)

Recognize that actual results will deviate from those predicted by the trend line due to

(a) individuality in buying decisions, and
(b) the fact that income is not the only factor that relates to cosmetic purchases, and for individual cases it may not even be an important factor.

Notice that the vertical intercept is negative, -50.168, which means that it crosses the vertical axis below the horizontal axis. The point at which the regression line crosses the horizontal axis is where **Y*** = 0, and **X** will be:

$0 = -50.168 + 0.103\, X$
$X = 50.168/0.103 = \$486.12$

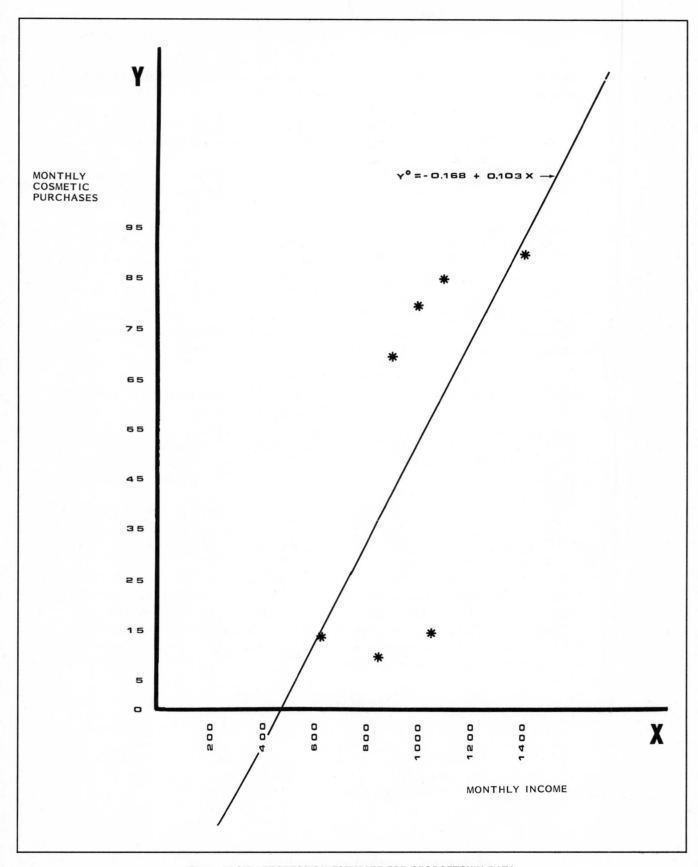

Figure VI.3.E: REGRESSION ESTIMATE FOR GEORGETOWN DATA

And we have already identified the other point through which the regression line passes, viz., $\overline{Y}$ = \$52 and $\overline{X}$ = \$990. Therefore, we can easily locate the line in the scatter diagram.

Recall that the correlation coefficient of 0.66 merely suggests some link-up between income and cosmetic purchases for the Georgetown sample, only at a 90 percent level of certainty.

With the regression equation we have developed a more analytical description of the cosmetic connection, a predictor line that projects purchases above income levels of around \$500 (or \$486, according to the equation) monthly.

If regression analysis can be checked against historical data (prices, national income, population, etc.), and if we can "predict" a result of the past about which you already have data, you may feel more confident about predictions for the immediate future if past predictions check out.

The underlying assumption in linear regression is that the future will be similar to the past. That may not always be true. Changes produce new trends.

• *Step VIII*: Evaluate the regression equation; calculate the coefficient of determination, the variation of the dependent variable about its mean.

Coefficient of Determination

How well does the regression line explain data variance? Like the standard deviation (Section V.1) and the variance (Section V.4) of the mean (Section IV.1), here, too, we need to calculate some measure of dispersion.

Also, as in other symmetrical bivariate distributions, where both variables have normal distributions, about 95 percent of the observations will fall between the regression line and plus or minus two standard deviations of the regression. (Refer to Sections IV.1, V.1, and V.2 for more on this topic.)

Total variance of the regression consists of the explained variance plus unexplained variance. It is equal to $\Sigma(Y - \overline{Y})^2$ divided by the number of observations. The unexplained variance is the measure of the deviations of actual sample observations from the regression line.

In correlation analysis, the coefficient of correlation was the concept used to account for explained and unexplained variance. In regression analysis, the coefficient of determination, the square of the correlation coefficient, is the measure employed to evaluate the closeness of variable relationships.

The coefficient of determination is the explained variance divided by total variance. The coefficient is designated by r^2.

$$r^2 = 1 - \frac{\text{Unexplained variance}}{\text{Total variance}} = 1 - \frac{\sigma_u^2}{\sigma^2}$$

If the explained variance equals total variance, so that no unexplained variance arises, then r^2 = 1.00. The regression line is a moving average, while the $\overline{Y}$ is a stable average. Therefore, if every bit of observed data—every point in the scatter diagram—falls precisely along the regression line, then there is no unexplained variance, and the coefficient equals 1.00.

The mean value itself, $\overline{Y}$, is really a line with zero slope. If the independent variable (income) fails to explain any additional variation in the dependent variable (sales), then $Y^* = \overline{Y}$, the explained variance is zero, and the coefficient of determination will be zero, $r^2 = 0.00$.

We will be concerned with an interpretation of those values between these extremes. Hence, the closer to 1.00, the better the coefficient accounts for explained variation; the closer to 0.00, the greater is the unexplained variation.

In terms of product sums, the formula for the coefficient of determination is:

$$r^2 = \frac{\Sigma(Y_i - \overline{Y})^2 - \Sigma(Y_i - Y^*)^2}{\Sigma(Y_i - \overline{Y})^2}$$

Data for calculating the coefficient of determination are summarized in Figure VI.3.F. Set up in a fashion similar to the tables in Figure VI.2.A, these data summarize the squared deviations of each person's cosmetic purchases from the

	DATA FOR COMPUTATION OF COEFFICIENT OF DETERMINATION						
Person (i)	Actual Monthly Cosmetic Purchases (Y_i)	Actual Monthly Incomes (X_i)	Predicted Cosmetic Purchases (Y^*_i)	Deviation of Actual from Average Purchases $(Y_i - \overline{Y})$	Deviation Squared $(Y_i - \overline{Y})^2$	Residual Variation $(Y_i - Y^*_i)$	Residual Squared $(Y_i - Y^*_i)^2$
1	$15	$1050	$58.19	−37	1369	−43.19	1865.52
2	70	900	42.71	18	324	27.29	744.60
3	14	630	14.85	−38	1444	−0.85	0.72
4	10	850	37.55	−42	1764	−27.55	759.15
5	90	1400	94.31	38	1444	−4.31	18.57
6	80	1000	53.03	28	784	26.97	727.28
7	85	1100	63.35	33	1089	21.65	468.66
TOTALS	364				8218		4584.50

$Y^*_i = -50.168 + 0.103\ X_i$, for each predicted cosmetic purchase.

$\Sigma Y_i = 364$, and $\overline{Y} = \dfrac{\Sigma Y_i}{n} = \dfrac{364}{7} = \$52$, average actual purchases.

$\Sigma(Y_i - \overline{Y})^2 = 8218$, the total variance in the dependent variable.

$\Sigma(Y_i - Y^*)^2 = 4584.50$, the variance not explained by the regression equation.

$r^2 = \dfrac{\Sigma(Y_i - \overline{Y})^2 - \Sigma(Y_i - y^*)^2}{\Sigma(Y_i - \overline{Y})^2} = \dfrac{8218 - 4584.50}{8218} = 0.442$

Figure VI.3.F: DATA FOR COMPUTATION OF COEFFICIENT OF DETERMINATION

sample average, which is the total variance in the dependent variable (purchases). And the table in Figure VI.3.F records the squared deviations of the residual, that portion of the variance not explained by the regression equation.

Of course, in practice, devising such a table is not required. Even with a professional hand calculator, most of these intermediate steps are performed internally within the circuits. But the table makes it easier to see the analytical process.

The coefficient of determination is the correlation coefficient (or index) squared: $r^2 = (r)(r) = (0.66)^2 = 0.44$. (The correlation coefficient was previously computed in Section VI.2.) Compare this answer with the formula for the coefficient of determination:

$$r^2 = \frac{\Sigma(Y_i - \overline{Y})^2 - \Sigma(Y_i - Y^*)^2}{\Sigma(Y_i - \overline{Y})^2} = \frac{8218 - 4584.50}{8218} = 0.442$$

What does it all mean? With an r^2 of 0.44, we can say that 56 percent (1 − 0.44, expressed as a percent) of the total variation in cosmetic purchases is *not* explained by the regression equation. On the positive side, 44 percent of the variation is explained by monthly income levels.

Now what do we do? We tossed out the Johnstown data back in Section VI.2 because of weak correlation between incomes and purchases, but, with some reservations, we have kept the Georgetown data.

Now we discover, after much work and computations, that the regression equation derived by the least squares method explains a mere 44 percent of purchase decisions. I am inclined to follow the less risky course of action, in the absence of other supporting information, and file away the regression equation, too —at least for now.

For marketing purposes, a coefficient of determination of 0.25 to 0.50 has marginal value at the lower end of this range and a risky value at the upper end. *Handle with care.* Don't even consider values approaching zero, say, values below 0.25. Interest in the regression equation begins to develop when the coefficient surpasses 0.50.

Of course, you are not restricted to a single test when evaluating data. Several other tests of significance are explained in Sections V.3 and V.4. If the data are not continuous, or for some reason cannot be applied to correlation/regression techniques, then the cross-tabulation method described in Section IV.6 may offer the best solution to analysis.

Because the regression line is really a kind of moving average, it applies to trend analysis and time series data detailed in the next subsection.

VI.4 THE TIMELESS RICHES IN TIME SERIES ANALYSIS*

Among the profit solutions sought through market research design and analysis, generally you will encounter two types of data: (1) cross-sectional, or (2) time series.

Cross-Sectional

In cross-sectional research designs, information is collected on persons or products or observations during a rather brief span of time—a few days, or at most, a few weeks. Results from such studies often are expressed as a ratio, the variation over some other variable. Some examples referred to in earlier sections of this book include sales-to-advertising outlay, or product revenue-to-age.

Time Series

In time series analyses, time is the key term. The data involve observations on variables over some time lapse; but the interval of time between observations is usually kept constant to avoid variations in results due to variations when the data are recorded. Recall the survey where the respondent was required to register purchases once a week, or where store audits are carried out on a regular schedule. Time series analyses that you are probably most familiar with are moving averages and sales projections.

Of course, you may have noticed that some solutions call for data of both types. Although these may arise from two distinct sets of data, the information is combined to convey one set of decisions.

Fortunately, regression techniques apply to both cross-sectional and time series analysis. But a few problems peculiar to time series analysis crop up when regression techniques are applied. Special techniques resolve these problems. We will show you how to do it.

The Problem of Trends

If a variable shows a tendency to grow in a systematic way over time, this systematic component may be called the trend in the variable.

Trends receive much attention in the analysis of economic time series. One approach to the problem of analyzing time series is to regard the observations as comprising a number of components which can be identified with different kinds of causes.

---

*Section VI.4 was prepared by Professor Kimon Constas, Department of Management, Fayetteville (North Carolina) State University.

In a simple but practical model of this kind, a series of observations, X_t, is expressed as the sum of four independent components:

$$X_t = T_t + C_t + S_t + R_t$$

T_t is the trend component of the series; C_t a cyclical pattern in the observations; S_t the seasonal component; and R_t the random component. A couple of applications should make it clear. We will look at a familiar one: moving averages.

Moving Averages

The moving average method is illustrated with the data in Figure VI.4.A, which tabulates food sales in a given geographical area over 17 years. The trend will be estimated by using a straight line (linear) moving average of three years' length.

ORIGINAL DATA TOGETHER WITH THE THREE-YEAR AND FIVE-YEAR TRENDS					
		Three-Year Moving Average		Five Year Moving Average	
Years	Y	$\Sigma^3 Y$	Trend	$\Sigma^5 Y$	Trend
1961	59	—	—	—	—
196J	60	177	59	—	—
197A	58	184	61	321	64
197B	66	202	67	364	73
197C	78	246	82	425	85
197D	102	301	100	510	102
197E	121	366	122	606	121
197F	143	426	142	720	144
197G	162	497	166	834	167
197H	192	570	190	958	192
1971	216	653	218	1059	212
197J	245	705	235	1181	236
198A	244	773	258	1305	261
198B	284	844	281	1446	289
198C	316	957	319	1566	313
198D	357	1038	346	—	—
198E	365	—	—	—	—

Fig. IV.4.A ORIGINAL DATA TOGETHER WITH THE THREE-YEAR AND FIVE-YEAR TRENDS

To compute the trend using a three-year average, we add the first three terms (Column 2). The mean of these terms is 59 (Column 3). To find the second mean we skip the first observation and consider the next three. Their sum is 184;

their mean is 61. Advancing along the data, we drop the oldest year of the three but add the next most recent year.

Similarly, for a five-year (or any other time span) moving average, an arithmetic mean is computed for each moving block of five years. The means represent the trend values (Columns 3 and 5).

These trend values may appear as dots or stars in a scatter diagram. A line connecting these values provides clearer visualization of the direction of the trend. Or a trend line can be linearly constructed.

Linear Trend

Let us assume that the successive differences of the variable Y_t are constant, or are approximately constant. Then, to represent the trend of the variable, we must run the following *regression*:

$$Y = a + bt,$$

where t stands for the time variable, the independent variable (Section VI.3).

Case 1: *Odd Number of Observations*

The table in Figure VI.4.B gives the annual output of a manufacturing company for the 15-year period. The median year is 197F.

Assigning 0 to the median year, -1 to 197E, -2 to 197D, etc., and $+1$ to 197G, $+2$ to 197H, and so on, we get a table with t ranging from -7 to 7. Now solving for a and b, we get:

$$Y^* = 145.75 + 7.23t,$$

where $t = 0$ for 197F.

LINEAR TREND WHEN THE NUMBER OF OBSERVATIONS IS ODD					
Year (X_i)	Output (Y_i)	(t_i)	$t_i Y_i$	t^2	Y_i^2
196I	110.2	-7	-771.4	49	12,144.04
196J	143.3	-6	-859.8	36	20,534.89
197A	143.3	-5	-716.5	25	20,534.89
197B	134.5	-4	-538.0	16	18,090.25
197C	138.0	-3	414.0	9	19,044.00
197D	55.0	-2	-110.0	4	3,025.00
197E	74.0	-1	-74.0	1	5,476.00
197F	129.0	0	0	0	16,641.00

Figure VI.4.B: **LINEAR TREND WHEN THE NUMBER OF OBSERVATIONS IS ODD**

Year (X_i)	Output (Y_i)	(t_i)	$t_i Y_i$	t^2	Y_i^2	
197G	150.0	1	150.0	1	22,500.00	
197H	140.0	2	280.0	4	19,600.00	
197I	145.0	3	435.0	9	21,025.00	
197J	160.0	4	640.0	16	25,600.00	
198A	210.0	5	1,050.0	25	44,100.00	
198B	225.0	6	1,350.0	36	50,625.00	
198C	229.0	7	1,603.0	49	52,541.00	
TOTAL	2,186.3	0	2,024.3	280	351,381.07	

Note: To compute a and b, use the following system of equations

$$Y = na + b\Sigma t \quad \text{or} \quad 2{,}186.3 = 15a + 0$$

$$\Sigma tY + a\Sigma t + b\Sigma t^2 \qquad 2{,}024.3 = 0 + 280b$$

$$\text{Hence,} \quad a = \frac{2186.3}{15} = 145.75$$

$$b = \frac{2024.3}{280} = 7.23$$

Figure VI.1.4.B (continued)

Case 2: *Even Number of Observations*

The table in Figure VI.4.C gives the number of branches of a discount store over a 16-year period. The median year is half a year from 197F and half a year from 197G; 197E and 197H are −1.5 and 1.5 years, and so on. Therefore, the neutral point, 0, lies between the years 197F and 197G, and the *t* designation of all years must end in 0.5.

For arithmetic convenience, the time variable is multiplied by 2. As Figure VI.4.C indicates, −1 is now assigned to 197F and −3 to 197E. Naturally, all values in Column 3, now no longer fractional, are odd numbered.

The regression equation is found to be:

$$Y^* = 1370.12 + 34.27t$$

Where t = 1/2, 3/2, 5/2, . . .
Now the year starts on January 1, 197G, and t becomes half a year.

To shift the data to July 1, 197G, we work as follows:

$$Y^* = 1370.12 + 34.25\,(1) = 1404.4$$

Hence, the equation with July 1, 197G, as a base, becomes

$$Y^* = 1404.4 + 34.27\,t'$$

LINEAR TREND WHEN THE NUMBER OF YEARS IS EVEN

Year (X_i)	Number of Branches Y_i	t_i	t'	t'Y	t'^2
196I	920	-7.5	-15	$-13,800$	225
196J	1,000	-6.5	-13	13,000	169
197A	1,039	-5.5	-11	11,429	121
197B	1,081	-4.5	-9	9,729	81
197C	1,111	-3.5	-7	7,777	49
197D	1,137	-2.5	-5	5,685	25
197E	1,176	-1.5	-3	3,528	9
197F	1,261	-0.5	-1	1,261	1
197G	1,364	0.5	1	1,364	1
197H	1,420	1.5	3	4,260	9
197I	1,484	2.5	5	7,420	25
197J	1,588	3.5	7	11,116	49
198A	1,727	4.5	9	15,543	81
198B	1,828	5.5	11	20,108	121
198C	1,890	6.5	13	24,570	169
198D	1,896	7.5	15	28,460	225
TOTAL	21,922	0	0	46,612	1,360

Note: As in Table VI.4.B, to find a and b we use a system of equations, therefore:

$$\Sigma Y = na + b\Sigma t' \quad \text{or} \quad 21{,}922 = 16a + 0$$

$$\Sigma t'Y = a\Sigma t' + b\Sigma t'^2 \quad 46.612 = 0 + 1{,}360\, b$$

$$a = 21{,}922/16 = 1370.12, \quad \text{and} \quad b = 46.612/1360 = 34.27.$$

Figure VI.4.C: **LINEAR TREND WHEN THE NUMBER OF YEARS IS EVEN**

where $t' = 1/2, 1, 3/2, \ldots$

To get the annual increase in branches, we write

$$\beta = 2 \times (34.27) = 68.54$$

Therefore, the equation of the trend line is:

$$Y^* = 1404.4 + 68.545t'',$$

where $t'' = 1, 2, 3, \ldots$ and with July 1, 197G as a base period.

Index Time Series

In studying a time-series representing the time behavior of some variable X, it is often of interest to know how X_t, the value of X at time t, compares with X_o, the value of X at some period time O. A convenient way to do this is to compute the ratio:

$$\frac{X_t}{X_o}$$

Or expressed as a percentage of X_o,

$$\text{Index Time Series} = 100 \left(\frac{X_t}{X_o}\right)$$

This ratio is called the index time series for X_t, when O is used as a base.

EXAMPLE: If sales currently amount to $17.3m, as compared with $16m, then the index for current sales is:

$$100 \left(\frac{17.3}{16}\right) = 108.1\% \text{ or } 1.081$$

Moreover, to obtain the percentage change in a sales we subtract 100 from the index. Here 8.1 percent is a percentage increase in sales.

Price Index

One of the most frequent errors of the application of statistical techniques in time series situations arises with price index numbers. Here data are collected, say, for sales over several years, and are used for deriving trends without any purification.

Over time, the price index changes. Therefore, unadjusted data cannot be compared. Look at the sales of a major food wholesaler. The sales manager goes ahead with his computations and announces that sales rose 84.4 percent between Years A and E.

	A	B	C	D	E
Sales	$16.0m	17.3	23.3	25.4	29.5
Index	100.0	108.1	145.6	158.8	184.4

There is a flaw here because during that period the food wholesale price index did not remain constant. In fact, the price index rose 29.2 percent. As a consequence, sales, in constant Year A prices, rose less than 84.4 percent.

	A	B	C	D	E
Price Index	146.4	166.9	181.0	180.2	189.1
Index of Prices	100.0	114.0	123.6	123.1	129.2

To find the increase in sales in constant prices we proceed as follows:

• First, we select the appropriate price index.

• Second, since it is possible that the first year of our sales figure does not correspond to the base year of the price index, we shift the base. In our example the new base is Year A (=100). Thus, the values of the index are computed by dividing each year by the base index.

• Third, we divide the sales figures by the new price index to obtain constant-value-sales.

• Finally, we compute the growth of sales by dividing constant-value sales by the base year sales.

	A	B	C	D	E
Constant Sales (Year A)	16.0m	15.2	18.9	20.6	22.8
Index of Sales	100.0	95	118.1	128.8	142.5

First Differences

A variable should be measured not at its actual level, say millions of Year A dollars, but as a deviation over the level of the preceding year. For example, if revenue is $150 million in one year, and $160 million the following year, we use the difference ($10 million) as the value of the variable.

There are several reasons for using differences. First, for some goods, especially durables, data on stocks are unobtainable. There is no public record of the stock (i.e., the total number in use) of electric refrigerators, TV sets, radios or other durables. Also for the current stock of automobiles no data are available from the Bureau of Public Roads. Since such data are not available, we must find some alternative to direct knowledge about their stocks of derived durables.

If the annual amount of scrappage of a durable good is stable, then the big variation in the stock arises from acquisitions. Thus, last year's purchases can be used as a proxy variable for the increase in stock. This enables us to escape the lack of direct information about the total stock of the durable.

A second reason for the use of first differences is to isolate the model from the impact of slowly moving variables like population, tastes, technology, habits, and similar factors.

A third reason is that forecasting with first differences takes full advantage of autocorrelated residuals. Actually, if there is a high positive deviation from the regression one year, it tends to be followed by a positive deviation the second year. This property of deviations is called positive autocorrelation, because the value of the deviation in any one year is positively correlated with its value in the preceding year.

As the Table in Figure VI.4.D shows, the first four residuals are negative; the next one is positive; the following three are negative, etc.

To remove autocorrelation we compute the first differences as in Figure VI.4.E. Now using a regression with 14 terms we get the following regression equation.

$$y^* = 2.271 + 2.43x$$

This equation is free of autocorrelation because the computed residuals do not show blocks of positive or negative signs.

DETECTING AUTOCORRELATION

Year	Income X (1)	Sales Y (2)	XY (3)	X^2 (4)	Y* (5)	Residuals e = Y* − Y (6)
1	4.2	41	172.2	17.64	43.572	⌐−2.572
2	3.5	36	126.0	12.25	36.950	−0.450
3	5.2	44	228.8	27.04	53.032	−9.032
4	5.5	50	275.0	30.25	55.370	⌐−5.870
5	4.6	50	230.0	21.16	47.356	2.644
6	5.5	54	297.0	30.25	55.870	⌐−1.870
7	6.4	57	364.8	40.96	64.384	−7.384
8	6.9	61	420.9	47.61	69.114	⌐−8.114
9	4.7	61	286.7	22.09	48.302	12.698
10	6.8	70	476.0	46.24	68.168	1.832
11	8.2	77	631.4	67.24	81.412	⌐−4.412
12	8.1	79	639.9	65.61	80.466	⌐−1.466
13	6.5	72	468.0	42.25	65.330	6.670
14	7.3	81	591.3	53.29	72.898	8.102
15	7.4	83	614.2	54.76	73.844	9.156
Total	90.8	916	5,822.2	578.64		

Notes: Regressing Sales (Y) on income (X) we get Y* = 3.84 + 9.46 X. The values of Y for different X values appear in Column (5). Residuals are shown in Column (6).

Figure VI.4.D: DETECTING AUTOCORRELATION

Differences $\Delta X = x$ (7)	Differences $\Delta Y = y$ (8)	xy (9)	x^2 (10)	y* (11)	Residuals $E = y^* - y$ (12)
−0.7	−5	3.5	0.49	0.570	5.570
1.7	8	13.6	2.89	6.402	−1.598
0.3	6	1.8	0.09	3.000	−3.000
−0.9	0	0	0.81	0.084	0.084
0.9	4	3.6	0.81	4.458	0.458
0.9	3	2.7	0.81	4.458	1.458
0.5	4	2.0	0.25	3.486	−0.514
−1.2	0	0	1.44	−0.645	−0.645
2.1	9	18.9	4.41	7.374	−1.623
1.4	7	9.8	1.96	5.673	−1.337
−0.1	2	−0.2	0.01	2.028	0.028
−1.6	−7	−11.2	2.56	−1.617	5.383
0.8	9	7.2	0.64	4.215	−4.785
0.1	2	0.2	0.01	2.514	0.514
4.2	42	51.3	17.18		

In columns (7) and (8), differences are reported. Now regressing ΔY on ΔX we get ΔY^* or $y^* = 2.271 + 2.43x$. As before, the residuals are reported in the last column (12).

Now we set up the systems of equations:

Let $\Delta X = x$ and $\Delta Y = y$. Then

$$\Sigma y = na + b\Sigma x$$
$$\Sigma yx = a\Sigma x + b\Sigma x^2$$

Where $n = 14$, $\Sigma y = 42$, $\Sigma x = 4.2$

$\Sigma x^2 = 17.18$ and $\Sigma xy = 51.3$

(1) $\quad 42 = 14a + 4.2b \quad | \quad -4.2$

(2) $\quad 51.3 = 4.2a + 17.18b \quad | \quad 14$

or $\quad -176.4 = -58.8a - 17.64b$

$\qquad 718.2 = \quad 58.8a + 240.52b$

Therefore, $541.8 = \qquad 222.88b$

Dividing by 222.88, we get

$$\frac{541.8}{222.88} = b = 2.43$$

Now, to estimate a, we return to equation (1), substitute 2.43 for b, and solve for a:

$\qquad 42 = 14a + 4.2 (2.43)$

$\qquad 42 = 14a + 10.206$

or $\qquad 31.794 = 14a$

Thus $\qquad \dfrac{31.794}{14} = a = 2.271$

Now we write the estimated equation:

(3) ... $\quad y^* = 2.271 + 2.43x$

Where

$\qquad y^* = \Delta Y^*$ and $x = \Delta X$.

The values of y* appear in column (11).

To get the residuals, we subtract (11) from (8), and report the differences in Column 12.

Figure VI.4.E: REMOVING AUTOCORRELATION

LIST OF APPENDICES

APPENDIX A

RANDOM NUMBERS TABLE

205	230	533	132	996	784	742	398	710	678
991	451	789	674	942	588	051	014	623	612
013	138	714	043	834	611	165	488	446	278
097	897	503	950	173	487	359	773	410	504
768	421	614	892	827	935	169	604	099	162
029	850	836	364	658	675	130	705	060	016
661	647	935	786	301	735	699	577	171	831
143	379	986	511	189	536	513	253	903	140
341	768	534	294	961	121	078	380	575	029
074	393	689	598	383	915	043	023	755	322
687	416	309	113	899	374	151	545	907	541
759	698	357	858	940	915	032	953	432	010
069	703	595	245	116	494	922	084	207	489
944	536	716	476	414	199	463	988	766	701
115	514	048	662	535	251	696	915	228	131
206	634	953	009	477	778	375	249	120	484
979	309	044	485	516	727	722	782	199	154
465	756	352	308	682	316	758	705	407	095
101	412	561	653	874	366	329	675	091	473
001	741	435	942	733	924	944	349	600	455
481	817	574	094	394	519	571	754	386	530
971	057	605	115	248	455	493	865	751	723
435	477	948	396	842	491	365	771	337	087
420	844	282	095	026	303	589	801	508	840
868	106	823	983	490	090	133	989	738	525
804	464	551	128	809	701	926	244	128	575
038	474	509	784	120	671	941	610	188	641
997	544	295	868	554	515	103	987	993	077
817	205	874	403	552	684	141	688	856	944
814	527	839	290	192	540	511	205	626	915
464	069	236	796	648	724	513	560	749	452
022	715	092	122	900	304	726	624	208	630
886	788	755	438	836	071	900	762	475	989
858	818	186	755	859	355	398	196	591	780
403	324	319	999	122	743	356	452	509	984
044	002	616	678	528	066	643	268	816	486
016	681	940	511	606	040	782	334	962	764
302	433	881	388	403	927	932	253	126	482
173	200	641	044	499	593	069	076	840	353
370	326	626	820	287	344	484	807	486	656
032	357	848	878	634	907	734	237	816	768
519	491	281	170	490	413	067	683	494	819
229	057	281	170	490	413	067	683	494	819
565	381	204	790	906	330	823	968	397	672
142	437	343	132	700	011	769	515	172	401
389	637	317	169	163	461	296	630	112	004
657	154	014	699	068	117	089	485	110	293
951	135	251	293	501	365	682	813	734	091
434	191	236	702	089	212	472	924	295	458
803	535	986	101	731	478	292	448	058	315
205	682	991	059	013	657	097	331	768	077
784	186	588	084	611	424	487	295	935	379
533	204	555	488	503	098	343	710	674	846
398	789	330	725	773	614	195	915	623	043
806	014	714	944	749	604	132	408	706	446

Appendix A: RANDOM NUMBERS TABLE

This partial random numbers table was prepared for the author by Duane B. Reutter, Data Control Manager, Electro-Methods, Inc.

Appendix (continued)

682	991	806	915	237	186	980	204	408	610
059	847	555	706	240	084	348	330	846	104
657	440	725	391	824	424	127	944	522	632
331	455	749	398	645	295	958	098	966	910
077	007	343	995	890	379	268	195	762	814
558	207	217	445	712	270	207	815	024	813
446	199	180	291	122	118	603	563	945	609
714	028	738	180	435	992	041	318	538	364
996	717	338	576	419	330	204	256	699	895
139	935	362	754	272	840	595	012	717	190
082	624	008	434	525	250	772	383	349	651
175	959	179	441	039	259	207	910	601	412
071	023	496	774	174	079	910	750	312	125
312	565	585	428	297	935	933	183	704	575
734	222	731	384	727	905	883	155	985	511
822	575	048	113	247	465	566	208	155	063
133	413	282	977	319	127	889	189	136	115
908	590	369	907	115	531	148	111	337	022
016	837	877	731	493	376	819	528	797	030
335	912	455	523	046	567	987	819	026	785
705	461	416	347	344	937	528	734	653	308
579	965	577	781	495	939	175	602	036	792
488	147	485	587	158	670	596	550	929	631
462	217	142	899	116	608	599	125	356	011
509	325	375	322	555	432	598	694	789	484
297	604	954	291	154	308	460	988	792	861
156	167	598	085	127	002	863	165	218	826
523	449	984	865	334	215	286	780	109	633
958	253	898	110	581	497	749	027	417	262
853	885	631	822	253	121	451	622	668	413
969	748	770	885	377	299	401	717	695	713
908	777	490	946	270	103	190	213	570	503
663	074	477	194	870	475	019	838	855	592
361	144	618	410	897	698	110	381	295	344
323	078	562	668	952	699	624	451	089	473
576	081	299	064	691	572	212	125	844	935
931	707	866	830	191	674	324	881	365	264
752	180	310	239	640	694	402	166	376	760
559	179	042	641	470	052	079	006	321	877
559	453	686	039	060	008	511	992	355	204
262	654	573	548	133	860	966	059	655	402
281	752	985	141	979	602	803	402	183	480
463	409	286	032	618	417	946	921	012	779
457	694	057	091	033	383	002	560	348	046
852	506	367	652	604	761	129	923	379	967
020	080	304	098	855	248	795	536	059	532
767	964	879	593	651	566	538	136	974	619
940	819	451	336	964	756	859	354	390	157
094	436	774	716	335	566	378	173	635	253
363	346	808	738	157	297	368	539	918	655
230	991	451	847	138	440	897	455	421	007
742	980	051	348	165	127	359	958	169	268
399	410	892	762	237	612	834	632	645	162
522	398	099	996	610	240	278	173	910	890
950	966	995	678	942	104	824	504	827	814

Appendix A (continued)

APPENDIX B

T-VALUES

DEGREES OF FREEDOM	LEVEL OF CERTAINTY			
	80%	90%	95%	99%
1	3.08	6.31	12.71	63.66
2	1.89	2.92	4.30	9.92
3	1.64	2.35	3.18	5.84
4	1.53	2.13	2.78	4.60
5	1.48	2.02	2.57	4.03
6	1.44	1.94	2.45	3.71
7	1.42	1.90	2.36	3.50
8	1.41	1.86	2.31	3.36
9	1.38	1.83	2.26	3.25
10	1.37	1.81	2.23	3.17
11	1.36	1.80	2.20	3.11
12	1.35	1.78	2.18	3.06
13	1.35	1.77	2.16	3.01
14	1.34	1.76	2.14	2.98
15	1.34	1.75	2.13	2.95
16	1.33	1.75	2.12	2.92
17	1.33	1.74	2.11	2.90
18	1.33	1.74	2.10	2.88
19	1.32	1.73	2.09	2.86
20	1.32	1.73	2.08	2.84
21	1.32	1.72	2.07	2.83
22	1.32	1.72	2.07	2.82
23	1.31	1.72	2.06	2.81
24	1.31	1.71	2.06	2.80
25	1.31	1.71	2.06	2.79
26	1.31	1.71	2.06	2.78
27	1.31	1.70	2.05	2.77
28	1.31	1.70	2.05	2.76
29	1.31	1.70	2.05	2.75
30	1.31	1.70	2.04	2.75
40	1.30	1.68	2.02	2.70
60	1.29	1.67	2.00	2.66
120	1.28	1.66	1.98	2.62
∞	1.28	1.64	1.96	2.58

Appendix B: T-VALUES

APPENDIX C

Z-VALUES: PERCENT AREA UNDER NORMAL CURVE

Z	%	Z	%	Z	%	Z	%
0.00	00.00	0.76	27.64	1.52	43.52	2.28	48.87
0.02	00.80	0.78	28.23	1.54	43.82	2.30	48.93
0.04	01.60	0.80	28.81	1.56	44.06	2.32	48.98
0.06	02.39	0.82	29.39	1.58	44.29	2.34	49.04
0.08	03.19	0.84	29.95	1.60	44.52	2.36	49.09
0.10	03.98	0.86	30.51	1.62	44.74	2.38	49.13
0.12	04.78	0.88	31.06	1.64	44.95	2.40	49.18
0.14	05.57	0.90	31.59	1.66	45.15	2.42	49.22
0.16	06.36	0.92	32.12	1.68	45.35	2.44	49.27
0.18	07.14	0.94	32.64	1.70	45.54	2.46	49.31
0.20	07.93	0.96	33.15	1.72	45.73	2.48	49.34
0.22	08.71	0.98	33.65	1.74	45.91	2.50	49.38
0.24	09.48	1.00	34.13	1.76	46.08	2.52	49.41
0.26	10.26	1.02	34.61	1.78	46.25	2.54	49.45
0.28	11.03	1.04	35.08	1.80	46.41	2.56	49.48
0.30	11.79	1.06	35.54	1.82	46.56	2.58	49.51
0.32	12.55	1.08	35.99	1.84	46.71	2.60	49.53
0.34	13.31	1.10	36.43	1.86	46.86	2.62	49.56
0.36	14.06	1.12	36.86	1.88	46.99	2.64	49.59
0.38	14.80	1.14	37.29	1.90	47.13	2.66	49.61
0.40	15.54	1.16	37.70	1.92	47.26	2.68	49.63
0.42	16.28	1.18	38.10	1.94	47.38	2.70	49.65
0.44	17.00	1.20	38.49	1.96	47.50	2.72	49.67
0.46	17.72	1.22	38.88	1.98	47.61	2.74	49.69
0.48	18.44	1.24	39.25	2.00	47.72	2.76	49.71
0.50	19.15	1.26	39.62	2.02	47.83	2.78	49.73
0.52	19.85	1.28	39.97	2.04	47.93	2.80	49.74
0.54	20.54	1.30	40.32	2.06	48.03	2.82	49.76
0.56	21.23	1.32	40.66	2.08	48.12	2.84	49.77
0.58	21.90	1.34	40.99	2.10	48.21	2.86	49.79
0.60	22.57	1.36	41.31	2.12	48.30	2.88	49.80
0.62	23.24	1.38	41.62	2.14	48.38	2.90	49.81
0.64	23.89	1.40	41.92	2.16	48.46	2.92	49.83
0.66	24.54	1.42	42.22	2.18	48.54	2.94	49.84
0.68	25.18	1.44	42.51	2.20	48.61	2.96	49.85
0.70	25.80	1.46	42.79	2.22	48.68	2.98	49.86
0.72	26.42	1.48	43.06	2.24	48.75	3.00	49.86
0.74	27.04	1.50	43.32	2.26	48.81	3.50	49.97

Appendix C: Z-VALUES: PERCENT AREA UNDER NORMAL CURVE

APPENDIX D

CRITICAL VALUES OF CHI-SQUARE

Degrees of freedom	Level Of Certainty			
	80%	90%	95%	99%
1	1.64	2.71	3.84	6.64
2	3.22	4.61	5.99	9.21
3	4.64	6.25	7.82	11.35
4	5.99	7.78	9.49	13.28
5	7.29	9.24	11.07	15.09
6	8.56	10.58	12.59	16.81
7	9.80	12.01	14.07	18.48
8	11.01	13.44	15.51	20.09
9	12.16	14.71	16.92	21.67
10	13.42	15.98	18.31	23.21
11	14.64	17.31	19.68	24.73
12	15.76	18.49	21.03	26.22
13	16.95	19.82	22.36	27.71
14	18.20	21.09	23.69	29.12
15	19.32	22.34	25.00	30.64
16	20.47	23.45	26.30	32.01
17	21.61	24.83	27.59	33.41
18	22.78	25.97	28.87	34.81
19	23.94	27.20	30.14	36.20
20	24.96	28.39	31.41	37.57
21	26.18	29.55	32.67	38.89
22	27.34	30.82	33.92	40.31
23	28.44	32.03	35.17	41.59
24	29.56	33.19	36.42	43.00
25	30.69	34.44	37.65	44.29
26	31.82	35.61	38.89	45.64
27	32.89	36.70	40.11	46.97
28	34.03	37.88	41.34	48.31
29	35.11	39.10	42.56	49.60
30	36.25	40.34	43.77	50.89

Appendix D: CRITICAL VALUES OF CHI-SQUARE

APPENDIX E

CRITICAL VALUES OF THE F-DISTRIBUTION

Table (1): 95% Level of Certainty

DEGREES OF FREEDOM OF THE NUMERATOR →

Denom \ Num	1	2	3	4	5	6	7	8	9	10	15	30	60	120	∞
1	161.40	199.50	215.70	224.60	230.20	234.00	236.80	238.90	240.50	241.90	245.90	250.10	252.20	253.30	254.30
2	18.51	19.00	19.16	19.25	19.30	19.33	19.35	19.37	19.38	19.40	19.43	19.46	19.48	19.49	19.50
3	10.13	9.55	9.28	9.12	9.01	8.94	8.89	8.85	8.81	8.79	8.70	8.62	8.57	8.55	8.53
4	7.71	6.94	6.59	6.39	6.26	6.16	6.09	6.04	6.00	5.96	5.86	5.75	5.69	5.66	5.63
5	6.61	5.79	5.41	5.19	5.05	4.95	4.88	4.82	4.77	4.74	4.62	4.50	4.43	4.40	4.36
6	5.99	5.14	4.76	4.53	4.39	4.28	4.21	4.15	4.10	4.06	3.94	3.81	3.74	3.70	3.67
7	5.59	4.74	4.35	4.12	3.97	3.87	3.79	3.73	3.68	3.64	3.51	3.38	3.30	3.27	3.23
8	5.32	4.46	4.07	3.84	3.69	3.58	3.50	3.44	3.39	3.35	3.22	3.08	3.01	2.97	2.93
9	5.12	4.26	3.86	3.63	3.48	3.37	3.29	3.23	3.18	3.14	3.01	2.86	2.79	2.75	2.71
10	4.96	4.10	3.71	3.48	3.33	3.22	3.14	3.07	3.02	2.98	2.85	2.70	2.62	2.58	2.54
11	4.84	3.98	3.59	3.36	3.20	3.09	3.01	2.95	2.90	2.85	2.72	2.57	2.49	2.45	2.40
12	4.75	3.89	3.49	3.26	3.11	3.00	2.91	2.85	2.80	2.75	2.62	2.47	2.38	2.34	2.30
13	4.67	3.81	3.41	3.18	3.03	2.92	2.83	2.77	2.71	2.67	2.53	2.38	2.30	2.25	2.21
14	4.60	3.74	3.34	3.11	2.96	2.85	2.76	2.70	2.65	2.60	2.46	2.31	2.22	2.18	2.13
15	4.54	3.68	3.29	3.06	2.90	2.79	2.71	2.64	2.59	2.54	2.40	2.25	2.16	2.11	2.07
16	4.49	3.63	3.24	3.01	2.85	2.74	2.66	2.59	2.54	2.49	2.35	2.19	2.11	2.06	2.01
17	4.45	3.59	3.20	2.96	2.81	2.70	2.61	2.55	2.49	2.45	2.31	2.15	2.06	2.01	1.96
18	4.41	3.55	3.16	2.93	2.77	2.66	2.58	2.51	2.46	2.41	2.27	2.11	2.02	1.97	1.92
19	4.38	3.52	3.13	2.90	2.74	2.63	2.54	2.48	2.42	2.38	2.23	2.07	1.98	1.93	1.88
20	4.35	3.49	3.10	2.87	2.71	2.60	2.51	2.45	2.39	2.35	2.20	2.04	1.95	1.90	1.84
21	4.32	3.47	3.07	2.84	2.68	2.57	2.49	2.42	2.37	2.32	2.18	2.01	1.92	1.87	1.81
22	4.30	3.44	3.05	2.82	2.66	2.55	2.46	2.40	2.34	2.30	2.15	1.98	1.89	1.84	1.78
23	4.28	3.42	3.03	2.80	2.64	2.53	2.44	2.37	2.32	2.27	2.13	1.96	1.86	1.81	1.76
24	4.26	3.40	3.01	2.78	2.62	2.51	2.42	2.36	2.30	2.25	2.11	1.94	1.84	1.79	1.73
25	4.24	3.39	2.99	2.76	2.60	2.49	2.40	2.34	2.28	2.24	2.09	1.92	1.82	1.77	1.71
26	4.23	3.37	2.98	2.74	2.59	2.47	2.39	2.32	2.27	2.22	2.07	1.90	1.80	1.75	1.69
27	4.21	3.35	2.96	2.73	2.57	2.46	2.37	2.31	2.25	2.20	2.06	1.88	1.79	1.73	1.67
28	4.20	3.34	2.95	2.71	2.56	2.45	2.36	2.29	2.24	2.19	2.04	1.87	1.77	1.71	1.65
29	4.18	3.33	2.93	2.70	2.55	2.43	2.35	2.28	2.22	2.18	2.03	1.85	1.75	1.70	1.64
30	4.17	3.32	2.92	2.69	2.53	2.42	2.33	2.27	2.21	2.16	2.01	1.84	1.74	1.68	1.62
40	4.08	3.23	2.84	2.61	2.45	2.34	2.25	2.18	2.12	2.08	1.92	1.74	1.64	1.58	1.51
60	4.00	3.15	2.76	2.53	2.37	2.25	2.17	2.10	2.04	1.99	1.84	1.65	1.53	1.47	1.39
120	3.92	3.07	2.68	2.45	2.29	2.17	2.09	2.02	1.96	1.91	1.75	1.55	1.43	1.35	1.25
∞	3.84	3.00	2.60	2.37	2.21	2.10	2.01	1.94	1.88	1.83	1.67	1.46	1.32	1.22	1.00

← DEGREES OF FREEDOM OF THE DENOMINATOR →

Appendix E: CRITICAL VALUES OF THE F-DISTRIBUTION

APPENDIX E (continued)

Table (2): 99% Level of Certainty

DEGREES OF FREEDOM OF THE NUMERATOR →

df	1	2	3	4	5	6	7	8	9	10	15	30	60	120	∞
1	4052.00	4999.50	5403.00	5625.00	5764.00	5859.00	5928.00	5982.00	6022.00	6056.00	6157.00	6261.00	6313.00	6339.00	6366.00
2	98.50	99.00	99.17	99.25	99.30	99.33	99.36	99.37	99.39	99.40	99.43	99.47	99.48	99.49	99.50
3	34.12	30.82	29.46	28.71	28.24	27.91	27.67	27.49	27.35	27.23	26.87	26.50	26.32	26.22	26.13
4	21.20	18.00	16.69	15.98	15.52	15.21	14.98	14.80	14.66	14.55	14.20	13.84	13.65	13.56	13.46
5	16.26	13.27	12.06	11.39	10.97	10.67	10.46	10.29	10.16	10.05	9.72	9.38	9.20	9.11	9.02
6	13.75	10.92	9.78	9.15	8.75	8.47	8.26	8.10	7.98	7.87	7.56	7.23	7.06	6.97	6.88
7	12.25	9.55	8.45	7.85	7.46	7.19	6.99	6.84	6.72	6.62	6.31	5.99	5.82	5.74	5.65
8	11.26	8.65	7.59	7.01	6.63	6.37	6.18	6.03	5.91	5.81	5.52	5.20	5.03	4.95	4.86
9	10.56	8.02	6.99	6.42	6.06	5.80	5.61	5.47	5.35	5.26	4.96	4.65	4.48	4.40	4.31
10	10.04	7.56	6.55	5.99	5.64	5.39	5.20	5.06	4.94	4.85	4.56	4.25	4.08	4.00	3.91
11	9.65	7.21	6.22	5.67	5.32	5.07	4.89	4.74	4.63	4.54	4.25	3.94	3.78	3.69	3.60
12	9.33	6.93	5.95	5.41	5.06	4.82	4.64	4.50	4.39	4.30	4.01	3.70	3.54	3.45	3.36
13	9.07	6.70	5.74	5.21	4.86	4.62	4.44	4.30	4.19	4.10	3.82	3.51	3.34	3.25	3.17
14	8.86	6.51	5.56	5.04	4.69	4.46	4.28	4.14	4.03	3.94	3.66	3.35	3.18	3.09	3.00
15	8.68	6.36	5.42	4.89	4.56	4.32	4.14	4.00	3.89	3.80	3.52	3.21	3.05	2.96	2.87
16	8.53	6.23	5.29	4.77	4.44	4.20	4.03	3.89	3.78	3.69	3.41	3.10	2.93	2.84	2.75
17	8.40	6.11	5.18	4.67	4.34	4.10	3.93	3.79	3.68	3.59	3.31	3.00	2.83	2.75	2.65
18	8.29	6.01	5.09	4.58	4.25	4.01	3.84	3.71	3.60	3.51	3.23	2.92	2.75	2.66	2.57
19	8.18	5.93	5.01	4.50	4.17	3.94	3.77	3.63	3.52	3.43	3.15	2.84	2.67	2.58	2.49
20	8.10	5.85	4.94	4.43	4.10	3.87	3.70	3.56	3.46	3.37	3.09	2.78	2.61	2.52	2.42
21	8.02	5.78	4.87	4.37	4.04	3.81	3.64	3.51	3.40	3.31	3.03	2.72	2.55	2.46	2.36
22	7.95	5.72	4.82	4.31	3.99	3.76	3.59	3.45	3.35	3.26	2.98	2.67	2.50	2.40	2.31
23	7.88	5.66	4.76	4.26	3.94	3.71	3.54	3.41	3.30	3.21	2.93	2.62	2.45	2.35	2.26
24	7.82	5.61	4.72	4.22	3.90	3.67	3.50	3.36	3.26	3.17	2.89	2.58	2.40	2.31	2.21
25	7.77	5.57	4.68	4.18	3.85	3.63	3.46	3.32	3.22	3.13	2.85	2.54	2.36	2.27	2.17
26	7.72	5.53	4.64	4.14	3.82	3.59	3.42	3.29	3.18	3.09	2.81	2.50	2.33	2.23	2.13
27	7.68	5.49	4.60	4.11	3.78	3.56	3.39	3.26	3.15	3.06	2.78	2.47	2.29	2.20	2.10
28	7.64	5.45	4.57	4.07	3.75	3.53	3.36	3.23	3.12	3.03	2.75	2.44	2.26	2.17	2.06
29	7.60	5.42	4.54	4.04	3.73	3.50	3.33	3.20	3.09	3.00	2.73	2.41	2.23	2.14	2.03
30	7.56	5.39	4.51	4.02	3.70	3.47	3.30	3.17	3.07	2.98	2.70	2.39	2.21	2.11	2.01
40	7.31	5.18	4.31	3.83	3.51	3.29	3.12	2.99	2.89	2.80	2.52	2.20	2.02	1.92	1.80
60	7.08	4.98	4.13	3.65	3.34	3.12	2.95	2.82	2.72	2.63	2.35	2.03	1.84	1.73	1.60
120	6.85	4.79	3.95	3.48	3.17	2.96	2.79	2.66	2.56	2.47	2.19	1.86	1.66	1.53	1.38
∞	6.63	4.61	3.78	3.32	3.02	2.80	2.64	2.51	2.41	2.32	2.04	1.70	1.47	1.32	1.00

← DEGREES OF FREEDOM OF THE DENOMINATOR →

Appendix E (continued)

APPENDIX F

R-VALUES

n	Level of Certainty	
	95%	99%
3	0.997	0.999
4	0.950	0.999
5	0.878	0.959
6	0.811	0.917
7	0.754	0.875
8	0.707	0.834
9	0.666	0.798
10	0.632	0.765
11	0.602	0.735
12	0.576	0.708
13	0.553	0.684
14	0.532	0.661
15	0.514	0.641
16	0.497	0.623
17	0.482	0.606
18	0.468	0.590
19	0.456	0.575
20	0.444	0.561
21	0.433	0.549
22	0.423	0.537
27	0.381	0.487
32	0.349	0.449
37	0.325	0.419
42	0.304	0.393
47	0.288	0.372
52	0.273	0.354
62	0.250	0.325
72	0.232	0.302
82	0.217	0.283
92	0.205	0.267

Appendix F: R-VALUES

INDEX